SHOVELING SMOKE

SHOVELING SMOKE

Advertising and Globalization in Contemporary India

WILLIAM MAZZARELLA

DUKE UNIVERSITY PRESS   DURHAM AND LONDON 2003

3rd printing, 2006
© 2003 Duke University Press   All rights reserved
Printed in the United States of America on acid-free paper ∞
Designed by Rebecca M. Giménez   Typeset in Sabon by
Keystone Typesetting, Inc.   Library of Congress Cataloging-in-
Publication Data appear on the last printed page of this book.

ILLUSTRATIONS

ACKNOWLEDGMENTS

I would first of all like to thank the members of my dissertation committee, Lawrence Cohen, Nelson Graburn, Allan Pred, and Brian Moeran, for their advice and unstinting support throughout the sometimes turbulent times that saw the gestation and production of the Ph.D. thesis that was the first *avatara* of this book.

During the last few years, several others have also offered me the privilege of their direct critical engagement with the ideas and materials presented in the following pages, and I wish to extend my deepest gratitude to them: Kalman Applbaum, Dipesh Chakrabarty, Jennifer Cole, Michael Cole, John Comaroff, Vikram Doctor, Wendy Doniger, Robert Foster, Susan Gal, Keith Hart, Raminder Kaur, Tanya Luhrmann, Merete Mazzarella, Rebecca McLennan, Jennifer Moore, Christian Novetzke, Peter Phipps, Arvind Rajagopal, Peter Redfield, Danilyn Rutherford, Kathleen Stewart, James Watson, Kimberly Wright, and two anonymous readers for Duke University Press. More generally, my colleagues at the University of Chicago Department of Anthropology have, during the latter stages of writing this book, provided me with an incomparably stimulating intellectual environment.

Christian Hellman and Jan Åkerwall were crucially involved in the very earliest stages of conceiving and facilitating the project. Raminder Kaur and Shoma Munshi provided me with invaluable leads at a time when I still had only the vaguest notions of what and whom I was seeking. The incomparable hospitality of the Wagh family and Arijit Sen made my stay in Bombay more comfortable than I could have hoped for. Lara Charles, Janet Fine, Amrita Shah, Anuradha Tandon, Anand Thakore, and Jeet Thayil all helped me to understand and appreciate Bombay life beyond the narrow confines of the agency walls.

In and around the Bombay advertising and marketing business, I would like to thank Anvar Alikhan, Jayant Bakshi, Usha Bhandarkar, Rama Bijapurkar, Sylvester da Cunha, Prabuddha Das Gupta, Santosh Desai, Aniruddha Deshmukh, Clarinda D'Souza, the late Subhas Ghosal, Kersy Katrak, Praveen Kenneth, Kiran Khalap, Mohammed Khan, Anil Nair, Suresh Nair, Alyque Padamsee, Piyush Pandey, Adi Pocha, Navonil Roy, Ravikant Sabnavis, Debadatta Sen, the late Frank Simoes, and Rohit Srivastava. I bear a special debt of gratitude to Vikram Doctor, Neeraj Mehra, Sorab Mistry, Madan Mohan, Rajendra Mohoni, Elliot Moss, Gautam Rakshit, and Peter Rodenbeck.

The practical and financial assistance of the Social Science Research Council, through their International Dissertation Research Fellowship program, and the American Institute of Indian Studies made this research possible. Its transformation into a book was rendered a pleasure through the assistance of Katie Courtland, Christine Dahlin, and Leigh Anne Couch. I want to thank my editor, Ken Wissoker, for being so enthusiastic about the project and for his exemplary patience. Ellen Gartrell provided me with invaluable help in accessing and negotiating the Hartman Center Archives at Duke University.

Gratitude is also due to my in-laws, Michael and Sheila Cole, who, in addition to valuable conversations, repeatedly went far beyond the call of duty in their willingness to provide practical assistance at times of great stress and instability.

My parents, Merete and Silvester Mazzarella, are naturally to blame for this whole farrago in the first place — they brought me to India in 1969 and again in 1972, thus setting off the complex chains of cause and effect that would bring me back in January 1997. I want to thank them here for their unflagging support, staunchly maintained in the face of my no doubt somewhat perplexing peregrinations over the last few years.

For my children, Amelia and Jacob, my "work in Bombay" has literally been a fact of life. Amelia, at the tender age of two, struggled through repeated illness for the sake of both her parents' ethnographic preoccupations; Jacob, for his part, was, as the contemporary Indipop song would have it, "made in India."

Finally, my wife and partner, Jennifer Cole, embodies the model life companion — combining an unconditional emotional commitment with an exquisitely particular and critical intellectual engagement. This work is dedicated to her.

INTRODUCTION

1

Locations: Advertising and the New Swadeshi

This book is an ethnographic study of globalizing consumerism. It is set in the world of the Indian advertising business, and the arguments that I develop emerge out of that specific context. At the same time, this is also a book about processes and institutions that are today quite general, if not ubiquitous. Indeed, my initial intuition, as I started my research, was that the advertising business is a particularly compelling point of mediation between the local and the global, between culture and capital. This turned out to be true, but its mediations were far more complex and unpredictable than I had anticipated.

In the chapters that follow I develop detailed analyses of the shapes taken by some of these mediations: the rise of mass consumerism in India in the 1980s as an explicit challenge to the developmentalist dispensation of the post-Independence years; the articulation of a concomitant social ontology around what I call "the commodity image"; the crises of value brought on by the decisive opening of Indian consumer markets to foreign brands after 1991; and the associated retooling of Indian marketing professionals as cultural consultants.

In part, this book is an account of how national consumer goods advertising is produced in metropolitan India, and the anxieties, commitments, and contradictions that animate that practice. By the same token, this is also an inquiry into some of the broader transformations in Indian public culture with which the rise of mass consumerism came to be identified. In some ways, the Indian advertising business's discourse is self-consciously modeled upon a global paradigm: consumerism as an inclusive formal system that strives to appropriate—and thereby also produce—local cultural difference as content. At the same time, the density of the cultural material that advertising is made of necessarily troubles such neat divisions. As an aesthetic interface of postcolonial capitalism, the everyday practice of advertising constantly calls into question the conceptual alignments that ground business discourse: local and global, culture and capital, particular and universal, content and form.

This is a book about the people who make advertising. I theorize the practice of advertising as a kind of public cultural production, centered on a distinctive form of commodity production, the production of commodity images. I certainly do not deny the importance of consumption as social practice, but I would prefer to situate it within a range of practices—commercial, political, subversive, disciplinary—that shape contested, and often internally contradictory, public fields of representation and discourse. And while we have a large and growing ethnographic literature on the cultural politics of consumption, a critical anthropology of the culture industries is only beginning to emerge.[1]

The New *Swadeshi*

Speaking to a journalist in 1995, George Fernandes, leader of the Samata Party, recalled a watershed moment in his public career:

> The idea of getting Coke out struck me [in 1977] when I was the Minister of Communications, prior to being Minister of Industry. I was visiting a village in my constituency. It was summer and hot, and the first thing I did when I reached that particular village was to ask for a glass of water. Someone brought me a glass of water, but the District Magistrate, who is the highest district government official, came and prevented me from taking the glass of water. He said "No sir, this is not for you, you can't drink this water. We have Coke for you." I was very upset and angry. I said "Thirty years of freedom and planning and we have Coke that has reached the villages, but we do not have drinking water that the villagers can consume." That is when my mind said something is wrong. (Coke Returns from India Exile 1995)

Within months, Fernandes, having assumed the Ministership of Industry in the newly elected Janata Party coalition, effectively forced the Coca-Cola Company out of India.[2] Fernandes's subsequent recollection of the episode located his action squarely within the developmentalist discourse of national self-sufficiency that had informed official policy in India from Independence through to the early 1980s. The historical conjuncture from which he spoke, the mid-1990s, was, in contrast, marked by what appeared to be a complete reversal of this position.

Starting in the mid-1980s, a series of economic reforms, implemented under the banners of "liberalization" and, subsequently, "globalization," had brought a movement toward a new, externally oriented, consumption-led path to national prosperity.[3] Coca-Cola, along with many other multinational companies (MNCs), was back. And yet by the time I arrived in Bombay to start my fieldwork, a backlash of sorts had already set in.[4] It was a period of political turbulence: the national Congress government of P. V. Narasimha Rao, which had implemented the most radical wave of reforms starting in 1991, had been banished from office in 1996. It was succeeded by a coalition that lasted for approximately a fortnight, led by the "Hindu nationalist" Bharatiya Janata Party (BJP). By late 1997 the second in the series of equally fragile coalitions that had replaced the BJP was in its turn crumbling, and the BJP was once again about to grasp power at the center in the national elections that were held in the spring of 1998. It was then that a word that had not been used seriously in national public debate since well before the economic reforms gained a new prominence: *swadeshi*.

Harking back to an older nationalist idiom, this new swadeshi represented an attempt to come to terms, in political discourse, with a predicament with which my informants in the advertising and marketing world were grappling every day. In brief, the challenge that faced them was to capitalize upon a world in which globalization was, in unpredictable ways, heightening rather than effacing the importance of locality and local identity.

Ostensibly, swadeshi (which literally means "of one's own country") and globalization were radically opposed. M. K. Gandhi had, starting in 1919, appropriated the term for a series of nationwide nationalist agitations against British industry, most notably the mill-woven cloth of Manchester.[5] Encapsulated by Gandhi's most potent symbol, the *charkha* or hand-operated spinning wheel, swadeshi came to denote the desire for self-sufficiency and self-reliance. But it was also from the very beginning connected to Gandhi's adaptation of the concept of *swaraj* (self-rule), which drew a philosophical and political analogy between mastery of individual bodily appetites and desires on the one hand and national independence on the other.[6] On the basis of this analogy, the desires of Indian consumers were understood as one of the deep foundations of foreign domination. Therefore, sublimating these desires for the greater good of the nation became, for Gandhi, every Indian's first duty. In his own words: "How can Manchester be blamed? We wore Manchester cloth, and that is why Manchester wove it" (Gandhi 1997, 107).

The term *swadeshi* re-entered national political discourse in 1997–98 primarily through the influence on the BJP's policy of an organization known as the Swadeshi Jagaran Manch (SJM, or "Forum for Swadeshi Awakening"), which itself was part of a diverse coalition of BJP-affiliated groups collectively known as the Sangh Parivar (or "Family of Coalitions").[7] Swadeshi once again became a lightning rod for ongoing public debates around the meaning and desirability of consumerist globalization. The discursive field of these debates was extremely complicated, and I can only provide the briefest of outlines here.

At one pole, there was the key ideologue of the SJM, S. Gurumurthy, who took an uncompromisingly anti-globalization position. Gurumurthy argued that both Nehruvian state planning *and* the consumerist dispensation that had replaced it represented the imposition, by a Westernized Indian elite, of foreign models that were unsuited to Indian cultural conditions and deleterious to native entrepreneurial energies.[8] Indeed, for Gurumurthy, imported social arrangements were a priori not compatible with the realization of Indian needs: "Each country's situation being different, there is no universal model of development available off the shelf" (Swadeshi Jagaran Manch, n.d.b). India's challenge was to articulate a path that arose organically out of "traditional" Indian life-worlds. Globalization, according to Gurumurthy, meant Americanization: "The new model of capitalism is the American variety—fabricated in USA, a State which is devoid of wholesome traditions and community life and has opted for atomized individualism" (ibid.). Indian "tradition," in contrast—and here the Gandhian critique blended with the Hindu nationalism of the ascendant cultural

1. Swadeshi in an age of globalization. This ad appeared in the autumn of 1997 at the time of the celebration of the fiftieth anniversary of Indian independence. With varying degrees of opportunism, companies were falling over themselves to stress their patriotic credentials. Nehru's famous words about "freedom at midnight" were, for instance, made banal in the service of nocturnal bodily comforts — coils promising freedom from mosquitoes, air conditioners promising freedom from heat. In this case, Tamilnad Mercantile Bank is self-consciously attempting to reconcile the historical gravitas of the nationalist theme with the contemporary frisson of globalization: "Kindled by the Swadeshi spirit in the globalized economic scenario."

right wing—rendered "true" needs as a function of the community rather than the individual:[9]

> The lowest socio-economic unit of society in the swadeshi view is not the individual but the family. . . . The unbridled and unbalanced individualism of the West is destructive of community living. The market has to be an instrument and not the master of the people. The smaller the size of the market, the better it is as an instrument. . . . [Swadeshi] commands needs-based life, and rules out unlimited consumption as an end. . . . It is not autarky; but a global alternative which accepts only need-based transnationalism. (Swadeshi Jagaran Manch, n.d.a)

From such a standpoint, Indian advocates of economic deregulation and globalized consumerism were simply victims of a postcolonial inferiority complex and therefore unable to recognize the superior value of their own heritage: "The nation needs psychotherapy," commented Gurumurthy (1998a). In line with mainstream BJP thought, the SJM advocated a movement away from the "pseudo-secularism" of previous administrations, which, in its alienation from Hindu/Indian "tradition," had brought about "a dual life: a formal modern life as the veneer and the age-old beliefs at the core" (Gurumurthy 1998c).[10]

At the other end of the discursive field, free-market apologists may have acknowledged Gurumurthy's dualism but preferred to give it a progressivist twist: Indians were not so much internally divided as torn between advocates of progress and the reactionary forces of tradition.[11] Amit Jatia, the managing director of the company that held the Indian franchise for McDonald's hamburgers, exasperatedly portrayed the swadeshi-ites as a fanatical group of Hindu renouncers: "For every explanation we give, there's a new objection. Tell me how do I convince a *sadhu* that we're okay?" (Jetley and Shastri 1998).[12] For another commentator, an investment analyst, bringing Indian policy into line with the requirements of foreign investors was simply the pragmatic thing to do. From this perspective, swadeshi represented an obsolete throwback to the days when George Fernandes, who was now back in power as a key member of the BJP-led coalition, had thrown out Coca-Cola: "His statements reflect an outdated mind-set which wants to take India backward. They have no foundation in or touch with [sic] economic reality and would send the wrong signals to foreign investors" (Xenophobic Investor Statements 1998). Privileging the "economic" in this way also enabled figures like Columbia University economist (and prominent pro-globalization theorist) Jagdish Bhagwati to dismiss swadeshi as merely "a cultural artefact" (Keshavan 1998).

Far from a cringing desire to please foreigners, many on the pro-globalization side saw a willingness to leap into global markets as the distinguishing mark of a self-confident nation. "Only a nation that lacks dignity and self-respect preaches swadeshi," wrote Pritish Nandy, Bombay publicist, marketing man, and political representative of the Hindu-nationalist Shiv Sena. "Because swadeshi means acknowledging one's inability to compete with the world. It means hobbling around on crutches and expecting others to pity you" (P. Nandy 1998). For Gurumurthy, legitimate Indian leadership meant an orientation toward "Indian" needs, defined as arising out of a "traditional" and indigenous sociocultural formation. For Nandy, conversely, the moral responsibility of the state was to ensure its citizenry access to a global marketplace: "Actually, the government owes it to the consumer to assist him in buying the best products in the world at the best possible price. In India. Irrespective of where they are made and who makes them" (ibid.).

In between these extremes, the debate about the merits of globalization offered several alternative positions. On the one hand, there were the economic pragmatists, who tended to suggest that the swadeshi position was both unrealistic and, in the words of Cornell University economist Kaushik Basu, "based on a bloated sense of national pride" (Basu 1999). The realistic option, then, was "to ask ourselves that given that the bias [of Western domination] is there, what is in our best interest? The answer that we would reach is that in today's world we have to attract foreign capital" (ibid.).[13] The former head of Procter and Gamble India, Gurcharan Das, similarly tried to emphasize that India was in no position to pick and choose between luxuries and necessities: "They [the BJP and the SJM] talk about potato chips versus computer chips. The global investment community is a linked one. You try to discourage Coca-Cola, you will see that your hi-tech industries will also get affected. Because India will get a bad name as a place to do business" ("I Won't Say That We Need a Strong Government" 1998).

On the other hand, several leading industrialists — known collectively as "the Bombay Club" — aligned themselves with the economic dimension of the new swadeshi. Their central contention was that the post-1991 reforms had favored foreign companies and investors but had done little to liberalize business conditions for *Indian* companies. The "level playing field" that they called for included a limited extension of domestic protectionism to compensate for the inefficiencies that had accumulated under the planned economy (inefficiencies that someone like Das would argue were precisely the result of domestic protectionism). S. Gurumurthy put it succinctly: "International business is not like swimming which you learn by first getting into the pool. It's like flying where you have to learn to operate the aircraft in simulated conditions before taking to the skies" (Jishnu et al. 1998).

Despite the fact that the reforms clearly had biased the field toward foreign investors in several ways,[14] and despite the preference shown by many commentators for seemingly objective economic data, the debate also involved many less quantifiable considerations. For the BJP and the SJM, swadeshi was never meant to be a purely economic concept; indeed, as we have seen, a Hindu-nationalist vision of Indian culture and identity underwrote it. But as we will see in the following chapters, appeals to cultural specificity could be mobilized in manifold ways. In fact, some of the staunchest critics of the new swadeshi used Hindu-nationalist and Orientalist-derived stereotypes of eternal India *against* its proponents. Gurcharan Das, for instance, admonished: "We should have confidence. Has our culture not survived the Moghuls, the British? Don't you think it will survive Coca-Cola?" ("I Won't Say . . ." 1998).

In practice, the statements made by key BJP figures both before and immediately after the 1998 general elections expressed a position that seemed far more ambivalent — not to say confusing — than Gurumurthy's line. Already in October 1997, BJP General Secretary N. Govindacharya proclaimed, with little apparent interest in converting the undecided: "Swadeshi movement is our electoral compulsion. Liberalization, foreign investments etc. are our necessities. Unless you understand this difference between compulsion and necessity, you will not understand the BJP strategy" ("Atalji Is Just a Public Face" 1997).

Ideologically, the BJP appeared to be adopting a policy that combined openness to foreign investment with a rhetorical commitment to social justice. Atal Behari Vajpayee, soon to be prime minister, explained: "What I and my party are opposed to is allowing the Indian market to be swamped by products that offer an illusion of prosperity but in reality meet the demands of a very narrow band of people. Putting it simply, we are against unlimited consumerism, which may appeal to cosmopolitan, upwardly mobile Indians, but ignores the needs of 75 percent of the country's population that lives in our villages" (K. Gupta 1997). Along similar lines, George Fernandes, who was now about to assume a position as minister of defense in the new government, attacked the pro-globalization camp's fixation on ensuring access to world-class quality consumer goods: "It is distressing that all the debates pertaining to the middle and upper middle class in India are on the quality of goods. People are arguing that protection should be removed so that there can be competition and we can get the best in the world. All those are important but as a nation we should see to it that no one goes to bed hungry. Our targets have to be in that direction" (Chaudhuri 1998).

Once in power, however, the BJP's spokesmen could be found stretching the concept of swadeshi to new levels of flexibility. Former BJP president Murli Manohar Joshi, for his part, was now arguing that "the swadeshi approach is the best approach to attract maximum foreign investment into the country" (Nanda 1998). Added the new finance minister Yashwant Sinha, speaking to Indian-American and American business leaders in New York:

> Swadeshi is pro-globalization because it's pro-Indian without being anti-foreign. And that's the important message from India. . . . Therefore, swadeshi is the best means of globalization. If every country were to follow this policy, and most countries *are* following it, we can have a better world. . . . We are not relapsing into protectionism. . . . Having recognized globalization as a fact of life we are merely saying that a calibrated approach is needed toward the process of globalization. (Keshavan 1998)

Back in India, many commentators saw the new juxtaposition of globalization and swadeshi as a cynical marriage of convenience or as a fumbling attempt to speak simultaneously to widely disparate constituencies. Under the rubric "BJP will kneel before world bank, and tout it as swadeshi," Ashok Mitra, formerly finance minister of West Bengal, characterized the BJP's increasingly important urban middle-class supporters thus: "Swadeshi is alright, but their eyes are agleam with avarice for the foreign goods the satellite television channels advertise night and day" (Mitra 1998). And once again, the figure of the famously absorptive capacity of Indian civilization was reworked, this time in order to describe the rudderlessness of contemporary public life: "India is famous for lolling in contradictions. It is, let us not forget, the land of tolerance and easy virtues" (ibid.).

Certainly, it would not be wrong to say that the rhetorical contortions around swadeshi arose in part out of a need to reconcile powerful foreign interests with a highly variegated electoral base in which up-and-coming consuming classes were becoming increasingly important.[15] But similar formulations, analogous attempts to be at once local and global, were also being produced at other institutional locations, not least in the Indian advertising and marketing industries. Taken together, they represented a series of attempts to deal with the predicament of globalizing consumerism.

Now, by "globalizing consumerism" I do not merely mean the extension of consumer goods markets across the globe, and the attempt by marketing and advertising interests to forge a globally coordinated method of publicizing them. Rather, the globalization of markets also required the assembly—in a piecemeal, contested, and multi-local manner—of a complex ideology of global consumerism, indeed an entire social ontology of global consumerism.

As key spokesmen for and direct beneficiaries of the new consumerist dispensation, the Indian advertising and marketing businesses rose to an unprecedented public prominence in the 1980s and 1990s.[16] As a consequence, both their practices and their statements increasingly became flash points for the key ideological issues of the day. Conversely, advertising and marketing ideologists could not avoid becoming entangled in debates that lay far beyond their habitual jurisdiction.

It is important to keep in mind that by this time the Indian advertising industry was already eighty years old. Most accounts suggest that the first agency was the Indian-run B. Dattaram and Co. of Bombay, which was founded in 1905. But the multinationals soon followed. The 1920s, in particular, saw a veritable boom: L. A. Stronach and Co. in 1926, Bomas Ltd. in 1928, and J. Walter Thompson in 1929 were just a few of the new entrants. Beginning in the mid-1960s, the Indian government tried to limit foreign equity in Indian operations, an effort that culminated in the Foreign Exchange Restriction Act (FERA) of 1974, the enforcement of which had ultimately caused Coca-Cola to depart in 1977. The agencies that stayed on during this period generally did so in "Indianized" versions; JWT, for instance, became Hindustan Thompson Associates. By the same token, the period extending from the late 1950s through to the mid-1980s saw the rise, consolidation, and in some cases, decline of several dynamic homegrown outfits, among them Clarion, Ulka, Mudra, Trikaya, Rediffusion, MCM, Enterprise, and Chaitra. The first post-FERA Indian agency formally to establish a new joint venture agreement with a multinational agency network was Trikaya, which in 1986 was allowed to enter into a formal arrangement with Grey. As it happened, it was the beginning of a deluge of joint ventures that gathered steam after 1991; by the time I got to Bombay six years later, an independent Bombay agency trying to sell to English-language consumers was already something of an anomaly.[17]

I have suggested that consumer and industrial goods had long served as powerfully concrete foci for political-cultural debates on questions of national versus foreign interests and the question of "legitimate" versus "illegitimate" needs. The 1990s were no different in this regard. But the rise of the new consumerist ontology had changed the rules of the game. In its initial phase of consolidation in the 1980s (see chapter 3), it had directly challenged the swadeshi distinction between the concretion of local community and the abstraction of the market. It had drawn upon a line of thought that went back to Adam Smith's *Wealth of Nations,* which posited that the market was in fact the ideal mediating mechanism through which the needs of individuals and communities could be realized. To this model, however, it added the affect-intensive power of advertising images as the tangible gateways (critics would say the seductive snares) that would reflect the truth of each individual consumer's desire and at the same time provide a generalized sounding board for the national community, now reconceptualized as an aesthetic community.

The consumerist ontology also deconstructed the crucial distinction between true and false needs, which had added a moral dimension to the distinction between necessities and luxuries and therefore served as the foundation for the dismissal of consumerism as inherently elitist.[18] In its place, the new dispensation offered an alternative populism based on the figure of the sovereign consumer as the final arbiter of all normative questions — "the customer is always right." Finally, it necessarily opposed the austerity embedded in the Gandhian interpretation of swaraj and by this route confronted the priorities and assumptions of the Nehruvian planned economy. Just as the BJP would promote Hindu nationalism as a means of releasing the innermost energies of an Indian population too long reined in by the abstractions of "pseudo-secularism," so the new consumerism pledged to liberate the consuming passions of the masses after decades of "socialism" (see Rajagopal 2001).[19]

The elementary forms of mass consumerism were, then, already in place by the time of the more or less simultaneous arrival of satellite television and the reforms of 1991. It was in this second phase that advertising and marketing people really began to grapple with many of the same questions that beset their apparent opponents, the ideologues of the new swadeshi. The dilemma took two forms. First, the sudden presence of a host of foreign brands on Indian shop shelves problematized the relative value of Indian brands in this newly globalized field (see part 2). Second, this same situation also created a kind of crisis of value for foreign brands in India (see part 3). I will show that Indian advertising and marketing professionals' attempts to deal with the problem of "Indianizing" foreign brands brought together the problem of devising a new source of value for products that were suddenly almost *too* available and the necessity of carving out a zone of professional autonomy vis-à-vis multinational clients. In practice, this conjuncture resulted in the promulgation of many of the same essentialized versions of Indianness that the proponents of the new swadeshi leaned upon. But rather than insisting upon the incommensurability of cultural integrity and globalization, the advertising and marketing industries — like the mainstream of the BJP in the wake of the 1998 election — were presenting them as eminently compatible and even mutually reinforcing.

The Anthropology of Globalization

One of the key propositions that emerged out of the anthropology of globalization in the 1990s was that established ways of thinking about the relationship between capitalism and culture had quite simply become inadequate. How, for instance, was one to interpret a statement like this, made by an executive at the Indian ad agency Mudra: "Only advertising which has an Indian soul and [an] international feel will work in the marketplace of tomorrow" (Arathoon 1996)?

Anthropologists had long argued that capitalism is a cultural system. And particularly since the 1970s, a fine body of ethnographic work had emerged on the various registers of resistance and/or adaptation that emerged out of the encounters between world capitalism and local cultural worlds. Nor was the realization that capitalism draws

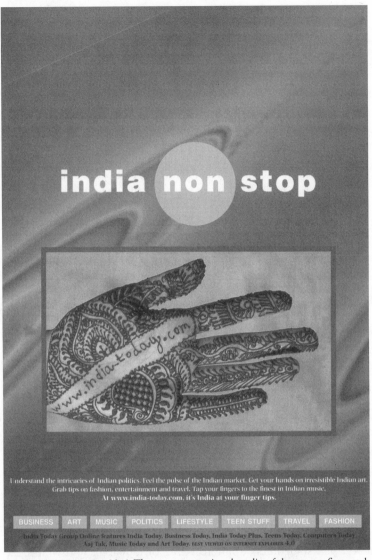

2. Indian soul, international feel. The new transnational media of the 1990s, first satellite television and then the World Wide Web, were the paradigmatic sites for experiments with commodity images that pursued the "Indian soul, international feel" equation. This ad, for www.india-today.com, employs a typical strategy: a "happening," cosmopolitan tone frames (and invades) a highly stereotypical visual icon of Indian "tradition."

upon and produces cultural difference in itself entirely new. Exoticism has for centuries been used to sell people goods from afar. In the last hundred years or so, it has become a vital component of the mass commodification of culture that we know as modern tourism.

But by the 1990s, a communications infrastructure had arisen that, for the first time, enabled marketers both to envisage and, more importantly, to *address* the global population as one big market. At the same time, and for reasons that this book will explore, this single market was also increasingly appearing as an infinitely divisible mosaic of "culture areas," in which consumers would have to be approached by means of culturally appropriate messages. This double-edged vision was succinctly, if rather gracelessly, captured by the marketing neologism "glocal."

In the 1960s and 1970s, the term *cultural imperialism* described the assumption, held by many critical theorists, that the global spread of capitalism entailed cultural homogenization, often understood simply as "Americanization."[20] This was the "McDonaldization" or "Coca-Colonization" of the world (cf. Watson 1997). Had not Karl Marx himself, in *The Communist Manifesto,* declared that European bourgeois civilization "creates a world after its own image" (Tucker 1978, 477)? Anthropologists had, of course, for a long time pointed out both the resilience of local cultural worlds[21] and the Eurocentric myopia of those critical theorists who insisted upon seeing what Immanuel Wallerstein called "the modern world system" as the only game in town (Wallerstein 1976; but see also Abu-Lughod 1989; Frank and Gills 1993; Friedman 1994; Mintz 1985; and Wolf 1982). But by the 1980s, even mainstream social theorists, spurred on by the controversies surrounding the diagnosis of the "postmodern" condition (Harvey 1989; Jameson 1991; Lyotard 1984), were grappling with intriguing questions about the ways in which capitalism seemed increasingly reliant upon the (sometimes) ironic recycling of (apparently) disembedded cultural references and the production of ever-more differentiated subvariants of existing repertoires.

Within anthropology, the so-called postmodernist critique had initially led to a wave of epistemological anxiety about the ways in which anthropologists themselves constructed representations of local lifeworlds, how they "wrote culture" (Clifford and Marcus 1986 being the watershed text). The rising interest in globalization around the turn of the 1990s was a generative response among anthropologists both to concrete changes in the world and to their own disciplinary predicament. The representation of the local was now, to invoke Paul Rabinow's (1986) ironic invocation of Durkheim, increasingly recognized as a social fact. Ethnographically, the challenge was to conceptualize and describe the ways in which the construction and experience of locality is frequently a product of struggles by cultural producers (anthropologists and their informants among them) to generate value out of translocal circuits of images, objects, and money.

By the end of the millennium, then, both marketers and anthropologists understood that "the local" and "the global" are not opposites; rather, they are mutually constitutive imaginary moments in every attempt to make sense of the world, whether for disciplinary, commercial, scholarly, or radical purposes. Neatly symmetrical summations of this dynamic flowed out of the emerging literature. Sociologist Roland Robertson spoke of "the twofold process of the particularization of the universal and the universalization of the particular" (Jameson and Miyoshi 1998, xi). Anthropologist Arjun Appadurai commented that "the central problem in today's global interactions is the tension between cultural homogenization and cultural heterogenization" (1996, 32).

On a concrete empirical level, however, much of the available material seemed impressionistic, as if the mere reporting of hybridity, mixture, and juxtaposition was enough. John Hutnyk captured the predicament well: "Much gee-whiz apocalyptic tone, but little more than lists. . . . The question to be asked is whether or not we are in a position to describe and evaluate, not just list, some of these global technological processes?" (2000, 41, 42). George Marcus (1998) rightly cautioned against slipping back into a habitual opposition between differentiated and resistant local worlds versus homogenizing and hegemonic global systems. This is not to deny that the cultural work that constructs our places in the world is shot through with power relations and inequalities. Rather it is to stress that the global is constructed locally just as much as the local is constructed globally.

Among the various projects that seek to manage and profit from cultural difference, the global marketing and advertising apparatus is uniquely positioned in terms of its access to the mass media. In addition, the power of advertising images to play on desire — coupled with the fiction of consumer sovereignty — frequently makes it look as if the world according to marketing is merely a reflection of the deepest and truest needs of the people to whom it is addressed.

Certainly it would be a mistake to equate the globalization of consumerism with globalization *tout court*. And yet I think that an examination of the institutions of contemporary consumer capitalism is of special interest. This is not simply because its products are so omnipresent. It is also because these institutions — marketing and advertising agencies, commercial mass media, and all the auxiliary services that accompany them — are perhaps the most efficient and successful contemporary practitioners of a skill that no one can afford to ignore: namely, the ability to move fluently between the local and the global, as well as between the concrete and the abstract. David Harvey makes the point forcefully:

> Capitalism is replete with mechanisms for converting from the particular (even personal) to the universal and back again in a dynamic and interactive mode. . . . No social order can, therefore, evade the question of universals. The contemporary "radical" critique of universalism is sadly misplaced. It should focus instead on the specific institutions of power that translate between particularity and universality rather than attack universalism *per se*. Clearly, such institutions favour certain particularities . . . over others . . . and promote a specific kind of universal. (Harvey 2000a, 242)

Of course such partiality is true of *any* project; the field of contemporary cultural politics as a whole must consequently be understood as a struggle between a multiplicity of such translation-projects, at locations ranging from provincial street corners to the WTO, and involving an enormous spectrum of interests and claims to authority.[22] I will be arguing, however, that we frequently make the mistake of assuming that this process of translation occurs smoothly and without remainder. In this regard, the critique of the cultural politics of global capitalism has some philosophical lessons to learn from the scholars who, in literary studies and history, have brought the tools of critical theory to bear on South Asian colonial conjunctures.

Globalization and Difference

In the context of South Asian scholarship, Homi Bhabha has given us a wonderfully subtle set of tools with which to make sense of the ambivalent relationships between power, knowledge, and desire that structured the cultural politics of colonialism. Specifically, he has demonstrated that the taxonomies and discourses through which colonial power operated always struggled with excess elements that escaped their definitive control, but which were nevertheless essential to their operation (Bhabha 1994). How might we adapt these insights to the transnational workings of contemporary consumer capitalism?

One point of departure might be Dipesh Chakrabarty's reflections on the relation between the commodity form and cultural difference. Histories of capitalism, Chakrabarty argues, are conventionally written on the basis of an imagined dualism: either the agents of globalizing capital are seen to dismiss/destroy difference entirely (the cultural imperialism thesis again) or they seize upon cultural difference for their own purposes, domesticating it by means of commodification and offering it up for consumption. This second possibility, which Chakrabarty calls the "consumerist" vision of capitalism, is, he argues, characteristic of the marketing imagination.

> [It is] the idea that capitalism works not so much by canceling out historical differences as by proliferating and converting differences into sets of preference, into taste. Difference becomes a matter of benign, consumable choice. . . . "Repeat after me," *The Wall Street Journal* of 11 October 1996 has the Indian "marketing guru" K. M. S. (Titoo) Ahluwalia saying to potential American explorers of the Indian market: "Repeat after me: India is different, India is different, India is different." Clearly, Ahluwalia, a person from the business world, has not yet learnt the academic fear of essentialism. The aim of his statement is to help transnational capital transform (Indian) differences into tastes, so that making different life-choices — in a capitalist or liberal utopia — could be like choosing between brands of shampoo. (Chakrabarty n.d., 3)

Here are several themes that will be of crucial importance in the chapters that follow: the reworking of "Indian difference" through marketing, the strategic benefits and/or liabilities of essentialism as a source of value, and the "hinge" position claimed by Indian marketing professionals as expert consultants vis-à-vis foreign corporations. But for the purpose of the present discussion, what we should note is that Chakrabarty deploys a close reading of Marx's notion of the commodity form in order to show why both of the conventional ways of writing the relationship between world capitalism and local difference are mistaken. Certainly, capitalism must always depend upon local resources, whether material, physical, or symbolic, to reproduce itself. But just as the rationalized extraction of labor power from the living body of the worker can never completely exhaust his or her concrete being, so the commodification of culture — as "lifestyle" — can never comfortably or completely encompass the life-worlds upon which it draws. On one level, the process of commodification requires a suppression of embodied idiosyncrasies and local conjunctures — the particularity of use-value is in this sense subordinated to the generality of exchange value. On another level, however, commodification *needs* the concretion and tangibility of objects and people — a "corporeal index" of sorts (Povinelli 2000, 509) — to lend credibility and desirability to its abstract claims.

Chakrabarty is highly aware of this generative aspect of the "gap" at the heart of the commodity form. Caught between embodiment and abstraction, the process of commodification (which is itself as ongoing as the circulation of the elements that comprise the commodity) is not simply "flawed." Rather, the very attractiveness of consumer commodities in some sense arises out of their uncanny inability to reify completely the materials upon which they draw. Otherwise, he remarks, "there would be no room for enjoyment in the rule of capital, no play of desires, no seduction of the commodity" (Chakrabarty n.d., 28).[23] The vulnerability of the commodity form, in other words, is also its greatest strength, its means of generating value.

In chapter 2, I will explore the theoretical implications of this insight in some detail, particularly with reference to the fact that an advertisement is itself a very particular kind of commodity, a commodity built on images, a commodity image.[24] For now, I simply want to suggest that what advertising and marketing professionals do is to attempt to manage the fault line at the heart of the commodity form in such a way that profit will accrue first to them, and subsequently, perhaps, to their corporate clients. Consequently, the ethnographic problem is how to make sense of these processes in particular places and at particular times. What is needed is an approach that will be sensitive to the highly concrete resonances that images have at particular times and places, to the complex ways in which these resonances are elaborated in discourse at each of these spatial and temporal junctures, and how all these multiple elaborations intersect to produce something like a public cultural field.

An advertisement, taken as a kind of commodity, is never finished; its elements are sourced from an existing repertoire of resonances and meanings, and after being "produced," it continues to be made and remade throughout its public career. This career, as we will see in the case of the KamaSutra condom campaign, sometimes far exceeds the formal life span of the advertisement itself. One of the entailments of this fact is that the structural "gap" at the heart of the commodity form is never resolved in any definitive way; rather, the way in which a particular image generates juxtapositions of embodied resonance and discursive elaboration is reopened and reworked every time an advertisement "touches down" in a particular setting. At the same time, a great deal of corporate money and effort is spent on trying to establish authoritative — and legally protected — interpretations (see Coombe 1998). The commodity image will not sit still; it must be understood in the flow of practice.

The Limits of Structure

Structuralism had a resounding impact on the critical/interpretive study of advertising, from the seminal works of Roland Barthes (1972, 1977, 1983) through the earlier writings of Jean Baudrillard (1981, 1996, 1998), and on to Judith Williamson's highly influential study, *Decoding Advertisements* (1978). Its great advantage was that it moved the debate on advertising away from a vulgar-materialist and dubiously moralistic preoccupation with "true" versus "false" needs. Earlier critics had frequently suggested that advertising diverted people from a healthy (and, it was implied, honest) relationship with objects by raucously encouraging unnecessary and harmful desires. This line of thinking was in fact held in common by both liberal and radical thinkers; it was a basic tenet of John Kenneth Galbraith's *The Affluent Society* (1958) and it even informed the reflections of as sophisticated a cultural critic as Raymond Williams.[25]

The structuralists, in contrast, started from the premise that goods — and representations of goods — were signifiers. As such, they had no inherent meaning; rather, it was their positions within shifting structures of signification that rendered them meaningful in particular settings. Some of the structuralists, particularly in the 1950s and 1960s, stayed true to elements of a Marxist optic, not least to rather vague references to the relationship between "base" and "superstructure." But structuralism had its own internal logic to fulfill. The structural properties of advertising considered as a kind of text were the real object of interest; the social relations that comprised their contexts of production were sometimes acknowledged, but never directly engaged.

Some tried to turn the vice into a virtue by drawing an analytical *cordon sanitaire* around the ads. While ultimately acknowledging that "the danger in structural analysis [is] its introversion and lack of context," Williamson nevertheless insists upon "simply analyzing what can be *seen* in advertisements. . . . Analyzing ads in their *material form* helps to avoid endowing them with a *false* materiality and letting the 'ad world' distort the real world around the screen and page" (Williamson 1978, 178, 11).

In Baudrillard's work, we see the logical conclusion of this trend: increasingly, the "real world" — however understood — is entirely dispensed with on the grounds that is in any case only a kind of ideological fiction. As I have suggested, this move is useful insofar as it raises questions about any claims about objects having inherent or natural uses — values that advertising then distorts — what Baudrillard calls "a spontaneous vision of objects in terms of needs and the hypothesis of the priority of their use value" (Baudrillard 1981, 29). But by equating use-value only with functionality, Baudrillard effectively eliminates the entire dimension of concretion, embodiment, contingency, and practice from his analysis. He demands an understanding of goods according to "social logic and strategy" (36), terms that suggest an engagement with specific conjunctures and located struggles. In Baudrillard, however, these terms always tend to refer back to a seamless and self-fulfilling "code," a system of signification which pervades all aspects of contemporary social life, and which admits of no interference or interruption. The greatest irony of all is that Baudrillard's position, while ostensibly critical, in fact resembles nothing so much as the totalizing vision of marketing itself. There, too, we find a world mapped entirely according to the structurally relative signifying relations of brands and product categories, indeed a "code" according to which social relations are matched, quasi-totemically, with relations between goods. In marketing such a model has long been enshrined as the science of "positioning" (Ries and Trout 1981; Trout 1995).

The crucial "gap" in the commodity form, which I have argued is essential to understanding the everyday politics of the circulation of advertisements, is in Baudrillard reduced from a dynamic principle to a ghost of logic, always surmised but never encountered.[26] In all essentials, structuralism leads us into a dead end, in fact into the hands of its avowed opponent: what Chakrabarty terms the "consumerist" vision of capitalism. So to what extent might an ethnographic approach reinstate the dialectic between practice and signification, between embodiment and abstraction?

Marshall Sahlins was the first anthropologist to think seriously about the social place of the advertising and marketing industries (although brief reflections upon the parallels between advertising and magic can be found in Malinowski [1965; cf. the discussion in McCreery 1995]). Sahlins too starts from the structuralist premise that the meaning of goods in any society is a function not of any objective material features, but rather of an independently determined cultural logic: "The material appropriation of nature we call 'production' is a sequitur to its symbolic appropriation" (Sahlins 1976, 196). But where Baudrillard sees only an ideological "alibi" of "functionality" in the concept of use-value, Sahlins argues that Marx had understood that uses were culturally and socially relative. Marx's mistake, according to Sahlins, was to sacrifice this insight because it didn't square with his universalist conception of history.

Sahlins identified an ambivalence in Marx's own writings on the subject of use-values and their attendant social meanings and human "needs." Marx had written: "The usefulness of a thing makes it a use-value. But this usefulness does not dangle in mid-air. It is conditioned by the physical properties of the commodity, and has no existence apart from the latter. It is therefore the physical body of the commodity itself, for instance iron, corn, a diamond, which is the use-value or useful thing" (Marx 1976, 126). At the same time, the "physical body," which is identified with the use-value of a commodity, is "only realized in use or in consumption" (126). The needs that spurred this use or consumption, however, are themselves ambiguous. Right at the outset of *Capital*, in his opening remarks on the commodity-form, Marx introduced this element of indeterminacy into his analysis of the basis of human needs: "The commodity is, first of all, an external object, a thing which through its qualities satisfies human needs of whatever kind. The nature of these needs, whether they arise, for example, from the stomach, or the imagination, makes no difference" (125).

If needs for Marx are as much legitimately a product of the "imagination" (and therefore in anthropological terms "culturally produced") as physiologically determined, Sahlins reasoned (1976, 148–65), then the use-values that "inhered" in the material bodies of objects, yet were only "realized" in relation to human needs, would themselves have to be understood as socioculturally relative. Why, then, did Marx insist upon an "anthropological deception" in which use-values appeared as unproblematic as compared with the great riddle of abstraction, of spectral equivalence, of exchange value? Certainly, the great contribution of the theory of exchange value is that it allows us to conceptualize the process through which incommensurable objects/commodities are made potentially equivalent. But, in Sahlins's words, "It does not tell us why wheat and why iron" (149). Sahlins's own explanation is that Marx effectively needed to repress his own concerns over the problem of the relativity of use-value because otherwise historical materialism would not have been able to offer a universal narrative of human emancipation. This is not to say, however, that Marx did not take into account the multiple factors that might determine production; rather, he tended to relegate many of these to the domain of the ephemeral and the unnecessary, as in the following passage from the 1844 Manuscripts:

> The Say-Ricardo school [of political economy] is hypocritical in not admitting that it is precisely whim and caprice which determine production. It forgets the "refined needs;" it forgets that there would be no production without consumption; it forgets that as a result of competition production can only become more extensive and luxurious. It forgets that it is use that determines a thing's value [Marx would, of course, no longer maintain this position by the time of *Capital*], and that fashion determines use. (Tucker 1978, 96)

The larger context of Sahlins's intervention was a concerted polemic against materialist modes of explanation. Consequently, having pointed to the social embeddedness of use-value, he proceeded to offer advertising and marketing as key sites not so much for a contested construction of cultural meanings, but for the *instantiation* and *discovery* of an underlying and always-already operational cultural logic. Just as Baudrillard's approach ironically ends up aligned with, rather than opposed to, the logic of marketing, so Sahlins suggested that anthropologists, advertising people, and marketing professionals are fundamentally engaged in the same task: that is, mapping the hidden correspondences of an already given cultural order. Sahlins moved from the indisputable fact that advertising does not emerge out of nowhere to the disputable suggestion that it is an index of an existing cultural organization.

> The anthropologist, in arranging [the elements of the cultural order] in a way faithful to experience does no more than discover that order. In doing so . . . he acts in something of the same way as a market researcher, an advertising agent, or a fashion designer, unflattering as the comparison might be. For these hucksters of the symbol do not create *de novo*. In the nervous system of the American economy, theirs is the synaptic function . . . like Lévi-Strauss' famous bricoleur, he uses bits and pieces with an embedded significance from a previous existence to create an object that works, which is to say that sells — which is also to say that objectively synthesizes a relation between cultural categories, for in that lies its salability. (Sahlins 1976, 217)

As I will show in subsequent chapters, the advertising that works is not necessarily the advertising that sells goods.[27] But the more troubling issue is the one that I have already identified in relation to Baudrillard: the critically disabling affinity between structuralist analyses and marketing dogma. For better or for worse, the story has it, advertising makes sense because culture makes sense. As Bharat Dabholkar, a senior Bombay advertising professional, has put it: "Ads do not go against accepted social norms, they reflect society. If I want to show a woman wearing a mini-skirt, which I couldn't do ten years ago, but I can today, it is because society accepts it. I see it all around me, so I can do that" (Dabholkar 1997, 165). Thus, questions of ideology, power, and agency are elided. Advertising professionals are, in Stephen Fox's phrase, merely "mirror makers." "Society" and, in particular, "culture" assume an a priori status, absolving commentators of the need to reflect upon their contested constitution, the dialectical play of reification and deconstruction that is everyday cultural politics. That it is at least rhetorically possible to maintain such a position while at the same time acknowledging the internal complexity of advertising practice — and thereby apparently absolving the industry of mind-controlling motivations — is borne out by Fox, who writes: "Outsiders see only the smooth, expertly contrived finished product, often better crafted than the programming and editorial matter it interrupts. Insiders know the messy process of creating an ad, the false starts, rejected ideas, midnight despair, the failures and account losses and creative angst behind any ad that finally appears. In particular, the insiders know that no successful ad can stray very far from where the audience already lives" (S. Fox 1990, 329).

In practical terms, this position precludes any critical consideration of the contingencies that actual practice might bring to the relationship between culture and advertising. One does not have to posit any dubiously autonomous agentive consciousness or will to resistance for this criticism to matter. Rather, one might argue, as I do, that the very intersection between the internal instability of the commodity form and the exigencies of situated practice in themselves disrupt any simple one-to-one relationship between advertising and culture. Precisely the fact that culture and locality have become dominant objects of representation and problematization in contemporary marketing and advertising practice — frequently in a mode reminiscent of a rather unreflexive brand of anthropology — should alert us to the importance of understanding the relation.

Sahlins's path-breaking move was to point to the ambivalence in Marx's analysis of needs, uses, and goods, to his realization that use-values were necessarily socially and historically constructed. But his insight was then subordinated to the requirements of a structuralist polemic. The predicament of globalization has only made more obvious what was true all along: that objects and goods serve as deceptively concrete boundary-markers in the ongoing and ubiquitous struggle to establish definitive worlds of reference, belonging, and power. What is required, then, is an ethnographic practice that goes to the heart of this struggle and that, in so doing, brings back into focus the question of the relationship between the thingness of things and the meanings with which they are invested.

The Practice of Advertising

Michael Schudson's *Advertising, the Uneasy Persuasion* fruitfully paved the way for subsequent ethnographic studies of the industry by stressing the contingency at the heart of the enterprise. Schudson cites an advertiser (that is, a client) who remarked: "[Corporate] executives go on the assumption that advertising is doing something, just like praying or going to church is doing something" (Schudson 1984, 86). In Schudson's wake, Brian Moeran and Daniel Miller, in particular, have produced studies that concentrate on the complex dynamics of the media system of which advertising is a part, on the internal structural tensions of the business, and on the ambiguous role played by market research in the making and selling of advertising.

Against postwar paranoiac discourses on advertising as a sinister centralized agency of mass manipulation,[28] Moeran emphasizes the conflicts and compromises that obtain on an everyday level both within agencies and between agencies and clients (Moeran 1996a, 32–33). This is not to say, of course, that what emerges from agencies is entirely contingent; in part 2, I show that it is often precisely out of this process of conflict and compromise that stereotypical and overdetermined advertising emerges.

One of the key structural features of the advertising business is the perpetual tension between creative personnel (art directors and copywriters) and account executives. Miller describes how executives and creatives "perform" in client meetings and relate to each other more informally via a set of conventionalized role expectations according to which creatives are invariably precious failed fine artists and executives are always business-headed boors. (Certainly my own fieldnotes contain several instances of such role-playing, often executed with all the malicious affection of high-school name-calling rituals.)

This structural relationship extends to the manner in which agencies sell their services to clients, producing a kind of professional ambivalence that insists at once upon scientific precision and ineffable creative inspiration.[29] The former takes the form of the fetish of market research, regarding which Moeran notes: "The Agency had spent a lot of time and money developing what it regarded as a marketing 'science,' designed to facilitate communication and advertising strategies. ... This ... was not simply a matter of general quality control, but was seen to demonstrate the Agency's overall power" (Moeran 1996a,

105). Moeran, Miller, and Schudson all note, however, that whatever the grandiloquent claims made for market research, its findings are more often than not used retrospectively to justify or rationalize decisions made on an executive hunch.[30]

In part 2, I will present a situation in which market research and the discourse of brand management played a crucial role in mediating the relationship between agency and client, almost irrespective of what the advertising itself was doing in the course of its public journey. But I would also suggest (and this will be an important point in part 1) that marketing discourse can function as a crucial idiom of legitimation for the advertising industry as a whole when it is faced with the need to justify its social role. This is, however, a double-edged sword, since "scientific marketing" can easily begin to raise the specter of social control, the administered society. Its place within the public repertoire of the industry is therefore highly ambivalent.[31]

The advertising business may choose to downplay connotations of frivolity, prurience, and opportunism by appealing to the "rigor" of market research. But it is just as likely — depending on the needs of the moment, and the specific agency involved — to distance itself from images of corporate routine and predictability. British creative star John Hegarty, on a visit to India, described his own operation: "We have . . . developed a unique style and work culture. We are youthful and we like to have fun. . . . And we are irreverent — that's why we have opted for the black sheep as our logo. Independence is our positioning. . . . I keep saying 'When the world zigs, you should zag' " ("Interview with John Hegarty" 1998).[32] The cult of creativity is as crucial a component of the ideological armature of the advertising business as is the fetish of research.

This doubling, this simultaneous appeal to inspiration and rationality, is of the essence both in promoting advertising as a crucial component of a nascent consumerist dispensation *and* in positioning the advertising business as the ideal arbiter between translocal brands and local "culture." For all that we realize the complexity and contingency at the heart of the production of advertising, we should not forget that the process is also highly ideological. This is because it cannot function without constantly intervening in a wider public cultural field.

As the chapters that follow will show, one of the areas in which advertising cannot help but intervene is in the visual and discursive articulation of national cultural identity. Indeed, on one level, the

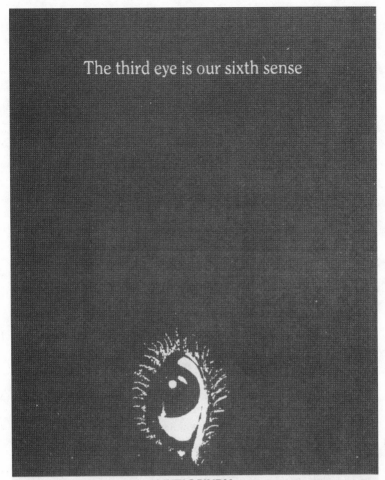

The third eye is our sixth sense

LINTAS :: INDIA
A member of the SSC&B-Lintas Worldwide advertising network

3. The cult of creativity given civilizational legitimation. As a business, advertising is generically torn between the cult of ineffable creative inspiration and the reassuring fetish
of scientific market research. This particular ad, for the Indian operations of the
transnational advertising agency network Lintas, draws on a vaguely civilizational
reference to spiritual enlightenment as a localizing support for the "creative edge"
to which the agency lays claim. Several years later, during the crisis of value brought
on by the globalization of Indian consumer markets (see part 3), many Indian
marketing professionals would explicitly extend this idea to make themselves indispensable as "cultural consultants" to multinational corporations.

global marketing and advertising business seeks to construct a global model of the world, in which each "culture area" (sometimes isomorphic with nation-state boundaries, sometimes not) occupies a particular position within a total structural system of signification. Just as economics suggests that each country will enjoy a comparative advantage with particular goods or services, so marketing conjures a world apprehended according to a global division of identity: the French are fashionable, the Americans are rugged, the Indians are spiritual.

How this utopian view from corporate head office plays out in actual advertising strategies (let alone other sites of everyday life) is of course another matter. This is so for a number of reasons, some of which we will encounter again in the following pages. Local advertising agencies, even if they are part of transnational networks, frequently have a stake in championing cultural specificity, because it means more local input will be required (see part 3). At the same time, the credibility of local references will depend upon historically embedded associations between certain kinds of product categories, certain specific brands, and given countries of origin (see part 2). Moreover, in postcolonial settings the distinction between the local and the nonlocal connects issues that might otherwise seem unrelated, the politics of the new swadeshi being a case in point (see also Kemper 2001). As Miller points out, his Trinidadian advertising executive informants were leery about positioning cocoa as explicitly local despite "international adjudication that suggested that Trinidadian-grown cocoa, for example, was of quite unusual excellence" (Miller 1997, 201). Moreover, national states and transnational corporations are constantly engaged in a tug of war over access to markets and the permissibility of certain kinds of products or messages.

Anthropologists, area studies scholars, and market researchers have sometimes been unwittingly complicit in the perpetuation of an image of the world as a mosaic of bounded "culture areas," each with their own, relatively stable set of traits. The everyday course of local life, it followed, could be read as a kind of performance or instantiation of these traits. Against such a "trait geography," Arjun Appadurai has proposed a "process geography," a critical optic that would help us to see "significant areas of human organization as precipitates of various kinds of action, interaction, and motion — trade, travel, pilgrimage, warfare, proselytisation, colonisation, exile and the like. . . . Regions are best viewed as initial contexts for themes that generate variable geographies, rather than as fixed geographies marked by pre-given themes" (Appadurai 2000, 7). The attention to process has the critical advantage of allowing us to understand how particular authoritative or would-be definitive statements about local culture or identity — whether they are made by scholars, governments, activists, or corporations — arise and circulate. And as David Harvey argues, this also means acknowledging that the local inevitably arises not out of itself, as it were, but rather in relation to translocal processes (Harvey 2000b).

In the Field . . . But Where Is It?

Doing ethnographic research on the advertising business involves both practical and more existential challenges.[33] Throughout my time in Bombay, I found myself constantly re-imagining the shape, or space, of the field in which I was doing fieldwork. On the one hand, I was working in several quite concrete places and with several types of quite clearly distinguishable data. I spent an extended period of time being a participant-observer in the Bombay office of a transnational advertising network, as well as spending a significant amount of time with some of its employees outside of work hours.[34] During and after this period, I was also interviewing media, marketing, and advertising people in other Bombay companies, as well as pursuing a program of archival research that was concluded at the Hartman Center Archives at Duke University.

On the other hand, the question of the dynamic relationship between these various sites remained open; increasingly, I found myself exploring a kind of force-field, a space of circulation comprising sites that were public, private, and ambiguously located along the continuum. I imagined myself following images and discourses as they moved through this field. Sometimes, they would disappear from view altogether; at other times, they would pop up simultaneously at multiple locations — on billboards, in magazine articles, in private conversations. Sometimes they appeared in surprising combinations; often, their avataras seemed heavily overdetermined. Always, I had the sense that I was trying to inhabit and understand (not "overview") a kind of totality, but one that was open-ended and part of larger networks that reached out far beyond Bombay. Obviously, I could not describe or record everything; my aim instead became to look for telling juxtapositions (cf. Cohen 1998), critical "nodes," as it were, that might provide access to the various projects of value that commodity images inhabit and refract.

As George Marcus (1998) points out, as anthropologists branch out beyond their habitual study of marginalized peoples, the ethics of the field encounter become more complicated. On the one hand, I was a meddling visitor in a world that was quite clearly distinct from the one that I would call home. On the other hand, my informants and I were, in each others' eyes, also occupants of categories—ad man, academic—that were translatable (if not quite equivalent) across our respective life-worlds. With the handful of my informants who gradually became personal friends, these categories became less important. But in more formal situations, such as when conducting interviews, I frequently found that this apparent categorical transparency in practice led to a kind of opacity. As senior members of a global business elite speaking to a junior member of a global academic elite, many of these informants, unsurprisingly, chose to address me in an idiom—marketing discourse—that acknowledged our mutual professional standing, yet, to my initial frustration, appeared to give nothing away.

As an anthropologist I had been socialized to look for the contingent detail, the apparently trivial element that would provide the concrete connection between reified abstractions ("the Indian consumer," "the market," etc.) and everyday lives. But there I was, confronted with informants whose very livelihood depended on their skill at information management, at making contingencies appear as if they had been part of the plan all along. Sometimes, it seemed to me as if our conversations had taken on the quality of illumination characteristic of advertisements: full-on and depthless, with the attention focused on hyperrealistic surface detail at the expense of shadow and perspective.

But of course my own position was, if anything, equally troubling to some of my informants. I have already pointed to the way in which anthropology and marketing can jointly constitute "culture" as an object of expertise and potential intervention (indeed, this affinity is the basis for the now prevalent employment of anthropologists in advertising agencies). From this point of view, anthropologists in advertising agencies make perfect sense; perhaps they can even make themselves useful by clarifying some of the "cultural factors" that might help the agency's clients sell products to hitherto recalcitrant consumers. In this respect, I was, I'm afraid, a great disappointment; it became increasingly clear to me and to my informants alike that I was more interested in the professional construction of these "cultural factors" within the marketing enterprise than in developing models that clients might find useful. As in any fieldwork situation, the informants with whom I continued to have the most immediately stimulating exchanges were the "insider-outsiders," those who were the most ambivalently or ironically positioned in relation to their work.[35]

As time wore on, however, I also came to realize that the conversations that I had initially interpreted as depthless and predictable were nevertheless important insofar as they comprised the constitutive discourse of the professional "field," in Pierre Bourdieu's sense (Bourdieu 1993). Soon I began to understand them as enunciations comprising one node in a relational field of other nodes — for example day-to-day practices, advertisements, political discourse, and informal conversations. And by the same token, I came to see my own study — and the texts that would emerge from it — as occupying another position within this same relational field, a critically engaged commentary that was of relevance to the broader context that my informants operated in, even if it was not immediately useful to their work.

Bourdieu's idea of a "field" is valuable in that it requires that we understand how statements that we might otherwise take to be "merely" ideological or smokescreens ("India is different") actively operate to make possible the stakes, dispositions, and values of the field itself. For Bourdieu, it is in fact both the duty and the privilege of the social scientist to interrogate the conditions of possibility of that field, since for those for whom it is their life-world there are certain truths that cannot be uttered, that constitute, as it were, the very normative and ontological boundaries of that world.

Now it is certainly true that the advertising business, like any business, encourages only the sort of critical reflection that is likely to be profitable within the terms of the enterprise as a whole. For all the talk about "thinking outside the box," this thinking must still take place *within* a box, a box marked "Dove," or "Ray-Ban," or "Videocon." But to say that participants in a field are not rewarded for the kind of reflexivity that calls the borders of that field into question is not to say that they do not regularly, and sometimes agonizingly, engage in this kind of reflexivity. Many of the executives I knew in Bombay loved the adrenaline rush and high salaries that came with the job. But they would also regularly turn despondent about what some of them perceived as the limitations of the enterprise as a whole.

Equally, most contemporary anthropologists would balk at Bourdieu's implication that the social scientist can or should establish some kind of objectivistic distantiation from the field. To be sure, all fieldwork involves a dialectic of familiarity and distance. But in a world where it is less and less feasible for us to pretend that we are radically separated from the people we study, we must acknowledge — with all due disclaimers about the limited audiences that most of us are likely to be addressing — that our work is necessarily an intervention, one among others, into the fields that we describe.

The greatest stumbling block, to my mind, is the unfortunate but widespread tendency to imagine a radical categorical divide between an ivory tower — within which a rarefied "life of the mind" can thrive — and a "world of business" — where all is cutthroat instrumentality. It is this kind of binary (not unrelated to that of observer and observed) that leads to the incessantly proclaimed idea that the public relevance of anthropology depends upon dragging hapless professors, blinking like moles in the sunlight, into the so-called real world. By the same token, it is this kind of binary that encourages those who work in business to believe that public debate is a kind of inessential good, a luxury, or — worst of all — "politics." The distinction between the ivory tower and the real world is not simply a habit of mind; rather, its reproduction is insured by institutionally embedded interests.[36]

The really important point of intersection between anthropology and advertising, then, is not that they share an abiding interest in understanding an entity known as "culture." On the contrary, it is that they are both public cultural interventions that necessarily intervene in areas that — whether they wish it or not — extend far beyond the narrow instrumentalities of their working environments. As such, they both point to the possibility of a critical engagement that would problematize the boundaries of expertise and authority that today help to police our public conversations.

Shoveling Smoke

Finally, a word about the title. While examining documents in the J. Walter Thompson archives at Duke, I came upon a memo written in

1949 by a social scientist named Vergil Reed. The agency's legendary director Stanley Resor had appended it to his response to a somewhat agonized missive from a young American executive posted in the agency's Bombay office. This young man was particularly concerned about the exact role that a powerful advertising network like his should play vis-à-vis the growing pains of the new Indian nation. In reply, it seems, Resor had sought to rein in the young man's idealism and to focus his mind on the matter at hand: shifting product. According to Resor,

> Part number 1, as I see it *is* "the problem of moving merchandise." Part number 2 is the doing of part number 1 in such a way that it contributes both directly and indirectly to part number 2, which is the delivering of the child. Only by doing part 1 in an efficient, farseeing, and practical way can one hope to contribute to part number 2 — the birth and development of the nation. . . . To see absolutely sharply, let us think of part number 1 as being 100 percent and part number 2 some fourth dimension which arises out of and is a product of part number 1. It is, as it were, an extra dividend.

Vergil Reed's lengthy memo, appended to Resor's note, was in essence a scathing summation of the hurdles in the way of Indian national development, most particularly the Indian "mind-set," which, in classical sociological mode, he understood as fundamentally inimical to the great task of the day: modernization. If advertising had a role to play, aside from "moving merchandise," he seemed to be suggesting, then it might well be in the territory of encouraging a change in cultural fundamentals. But the prospects, he cautioned, were bleak:

> Indian genius runs more to introspection than to the practical. It has concerned itself mainly with abstract ideas and speculation on the nature of the soul rather than with physical laws, the properties of matter and the mastery of environment. Two meals a day and decent houses for India's millions are problems far removed from this high plane of thought, — and entirely too materialistic. Lethargy and lack of initiative in practical pursuits are a further sedative to conscience and a palliative to misery. . . . Did you ever try to shovel smoke or put a rubber band around a gaseous mass? It's easier than convincing Indians what they *must do* to become a modern nation. . . . Stress the fact that American technicians are available and

will continue to be so with U. S. Government encouragement — but they expect immediate steps to be taken to make the improvements they recommend rather than ten years of talking mostly explaining why it can't be done in India. It can, and no self-respecting technician is going to remain through years of unadulterated frustration. Five years is really a long time to an American, regardless of any comparisons with how short a period that represents in history [reference to earlier complaint that Indians will always go on about eternity, etc]. The medicine of modernization may taste strange and bitter at first, but it can't help the patient until taken. Modernization will hurt quite a bit and will require action rather than philosophy.[37]

Reading these words half a century after they were written, I was struck by Reed's complaint about "shoveling smoke." To be sure, Stanley Resor's advice, to see the project of selling as a concrete set of measures that may, as an "extra dividend," produce national progress, would, as we will see in the following chapters, begin to supplant the Nehruvian developmentalist model in India in the 1980s. But beyond the arrogant impatience of Reed's modernist teleology, so distinctively of its time, there was something else about his phrase that, ironically, resonated with my own thinking about contemporary advertising practice. This was its aptness as a description of the commodity-imaging project, a project in which the linear structures of technique and narrative are forever attempting to coordinate, encircle, and domesticate the evanescent substance to which they are applied. The "smoke" that Vergil Reed had seen as an apt metaphor for the resistance offered by Indian tradition to the "strange and bitter" medicine of modernization, had, however, in the meantime been transformed into part of the very substance of a new conception of progress: the commodification of culture itself.

2

Elaborations: The Commodity Image

In chapter 1, I laid out the general context both for my experience in Bombay and for the conceptual tools that I brought with me. In doing so, I pointed toward the commodity image as a tool for theorizing advertising as public cultural commodity production. The present chapter is devoted to elaborating what I mean by "the commodity image," and how my understanding emerges out of—and calls into question—the tradition of thought on capitalism and aesthetics that moves from Kant, through Hegel, Marx, and the Frankfurt School, on to more recent reflections on photographically mediated modernities. Most generally, my discussion takes the form of an immanent critique of the teleological "totalization narrative" that has dominated this tradition, in particular the idea that commodification entails the subsumption of concrete particulars to abstract universals. This discussion will be an invaluable key to some of the analytical moves that I make in the following chapters. That said, those readers impatient for ethnographic substance may wish to skip directly to chapter 3.

We might understand contemporary globalizing consumerism as a chapter in a world historical process that we can trace further and further back in time: the consolidation of the U.S. position of hegemony, the rise of mass consumerism in the West, the infrastructural and experiential shifts entailed by the coming of industrial capitalism, the consolidation of a philosophical and a geopolitical European modernity, and the whole long and complex history of the foundations of European colonialism.

Indeed, outside of anthropology and postcolonial studies, the story is usually told in precisely these terms: the virgin birth of modernity in Europe and its subsequent embrace of the globe. The white man's burden is indeed alive and well, nowadays appearing as "modernization" and "globalization," stalking the corridors of the World Trade Organization. Anthropologists have of course been at the forefront of rethinking this totalizing story, not least in partial atonement for their earlier complicity with its foundations. But as Enrique Dussel (1995) argues, our response to the arrogant complacency of existing universalist histories should not be a reactive championing of the local. Rather, if we reexamine the universalizing project of Western modernity at its core as well as at its peripheries, we will see that the story of the virgin birth has been a long and ongoing attempt to deny an actuality of miscegenation. The universalist categories of modernity arose and today continue to be reinvented in an attempt to manage the otherness of the worlds that the Europeans confronted. The important point is that locality and difference *constitute* modernity; they are not *subsumed* by it.

Dussel's argument about the relational invention of modernity resonates closely with Dipesh Chakrabarty's argument (see 19–20) about the "gap" at the heart of the commodity form. Indeed, by generalizing the commodity form to an unprecedented extent, contemporary consumerist globalization in a sense represents a staggering intensification of the particular project of global difference-management that was inaugurated when Columbus reached the New World. One need only consider the way in which marketing plans for global brands today seek to tabulate and incorporate the cultural particularities of consumers everywhere to discern a line of descent that connects contemporary marketing thought to the earliest efforts to ground world power in cosmopolitan knowledge (see chapter 7).

Even if we accept that capitalist modernity has always been about the ambivalent relationship between concrete particulars and abstract universals, the question of the possible uniqueness of the contemporary moment remains. Is the globalizing consumerism of today the latest installment of this history, or is it qualitatively different? My argument is that it is both. On the one hand, the tensions and contradictions that I will describe in the chapters that follow are both instantiations of—and responses to—the difference-management projects that define histories of modernity. On the other hand, the fact that mass-mediated images have now become indispensable to this project means that its central tension—the irreducible tension between the concrete and the abstract, the particular and the universal—is now played out in full public view.

Interestingly, many of those theorists who have formulated the most influential diagnoses of contemporary image- or "video-capitalism"[1] — frequently under the rubrics "postmodernism" or "postmodernity" — have come to the opposite conclusion (Harvey 1989; Jameson 1991). The fact that mass-mediated images have become indispensable to the reproduction of capital, they argue, is a sign of the increasing abstraction of capitalism away from concrete life-worlds, particular histories, and embodied experience. The more "culture" itself becomes commodified, the argument goes, the more total is the abstracting rule of exchange value. Signifiers that used to be anchored in particular sociohistorical locations increasingly float free of such local referents; instead, they function as tokens in a more or less self-referential, electronically mediated global culture.

I will be arguing against this interpretation of the present, not because I think it underestimates the resilience of local cultural worlds (although this is a charge worth pondering), but because I think it misunderstands capitalism. I should add, however, that my argument is inspired by many of the same thinkers who provide the intellectual foundations for the position I am attacking. Consequently, I will need to spend a little time considering these foundations, and the kind of recuperation that I have in mind.

The Totalization Narrative

The notion that the rise of Western modernity was, above all, a matter of the diffusion of universalizing processes and categories is central to both critical and affirmative versions of this story. Both interpretations owe their common foundation to the systematizing work of the German philosopher G. W. F. Hegel. Hegel made the case for understanding European imperialism, the work of philosophy, and historical progress as manifestations of a single process: the self-realization of Spirit. Let us call this the totalization narrative. Later, in part 1, I will have occasion to refer to his *Lectures on the Philosophy of History*, the work where Hegel most explicitly — and most infamously — offers an apologia for the world-historical triumph of Northern Europe. But for the purposes of this chapter, the following passage from *Elements of the Philosophy of Right* provides a forceful illustration of just how fundamentally Hegel connected progress — in thought as in history (for him, merely two sides of the same coin) — with the *possession* and *penetration* of the concrete and particular by the abstract and general.

> When I think of an object, I make it into a thought and deprive it of its sensuous quality; I make it into something which is essentially and immediately mine. For it is only when I think that I am with myself [*bei mir*], and it is only by comprehending it that I can penetrate an object; it then no longer stands opposed to me, and I have deprived it of that quality of its own which it had in opposition to me. Just as Adam says to Eve: "You are flesh of my flesh and bone of my bone," so does spirit say: "This is spirit of my spirit and its alien character has disappeared." Every representation [*Vorstellung*] is a generalization, and this is inherent in thought. (Houlgate 1998, 328)

Every undergraduate in the social sciences is told that Marx, inspired by Feuerbach, "turns Hegel on his head," thus apparently substituting a "historical materialism" for Hegel's "historical idealism." It is certainly not my intention to continue the interminable debate about the relative weight that Marx (or indeed Hegel) gives to "material" versus "ideal" determinations. What is important to me here is that Hegel's Big Picture, in all essentials, remains unaltered. (It is precisely for this reason that Cornelius Castoriadis argues that "a revolutionary surpassing of the Hegelian dialectic demands not that it be set on its feet but that, to begin with, its head be cut off" [Castoriadis 1987, 55]). True, Marx refuses to accept the bourgeois state as the culmination of world history, pointing to its internal contradictions and consequently insisting that the Big Resolution will arrive with the *following* stages of the story, "the dictatorship of the proletariat" and eventually — a tantalizing possibility hovering on the borders of the imaginable — a communist future. But the grand narrative persists, albeit with new protagonists. Hegel's Spirit is replaced in Marx with class struggle, and the work of overcoming concretion is shifted from the philosopher's study to the factory floor. Now it is the commodity form that brings everything that had once been merely concrete and particular into an abstract relation of equivalence and exchange. And according to the familiar logic of the historical dialectic, it is precisely this violent deracination of the world in the name of profit that will prepare the ground for the redemption of humanity through revolution. The bigger the lie, the closer we are to the truth; the more bourgeois civilization remakes the world in its own image, the closer we will come to the moment when the scales fall from our eyes and we suddenly see all fellow beings and objects clearly, in all their positive truth. In the famous words from *The Communist Manifesto:* "All that is solid melts into air, all that is holy is profaned, and man is at last compelled to face with sober senses his real conditions of life and his relations with his kind" (Tucker 1978, 476).

This vision of modern history as a one-way process of abstraction, with a messianic inversion at its conclusion, becomes a dominant leitmotif in subsequent Marxist cultural criticism. In the work of the "Western Marxists" (Lukács, Bloch, the Frankfurt School theorists, etc.), it comes to inform a new pathos arising out of the native ambivalence of a set of thinkers who formulated an aesthetic critique of mass society *before* they turned to Marxism. Lukács, in particular, leavens his hopes for the proletarian revolution with a strong dose of nostalgia for a more "organic" past, a world before the relentless and universal reification of industrial capitalism (Lukács 1971). Benjamin and Adorno are less prone to such nostalgic romanticism. But Adorno in particular is also far less optimistic about the revolutionary potential of the masses. His is the "administered society," where the progress of commodification, in the form of the booming "culture industries" — Hollywood movies, popular music, commercial journalism, advertising — diverts whatever transformative libidinal impulses once existed into a controlled dispensary of consumerist pleasures (Horkheimer and Adorno 1972; Adorno 1991).

The beautiful work of art, for Hegel, is *serene;* the artist's work of mediation — which prefigures, on a more elementary (because more concrete) level, that of the philosopher — depends upon transcending the merely contingent appearances of the object under consideration: "Accordingly, the Ideal is actuality, withdrawn from the profusion of details and accidents" (Hegel [1820s] in Houlgate 1998, 431). The critical cultural theorists who follow in the wake of Marx's materialist inversion come to understand this aesthetic serenity not as a transcendent ideal but as its mockery: a project of audiovisual deception that fulfills the ideological functions of the art-commodity in bourgeois society by concealing the ruptures and contradictions of everyday life.

A thought-provoking essay on the cinema by Susan Buck-Morss provides a recent example of this position: "The Hollywood star, with a new, non-ethnic name, and rhinoplastic surgery on nose and orthodontic surgery on teeth, fulfilled his/her mass function by obliterating the idiosyncratic irregularities of the natural body" (Buck-Morss 1994, 53). The point I wish to emphasize here is that while the evaluation of Hegel's totalization narrative is inverted, its adequacy as a means of understanding the cultural politics of capitalist modernity is not called into question. So it is that Guy Debord (1977) writes of a "society of the spectacle" in which everything that was once directly lived has moved away into a representation, Baudrillard's all-encompassing "code" erases any traces of the concrete in social life, and Fredric Jameson identifies as "postmodernity" the historical moment of the complete aestheticization of reality by means of the commodity form.

The totalization narrative, then, has reached its logical conclusion, for critics as well as for celebrants of the new order (see Fukuyama 1992 for an influential version of the latter). There is no longer any "outside" at all, any point of external leverage beyond the great abstracting machine of commodity capitalism. "Consumerist globality not only absolutely circumscribes but even produces resistance to itself as yet another possibility of consumption" (Moreiras 1998, 92). Horkheimer and Adorno were pessimistic about the revolutionary potential of "the masses," dulled as they were by the pleasurable anesthesia of Glenn Miller on the radio and Mickey Mouse at the movies. But they also clung to a counterpart, an inverse, of this soulless machinery: a domain of critical-aesthetic production and experience, relatively autonomous of the tyranny of the market.

It is precisely this quasi-autonomous space that Jameson declares defunct: "Postmodernism is what you have when the modernization process is complete and nature is gone for good. . . . What has happened is that aesthetic production today has become integrated into commodity production generally" (Jameson 1991, ix, 4). What kind of politics, what kind of critique might be adequate to such a moment? Jameson ruminates: "Modernism was still minimally and tendentially the critique of the commodity and the effort to make it transcend itself.

Postmodernism is the consumption of sheer commodification as a process" (x).

Precisely the notion of "sheer commodification" is, in my view, the problem. In its assumption of abstraction without remainder, it participates fully in the intellectual tradition defined by the totalization narrative. Indeed, it goes so far as to deny the problem of the concrete altogether, or, rather, to render it anachronistic, an intellectual survival from a period of high modernism. To the extent that we make the common mistake of assuming that global capitalism is today all about computerized bits, a virtual flow of digitized information, such a move may appear credible. But this is, in truth, a highly impoverished reading of contemporary capitalism. It misses the importance of concretion on two crucial levels. Firstly, it disregards the aspect of specific human beings performing specific kinds of work under specific sociohistorical conditions (the basis of Marx's original discussion of labor and surplus value). Secondly, it forgets the fact that the images that have become increasingly important to the reproduction of capital are *not* reducible to the calculi of value — whether economic or semiotic — by which cultural producers seek to manage them. The life-world of the worker and the image-as-object always necessarily retain concrete elements that exceed the abstracting requirements of exchange value.

Earlier theorists in the Marxist tradition recognized that this concrete excess was crucial both to the functioning of capitalism and to the possibility of its revolutionary overcoming. According to Cornelius Castoriadis: "A factory in which the workers were really and totally mere cogs in the machine, blindly executing the orders of management, would come to a stop in a quarter of an hour. Capitalism can function only by drawing upon the genuinely *human* activity of those subject to it, while at the same time trying to level and dehumanize them as much as possible" (Castoriadis 1987, 16). For Lukács, this is part of the "irrationality" of capitalism, a social order that presented itself, on an ideological level, as eminently rational. But it is also out of this "irrationality" that profound social change might emerge: "In moments of crisis the qualitative existence of the 'things' that lead their lives beyond the purview of economics as misunderstood and neglected things-in-themselves, as use-values, suddenly becomes the decisive factor" (Lukács 1971, 105). But even when the necessity of this concrete dimension is recognized, its sway is, by the historical logic of the totalization narrative, deferred into the future. A long-suppressed "truth" stands poised to realize the radical promise of history. But until then it must remain silent, or at best speak in muffled tongues. Perhaps it is not surprising that once the historical confidence of earlier Marxist cultural theory evaporated, the problem of the concrete evaporated with it.

Anthropologists, for their part, have for a long time seen themselves as occupying a kind of trickster position in the social sciences. They have taken it upon themselves to shoulder "the burden of the concrete,"[2] not least in the face of the hubristic, ethnocentric, and totalizing proclamations of many of their colleagues in the sister disciplines. In a humanist-realist mode, valorized concrete life-worlds (peasants, workers, "everyday life") have been pitted against demonized abstracting systems (capitalism, bureaucracy, "the state") and narratives ("modernization," "progress"). But in fact the upshot is that the binaries persist. The representation and understanding of capitalism per se is not challenged; rather, it is relativized as one social fact among others, not the only game in town. Moreover, this superficially liberal gesture has unfortunate philosophical implications: among them, the belabored and misleading distinctions between "inauthentic" (commodified) and "authentic" (organic) cultural forms,[3] and the peculiar but predictable corollary assumption that culture could somehow be a finite resource, threatened with extinction by commodification.[4]

However, many less humanistically inclined authors (frequently writing in a poststructuralist mode) have usefully called into question the philosophical and political foundations of this rhetoric of authenticity. Too frequently, however, in their zeal to demonstrate the discursive construction of the social world, they have reduced the entire messy field of practice, embodiment, and image to the ostensible linearity of text. In part, this move is descended from Hegel's stern dismissal of Kant's category of the *Ding-an-sich:* the "thing-in-itself" that Lukács evokes, the concrete and constitutive dimension in the object-world that necessarily resists or exceeds any attempt at translation into language or conceptual finitude. To be sure, the poststructuralists share little of Hegel's faith in the positivity of philosophy, history, or their mediating representations. But they do tend to share his skepticism regarding any notion of a positive materiality; if the truth of discourse is troubled, then it is not because of the intrusion of the concrete, but rather because of its own contradictory claims to authority.

In a sense, what I am calling for here is a return to taking the *Ding-an-sich* seriously; *not* as a route to some repressed "truth" of the object or of the human condition, but rather as a constitutive, historically grounded, yet always *excessive* dimension of the production of value, political and/or economic. This, in turn, means revisiting the irreducible ontological duality of Marx's original concept of the commodity form. In terms of an ethnographic project, this also means attending to the *process* of commodification. Indeed, one of the underlying assumptions of this book is that it is only in the flow of practice that the duality of the commodity form becomes properly apparent. Nowhere is this clearer than in the production of advertising, where the value is generated precisely out of provisionally harnessing the unpredictable concretion of images within linear narratives.

Jameson insists that "any sophisticated theory of the postmodern ought to bear something of the same relationship to Horkheimer and Adorno's old 'Culture Industry' concept as MTV or fractal ads bear to fifties television series" (Jameson 1991, x). Perhaps he is forgetting Walter Benjamin's lesson: that it is the detritus of the past (objects as much as ideas) that may offer us the most profound, and the most surprising, illuminations of the present.

The Sensible and the Intelligible

I have shown that Jameson's conception of postmodernity announces the passing of the zone of quasi autonomy that Horkheimer and Adorno still held out as a possibility for nonreified aesthetic experience. In fact, Adorno himself paved the way for Jameson's move by insisting upon a radical ontological distinction between commercial cultural production and "serious" artistic activity.

Some argue that Adorno's 1963 reconsideration of the culture industry essay that Horkheimer and he had written nearly twenty years before evinces a certain "softening" of his stance (see e.g., Huyssen 1975). I find little evidence of this. In the later essay Adorno states quite clearly that artistic technique requires and allows for careful attention to what he somewhat obliquely calls "the inner logic" of the object (Adorno 1991, 101). In the culture industries, conversely, technique is determined by considerations that are entirely external to the object at hand: profitability and the rationalization of markets foremost among them. In line with the generally accepted reading of his critique of the culture industries, Adorno presents us with the image of a streamlined apparatus of production in which the materiality of the finished product is entirely contained by its destiny as an object for sale.[5]

I would argue that it is in fact in the earlier essay that Adorno and Horkheimer appear to recognize the limits of such a totalizing interpretation of the culture industries. Kant, they reflect, had postulated a "mechanism" in the mind that served to fit sense experience (the particular) into concepts (the universal): the principle of judgment.[6] And it was now this judgment—in Kant the mark of the enlightened individual—that the culture industries were threatening to usurp, offering consumers a predigested world.[7] But then they add: "While the mechanism is to all appearances planned by those who serve up the data of experience, that is, by the culture industry, it is in fact forced upon the latter by the power of society, which remains irrational, however we may try to rationalize it; and this inescapable force is processed by commercial agencies so that they give an artificial impression of being in command" (Horkheimer and Adorno 1972, 124–25). This admittedly ambiguous passage appears, on one reading, to suggest that the work of the culture industries might, after all, not consist in serving up a completely rationalized and coherent cultural product. Instead, the culture industries appear as a node in a social circulation at which the *appearance* of rationality is imposed on necessarily "irrational" materials.

This position is still, of course, entirely consonant with Horkheimer and Adorno's notion of "mass deception"; the appearance of rationality disguises and represses the "irrationality" of the material to which it is applied. But it also suggests that the seamless reification that the authors generally attribute to the products of the culture industries is in fact only a matter of appearance. And if this is the case, are we not entitled to suppose that culture industry products carry the same dialectical tension between concrete materiality and discursive elaboration that characterizes other forms of cultural production? Perhaps the crucial factor is not, after all, a radical ontological distinction between "autonomous" and "commercial" forms of cultural production but rather the different considerations that are brought to bear upon particular, and always provisional, attempts to mediate the tension between the materiality and the avowed social meaning of an object.

What I am suggesting is that public culture, because it involves the circulation of images and objects as well as discourses, is always in part a matter of material culture. This does *not* mean that objects enter into public circulation with their meanings already defined according to some preexisting cultural matrix. Nor are these objects innocent of history. Rather, the public cultural careers of commodity image-objects involve a constant tension between the particular embodied memories that they evoke and more explicitly articulated projects of value. Sometimes these two levels are mutually reinforcing, at least for a time. Often, as we will see, they contradict each other. Always, they are mutually irreducible.

There are risks here. We might be tempted to imagine the distinction as coinciding with that often drawn between image and text (see Mitchell 1986 for a critical review of this relationship). Angela Cheater's evocative description of the way that visual images appeal to an embodied memory suggests such a division: "the potentially chaotic impact on the human memory of visually imagined action-gestalt, so much more mobile, complex, difficult to comprehend and yet easier to remember than neatly ordered letters or characters on a page" (quoted in Hawkins 1999, 139). Here we should remember the lesson of semiotics: that images are just as capable of constituting a kind of language as text is capable of being interpreted graphically.

We might, alternatively, be tempted to recognize a dimension of transcendent possibility in the image, a dimension that is not only irreducible to language but also to experience. Gilles Deleuze, in his remarks on the cinema, appears to move in this direction: "There are Lulu, the lamp, the bread-knife, Jack the Ripper: people who are assumed to be real with individual characters and social roles, objects with uses, real connections between those objects and these people — in short, a whole actual state of things. But there are also the brightness of the light on the knife, the blade of the knife under the light, Jack's terror and resignation, Lulu's compassionate look. These are pure singular qualities or potentialities — as it were, pure 'possibles'" (Deleuze 1986, 102). Now, as Herbert Marcuse reminds us, the category of "potentialities" has an ambiguous philosophical genealogy; in Aristotle, it referred to the possibility of access to ideal forms. In Marxist thought, it becomes mapped onto a historical narrative in which Marx and Engels's day of revolutionary reckoning is also the day on which the "truth" of things is *recalled*.[8] This teleology reserves such recall for revolutionary moments; for the same reason, it grants it a privileged relationship to truth. But if we divest ourselves of the teleology, might we not reconsider the idea of the "potentialities" of an image-object in terms of a kind of embodied memory that supports *and* disturbs the frameworks of discourse?

Brian Massumi's notion of "affect" may be useful here. Massumi distinguishes "affect," a nonsignifying response to a quality of intensity, from "emotion," the product of the insertion or harnessing of affect within particular narrative structures of meaning: "Emotion is qualified intensity, the conventional, consensual point of insertion of intensity into semantically and semiotically formed progressions, into narrativizable action-reaction circuits, into function and meaning. It is intensity owned and recognized" (Massumi 1996, 221).[9] Again, Massumi is not at all suggesting that affect or, as he also terms it, "intensity" is transcendent of context. It is not some "romantically raw domain of primitive experiential richness. . . . Intensity is asocial, but not presocial . . . the *trace* of past actions *including a trace of their contexts* were conserved in the brain and in the flesh" (223). In experience, affect/intensity *accompanies* explanation and narrative, but it is not governed by the same determinations: "It would appear that the strength or duration of an image's effect is not logically connected to the content in any straightforward way. . . . There is a disconnection of signifying order from intensity — which constitutes a different order of connection running in parallel. . . . Every event takes place on both levels — and between both levels, as they resonate together to form a larger system composed of two interacting subsystems following entirely different rules of formation" (218, 220). I would resist an *absolute* separation between the "rules of formation" that govern meaning and affect; after all, they must both emerge out of the same historical contexts. But certainly Massumi's acknowledgment of their relative autonomy admirably captures the dual social lives of the image-object, and in the case of the commodity image, its alignment with the duality of the commodity form.

The production and circulation of commodity images is all about achieving a provisional or temporary "fix" on this relationship, while at the same time relying on its lability for the harnessing of desire. As a culture-industrial (and, more generally, public cultural) practice, the work of advertising is marked by its constant oscillation between, precisely, affective resonances and the rationalizing work of "owning and recognizing" this intensity by means of elaborated and emotionally specified brand and product narratives. It is preeminently a dialectical movement, but not in the positive Hegelian sense. The two terms, affect and narrative, do require as well as undermine each other, but they do not resolve into a higher synthesis. There is no "forward" movement. The most that advertising professionals can hope for is that a fusion of affect and narrative will "hold" for as long as it takes to realize exchange value in one of the many arenas through which the advertisement must travel: the client-agency meeting, the media, the street corner.

The crucial point, for my argument, is that the power *and* the vulnerability of the commodity image lies in the fact that the gap between what Kant called the sensible and the intelligible persists. In contrast, in the theory of "late" capitalism defined by the totalization narrative, the power and the vulnerability of commodity images is defined by their ability to subordinate completely the concrete — even images — to the abstract calculus of exchange value. Many would argue that the centrality of photographic representation to contemporary commercial culture has simply intensified this process of reification. I disagree, and in the following section I will explain why.

Photography: Materiality and Meaning

On one level, photographs partake of an ancient history of ambivalence regarding images: from idolatry to iconoclasm, from fetishism to the prohibition on graven images (Davis 1997; Freedberg 1985; Goody 1997; Halbertal and Margalit 1992; Jay 1993; D. M. Levin 1993; Mitchell 1986). This is a history of the perennially tortured relationship between power, representation, and belief. It is a history of the ability of images to focus desire and identification, and, conversely, of human projects to animate images. But it is also a history of the contradiction between the quest of the powerful for transcendent legitimacy and the earthly finitude of physical embodiment.

On another level, photographs are something quite new. For the first time in history, photography made possible pictures that were not completely mediated by the hand and mind of the artisan; that were, instead, direct "prints," as it were, of a moment in time and space. Photographs, then, are at once deeply imbricated in social and political projects and yet in some sense still formally independent of them. What effect does this ambiguity have on their usage in advertising?

The *palpability* of photographic images made them ideal for the project of visual persuasion. According to Stewart Ewen: "At the same time that the image appeals to transcendent desires, it locates those desires within a visual grammar which is palpable, which *looks real*, which invites identification by the spectator, and which people tend to trust. According to John Everard, one of the pioneers of commercial photography, it is this trust that makes photography so forceful as an advertising medium" (Coombe 1998, 103). But is this "looking real" any different—except in degree—to the realism that obsessed European fine art after the invention of Renaissance perspective? Many argue that it is not, that the "truth" of photography too is a matter of cultural convention and institutional authority. John Tagg, for instance, insists that a photograph is nothing more than "an image produced according to certain institutionalized formal rules and technical procedures which define legitimate manipulations and permissible distortions in such a way that, in certain contexts, more or less skilled and suitably trained and validated interpreters may draw inferences from them, on the basis of historically established conventions" (Tagg 1988, 2).

Tagg's approach presents itself as a rigorous demystification of photography, an insistence upon the social construction of all its claims to transcendent truth. Susan Sontag, for her part, argues that "there can be no evidence, photographic or otherwise, of an event until the event itself has been named and characterized. . . . The contribution of photography always follows the naming of the event" (Sontag 1989, 18–19). In the light of ethnographic studies of the differences in evidentiary status accorded to photographs, as compared to, say, painted images (Pinney 1997; Srivatsan 1991), this insistence on the meaninglessness of the photograph per se seems all the more convincing.

We may on one level agree with Sontag when she says, "photographs are as much an interpretation of the world as paintings and drawings are" (Sontag 1989, 7). But we are still left with the mystery of the photograph's indexicality, the fact that, as Sontag subsequently acknowledges: "A photograph is not only an image (as a painting is an image), an interpretation of the real; it is also a trace, something directly stenciled off the real, like a footprint or a death mask. While a painting, even one that meets photographic standards of resemblance, is never more than the stating of an interpretation, a photograph is never less than the registering of an emanation (light waves reflected by objects) — a material vestige of its subject in a way that no painting can be" (154).

What to make of this footprint? Certainly, as film theorist André Bazin notes, the indexicality of photographs appears, in Western modernity, finally to satisfy (and retrospectively to justify) the centuries-old cultural obsession with representational realism.[10] And yet, he notes, as much as we may deconstruct this fixation, we seem to be *troubled* or *moved* by photographs in a particular way: "Photography affects us like a phenomenon in nature, like a flower or a snowflake whose vegetable or earthly origins are an inseparable part of their beauty.... In spite of any objections our critical spirit may offer, we are forced to accept as real the existence of the object reproduced" (Bazin 1967, 13).

Several theorists have spoken of a kind of shock or agitation when contemplating photographs. John Berger suggests that this experience has to do with their formal properties. On the one hand, they provide indubitable evidence of the "thereness" of that which they depict. This is true even if we have no idea what the object is, as well as under those conditions where we may be entirely deceived about the identity of the image. Roland Barthes characterizes this property of photographs as their "plenitude": "The photograph is violent, not because it shows violent things, but because on each occasion *it fills the sight by force,* and because in it nothing can be refused or transformed" (Barthes 1981, 91).

On the other hand, photographs abstract the images they carry away from the time and place of their production. "Every photograph presents us with two messages: a message concerning the event photographed and another concerning a shock of discontinuity" (Berger and Mohr 1995, 86). Just in passing, I would like to note the parallel here between Berger's characterization of the photograph and the duality of the commodity form: forceful presence coincides with radical absence, concretion with abstraction. A photograph, like a commodity, is an uncannily tangible riddle.

Barthes's contemplation is unabashedly "private": perusing snapshots of his late mother, he experiences the shock of disjuncture at the heart of the photograph in a manner that resonates with Massumi's definition of affect. "What it produces in me," writes Barthes, "is the very opposite of hebetude; something more like an internal agitation, an excitement, a certain labour too, the pressure of the unspeakable that wants to be spoken" (Barthes 1981, 19). This begs the question: might a more public circulation of photographs be subject to a similar kind of movement between agitation and articulation, less personal, perhaps, but no less complex? Might this not in fact be one of the tasks of a critical study of visual culture: to understand the politics of contending public versions of "the unspeakable that wants to be spoken?"

Berger suggests that photographs contain important keys to the complex connections between the experiential temporalities of subjective lives and the histories of social collectivities. But neither Berger nor Barthes will allow that the tension between the sensible and the intelligible might survive in commercial photography or "publicity." Here, not to put too fine a point on it, we run into a familiar brick wall: the totalization narrative. In private viewings, the mysterious concretion of photographs enjoys a certain life of its own. But in commercial or public photography it is suddenly entirely subordinated to the instrumental requirements of ideology. For Berger, therefore, commercial photography is tendentially fraudulent:

> We are surrounded by photographic images which constitute a global system of misinformation: the system known as publicity, proliferating consumerist lies. The role of photography in this system is revealing. The lie is constructed before the camera. A "tableau" of objects and figures is assembled. This "tableau" uses a language of symbols, . . . an implied narrative and, frequently, some kind of performance by models with a sexual content. This "tableau" is then photographed. It is photographed precisely because the camera can bestow authenticity upon any set of appearances, however false. The camera does not even lie when it is used to quote a lie. And so, this makes the lie *appear* more truthful. (Berger and Mohr 1995, 96–97)

The poetic potential of photographs is violated, in this vision, because their indexical quality is exploited without an acknowledgment of its inherent ambiguity. "Public photography . . . has been adopted by the opportunism of corporate capitalism," Berger laments (100). "In reportage and publicity, the coupling of text and image join each other in a mutual confirmation that neither of them could achieve alone" (92). The rupture, the internal incommensurability between presence and absence in the photograph, is papered over with "dogmatic asser-tion" (91).

Barthes, too, assumes that commodity images must deny all ambi-guity. In advertising, he remarks in an aside, "meaning must be clear and distinct only by reason of its mercantile nature" (Barthes 1981, 36–38). Publicity enforces a "banalization" and "generalization" of photography; the exquisite affect that Barthes savored in his private relation to particular images gives way to "mere" communication, deracinated at that. By this time, there is not much to separate Barthes from Baudrillard (except perhaps for their evaluation of American civilization): "We live according to a generalized image-repertoire. Consider the United States, where everything is transformed into im-ages: only images exist and are produced and consumed" (118). And the indexicality of the image serves now only as a fraudulent guar-antee. What film theorist Christian Metz wrote about the evidentiary effect of photography in film might, according to this logic, be applied to advertising as well: photography turns its "initially indexical power . . . into a realist guarantee for the unreal" (Metz 1985, 82).

It is perhaps Walter Benjamin who comes closest to a dialectical reading of the photographic image in the sense that I have suggested above. Through his much discussed category of "aura," Benjamin re-flects on the manner in which the concretion of particular images may, depending on both the image and the context of its deployment, over-turn our habitual assumptions *and* serve the most reactionary pur-poses. Perhaps the most important component of aura, according to Benjamin, is the experience of *distance,* a "unique phenomenon of dis-tance however close it may be" (Benjamin 1968a, 222). This distance may be the mark of the cultic image-object, the idol, the "unique" work of art, surrounded by all the prohibitions of ritualized exclusiv-ity. But it is also rooted in the very foundations of social life. In his essay on Baudelaire, Benjamin suggests that attributing aura to image-objects involves the projection of assumptions concerning social reci-procity onto the relationship between people and inanimate objects: "Experience of the aura thus rests on the transposition of a response common in human relationships to the relationship between the inani-mate or natural object and man. The person we look at, or who feels he is being looked at, looks at us in turn. To perceive the aura of the object we look at means to invest it with the ability to look at us in return" (Benjamin 1968b, 188). Distance, the mark of aura, is for Benjamin at one and the same time the medium of alienation and the condition of social reciprocity. And the advent of photography only heightens the ambivalence.

On the one hand, his discussion in both the "Work of Art" and the "Baudelaire" essays would seem to point to a positive *de*-auraticizing function for photography, a disruption of the mystifying distance that art images partake in. This is Benjamin at his most conventionally iconoclastic, reveling, as he does in "Experience and Poverty," in "a new, positive concept of barbarism" (Benjamin 1999c, 732). Here Benjamin celebrates the sheer, austere glass surfaces of Le Corbusier and Loos, who "reject the traditional, solemn, noble image of man, festooned with all the sacrificial offerings of the past. They turn instead to the naked man of the contemporary world who lies screaming like a newborn babe in the dirty diapers of the present" (733). Photography, too, feeds the hunger of this "naked man," the long-repressed citizen of the nascent mass society, in his need finally to abolish distance, "to pry an object from its shell" (Benjamin 1968a, 223) and to *bring things closer.*

On the other hand, for Benjamin photographs are also deeply implicated in the production and preservation of auratic distance. This, furthermore, is not simply a matter of the alliance between aura and reactionary politics, as in the increasingly stylized work of late nineteenth-century portrait photography, or in the more contemporary mobilization of photography and film for state authoritarianism (whether Stalinist or fascist). Photographs are also, as Benjamin argues in his "Little History of Photography," capable of the kind of "looking back" that defines the poetic potential of an image-object. In part this is a matter of history. Benjamin identifies this uncanny power in a set of portraits taken before the conventions of bourgeois practice set in. Here there is indeed a certain persistence of the uncanny density of the *Ding-an-sich:* "In Hill's New Haven fishwife, her eyes cast down in such indolent, seductive modesty, there remains something that goes beyond testimony to the photographer's art, something that cannot be silenced" (Benjamin 1999a, 510). This excess is, in Benjamin, frequently a function of history, of a forgotten past that erupts into the all-too-familiar present, a salutary estrangement: "No matter how artful the photographer, no matter how carefully posed his subject, the beholder feels an irresistible urge to search such a picture for the tiny spark of contingency, of the here and now, with which reality has (so to speak) seared the subject, to find the inconspicuous spot where in the immediacy of that long-forgotten moment the future nests so eloquently that we, looking back, may rediscover it" (527).

This temporal dialectic of aura and demystification allows Benjamin to move toward articulating his thinking on photography with a brand of post-Marxian historical materialism. And yet at the same time, both the enchanting and the disenchanting powers of the image-object have formal underpinnings. It is the mass mechanical reproduction of the image that separates it from the myth of the unique object; furthermore, photography brings art closer through portability and miniaturization: "Mechanical reproduction is a technique of diminution that helps people to achieve control over works of art — a control without whose aid they could no longer be used" (523). But the domestication of the art object goes hand in hand with its dialectical companion: the defamiliarization of the everyday world of instrumental purpose and objective knowledge: "Photography reveals in this material physiognomic aspects, image worlds, which dwell in the smallest things — meaningful yet covert enough to find a hiding place in waking dreams, but which, enlarged and capable of formulation, make the difference between technology and magic visible as a thoroughly historical variable" (512). This, perhaps, is the basis for a new, historically adequate, image-poesis, one that takes the everyday world as its source.

There is of course an argument that mass consumerism was, in the West, part and parcel of a historical deal, forged in the first couple of decades of the twentieth century, between the ruling classes and the toiling masses. The technological advances that had by then made the abolition of the exploitative social relations of capitalism possible were instead harnessed to the proliferation of creature comforts, and soon — in tandem with a vastly expanded bureaucracy — the domesticated socialism of the welfare state. Advertising played a crucial part in this transition as a kind of didactic theater for the new dispensation. The radical potential of the image was betrayed in favor of endless stereotypy; again, the culmination of the totalization narrative applied to capitalist visual culture. From here, it is no surprise that commentators turn either toward arguing against the supposed omnipotence of advertising and for the creative reworkings of popular reception, or persist in trying to locate less reified and banal kinds of images in self-proclaimedly avant-garde locations.

It is certainly possible to read Benjamin on photography as support-ing such interpretations. For my own part, however, I am inspired by the suggestion that the auratic dialectic is active in all domains of visual culture, not least in commodity images. This could be put in formal terms. Advertising relies on a ceaseless oscillation between reactionary mythos and everyday contingency. Contra the totalization narrative, these two elements are not fused; they remain poised in an uneasy and unstable alliance. The dialectical movement of shock and domestica-tion in the image-object is not necessarily so much a matter of genre or historical period; rather, it is, at every level, a constitutive feature of the circulation of commodity images.

In the course of these reflections on the commodity image, I have largely been concerned with formal properties. But the following chap-ters will show that it is only in the flow of historically situated practice that the public lives of the commodity image become fully intelligible. In the production as well as in the circulation of commodity images, we will see appeals being made — in the same breath — to a populist aes-thetic politics *and* a cultural logic of distinction. We will also examine how the image-object serves as an arena for the negotiation of another border: the imaginary — yet eminently historical — line between the lo-cal and the global. Two axes intersect each other here in the work of advertising: a politics of socioeconomic distinction, understood in uni-versal terms, and a politics of cultural difference, understood in geo-historical terms. These, then, are the stakes of the cultural politics of globalization in an age of consumer capitalism.

PART ONE

3

Citizens Have Sex, Consumers
Make Love: KamaSutra I

In the autumn of 1991, a "premium" brand of condoms called Kama-
Sutra was launched in India. My first encounter with the brand came
by way of a later installment of its advertising campaign, which I came
across during my first visit to Bombay in January 1997. At that time, I
had no knowledge of the notoriety of the brand or of the multiple
narratives that surrounded it. What struck my eye most forcefully
about the ads was their coupling of a brand name and quotations from
Vatsyayana's *Kamasutra,* with images that were nothing if not contemporary in styling and intent. At first this juxtaposition made me wonder about the commercial and cultural politics of what one might call
"trademarked tradition." What did it mean for a contemporary Indian
consumer product to be marketed to Indians through the use of an ancient Indian treatise on the science of the senses?[1] Could comparisons
be drawn between Vatsyayana's intended audience, the *nagaraka* —
roughly, the well-to-do man-about-town[2] — and the figure of the affluent, urban, Indian premium-brand consumer — crudely, the "Indian
yuppie" — that was being delineated in advertisements, press commentaries, and corporate conference rooms all around me?

Returning to Bombay in the autumn of 1997, I proceeded to im-
merse myself in the history of the campaign through informal conversations, archival research, and interviews with many of the main
players in the story. I quickly found that the launch of the KamaSutra
campaign in 1991 had attained a quasi-legendary standing. Everyone I

talked to remembered it; it was thought to be a watershed moment in Bombay public culture. At the same time, my giddier interpretive extrapolations regarding the cultural significance of the campaign were quickly checked by the skepticism of my industry informants. One agency art director shook his head and clicked his tongue impatiently: "Don't over-intellectualize it. What was important about the campaign was that, for the first time, Indians were being told that sex is fun. That and the pictures. Don't read too much into the words. They're just the product of some copywriter's overheated imagination." Others agreed: The campaign had been a thrilling scam. A corporation and its advertising agency had managed to outwit the prudish hand of the censors, challenging the public morality and aesthetic austerity handed down from Gandhi and Nehru, and, into the bargain, made *condoms*, of all things, seem sexy.

Yet these apparently straightforward recollections contained a more complex set of questions. After I had spoken with some of the people involved in the making of the campaign, it initially seemed as though I was being given two completely disparate sets of narratives regarding the significance of KamaSutra. The first was the one that I have already hinted at: KamaSutra as the harbinger of a thrilling new erotic sophistication in public communications. The second, however, suggested that KamaSutra was a model for a whole new approach to public service, confronting the stagnated aims and methods of centralized state planning with the alleged efficacy of the consumerist agenda. Eventually, however, I was to realize that these two narratives were in fact part of a larger unit; namely, a transformation of the social significance claimed on behalf of commercial images and a corollary shift in the legitimating strategies and discursive practices required of the Indian advertising industry. These shifts were themselves responses to — and strategic readings of — developments in the Indian political economy that came to a head in the 1980s. From the advertising industry's point of view, they were interesting insofar as they provided the social basis for a new and potentially very profitable regime of consumer spectacle. But the drastic expansion of the ambit of commodity images, made technologically viable through the spread of commercial television after 1982, also required an equally drastic reconfiguration of the industry's discourse on the social meaning of consumption. In the present chapter, I examine the outlines of this transformation and the impasses that it generated. I then move toward a consideration of the model that was offered as a resolution: an aestheticized, dehistoricized, and globalized vision of the relationship between individual citizenship and the national collective based upon the idea of the democratization of consumer aspiration.

A Marketing Man's Dream Come True: The Launch

In October 1991, the Bombay-based glamour magazine *Debonair* sold out its print run in a matter of days. That month's issue quickly became a collector's item, changing hands at premium prices. But it wasn't the editorial content that sparked this enthusiasm. Nor did it appear to be a direct result of the magazine's customary photo-features of half-naked women, inserted in between a characteristically eclectic assortment of literary efforts, surveys, and social commentary.[3] What was happening was a marketing man's dream come true: by all accounts, readers were actually buying the magazine for the advertisements it contained. That month, a company called J K Chemicals (JKC)[4] had launched a new product — a self-proclaimed "premium condom" called KamaSutra. And as part of the attendant media blitz, the company's ad agency, Lintas:India, had taken out every single page of advertising space in *Debonair*.

The ads that were featured in *Debonair* that month were in part the same ads that ran elsewhere: blue-tinted photographs of a half-clad couple clutching each other in a variety of urgently passionate poses. The aesthetic parameters were clearly derived from the visual repertoire of Western fashion shoots and the glossier end of pop videos, suggesting candidly captured yet carefully stylized moments. The man was invariably positioned in a supporting role as the ardent source of the female model's pleasure. Both of them had closed eyes, the man's face usually half-hidden, while the woman's head was thrown back, suggesting submission to a pleasure heightened by the discerning deployment of a KamaSutra condom. By way of guidance for the sophisticated lover, each ad featured one of a series of quotations from the text of the *Kamasutra* itself. In at least one case the text directly implied that the acquisition of the product might be the key to a woman's desire: "The man should do whatever the girl takes most delight in, and he should get for her whatever she may have a desire to possess."

4. From the launch campaign, 1991.

Invariably signing off with the baseline "For the pleasure of making love," the copy of the ads specifically sought to position the condoms themselves as a source of enjoyment.

But the centerpiece of the issue amounted to a veritable KamaSutra advertising supplement in the form of a multi-page photo-essay entitled "And Then Came KamaSutra (Or the Beginnings of a New Sexual Revolution Sparked Off by a Condom)." In addition to the ads that also ran elsewhere, the text of the copy was interlaced with glamour shots of the female model featured in the main ads, Pooja Bedi, as well as topless pictures of two other women. Several of these images were published in the fold-out format that *Debonair* used for its regular photo-features, but differed from the usual fare in that they echoed the smooth production values of the main KamaSutra ads, thus giving the impression that KamaSutra could bring a whole new level of gloss to erotic objectification. Lest the process remain at the level of looking, the text of the copy suggested that the refinement connoted by the brand in turn offered nothing less than self-realization. First, a quasi history was evoked, which would allow the brand to appear as a contemporary rediscovery of a timeless truth: "Over 3000 years ago, the Egyptians used linen sheaths. Casanova used condoms made out of animal intestines. World Wars I & II saw condoms issued in standard service kits for men in the armed forces. The Beatles and Rock 'n' Roll and the sexual revolution ignored the condom to the dark side of the moon [*sic*]. And for years, there was an uncomfortable silence. And then came KamaSutra. The condom. Dedicated to the partners of love-making. And their pleasures."[5]

One might note, in passing, the manner in which the passage used stereotypical images of Western postwar popular culture to cue the period that in the Indian context tacitly refers to the post-Independence years, here a time, apparently, of "uncomfortable silence." The body of the text went on to explain that KamaSutra condoms were specifically designed to enhance pleasure, that they were in themselves objects of desire, inseparable from sex, and to stress that it was up to the consumer to take the initiative: "The fact is that KamaSutra condoms are created for love-making. Pure fact. And that KamaSutra condoms are especially textured. Contoured. Dotted. On the outside. Also ultra-thin. And that the attraction begins with the aura around the Kama-Sutra condom itself. However, a lot will depend on you. And the ambiance in which you open the pack. And the manner in which you decide to wear KamaSutra. Or let someone else put it on for you. It's just the beginnings of the desire called KamaSutra."

The final lines presented the decision to purchase the condom as the first step in the consumer-citizen's duty to inaugurate a national erotic revolution: "The stage is set. The location is upto [*sic*] you. The fires have been on low for too long. KamaSutra condoms have been launched in October 1991, all over the country. It's your revolution. It's your condom. It's KamaSutra."

Amrita Shah was at that time the editor of *Debonair*. In November 1997, I asked her about the public stampede for the issue. She told me: "I was completely taken aback. I couldn't work out why this was happening. I mean, it wasn't as if we were featuring anything more explicit than what we had run before. But it got to the point where we were actually considering a second print run. The models in the launch campaign were girls that we had already featured in *Debonair*. So what was the big deal?"

As I amassed more information about the campaign, I continued to ask myself this same question. Unquestionably, KamaSutra *had* been a "big deal:" *Debonair* had flown off magazine sellers' racks at an unprecedented velocity, but the impact of the campaign had also been articulated in ways that, at first sight, appeared less commercially desirable but ultimately all added to the publicity that surrounded the event. There were complaints to the Advertising Standards Council of

India (ASCI), questions raised in parliament, a ban on Doordarshan (DD, the state-administered national television network), and a flurry of letters to the press. At this early stage, all I could surmise was that the *hangama* (uproar, commotion) surrounding the launch had less to do with the selling of erotica than with the eroticization of selling in a wider sense. As Wolfgang Fritz Haug puts it: "Here it is not the sexual object that assumes commodity-form, but instead the entirety of useful objects with commodity-form tends to assume in some way a sexual form" (Haug 1987, 120). Such, then, were the outlines of KamaSutra's public debut. But what were the origins of this infamy?

A Farewell to Rhinoceros Hides: The Origins of the Product

Gautam Singhania was the twenty-four-year-old scion of one of the most prominent industrialist families in India. "The condom project," as KamaSutra was referred to in the beginning, offered him a chance to stretch his entrepreneurial wings.[6] JKC, which was run by his father, had been casting around for a small investment opportunity for him, something on the order of five or six million U.S. dollars. It was the end of the 1980s, and several factors had conspired to make the condom market an attractive proposition. Under the Board of Industrial and Financial Reconstruction, ailing industries, many of them in "backward" areas, could qualify for grant money and tax incentives from the government. A factory site in the depressed city of Aurangabad appeared ideal for the project, particularly since the Singhanias had been able to strike a deal with a South Korean supplier for some high-tech condom-manufacturing equipment. Condoms seemed a promising bet both for the domestic market, where free government distribution required a supply of 700 to 800 million pieces a year, and for export, where the labor intensive nature of condom production put India at a comparative cost advantage.[7] Finally, the contemporaneous emergence of AIDS as a major issue seemed set to give the previously stagnant commercial condom market a fillip.[8]

Knowing next to nothing about the condom market, Singhania and his associates at JKC entrusted the promotion of the entire project to Lintas:Bombay, a large advertising agency that had already done work for the Park Avenue line of "suitings," a division of the prestigious Raymond brand, one of the most visible companies under the J K Group umbrella. Lintas found itself faced with a not entirely thrilling prospect: the billings for the account were rather meager (at least by its standards as one of the top two agencies in India),[9] and there was a widespread impression that the free and subsidized condoms distributed by the government under the brand name Nirodh had been instrumental in creating a great deal of popular resistance to the product category as a whole. One contemporary account describes it thus: "In the beginning there was Nirodh, a non-lubricated . . . government-manufactured condom that was as thick (and sensitive) as a rhinoceros-hide. Its sickly-yellow colour . . . was enough to put anyone off sex forever — little wonder that even today condoms are a good substitute for balloons in rural areas" (Kankanala 1991). Here, then, was the marketing problem: how to stimulate desire for a brand within a product category that was more or less universally thought to be an anti-aphrodisiac?

From Anathema to Accessory: The Agency Takes Charge

The official hero of the KamaSutra story was Alyque Padamsee, then close to the end of his reign as C.E.O. of Lintas:India. In this guise, he appeared as the Legendary Adman, routinely, almost casually revolutionizing the very basis of marketing through inexplicable flashes of inspiration. When eventually I got a chance to meet him, he told me: "[The government condom, Nirodh,] acted as a deterrent to sex, because as soon as you thought of Nirodh, you lost your erection! If you lose your erection, you can't put on a condom. The logic is simple, but nobody seemed to have stumbled upon it. So I said, 'How can the male think of the condom as a pleasure enhancer?' Nobody wants to sit down to a sumptuous meal, and then be told that you have to take medicine before it. [It] kills your appetite."[10] By the time I got my audience with Padamsee, however, I had already spoken to a number of the other key players in the KamaSutra story. In the process I had discovered that the "attraction [that] begins with the aura around the KamaSutra condom itself" had a complex and in some respects contradictory parentage.

Adi Pocha, now the head of a film scripting and production company called Script Shop, was the creative director on the KamaSutra account. He told me that the idea for a pleasure-enhancing condom had come to him in the course of brainstorming in preparation for a pitch for a *different* condom account at Lintas:Calcutta where he was at that time creative head, about eighteen months before the JKC project landed at his new job in the Bombay office.[11]

> I'll explain what the exact thinking was. If a guy is into sex, and he doesn't wear a condom, chances are he's doing it for a child. Or, just because he can't care less. But if a guy wears a condom, that means he's only into sex for the pleasure. Right? . . . But a condom is perceived as inhibiting pleasure. So we said, "Why don't we turn that around on its head, and see if we can associate some amount of sexiness with a condom so that a guy who's considering buying a condom says 'Okay, if I've got to wear a condom, why don't I at least go for the sexier one?' "[12]

In Pocha's narrative, Padamsee appeared as the mediator between an inspired creative idea and the cautious company-minded instincts of "the suits" at the agency:

> All these guys said, "You're crazy! How can you position a condom as an aphrodisiac?" To Alyque [Padamsee's] credit, when I surfaced it at the brainstorm, Alyque said [in expert impression of theatrical Padamsee cadences], "Yees, my boy! That's briiilliant! Just go with it!" And then of course everybody just piled onto that. Then in Bombay, when this whole KamaSutra thing — of course it was just a piece of rubber at the time — when the whole thing came up, again there was a lot of resistance from servicing [the account executives]. . . . I won't mention names, but there was [sic] a lot of people who went into, you know, "Let's water down the position a bit, let's make it love instead of sex," and "Let's have this woman reading poetry" and, you know, stuff like that. And again to Alyque's credit, he stuck by me right through and said, "Nooo! It wiiill be sex!" And that was it. Once Alyque had spoken, everybody just kind of fell into line.

Whether Jayant Bakshi was one of the "suits" that Pocha remembers struggling with is unclear; he was, however, the executive put in charge of the KamaSutra account (subsequently taking it with him when he left Lintas to form his own agency, HeartBeat Communications). The classic confrontation between creative and executive positions, I was to find, had survived this initial moment. From a perspective several years down the line, with KamaSutra an established success, Pocha — true to creative mythology — was still stressing the intuitive "leap" that had produced an irresistible idea for a particular

5. Political insatiability reworked in a consumerist register. Indian consumer-goods advertising has seldom dealt directly with contemporary events in the arena of formal politics. The long-running series of billboards for Amul Butter is an irreverent exception that ventriloquates satirical sentiments through the "cuteness" of its cartoon protagonist. This particular installment from the late 1970s is a retrospective comment on the political "excesses" of Indira Gandhi's experiment with dictatorship in 1975–77.

campaign. Bakshi, in contrast, had extended the lesson of KamaSutra beyond the product itself. Whereas Pocha and Padamsee narrated the triumphant eroticization of an inherent anti-aphrodisiac, Bakshi's exegesis capitalized upon the association between condoms, family planning, and the anti-erotics of government discourse. In effect he extended the dramatic reversal of the brand (anathema to accessory) from the product itself to the entire mode of communication that it exemplified: "The understanding of what will work for KamaSutra, the brand as we now know it, started off as a learning in 1976, which is a good fifteen years before the brand was finally launched."[13]

Bakshi had formed part of a task force, drawn from several agencies, to work in consultation with the government of India on a project to devise more effective methods for the communication of family planning messages to urban and semi-urban populations:[14] "in fact one of the biggest problems that family planning had was that we used to call it 'family planning.' After successive representations by the advertising field, we began to call it 'family welfare.' We started positivizing it. . . . The moment you said 'family planning' people said, 'Don't talk to me about it!' So when we were launching KamaSutra it was [with] that understanding."

Family planning was one of the paradigmatic projects of modernization and development within the dispensation of the post-Independence Indian state. Bakshi was suggesting that one of the government's greatest problems in this area was a lack of legitimacy grounded in an insufficient understanding of what made people "buy into" a particular venture. One of the cruelest manifestations of this legitimacy crisis was the authoritarian resolve of the Emergency declared by Indira Gandhi from 1975–77 with its ubiquitous and infamous sterilization camps. Doctors with quotas to fill left scars on the collective memory as well as on citizens' bodies.[15] The method advocated by advertising and marketing interests, conversely, posited a form of communication that would not simply disseminate information to passive recipients, but rather engage its audience aesthetically, with promises of pleasure and self-realization. In such a manner, a dialectic of reciprocal exchange — rather than force and refusal — might be created between citizen and state. During the days of the sterilization drives, Bakshi recalled:

> They would go into these areas, they would conduct a camp, they would invite people to the camp, not always by self-volition. Some of it was also forced. And they would say, "No, no, no, you have three children," *brakk!* [makes emphatic chopping motion], "you have to get into the camp!" So they put all these guys in there, women and men, irrespective of age, irrespective of caste, and then had them go through vasectomy or tubectomy or coerced them sometimes into having copper-Ts inserted, and so on and so forth. Consequently . . . the people didn't think very kindly to receiving advice on any sort of device or usage of contraceptive methods. They also didn't think very kindly of the government. . . . What these people used to say was "Look, if the government has done nothing for us, then who is the government to tell us what to do?"[16]

Condom publicity during this period, Bakshi and others argued, had similarly not made any concessions to seducing its audience; rather the emphasis was on getting across an unequivocal message through slogans like "Do ya teen bachche bas!" (Two or three children are enough!) or "You have two, that will do!" The stern tone of these communications, Bakshi implied, was a symptom of the government's distance from the sensate lives of the people. The understanding that the advertising and marketing industries could bring to the task, in contrast, was apparently based upon an empathy borne of direct experience. This experience was all the more profoundly attuned to the embodied preferences of the audience in that it was motivated not out of a desire to regulate, but rather to sell, and therefore to seduce. As Brian Barton, co-founder of U.S.-based advertising agency BBDO, once put it, "If you want to find out about people, try selling them something" (S. Fox 1990, 308). Conversely, even the *name* of the government product, Nirodh, a Sanskrit-derived word meaning "restraint" or "control," seemed detached and admonitory.[17] According to Bakshi, "It [communication] doesn't work like that, and in family planning . . . it had an adverse impact. This doesn't come across from any attitudinal survey. It comes when you travel from, you know, shantytowns to ivory towers. What we attempted to do was position KamaSutra for the pleasure of making love. Trying to tell couples that this was going to enhance sexual pleasure, and therefore they should use it. Not keep talking about the fact that 'it's for your own good, therefore do it.'"

Nirodh metonymically represented the government as a whole ("as soon as you thought of Nirodh, you lost your erection" — and, as Bakshi suggested, if you *listened* to the government, you could well stand to lose more than that), while KamaSutra stood for the pleasures of the consumer's market. Impotence and humiliation led to stagnation and alienation; virility and sensuous self-assertion to responsive and inclusive sociality.

Adi Pocha, the creative director, had stressed that the affective power of the images used for KamaSutra, channeled through the desirable connotations of a "premium" brand, was intended first and foremost to steal market share away from the closest competitor in the product category (then, as now, a brand called Kohinoor). But Jayant Bakshi's perspective was quite different. Certainly he was proud of the precise manner in which the KamaSutra brand — as an identifiable set of graphic and stylistic conventions — had been able to "take ownership" of — not to say domesticate — a particular area of consumer desire (I will discuss this point in greater depth in chapter 4).[18] But if KamaSutra was to be made a symbol of the wider social possibilities of marketing, then the relative exclusivity of its pricing and brand image had somehow to be made congruent with its universal significance. Family planning, as the quintessential government planning project, provided the crucial link between the supposed universality of sexual activity and the shared experience of subjection under an allegedly incompetent polity. Therefore, it could also provide the strategic point of intervention for an advertising industry bent upon reconfiguring the very terms of public communication. According to Bakshi:

> Men and women copulated, or had sex. They never really *made love*. It was more either a procreative necessity, or it was a diversion, or it was, you know, "I have to do this because what else?" or "I'm expected to do this." In many cases, in fact, the parents and the grandparents used to check, about fifteen years ago, after the wedding night [of their children], that "Did you have sex?" Not "Did you *enjoy* sex?" or "Did you have a satisfying night?" No, no — "Did you have sex?" Because, you see, what they wanted to know was, the boy was okay and the girl was okay. And somehow the certificate of that was the penile action. "Did you manage to penetrate the vagina?" — and it's all over![19]

This scene of gerontocratic inquisition dramatizes the ideological confrontation between the stereotypical government official — the census-taker or the family planning agent with his quota to fill, bored and hurried, interested above all in a quantitative result — and his imagined other: a service-oriented consumer industry representative, intimately solicitous about the qualitative evaluation that the customer may have of his or her "experience." Liberated by KamaSutra, the masses throw off the shackles of prudery: "It's your revolution. It's your condom. It's KamaSutra." Suddenly the aesthetic positioning of the product appears progressively inclusive. As Bakshi framed it: "Quality suffered in this country. Service suffered in this country. . . . I think a *latent* desire was always there with people to try and express it [dissatisfaction], and I think one of the expressions was this case [the KS campaign]. And coming as it did on the heels of this liberalization movement, I think it just fitted. It seemed that, at a very large level, the time was just right for somebody to say 'Hey, I'm going to express myself — I need a condom!'"

Here, then, was the apotheosis of the consumer-citizen: the civil franchise of the *right to choose* triumphs serenely over the arduous, contradictory, and messy procedures of representative democracy. In this version, the story of KamaSutra was the story of the present, that is, the story of liberalization: how the consuming energies of the people had been liberated from the paternalist grip of the state. The eroticized images contributed by advertising appeared primarily as facilitators, mediating between individual desires and the collective rationality of the market. The instant gratification promised by the consumerist dispensation looked like the direct antithesis of the perpetually deferred realization of the dream of development. The gleaming surfaces of the world according to marketing seemed a million miles from the grubby habitat of the bureaucrat.

But the more I delved into the history of the relationship between the advertising industry and the government, between the roles played by private and public sector interests in articulating a vision of a present and future India, the more I came to understand their complex entanglement, their ambiguous kinship. By the same token, it also became clear to me that the significance of the KamaSutra campaign was not primarily its emblematic status as a sign of a new era. Rather, its power resided in its ability to mediate some of the most persistent contradictions that arose in the transition between the developmentalist and the consumerist visions of the nation. To understand, as it were, the questions to which KamaSutra appeared as an answer, we will need to explore both the outlines of the rise of mass consumerism in India and some aspects of the changing relationship between the advertising industry and official state discourse.

Let's Enjoy Ourselves! The Origins of Mass Aspiration

Certain very broad trends can and should be enumerated. In particular, I want to mention the conditions that, in the early 1980s, created a contradiction that required a mediating discourse: the gap between the inclusive rhetoric of the consumerist agenda and the exclusive images through which it was expressed.

On a purely economic level, there was, to put it simply, more money around. The "green revolution" of the mid to late 1960s had created a whole new class of agricultural "bullock capitalists," many of them from the intermediate caste groupings that had been the primary beneficiaries of the limited land redistribution enabled by the abolition of the "feudal" Zamindari system a decade earlier (A. Gupta 1998, 109–12). Government policy since the Second Five-Year Plan had supported small business enterprise, even as the licensing restrictions and bureaucratic hurdles instituted by the "permit-license raj" ensured that only the most resourceful (and perhaps the least scrupulous) of entrepreneurs could flourish. Further assistance was given under Indira

Gandhi; in particular, the nationalization of banks undertaken in 1969 made capital available to small entrepreneurs at affordable rates. "By the mid-seventies," remarks Pavan Varma, "the small-scale sector had grown to within striking range of contributing almost half of the country's total industrial production. And the significant point is that its profitability was often higher than that of the corporate sector" (Varma 1998, 91).[20] In the late 1970s, many Indians began to seek work in the booming oil economies of the Middle East; as a consequence, foreign exchange flooded back into India. At home, an enormous informal economy consisting of traders, speculators, and middlemen sprang up in the interstices of this quickening growth. Finally, even the traditional inhabitants of the sociological box marked "the Indian middle class," the white-collar salariat, had, through a series of government pay raises, found themselves with noticeably more disposable income, not to mention whatever additional considerations were offered them in return for bureaucratic favours.[21]

The period stretching from the late 1960s to the early 1980s had also witnessed significant political changes (Brass 1990; Rudolph and Rudolph 1987). The ideological hegemony of the Congress Party started breaking down on a regional level in the 1960s and was brought to a crashing defeat at the center in 1977 after Indira Gandhi's less-than-two-year attempt at dictatorship. The hastily assembled coalition of opposition parties that defeated her collapsed in 1979; by 1980, Indira Gandhi and Congress (I) were back in office. Indira's last term (1980–84) saw a decisive shift in the idiom of politics. The overtly authoritarian populism that had characterized the mid-1970s had in some measure been delegitimated by the experience of the Emergency. By the early 1980s, the political fragmentation that had first expressed itself electorally in the 1960s was exploding in the form of a whole series of powerful regional secession movements. Facilitated by the political economic shifts outlined above, consumer spectacle now offered itself as a privatized outlet for frustrations for those who could afford to partake, a mirage of a new consensus based on desire rather than deliberation.

Technologically speaking, the event that made the construction of such a spectacle possible on a whole new level was the rapid spread, starting in 1982, of commercial color television.[22] "A television in every village" was the government's slogan. The official ideology that accreted around television combined the early idea that the mass deployment of communications technologies would encourage the realization of India's full democratic and developmental potential with the gradually more pronounced implication that this realization would in large part be manifested as a libidinal engagement with commodity images and their promise of a better life.

In the early- to mid-1980s, the primary symptom of the new dispensation was the intense media fixation on the "exploding middle class." Study after study of the habits and dispositions of this apparent sociological entity began the work of delineating the collective subject that would engage with the new consumer spectacle, an ever-expanding series of manifestations of "the Indian consumer," each with their own subcategories: "the Indian teenager," "the new Indian woman," and so on. The studies were spectacular news in themselves. In what Jean Baudrillard has termed "autointoxication" (Poster 1988, 210), the consuming public — to judge by the contents of the media through which it was being constituted as such — was hungry for nothing so much as itself, or rather, its imagined self-fulfillment. Thus the new media were the didactic theater, doubling as innocent mirror, in which the new Indian consuming classes found their public subjectivity as well as their objective form (see also Mankekar 1999). Tying the tactile concretion of modern surfaces and bodies to a generalized narrative of middle-class transformation, the commodity image was offered, for the first time in India, as a generalized social ontology.

From the beginning, commercial television in India involved a juxtaposition that required ideological legitimation: awesome reach and an overtly middle-class agenda. Arvind Rajagopal remarks: "State-sponsored TV entertainment aimed at the middle-classes symbolized some of the contradictions in this process [the consumption-led route to national prosperity]: a minority-oriented public apparatus projecting an image of harmony and unity" (Rajagopal 1993, 97). As we have already seen, the introduction of the consumerist dispensation was often legitimated in terms of the removal of libidinal constraints from the lives of the entire citizenry. Anand Varadarajan, the president of Pathfinders, a prominent market research organization, told me, in terms remarkably similar to the ones Jayant Bakshi at HeartBeat would use several months later: "Indians are a very serious people. We don't have a sense of fun. We're very fatalistic. You're born, you work — slogslogslog — you die. That's it. We used to exist; we never used to live. There's a lot more of 'let's enjoy ourselves' now."[23]

Television, as far as many in the marketing and advertising professions were concerned, had enabled this transformation. Mohammed Khan, head of Enterprise Nexus Lowe advertising, remarked:

> Historically, there's been a kind of guilt attached to consumerism. If you spend money then . . . they say that anything that's enjoyable or made you feel good was either illegal, or it was immoral, or it was fattening [laughs]. So there was a great deal of guilt attached to spending money, and I think, for example, even chocolates — no woman would admit that chocolates were brought into the home because she wanted to eat them or her husband wanted to eat them, you know? And we know from research that once a thing came into the house, then everybody had it in any case. But the woman had to justify . . . I mean, for the housewife to buy something for herself, was almost like she was depriving the entire family of something or the other. That kind of guilt feeling . . . I think in the last twenty years we've seen such dramatic changes in that kind of behavior that today I don't think that any housewife feels any kind of guilt at all about going and blowing Rs 10,000 *on herself*. Cosmetics. If you look at the sales of cosmetics and shampoo and stuff like that, which are not luxury items, you know, you find that in a country of that size with such a huge population of women, such a large *urban* population of women — *pathetic. Pathetic.* Even now it's not a huge market, although I think the potential's much bigger.[24]

This liberation from guilt was, for Khan, connected to a change in Indian attitudes toward expenditure, which was itself an outcome of the rise of commercial television.

> Television changed a lot of things. . . . I think the biggest change that happened was that people in India saved money for the sake of saving money. This thing of money was not a medium, it was an end. That to make money and to sit on it was really how people saw life. But money was not really a means to making your life better, making your life more comfortable, you know, satisfying your various needs. And there were whole communities, the Marwaris, the Gujaratis, and so forth who just made more money, and they used that money to make more money and that was the end thing. I think what television did was that it opened, for a few million people, whole new worlds which they never knew existed. And it made

them want and need things which they never bought before, you know. So from just saving money for the sake of saving money, I think for the first time people said, "Oh — I make money so that I can do things with it." And this is something which I think happened for the first time in our history. You know I think that's what television did.

Varadarajan similarly connected the freeing of the libidinal energies of the people not merely to spending, but to the sensory intensity and richness of television. In contrast (and with scant regard for the aesthetic polyvalence accorded to local performance idioms by anthropologists), he characterized "traditional" entertainments as monotonous and limited. "The village storytellers got killed in the process," he remarked. When I asked whether he did not think something was being lost as television apparently replaced older idioms, he waved his hand dismissively: "It is. It should. What is the repertoire [of the village storyteller]? It's highly limited. TV stimulates many of the senses. It's that much richer an experience."

The expansion of commercial television, then, was figured as the concrete infrastructure that allowed the national-healing-by-commodity image that Jayant Bakshi had already described to take place. Ostensibly, "the government" or "the bureaucracy" was the evil other, a bulwark of vested interests and politics that constantly threatened to block the transformative power of the market and its valiant champions in the private sector. This heroic narrative disguised a more ambivalent reality. The fact that the government effectively offered privileged access to markets through the permit-license raj meant that, despite real ideological differences, successful entrepreneurs and powerful bureaucrats necessarily shared key interests.

Because of the political economic shifts sketched above, by the early 1980s the old discourse of national development was increasingly coming into conflict with the consumerist agenda that was being offered to the ascendant "middle classes." As a result, Indira's last years in office saw the government taking what amounted to contradictory positions vis-à-vis consumerism. On the one hand, the desires of the new "middle classes" were acknowledged and even encouraged. On the other hand, advertising, as the visible face of consumerism, came under renewed attack for promoting "false needs." What from one point of view might be read as the desperate rhetorical zigzagging of a government trying to appeal to incommensurable interests could also be interpreted as a strategic compromise. By the early 1980s, after all, the government knew that the private sector would be grateful for whatever liberalizing reforms it saw fit to introduce.[25] In return, the government could expect to ventriloquate the new pro-consumerist discourse through the private sector, and in particular the media industries, thereby keeping enough strategic distance from this discourse to maintain electoral credibility with less affluent but numerically preponderant voters.

Government rhetoric on consumerism would shift markedly at the time of the accession of Indira's son Rajiv to the prime ministership in 1984; indeed, his inner circle of advisers included several young media, telecommunications, and advertising professionals. In fact this technophile coterie was in charge of the event that in hindsight embodies the locus classicus of the ambivalent discourses surrounding consumerist spectacle during Indira's last years: the 1982 Asian Games. Held in Delhi, and broadcast internationally, the so-called "Asiad" was the occasion for a massive push to introduce color television to India.

Achieving "world class" televisual spectacle became a crucial marker of national pride for the government. As Purnima Mankekar notes, "The Asiad provided the state with an opportunity to convey its image as a modern nation capable of hosting and organizing an international sports event, not just to the rest of the world but also to its own citizens" (Mankekar 1999, 56).[26] Customs duties were temporarily lifted on television sets to encourage importation. As Amrita Shah (1997) points out, many commentators at the time did indeed deplore the channeling of public resources and energies into such "frivolous" ends, particularly at a time when the government was facing crucial political problems in several parts of the country, not least among them the agitation in Punjab that eventually led to Indira Gandhi's assassination. And so, in order to counteract the growing impression of disjuncture between the government's approval of consumerism and its ongoing stated commitment to social justice, it proceeded, within just a few months, to displace blame onto the advertising industry.[27]

While presenting the 1983–84 budget to parliament, then finance minister Pranab Mukherjee suggested that "Hon'ble members must be aware of the lavish and wasteful expenditure by trade and industry, particularly on traveling, advertising, and the like" (Swamy 1984).

Proposing that 20 percent of such expenses no longer be tax deductible, Mukherjee explained that his aim was to "discourage conspicuous consumption at the individual and corporate level, inculcating an atmosphere of austerity and providing a disincentive to unproductive, avoidable and ostentatious spending in trade and industry" (T. Kumar 1984).

The advertising industry retorted, over the next year or so, with a flurry of lobbying. Out of this frenzy a new model for the social significance of advertising in India began to crystallize. Although Mukherjee's attack was intended as a quantitative curb on ad spending, the industry responded with a universalistic defense of the social relevance of the commodity image. In the following pages, I will present some of the forms that this defense took, as well as some of the ambiguities that it struggled to overcome. For now, let me simply introduce the problematic in the following way.

So far, we have encountered defenses of consumerism in India that have achieved much of their definition by opposing themselves to an image of a stagnant centrally planned economy and the discourse of development that legitimated it. Certainly, as we will see, the resentment of "red tapism," "adhocism," and "authorityism" has a long history in the Indian advertising industry's discourse on the government. But it is nevertheless a striking fact that, in the 1960s, when the advertising industry parried a series of attacks that were in substance very similar to those it faced in the 1980s, it appealed precisely to the planned economy and to the collective ideal of development to justify its activities. These appeals might of course be interpreted as a pragmatic adaptation to the prevailing public discourse of the day. It is tempting to conclude that the mass consumerist paradigm was simply waiting to emerge, half-formed, during the 1960s and 1970s, but that the social, infrastructural, and ideological changes that would enable it (those that I sketched at the beginning of the present section) had not yet taken place. This interpretation involves the dubious historicism of reading the life of the industry during these decades as simply a rehearsal for a future full flowering.[28] At the same time, we should also remember the ambiguous play with consumerist pleasures that the Hindi cinema had dabbled in, in shifting registers, since the 1950s.[29]

In Jayant Bakshi's appeal to the universality of sexual pleasure as a metaphor for consumption we have already seen the foundations of an alternative universal justification — one based on the "natural" and yet deeply cultural human capacity for sensual gratification. The specific way in which this aspirational yet universalist aesthetics took form in and around the KamaSutra campaign is the subject of chapter 4. To complete the groundwork for that discussion, I must first, however, explore the genealogy of the specifically *political* critique mounted by the ideologues of mass consumerism in India.

Sleeping with the Planned Economy: Politics and the Commodity Image

The Indian advertising industry's attempts to legitimate itself always involved three areas of ambiguity. Taken abstractly, these areas of ambiguity are generic to the project of advertising anywhere. In the Indian context, however, they took on a particular urgency with respect to the extreme social disparities in relation to which the dream of development had functioned as a kind of theodicy.

First, there was the question of what advertising actually *did:* Was it merely a neutral channel of information about useful products, or did it have the capacity to add value through persuasion, to generate needs and wants of its own? Second, there was the question of time: Did advertising-led consumerism promise immediate gratification, an instant plenitude, or did it hide a new deferral — a new "always not quite yet?" Third, did advertising encourage competitive and individualistic consumption over social solidarity, or did it contain its own principle of social harmonization? Adam Smith and G. W. F. Hegel had both explained how the mechanisms of the market and civil society, respectively, wrought collective benefit out of self-interested striving. But how was this to be squared with consumption driven by social distinction?

There was a certain irony to the Indian advertising industry's post-1980s fondness for attacking the planned economy as the very embodiment of "politics," inefficiency, and vested interests, since this very desire to transcend "politics" was one of the motivations for the creation of the Planning Commission in the first place. Jawaharlal Nehru himself wrote of the time he spent on the Commission: "I found it a pleasant contrast to the squabbles and conflicts of politics" (Chatterjee 1993, 201). Certainly, this impression of rising above particularistic interests was an effect of the specific vision of the social whole that the planning imagination required and constructed. This was society as mechanism/organism, visible "from above" and amenable to "scientific" intervention — in short, a Comtean sociology. In the wake of a more general disillusionment with the mid–twentieth century planning paradigm, critics on the political left have argued that this particular vision of the social suffered from excessive abstraction. Sudipta Kaviraj, for example, suggests that the price of the serenity experienced by Nehru from the elevated prospect of the Planning Commission was a growing disjuncture between the "expert" discourse of the state and the hearts and minds of the people.[30] As a consequence, the Congress Party gradually lost the motivating legitimacy that it had enjoyed as a social movement during the nationalist struggle. Invoking a Gramscian notion of political movements, Kaviraj elaborates upon what has been lost in the process: "A movement seeks to transform the commonsense of the people, negotiate their relationship with the social world through talking to them. And what is more important is that there is a necessity in this of developing some kind of common language between the elite of the movement and the common people" (Kaviraj 1990, 64).

At the other end of the political spectrum, the language of the proponents of deregulated markets at first sight bears striking similarities to that of the planners. Although the mechanism of the market itself takes over from the expert calculations of a centralized state body, a similarly exhilarating abstraction away from vested interests is evoked. Management guru Kenichi Ohmae, for example, writes: "When individuals vote with their pocketbooks . . . they leave behind the rhetoric and mudslinging" (Ohmae 1990, 3). My discussion of KamaSutra has already demonstrated how the consumerist vision includes a populist appeal, and a concomitant critique of centralized authority. Here, too, we see the crucial locus of agency being shifted from the state center to a rather more intimate location, namely the individual's pocketbook. Yet Kaviraj's Gramscian critique and Jayant Bakshi's celebration of the power of eroticized images remind us that both these social "logics" — the rationally planned society and the perfectly functioning market — are abstractions that downplay the concrete mediations that necessarily connect local interests with translocal projects. It may seem counterintuitive to compare revolutionary political mobilization with consumer goods advertising. But what connects them is the problem of aesthetic engagement: how concrete discourses and image-repertoires forge links between lived worlds and abstract social projects.[31] Advertising is, of course, par excellence such a medium of aesthetic engagement. But it is also promoted as a medium of information. And it is here that we find ourselves face to face with the first constitutive ambiguity in the public role of advertising.[32]

The advertising industry's involvement in family planning initiatives was, as we have seen, part of the prehistory of the KamaSutra campaign. In fact this engagement went back much further than the mid-1970s projects in which Jayant Bakshi had participated. Limiting the size of the Indian population was, within the neo-Malthusian schema of postwar modernization and development discourse, an article of faith (Caldwell 1976; Gwatkin 1979; Karkal 1992; Krishnaji 1998; Szerter 1993); by the time of the Third Five-Year Plan in 1961 it had become an explicit and important part of the Indian planning exercise (Vaidyanathan 1995). Family planning was a strategically attractive area of intervention for the advertising industry for three reasons: first, it offered social legitimation for an industry often accused of encouraging dubious desires; second, it provided a large-scale opportunity to demonstrate the radical communicative efficacy of marketing and advertising; and third, it held up the prospect of vast billings.[33] But from the very beginning, it also shaped up as a terrain of bitter confrontation between government and private sector interests.

The late Subhas Ghosal, formerly head of Hindustan Thompson Associates, was brought into a Nirodh-distribution project by his friend and client, Ajit Haksar of the Indian Tobacco Company (ITC), in the late 1950s. A handful of companies with extensive grass-roots networks, among them ITC, Hindustan Lever, Lipton, and Brooke Bond, were selected by the government to help make condoms available in villages. The plan had run aground for several reasons, including the government's policy of giving Nirodh away free while encouraging village stores to sell it, as well as the general social awkwardness associated with the product. Ghosal's recollections still seethed with the resentment of bureaucratic delay and political confusion that had become a standard feature of the advertising business's relationship to the government.

> We [HTA] produced lots of advertising, I remember, at his [Haksar's] behest. He and I went and made a presentation at the end of it, it must have been '58 or thereabouts, in Delhi. We made the presenta-

tion to the Home Secretary, Narayan, a very capable ICS man of the old cadre.[34] . . . I remember it was a one and a half-hour presentation and I took up with me something like 150 pieces of advertising material. This for the villages, this for the towns, you know. Really we had gone berserk. And it *was* something to go berserk about. We all believed in it. It was nothing commercial. We saw that this damn population thing was holding everything back. And the whole agency threw itself behind it. . . . And [Narayan] said, "Oh, you'll get a go-ahead on this from the Finance Ministry. I'll see that you get it by the end of January." It still hasn't come in January *1998!*[35]

Ghosal and HTA then turned to the Ford Foundation in an attempt to bypass the government altogether, but the Ford Foundation was itself, under the terms of Public Law 480, dependent upon USAID.[36]

USAID was full of bureaucrats. USAID used to strong-arm the Ford Foundation with grants and all kinds of things. It was a hive of bureaucrats and [yet,] they didn't know a *thing* when it came to the Indian bureaucrat. . . . The next thing [the government] roadblocked was, "Oh yes, you give us the material, and we will put it through . . . the Directorate of Advertising and Visual Publicity," DAVP.[37] [They were] the most *incompetent bastards* that I have ever come across. Both incompetent *and* bastards. They did nothing.

Similarly, Sylvester da Cunha, who today heads the Bombay agency that bears his name, found himself stymied when the lure of commercial television raised its head for the first time in the mid-1960s.

Well, the industry, that means advertising and marketing — in '66 in fact — the companies in advertising wanted TV to be commercial. TV had just started in Delhi, but it was very sort of didactic and farm programming . . . and it was just Delhi itself. They were about to go national and the private sector wanted to make a case for it to be commercial. That means education through entertainment kind of stuff, which involves also advertising — us being permitted to use the airwaves to sell our goods. And they mounted a three-day conference in Delhi, which was quite high-powered and attended by ministers and stuff like that, and our group — I was in my agency. I said, "Why don't we do something practical? Let's run a case [study] of how television can help promote an important national cause." Television per se; nothing else. So we did a campaign that was underpinned by one line: "You have two, that will do!" In those days, it was quite revolutionary because they were just running campaigns like "A small family is a happy family," sort of goody-goody, diffuse, meaningless kinds of efforts. . . . Let's get down to specifics. Mrs. Indira Gandhi was then the information and broadcasting minister. . . . She wasn't there, but she heard of it, and she asked us to make a presentation to her on the next day. . . . So I made this thing to her and her secretary, and she said, "Now can you blow this up? This seems okay; can you blow this up into a full-blown multimedia campaign and come and present it to us?" There were these films and posters and all that kind of stuff. So we did that and the next month we went down and we had this huge presentation, a day-long presentation to her. So she said, "Fine, I think there's something in this." She turned to her secretary and she said, "Who's doing our advertising at the moment?" So he said, "I think Ford Foundation are advising us." . . . Ford Foundation, to cut a long story short, stepped right between us and the job. Because they felt removed from their turf. All we wanted to do was make this one presentation. Finish it. But we had to be in consultation with the people who were hands-on. Ford Foundation was. . . . They picked holes in us. They said "Why 'two'? Should it be two boys or two girls?" Before we knew what, they had expanded it to two or three — "Do ya teen bachche bas!" Which mangled our entire communication, which was built on songs, village songs. It was built on posters and mnemonics and stuff like that."[38]

The trope of private sector expertise blocked by bureaucratic bungling was well established, then, by the 1960s. But unlike a later generation of advertising apologists, the industry's attempts to legitimate its activities during this period did not involve a rejection of either development or of state planning per se. If anything, the collective telos of modernization provided the industry with a convenient normative orientation.

For example, in 1965, when finance minister T. T. Krishnamachari attempted to restrict the tax deductibility of corporate expenditures on advertising, the industry actually responded by arguing that advertising was an indispensable component of the planning enterprise. The industry put out a series of advertisements for itself. "Do we need ADVERTISING in a Planned Economy?" asked one.[39] "Many people will tell you that in a planned economy such as ours ADVERTISING is not necessary. It is not so. In India today ADVERTISING is a vital part of industrial progress, as it is in every developing economy."[40] The usual suspects were rounded up to defend advertising: information, choice, productivity, and therefore jobs. The ads conceded to the government the centrality of a productivist logic (even though the critique of productivism had, by this time, already been a key plank of international industry discourse for decades). At the same time, they responded directly to the accusation of promoting "inessentials," so often leveled at the industry, by blurring the distinction between need and desire: "How does a Developing Economy develop? By continuously increasing production. Not just of steel and machine tools and locomotives and electric generators, but also of saris and suitings, of canned foods and biscuits, of soaps and cosmetics . . . of all the things you need and would like to have to make your life more enjoyable." Similarly, the distinction between information and persuasion was subordinated to the great drive for growth: "By making known what is available, and by encouraging people to buy, ADVERTISING is the vital link between the manufacturers and you, the consumer. By creating demand for goods and services which can be made available by industrial enterprise, ADVERTISING is an indispensable aid to a developing economy." Finally, even the most apparently manipulative aspects of advertising's play with consumer desires, its supposed capacity to channel desire in directions it might not otherwise travel, was — as a marketing man might say — "turned into a positive" in the context of an economy of shortages: "ADVERTISING is always needed to inform people and to guide them. A special function [when production falls short of demand] is to divert expenditure from things in short supply by creating demand for others which can be made readily available. Remember, it is not wasteful to create demand for things which 'are not really needed' when their manufacture, distribution, and consumption create jobs."

While the industry's public communications at this time stressed these general benefits of consumption (and therefore advertising) to production, its approaches to the government were more focused upon the interests of administration. To begin with, there were the apparently disastrous economic consequences of curtailing advertising. Growing industries would not be able to expand markets to keep up with capacity, and consequently exports would also suffer since home markets would be too small to support the high quality and low prices required for effective international competition. As a result foreign exchange would be in even shorter supply than it already was. An anticompetitive "lock-in" would arise in which well-entrenched brands would enjoy an unfair advantage over newcomers. Foreign joint ventures would be difficult to arrange since foreign partners would shy away from markets in which they would not be able to promote themselves effectively. Artificial shortages would arise as a result of inadequate distribution of product information, raising the likelihood of inflation, while — and this is among the oldest arguments for advertising and the legal protection of trademarks (Coombe 1998; Strasser 1989) — a lack of advertising and the quality enforcement that branding is supposed to bring would put consumers at risk of manufacturer malpractice and product adulteration.

Moreover, the advertising business was particularly keen, in its direct appeals to the government, to conjoin the legitimation of consumption with the regulation of its citizenry under the sign of development. R. K. Swamy, today at the helm of his own agency (R. K. Swamy/BBDO), was in the mid-1960s in charge of the Madras office of Thompson's. In a lengthy 1965 memo to the Finance Ministry, he sought to sell the advantages of advertising to the government. Whereas the advertising lobby's public ads had simply sought to efface the difference between "essential" and "inessential" goods, Swamy's argument placed them in a direct and necessary relation to each other. The "essential" means of production and the "inessential" markers of life-style and distinction were linked in a chain of production and consumption, a *perpetuum mobile* driving the expansion of the national economy.[41] Beyond giving conspicuous consumption a dynamic role in economic growth, the linkage was important in that it highlighted the advertising industry's apparent concern for consumers beyond the metropolitan areas:

> On the one hand, we have to promote the use of pumps, motors, poultry and animal feed, fertilizers and insecticides, tractors and other improved implements. This would best be done by a large number of manufacturers who produce them. On the other hand, the farmer must be given the necessary incentive to produce more, which can only come out of a desire for a better standard of living. Unless he is shown the advantages of owning and using bicycles, radios, grammophones [sic], electric table fans, garments, foot-

wear and other amenities of life, which he can buy only with the surpluses on what he produces now, he will have very little desire to exert for more.[42]

The advertising business's attempts at social legitimation did not stop at an assertion of the economic benefits of consumption. Rather, it suggested that an engagement with citizens' desires, an affective appeal, was a mode of communication inherently superior to the mere dissemination of information with which it identified the speech of the state. Thus, Swamy (with "independent" support from a study carried out by the Vidyalankar Commission) suggested in a 1966 memo that "aiming primarily on [sic] the dissemination of information, Plan publicity has failed to *touch* any section of the population."[43] The engagement made possible through such, as it were, haptic communication was at once a matter of affect, its careful monitoring, and its strategic supervision: "The root of all ills that beset Plan Publicity is the *absence of expertise* to plan the strategy and tactics of publicity campaigns and to ensure the most profitable utilization of mass media." In Swamy's terms, the application of market research techniques would allow government propaganda work to become a "two-way traffic of news, views, opinions and comments. Apart from furnishing news to the public to keep them informed of economic and social policies, there must function an intelligence service to obtain, study and analyze public comment, opinion, and reaction. . . . The resulting publicity should be so directed as *to persuade and inspire people* into accepting the social and material changes, and thus lead to local initiative for decisions." Swamy's 1965 memo concluded by equating market research with populist democracy, and the consumerist "good life" with the developmentalist aims of the Planning Commission.

> The concept of democratic planning implied that the citizens and local communities should be enabled to make their own decisions for the realization of the national aims and that *all sections of the population should be closely involved in the work of social and economic development.* It is only through such intensive exploitation of national human resources and ingenuity that we could hope to attain the kind of society we desire. . . . The fundamental aims of Plan publicity was [sic] to motivate group and individual actions for the realization of the "good life" that the Government sought to provide for the people.[44]

Already here, as the advertising industry attempted to legitimate itself under the sign of development, we see the key ambiguities of the enterprise bubbling under the surface, particularly the uncertain balance between information and persuasion, and the fuzzy connection between individual consuming desires and collective progress. By the 1980s, the precarious compact between advertising and the planned economy would be completely undone, most immediately because of the decline of the ideological persuasiveness, for the urban "middle classes" in particular, of the idea of national development as a collective task.

By contrasting the 1960s directly with the 1980s in this discussion, I am, in the interests of relative brevity, bracketing an intervening step in the genealogy of government attacks upon the advertising industry. In 1978, the Janata coalition that had replaced Indira Gandhi's electorally disastrous Emergency regime, sought once again to bring in restrictions on advertising expenditures. This time, rather than seeking to impose a ceiling on the ratio of permissible publicity expenditure to company turnover, finance minister H. M. Patel brought in legislation that stipulated that 15 percent of a range of different kinds of business expenses would no longer be tax deductible. These included newspaper advertising for personnel recruitment; newspaper publication of any notice required by law; maintenance costs for office space maintained for advertising purposes; publicity or sales promotion; salaries for employees engaged in advertising; costs of organizing or participating in press or sales conferences, trade conventions, fairs, and exhibitions; and the publication and distribution of journals, catalogs, or price lists (Krishnan 1984). The 1978 bill was passed, albeit in a watered-down version, but was subsequently entirely scrapped in 1980 under finance minister R. Venkataraman, when Congress (I) returned to power. Part of the rationale given at the time for the scrapping of the 1978 bill was that curbs on advertising were harmful to up-and-coming entrepreneurs; as such, the decision was congruent with Indira's consistent policy of attempting to assist small business interests. It is in this light that Congress's own 1983 version should be viewed; it proposed that the "disallowance" on tax deductibility kick in only at the level of amounts higher than Rs one lakh (Rs 100,000). Many advertising professionals at the time argued that this ceiling was so low as to reflect a total ignorance of contemporary advertising costs (Sheshadri 1983). Others suggested that the measure in fact hurt smaller businesses more than larger ones, since their advertising budgets theoretically reflected a higher percentage of their turnover (Shankar 1984; Sidhvi 1984).[45]

I have already suggested that, for all the private sector's rhetorical condemnation of centralized planning, the flagging fortunes of this idea created something of a crisis. The ability of the development project to construct national solidarity had always rested upon a rhetoric of sacrifice and deferral in the present in return for plenitude in the future. Its decline as a compelling discourse was, therefore, connected with a questioning of both the acceptability of this temporal deferral *and* the reality of the common purpose that it implied. As we will see, the advertising industry had no trouble substituting a discourse of immediate gratification for the increasingly resented deferrals of the post-Independence period. But the legitimation of this new discourse in terms of collective benefit proved more difficult. Once again, Kama-Sutra would provide some crucial connections.

Perceptual Utility: The Commodity Image Comes into Its Own

The discourse of development did not, of course, disappear from the advertising industry's repertoire overnight. This was, unsurprisingly, particularly true among the "old guard." In the early 1980s, Indira Gandhi, addressing the business at one of its functions, attempted to make sense of the ascendant discipline of marketing in terms of an older productivist idiom: "Advertising increasingly involves market research and consumer analysis. Looked at this way, advertising is a factor of production and, therefore, of technological development" (Shankar 1984). Similarly, in response to Pranab Mukherjee's 1983 attack on excessive ad spending, corporate veteran Prakash Tandon (quoted in this instance by the very same R. K. Swamy who had articulated the case for the defense almost two decades earlier) relied on tried-and-true turns of phrase:

> Communications have a crucial role for smooth development and progress, for which we have today mass media of newspapers, journals, radio, television, outdoor, cinema and a variety of other means to convey messages through the society. Media communications will help disseminate state plans and policies, inculcation of social desirables, national exhortation of rights and obligations, distribu-

tion of goods and services and generally assist the new dynamics that propel a society forward. (Swamy 1984)

The industry had appealed to consumption as a democratizing force in the 1960s, and would do so again in the 1980s. The importance of not severing the fragile ties between urban and rural worlds remained an important theme. But whereas in the 1960s the connection had been developed in terms of a cycle of production, by the 1980s the key issue appeared to be ensuring a collective participation in modernity, a joint entitlement to aspiration. Gurcharan Das, then head of Richardson Hindustan, the forerunner of Procter and Gamble India,[46] wrote: "The most unfortunate consequence of the advertising tax disallowance is that advertisers have had to cut off the already slender connection of the countryside with the modern world, depriving rural areas of the opportunity to share in the benefits of the twentieth century, which includes consumer products. This is almost as bad as depriving them of the right to free speech and the right to vote" ("Spotlight" 1983).

In the 1960s, Swamy had spoken of Plan publicity being about "attain[ing] the kind of society we desire." By the 1980s, the tone was decidedly more individualist, even libertarian. The very name of the lobbying organization that brought together advertisers, agencies, and the media against Mukherjee's tax proposal reflected this change: The Joint Action Committee to Protect the Freedom of Commercial Information. "Any measure which constricts the growth of advertising will cut at the very roots of democracy," wrote one commentator, suggesting that the interests and desires of consumers had a moral legitimacy that was autonomous of the will of the state (Sheshadri 1983). Gurcharan Das added: "The disallowance on advertising is, in fact, a tax on disseminating information in a country where the process of communication should be encouraged" ("Spotlight" 1983).

Previously, consumption had to be justified in terms of collective economic growth. But now, individual consumer desire began to take on an absolute moral priority. Asked Das, rhetorically: "How can I sit in judgment on the preferences held by certain people? If by an appropriate message advertising can 'create value' in the eyes of consumers, then it is the same thing as a product improvement or a reduction in the real price to that person" (ibid.). This mechanism was even given a name: "advertising . . . may be said to add perceptual utility" (Sheshadri 1983).[47] And R. K. Swamy closed the circle by arguing that if it could be said that advertising ensured freedom of choice, then freedom of choice should also reciprocally ensure advertising: "Where freedom of choice is guaranteed, the right to persuade cannot be discouraged" (Swamy 1984).

These claims were the discursive counterparts to the images that comprised the didactic theater of the "exploding middle class" (see pages 71–76). On the face of it, the libertarian rhetoric that suffused the new defense of advertising sat awkwardly with the highly standardized content of the images it offered. But in fact it was precisely here that the mass consumerist dispensation laid the foundations for its own vision of the social collective: a universal entitlement to aspiration concretized in the form of advertising images portraying a generalized middle-class imaginary.

The tension between individualism and standardization was justified in terms of *equity*: equal access to the dream of self-transformation. Piyush Pandey, one of the brightest stars of the Bombay advertising scene during the time of my fieldwork, put it to me like this: "I have always believed that it is not that the beggar on the road dreams of being the most well-off beggar. He has the right to dream of being a king. So he dreams of being a king, I dream of being a king. So everyone wants to get the sun and the moon and the stars. It's not that people dream in segments — that I will only dream this much because I am here. Everyone has the right to dream."[48] The new advertising, then, positioned itself as a democratizing force, theoretically opening the infinite transformations of consumption to all comers. In concert with the drive toward the "liberalization" of markets that was initiated by Indira but most strongly identified with her son Rajiv,[49] it figured itself as an expansive gesture of inclusion — a field of possibilities finally opened for those previously excluded ("the beggar on the road").[50]

I say "finally" because much of the euphoria embedded in the liberalizers' discourse arose out of a sense of a *temporal overcoming*, a rejection of the historical stalemate that the developmentalist/modernizing paradigm had bequeathed. Akhil Gupta adapts the term "allochronicity" from Johannes Fabian to characterize the sense of temporal lag that the narrative of modernization interposed between "developed" and "developing" countries (A. Gupta 1998). Dipesh Chakrabarty characterizes the roots of this formation thus: "Historicism — and even the modern, European idea of history — one might say, came to non-European peoples in the nineteenth century as somebody's way of say-

ing 'not yet' to somebody else" (Chakrabarty 2000, 8). On an experiential level, the sense was one of being perpetually behind in the game
of progress. While international development agencies might measure
such lags in terms of quantitative macroeconomic indicators, and his-
torians and social scientists according to received trajectories of social
transformation, my informants' conversations frequently bristled with
recollections of a sense of being viewed, in a global context, as qualitatively inferior.

Many advertising and marketing professionals at the peak of their
careers during the period of my fieldwork had identified strongly,
on a personal as well as a professional level, with the globe-trotting,
post-ideological, "professional" persona put forward by Rajiv Gandhi
during his first years in office. His frequently stated managerial dis-
taste for the Machiavellian intrigues of "politics" (or, according to
others, his naïveté) suggested to them a new modern age in which the
double indignities of the planned economy — privation at home, scorn
abroad — would finally be redressed. An independent marketing consultant told me:

> I think we went through the pain of building India. We went
> through three wars. And I remember very vividly, we went through
> rationing, we went through drought, we went through adulterated
> food, we went through being punished every year through increased
> excise duties, because you had the temerity to consume what the
> government considered as luxury. We had two television channels
> which showed Indira Gandhi on one and Rajiv Gandhi on the other,
> okay? . . . And the workforce . . . there was a whole generation who
> were about to become chief executives who were told that "now it's
> globalization" so you get a young brand manager from South Africa
> who will come to India and he will run this country 'cause it's a low-
> priority country in the scheme of things. . . . [My mother] said that
> "in our day, we were terrified of a Britisher. We stood up the minute
> he entered, and if he had fair skin it was like we were really in awe."
> My generation [this informant was born in the 1950s] was also in
> awe, except that I think we tried to hide it in many ways by fighting
> discrimination. For example, I've always hated going to England
> because there's always that imperceptible shift away from a brown
> when you're sitting in the tube. People tell me it's a chip on my
> shoulder, but it was also the way I felt because I never had enough

money when I went over, because we were constrained in terms of how many dollars you could take out. And if you took it out you took it out in ways that were not legal. So you were just made to feel like a shit when you went out, and I think that was reflected in the way that you were treated as well.

It is against this background that the spectacular importance of, and controversy surrounding, an event like the international broadcasting of the 1982 Asian Games (see pages 72–76) should be understood. The linear dream of development was increasingly being painted as a cycle of infinite deferral. The consumerist dispensation, in contrast, offered the powerful promise of immediate gratification, of *arrival,* if only through the (not inconsiderable) enjoyment of consuming affect-intensive images. Pleasure was a powerful weapon indeed. But it was the sense of historical overcoming that allowed the advertising industry to borrow the legitimating discourse of a popular movement. Remarks Chakrabarty: "Historicism has not disappeared from the world, but its 'not yet' exists today in tension with this global insistence on the 'now' that marks all popular movements toward democracy" (Chakrabarty 2000, 8).

And yet the "now" that seemed so tangible in the realm of representations, and which was in the process of configuring an entire imaginary vernacular around the idea of the "middle class," nevertheless faced a crucial problem. Previously, legitimating advertising had been a matter of demonstrating its efficacy as an accelerator of the project of centrally planned economic development. The idea of development itself had provided the conceptual umbrella under which the entirety of the Indian population could be seen as engaged in a common goal that justified itself in the name of the interests of the very poorest sections of society. Now that this idea was in decline, how could the consumerist dream fill the gap?

I will argue that the role played by the family planning experience in the prehistory of KamaSutra was a versatile one. It provided a way to forge that most difficult of connections: between public service and aspirational consumerism. But it was only able to do so because the advertising business, as a complement to the mass consumerist boom in the first half of the 1980s, had already done a great deal of work to demonstrate the power of the commodity image in public service. The locus classicus of this demonstration was the genre known as public

service advertising. And it was no accident that one of its most prominent spokesmen was the future hero of the KamaSutra story, Alyque
Padamsee.

Electricity Versus Information:
The Erogenous Public Sphere

Obviously, as we have seen, Indian public service advertising did not
start in the 1980s. But Padamsee's version of the form had a particular
strategic affinity with the rise of television, the liberalization of consumer markets, and the need to lend social legitimacy to the social
vision that the new dispensation entailed.

This reaching for legitimacy was marked, in 1984, by the institution
of a national awards competition dedicated to public service campaigns. Much media commentary was favorable; Jacob (1985) spoke
of a new "maturity" on the part of the advertising industry. Others,
including industry spokespeople, have been more frank about the pay-
offs involved. Santosh Desai, former general manager at Mudra Communications in Delhi, offered: "Cause-related communication strategies prove to be a public relations insurance for companies producing
cigarettes and alcohol. It helps in building an image of their being
socially conscious companies" (S. Gupta 1996).

Although public service campaigns offer NGOs and their related
activities a kind of publicity that would otherwise be hard to come by,
"it is not easy to convince corporations to part with funds. Therefore,
what the NGOs are now doing is identifying core social cause areas, and
tailoring them to meet the needs of corporates or project benefactors"
(ibid.). A spokesperson for Delhi-based NGO Action Aid, in contrast,
put a diplomatic face on it, and adopted the rhetoric of efficiency and
professionalism: "It takes a more professional outlook, efficient management of funds and positive results to hold a company's interest for
continuous inflow of funds" (ibid.).

The attention-grabbing style of the new public service advertising,
particularly insofar as campaigns like KamaSutra were identified with
it, also came in for critique from cultural conservatives: "What is
shocking is that some social campaigns try to usher in questionable
social values under the garb of respectability. AIDS has been used to
put in questionable ads by a host of agencies. Casual sex is all right,
they seem to be saying, only wear a condom" (D. Kumar 1996). Per-

haps the most straightforward statement of the situation in the mid-1980s came from Tara Sinha of Tara Sinha Associates, known inside and outside the advertising business for her uncompromising style: "It is time to be businesslike about public service advertising" (Shekhar Ghosh 1987). (One might reflect that, according to the logic of the consumerist dispensation, *all* advertising is, in a sense, a kind of public service.)

Padamsee's version of public service advertising was based on principles similar to those that Jayant Bakshi was to attribute to the thinking behind the KamaSutra campaign. A population grown tired and alienated from years of government exhortation needed to be stirred into action through a more visceral appeal. The potential of the commodity image to effect social change depended upon extending the logic of consuming pleasures to social action more generally. Once again, self-interest was the source of collective value, now figured as ethical rather than merely commercial. And in fact the advertising industry's involvement in public service advertising was the first example of the principle. Padamsee himself framed it in terms of a kind of reciprocity: "Everyone who's making a profit has a special responsibility to the public at large. . . . The idea is not to win prizes — although you may win them incidentally — but to put back into society something you take out" (quoted in Jacob 1985).[51]

Once again, the key premise was the power of the striking commodity image to transcend tired discursive appeals and *shock* the spectator into self-motivation. What the government had hitherto been dispensing, Alyque Padamsee opined, was mere information: "You have to put electricity into it to make it communication" (Thakur 1985).[52] This "electricity" was the conductor of motivation, and the key to consensual engagement: "Motivation is the only difference between advertising and propaganda" ("Padamsee" 1988). Precisely the kind of family planning communication that da Cunha and his associates had been involved in crafting in the mid-1960s was among Padamsee's favorite object lessons: "Take that family planning slogan itself, 'ek ya do bas,' it said. I do not say it was bad or unsuccessful — perhaps people got bored with it — but something could be done to it. Something that could communicate better. And then we made this film. We took a jar, put one tomato into it, put another, and a third one. Then we show this hand trying to shut the lid and all the tomatoes burst up. And then we show this line: 'ek ya do bas' " (Thakur 1985).

6. Advertising: A public service? From the perspective of the consumerist dispensation, *all* advertising is of course a kind of public service. Internationally, the rise of the normative figure of the consumer-citizen has, however, also required the advertising business to position itself as an incomparably effective—because directly *affective*—mode of communication on issues of public concern. In India, this meant taking on all the classic goals of the developmentalist state: hunger, literacy, and employment. This ad for Hindustan Thompson Associates (the Indian office of the transnational agency network J. Walter Thompson) dramatizes the effortlessness of advertising-mediated social communication, in implicit contrast to the artificiality and abstraction of the exhortations of the state.

Formally, then, the efficacy of the commodity image was the same whether its task was realizing "social" or "commercial" value. But the problem of pleasure remained a formidable aporia to the linkage between consumption and public service. The pleasures of seduction and the indulgence of desire that drove consumer goods advertising were quite simply absent from exhortations to public service, much as the latter might otherwise demonstrate the ability of the well-deployed image to harness self-interest productively.

This is where KamaSutra was able to provide the crucial connection. Qua condom, KamaSutra provided a unique connection between the critique of government communications and the metaphorical equation of the universality of sexual activity with the inclusiveness of consumer desire. In this capacity it supplied the missing link in the campaign to eroticize not simply consumer goods, but public speech in general. Precisely the government's family planning initiatives continued, well into the 1990s, to provide the material for morality tales about the price of being prudish about public service.

In 1993, for example, it was discovered that the Madras branch of the Family Planning Association of India had simply been burying vast numbers of government condoms in ditches and elsewhere in order to avoid admitting that they were unable to interest their constituency in them and thus risk losing their funding. On the defensive, local medical authorities ended up blaming the government for not providing adequate resources with which to educate the people in the proper usage of condoms.[53] Two years later, another story described a solution that was at once more bizarre and more creative. A reporter in Uttar Pradesh found that the State Health Directorate was selling off its supply of Nirodhs to, of all things, toy manufacturers, who were apparently only too happy with this cheap supply of high quality rubber. "The volume of diversion . . . is so high that almost all the rubber toys manufactured in Meerut or Kanpur are made from recycled Nirodh" (B. Banerjee 1995). Even the government's concerted efforts at overcoming the awkwardness surrounding condom distribution seemed only further to confirm its ineptitude. For example, it was reported that the Ministry of Health in Delhi was, in all seriousness, pondering "the question of evolving a commonly-understood sign which will indicate to the shopkeeper that his customer wants to buy condoms" (Lankesh et al. 1992).

These narratives, and others in the same genre, served the interests of the advertising business and its clients by sketching a critical portrait of the contemporary polity in which a communicatively incompetent government faced a cynical and sullen citizenry. After the publicity and attention generated by the KamaSutra campaign, public sector executives were also regularly painted as hostages to an antiquated public morality. Hindustan Latex's marketing strategy, for instance, "has been hampered by its existence as a public-sector company. Though there are no specific guidelines, HL managers say they cannot just come out with a provocative or sexy campaign to combat their competitors. There is always the fear that some member will raise the issue in Parliament, charging the . . . company with debasing Indian morals" (K. G. Kumar 1993). Provocation and attention-grabbing were themselves now essential tools of the trade. Pleaded the marketing manager at HL: "We're only trying to be more businesslike" (K. G. Kumar 1993). The misplaced and anachronistic austerity of government ideology was the root of the problem as far as the private sector was concerned, but the focus for all the resentment was the advertising industry's old bête noire: its own counterpart within the administration, the Directorate for Advertising and Visual Publicity (DAVP). "The dull and unimaginative advertisements that the DAVP regularly churned out," complained one commentator, "were probably responsible for the cynicism with which they were greeted" (Shekhar Ghosh 1987).[54]

For KamaSutra, on the contrary, there was apparently no contradiction between acknowledging, along with one journalist, that the brand was "selling the notion that sex is fun, safe, and somehow upmarket to young, high income yuppies" (Sengupta 1991) and at the same time making public service claims on behalf of the product, as did Gautam Singhania himself at the time of the launch:

India has been one of the largest contributors to the world population. With only 2.4 per cent of the world area, we account for about 15 per cent of it! Besides this there is also a high incidence of sexually transmitted diseases. It is a proven fact that of all the ways of contraception, condoms are the most reliable not only in birth control, but also in preventing diseases. And talking of AIDS, it's not a problem of the future or anything. KamaSutra with its bold advertising is our contribution to doing social good. The 15 crore (Rs 150,000,000) investment that we have made to set up the factory in Aurangabad is a very small sum, considering the amount of good that we can do (Menon 1991).

The fiction that high-end consumerism could comfortably be aligned with public service was of course never going to be a stable one. Indeed, one price of the union was the inability of the advertisements to refer overtly to any social "issues," since these would have been perceived as "negatives," dampening the erotic potential of the brand. Adi Pocha, the creative director, suggested to me that AIDS wasn't yet "big enough to position a brand on" in India in 1991. But Aniruddha Deshmukh, executive director at JKC, conceded that the cultural politics of branding precluded such options, couching his explanation in terms of a concern for public propriety. I asked him why they had not chosen to market KamaSutra on an anti-AIDS platform given that growing awareness of the epidemic had been one of their reasons for getting into the condom business in the first place. While conceding that condoms as a generic category could, indeed should, be marketed on such a platform ("so it's there in the back of the mind that *all* condoms are good against AIDS"), he opined that the life-style connotations of someone *choosing* a particular brand on the basis of its protection against AIDS — and thus himself being identified with that choice ("it would be a giveaway to his life-style") — would not be socially acceptable:[55]

> If you have a condom, which you're promoting, saying that this is very good as a prevention against AIDS . . . saying that it has got nonoxynol-9 or something like that, and if you have consumers buying that, it's a very strong indication that here's a person who's promiscuous or is visiting commercial sex workers. Now that's not accepted over here as yet. So you would have a very, very, very, very limited segment for that. . . . We don't believe that there is a segment that you can market a condom to on those lines.[56]

The reporter who interviewed Gautam Singhania at the time of the KamaSutra launch, however, came to his own succinct conclusion: "Gautam Singhania has discovered an erogenous place in the market which, when stimulated, he hopes, would yield pleasurable results" (Menon 1991).

Conclusion

This chapter has traced the background of the apparently paradoxical union of two discourses in discussions of the KamaSutra campaign:

one of aspirational luxury consumption and one of public service. Focusing particularly on the latter, I have described the shifting basis of the Indian advertising industry's operations in the 1980s and the problems of legitimation and representation that these changes gave rise to. I argued that the rise of commercial television from 1982 onward formed the basis for a new notion of collectivity, which was expressed as "the middle class" and was based on the idea of the democratization of aspiration. This new formation was one response to the decline of the paradigm of planned development, and while it initially served the government's interests in addressing its more affluent constituents, it came with universalistic pretensions. At this point, however, the ideologues of consumerism found themselves having to incorporate both aspirational consumption and public service within the discourse of the commodity image and were thus presented with a contradiction: the discontinuity between pleasure and obligation. The importance of KamaSutra rests in part upon the brand's apparent ability to overcome this contradiction.

The problems I have discussed in this chapter were very much problems of the 1980s: in broad strokes, they smoothed the reconciliation of a developmentalist and a consumerist model of society. In this regard, KamaSutra, when it emerged in 1991, offered a kind of retrospective summation. But as I will show in the next chapter, KamaSutra also anticipated themes that would become important to the advertising industry in the 1990s. Perhaps the most important of these was the commodification of "Indianness" in a globalizing world. For thoroughly pragmatic reasons, KamaSutra itself ended up providing a model for how a "world-class" or "aspirational" — and yet at the same time *Indian* — commodity aesthetic could be constructed. And in so doing, it also offered one solution to a problem that I will focus on in parts 2 and 3: the ambivalent value of "Indian" as a differentiator in a globalizing landscape of brands.

4

The Aesthetic Politics of
Aspiration: KamaSutra II

One of the central claims made on behalf of advertising, as I suggested in chapter 3, is that it is uniquely capable of engaging with the embodied preferences of its audience. Apparently bypassing the abstractions of discourse, it speaks directly to the senses. I have shown how this aesthetic engagement, promising an instantaneous gratification, was offered by the Indian advertising business as an alternative to the increasingly sclerotic discourse of state-centralized planning. But the challenge was not simply a matter of replacing the perpetual deferrals of the goal of development with the present plenitude of consumer pleasure. Rather, the "aspirational" orientation of the new consumerist dispensation was also a matter of *content*.

What were the cultural politics of the specific images that were being proliferated? I have hinted that KamaSutra generated a great deal of public controversy at the time of its launch, ostensibly because of its visual boldness. In the present chapter, I will argue that the controversy over KamaSutra that was played out before, during, and long after its launch involved the negotiation of a new vision of citizenship based on aspirational consumption.

The effect of commercial communication, or "publicity," has been a central bone of contention in debates on citizenship and "the public sphere." At one end of the spectrum we find the position associated with the early work of Jürgen Habermas (1989), according to which the rise of commercial publicity necessarily threatens the integrity of the kind of discursive — and therefore "rational" — public sphere invented by the bourgeois revolutions in seventeenth- and eighteenth-century Europe.[1] Critics have questioned both the desirability of the *particular* discursive forms that Habermas evokes (see, in this connection, Chakrabarty's [2000] discussion of the institution of *adda* in Bengal; Kaviraj 1997) and his *general* privileging of discourse over images. On the latter count, analysts of consumerism in Europe and the United States have frequently argued that commodity images have provided a crucial — if not innocent — idiom of public agency and expression for individuals and groups marginalized by mainstream forms of public discourse. The idioms and interests are diverse — from women at various socioeconomic locations through youth subcultures to ethnic and sexual minorities — but the common factor is the way in which commodity images add a dimension of sensuous embodiment to an otherwise abstract ideal of citizenship. "Responding to an immanent contradiction in the bourgeois public sphere," Michael Warner writes, "mass publicity promises a reconciliation between embodiment and self-abstraction" (Warner 1992, 396). This, then, is precisely the domain in which the advertising business operates.

In the last chapter, I described how the Indian advertising industry sought to make the case for this more sensuous, "electric" form of public address. I suggested that part of the great appeal of the Kama-Sutra campaign, from the industry's point of view, was that, by making a universalistic claim on the basis of sex and the collective trauma of family planning, it bolstered the image of advertising as a universal language, even as the actual content of the most eroticized advertising was clearly oriented toward an upscale minority. Public service advertising was one of the few arenas in which the advertising industry could argue that the *content* of its communications might provide the kind of mass stimulation that it had already attributed to advertising as a *medium*. But most of the highly eroticized aspirational consumer goods advertising of the period could make no such mass claims. Here too, KamaSutra, a quintessentially "aspirational" brand, proved a powerful mediator. I argued that the consumerist dispensation promised immediate gratification in place of the deferrals of development. This promise, however, contained its own undoing insofar as the full realization of the gratification evoked in advertising would, for the great majority, necessarily not be immediately attainable. The language of "aspiration" provided a twofold solution. First, it attempted to equate the generality of consumer desire with the particular norms and forms of the nascent middle-class imaginary. And second, it introduced an alternative temporality with its own language of progress and evolution. Certainly the ultimate goal of aspirational consumption was just as chimerical as that of development. But there was an important compensation: the aspirational consumer was being exhorted to individual and collective self-fulfillment by means of pleasure rather than sacrifice.[2]

Thus far, there was nothing much to distinguish the Indian version of this aestheticized citizenship from its counterparts elsewhere. As we will see, however, the figure of the Indian consumer-citizen cannot, as in the Habermasian debate, be read as a radical and/or reactionary shadow of bourgeois civic man. This is so for at least two reasons. First, unlike in Europe, a professional bourgeoisie was never able to establish hegemonic control over the political imagination in India (see Chakrabarty 2000; Chatterjee 1993; Chatterjee and Mallik 1997). Second, the idealized model of citizenship that emerged out of the nationalist struggle in India involved not so much a disembodied abstraction as a powerfully elaborated regime of bodily self-discipline that combined the austerities of Gandhian swaraj[3] with those of Nehruvian socialism (Alter 2000). To many of my informants, this ideal had long since lost its potency; indeed, its failure was widely perceived as both "material" (economic stagnation) and "spiritual" (a loss of national pride). In effect, KamaSutra appeared as a distilled response to both these frustrations. Flagship of aspirational consumerism, it embodied the new aesthetic teleology: progress through pleasure. But more than this, in its strategic deployment of "Indianness," it prefigured the ways in which this universal model of progress would inevitably confront the specificity of the preferences and pleasures of Indian consumers.

Aspiration

What some in the marketing world called "aspirational" consumerism, then, mediated between the particular and the universal in two ways. First, it promised to link the particularity of individual consumer desire with universal progress, imagined at once as material and aesthetic. Second, it offered to mediate between the particularity of local or national "culture" and a global repertoire of images. Both of these mediations were made possible by advertising images. It is therefore hardly surprising that the advertising industry became both source and target of debates around the new dispensation.

We can see how such notions of personal and collective transformation are embedded in the way in which the word "aspirational" operates in marketing discourse. In this adjectival form, it appears to be virtually exclusive to marketing, although to some extent it crosses over to and borrows from ethics, as in theologian K. L. Patton's expression "an adequate moral and aspirational life."[4] In the language of advertising and marketing, this adjectival usage is important because it attaches a quality that is usually understood to be a state of mind to objects and images. The noun "aspiration" and the verb "to aspire" — aside from their medical and phonetic senses — both connote a desire for transformation, for the realization of particular exalted ends, whether abstract or concrete, predominantly sacred but also profane: "a strong desire for realization; an end or goal aspired to; a condition strongly desired";[5] "earnest longing or an earnest wish for that which is above one's present reach or attainment, especially for what is noble, pure, and spiritual";[6] "yearning and craving."[7]

The statement that objects or images may be "aspirational" implies that an orientation toward such objects or images indicates a desire for personal transformation, in line with a widely diffused and thus generally recognized index of advancement. Aspirational qualities appear, on the face of it, to be inherent properties. Thus marketing theorist David Aaker writes: "The brand [Nike] is very aspirational in the sense that wearing Nike represents what the users aspire to be like rather than their current self-image" (Aaker 1995, 154–55, original parentheses omitted). Aspirational qualities are, moreover, associable not only with particular brands but also with whole quasi-geographical imaginaries. In this way — and this is a point that I will explore in greater detail in part 3 — a geographical hierarchy still intersects the apparent "leveling" effect of globalization. " 'The U.S.A. is still a very aspirational place,' says Michael Conrad, [global ad agency] Leo Burnett's German-born chief creative officer. 'People love it, especially when [you're talking] about the new, emerging countries. For them, getting into the West is very desirable' " (Wells 1998).

But a brand like Nike is clearly the carefully husbanded creation of teams of marketing and advertising professionals. And "the U.S.A." understood as "a very aspirational place" must equally clearly be understood as an image-object, distilled from multiple sources — advertising, movies, journeys, conversations — and circulated through multiple social contexts. Insofar as we interpret either of these entities as *inherently* aspirational we are missing the multi-sited work of the imagination — both amateur and professional — that goes into constructing them as desirable objects.

In fact, the perpetual dilemma of the advertising business in this regard is that it must insist at one and the same time on its own exclusive expertise in discovering and articulating this aspirational quality *and* on its objective and universal aesthetic basis. This is why advertising industry discourse frequently comes across as a curious blend of elitist pedagogy and populist appeal — a combination that should not surprise us in a form of cultural production that, more acutely than any other, straddles the realms of "art" and "commerce." As a commercially motivated practice, advertising cannot fall back on the kinds of claims to aesthetic "autonomy" that are typically made on behalf of fine art, and around which Pierre Bourdieu has constructed a critical sociology (Bourdieu 1984, 1993). At the same time, because it deals in the concrete currency of images and because it is always involved in a project of aspirational *transformation,* it cannot be reduced to the purely instrumental calculus of the market either.

What from one perspective looks like a tension between autonomy and instrumentality in the production of advertising appears, from another angle, as a tension between exclusiveness and inclusiveness. Both of these tensions are, in fact, internal to what Terry Eagleton calls "the ideology of the aesthetic" (Eagleton 1990). And it is in terms of an aesthetic politics that I will examine the production and circulation of KamaSutra in the pages that follow. But before I can return to the concrete conjunctures of the campaign, I must show how the rise of mass marketing in India, as outlined in the previous chapter, profoundly transformed the aesthetic politics of the Indian advertising business during the 1980s.

The Aesthetic and the Politics of Taste

We have grown accustomed to thinking of aesthetics as an inquiry into a rather rarefied level of cultural production, typically "fine" or "autonomous" art. But as Eagleton reminds us, this equation is in fact the product of a specifically modern European experience (cf. Buck-Morss

1992). Furthermore, it creates the impression that there is a radical separation between a domain of fine art and a domain of everyday life, between artistic "freedom" and everyday "utility." While such a division from one perspective appears designed to safeguard human creativity from the encroachment of instrumentality, it also provides the conceptual basis for authorizing a set of expert discourses on what constitutes "good taste." And it is no surprise that precisely because the category of taste purports to be both objective and universally grounded in basic human faculties, it frequently serves as a particularly insidious (because deeply embedded) way of naturalizing power relations. By the same token, no matter how formalized and refined aesthetic discourse on the good or the beautiful becomes, it must always, in the final analysis, appeal to a basic and universal capacity for sensuous experience, a capacity which — in its infinite diversity of concrete locations — will never be reducible to authoritative formulae.

The category of the aesthetic, therefore, inhabits the cultural politics of the commodity image. A level of visceral concretion — embodied experience, the given image — both enables and exceeds formal projects of value-extraction, whether "commercial" or "political." Eagleton's account of the duality of the aesthetic makes the point nicely. On the one hand, the aesthetic is "the whole region of human perception and sensation. . . . That territory is nothing less than the whole of our sensate life together — the business of affections and aversions, of how the world strikes the body on its sensory surfaces, of that which takes root in the gaze and the guts and all that arises from our most banal, biological insertion into the world" (Eagleton 1990, 13). The aesthetic as concrete, embodied experience is the basis for a kind of "deep subjectivity" (28). As such, it is both an indispensable resource for hegemony but also ultimately — precisely because of its concretion — resistant to all reifying agendas: "Deep subjectivity is just what the ruling social order desires, and exactly what it has most cause to fear. If the aesthetic is a dangerous, ambiguous affair, it is because . . . there is something in the body which can revolt against the power that inscribes it; and that impulse could only be eradicated along with the capacity to authenticate power itself" (28).

Immanuel Kant inaugurated the line of modern aesthetic discourse that sought to establish an objective and universal basis for judgments of taste. Insofar as we are post-Nietzscheans, we may well today be skeptical as to the political innocence of the faculty that Kant hoped would provide the foundation — by way of an objective assessment of the beautiful — for a noncoercive social order. And if we use this skepticism to inform a post-Marxian critical social theory, then we are also soon in a position to understand the ways in which judgments of "taste," manifested as a scaled normative discourse of distinction, may exploit the given concretion of "the whole of our sensate life together" to naturalize a would-be hegemonic cultural scheme. Wolfgang Fritz Haug effectively shows how Kant's recipe for community slips into the means of domination:

> In positive terms, the focus in this space of the aesthetic is to find — via a sort of common sense, *sensus communis* . . . — the connection to a human community. The focus here is on participation in something common to all, in a universality; it should not proceed through intellect but through the senses. That which presents itself in such a contradictory way can be grasped as an *imaginary community in the mode of the aesthetic*. The aesthetic is anchored in the individual as taste. Taste means not only the link to the aesthetic community but also to Good Society. To have taste means to belong to it. Taste is a form of socialization in which the top/bottom of power and domination is transposed into the "aesthetic" opposition of taste vs. tastelessness. (Haug 1987, 136)

Advertising transforms desire into aspiration by routing it through a symbolic field defined with reference to taste. In line with the operation of the aesthetic, this symbolic field manages at once to appear naturally inclusive and socially exclusive. In Hegelian terms, advertising is a kind of *Bildung*, a project of education: it purports to transform the "first nature" of subjective desire into the "second nature" of objective social truth. The crucial point here is the *naturalization* of both individual desire and the socially mediated goal of aspiration, as well as the harmonization of the relationship between the two. In a footnote, Jean Baudrillard notes how the French term *concurrence* captures this dialectical movement in the ideology of consumerism: "The term competition (*concurrence*) is ambiguous: that which 'competes' *(concourt)* at the same time rivals and converges. It is through relentless rivalry that one 'concurs' *(concourt)* most assuredly towards the same point" (Poster 1988, 25fn).

The tension between universality and exclusivity in advertising must be diligently managed in any consumerist project. In India, this aesthetic calculus was particularly problematic for the advertising industry for several reasons, including the extreme diversity of cultural idiom and educational attainment among the inhabitants of the subcontinent taken as a whole and the extreme disparities in wealth, with hundreds of millions of citizens living lives precariously perched on the edge of starvation and tens of millions enjoying levels of luxury hardly imaginable by the majority of their compatriots. When, in the early 1980s, a more mass-based defense of advertising-led consumerism was needed (see chapter 3), the Indian advertising industry found itself obliged, first of all, to address the way these social contradictions structured its own operations. As I will show in the following section, this spelled the end of a formative era in Indian advertising. But it also brought new contradictions to the surface, contradictions that could only be resolved by appealing precisely to the mass foundation of the aspirational aesthetic community.

A Historical Dialectic:
Creativity, Rationalization, and the Big Idea

In the 1960s and 1970s, the appeal of Bombay advertising images duplicated and reinforced the social profile of the men and women who produced them. The industry was strongly identified with the creative talents of a small group of South Bombay Anglophile writers and visualizers. This was the so-called "Churchgate Set," the likes of Frank Simoes and Kersy Katrak, whose urbane insouciance borrowed heavily from the "creative revolution" that swept Madison Avenue in the 1960s. The U.S. version—led by admen such as Bill Bernbach and George Lois—was a reaction against the banality and corporate stolidity of 1950s mass marketing and it identified with (some even say it invented—see Frank 1997) the American counterculture of the period. The Churchgate Set similarly revolted against what they perceived to be the mediocrity of the industry that had spawned them. On the one hand, as Mohammed Khan (now of Enterprise Nexus Lowe) remembered, it was a matter of the product itself: "It was just *there,* you know, and I think it didn't even attract attention because it was so bad! We didn't have any television in those days, for instance. There was cinema, but very poor. The kind of advertising then was very *factual,* it was very boring. . . . The one thing it was supposed to do, it did not do.

Which is attract attention to itself!"[8] On the other hand, the new creative stars of the 1960s were reacting against the specific social context of the Indian advertising profession in the late 1950s and early 1960s, a world that was still in some respects an outpost of the British Empire. The late Frank Simoes remembered joining S. H. Benson's in Bombay as a copy trainee:

> There was somebody called Geoffrey Bell in charge. He was co-lossally ill equipped to do the job, and he had around him a coterie of expatriate Brits, who were if anything even *worse* at their jobs than he was! You were really on your own, you know. There was nobody to teach you, to guide you. The entire business was extremely primitive, and you were left to your own devices. And this was a two-edged situation: on the one hand, one was deprived of proper professional guidance, of training; on the other, you had to learn on your own, which sometimes I think is the best way of learning if you are motivated. So I was left largely to my own devices. . . . It was actually the top of the expat parabolic curve. They were here in vast numbers. Most of them were colonially biased in various ways. They were perfectly happy to allow competent Indians to do the work and live a fairly sybaritic life. They had large houses, they had servants, they had club memberships, they had . . . all the privileges. They also had an income structure at the agency which was about five to six hundred percent higher than the Indians who were doing the work. And they had a very good life. . . . I never had a head for managing money. I was terrible at administration. I abhorred systems. I was a maverick. I went my own way. And under the protection of Benson's—one thing the British had going for them: they had a very tolerant attitude towards people who should have been axed at birth. Within a year I was copy chief, and within a[nother] year I was creative director in Calcutta. After a year I came back as creative director in Bombay, in a year I was account director, and then three years after that I was on the board of the company. Handling 70 percent of their business, all-India. The only reason this happened is because they allowed it to happen. They never interfered.[9]

MCM (Mass Communications and Marketing), an agency started by Kersy Katrak in 1965, is still discussed in reverential tones in Bombay advertising circles. It was, for those of Katrak's generation, the path-breaking institutional realization of their generational and professional self-identity. Katrak, who started his own career at Lintas in 1959, and today occupies a semi-honorary position at that same agency, told me:

> We always thought of MCM as a kind of Indian Doyle Dane and Bernbach, which was the great white-hot shop in the U.S. of A. at that point. . . . Hopelessly romantic . . . one sort of saw it as a kind of advertising Bauhaus. It brought a whole set of forces together and started something completely new. As it happened, that is what *did* happen. But as I say, it's hopelessly romantic to think of yourself like that, a sort of Bauhaus, which is putting architecture and the arts and painting and everything else together. But we did create a minor revolution.[10]

Frank Simoes, a close friend and competitor of Katrak's, also remembered the impact of MCM in terms that resonated with those of the Madison Avenue creative revolution:

> Kersy was the first Indian in the advertising business to start a seemingly different advertising operation, which was based not on contacts, not on servicing, but on the actual content of the communication, which was as shockingly different from anything being done in India as the work being done by Doyle Dane and Bernbach and other agencies in America at that time. And yet [it was] not imitative of their work. It was very original work. Startlingly original. And the rest of us, who were all creative people in advertising, were not just heartened by this, but certainly . . . it gave us pause for thought. Because we all had Olympian egos, we all thought we were better than each other. And we all thought that if Kersy could do it, we could do it standing on our heads. So a lot of us broke away and started our own agencies. Sylvie da Cunha started his own agency, I started my own agency. . . . We believed in creativity more than anything else. And [were] very cocky in our belief and the success that brought us so far. And we brooked no nonsense from our clients. We said, "Take it or leave it. This is what we think you need. That's why you've come to us. If you want to buy it, buy it. If not, farewell." And this attitude, I think, worked with at least 70 percent of new agencies and their clients. And this led in the 60s and 70s to a

bold new wave of advertising in India, which was really a paradigm shift in terms of creativity in advertising communications. Or in corporate communications.

The brashness of this new professional attitude was reflected in the sheer effrontery of the advertising they created. Mohammed Khan, who passed through MCM in the early 1970s, remembered:

They were trying to be different. . . . The layouts were what made the advertising stand out because people hadn't seen those kinds of layouts. *Huge* big ads. That was another thing that was new. When I came [back] to India [having spent several years working in London in the 1960s], the average size of the ad used to be fifteen by two columns. Or twenty by three, which was the kind of thing where people would fall off their chairs. And I was trying to flog twenty-five by four layouts and people thought I was nuts, you know! MCM advertising stood out, I think, because one of the things that Kersy understood was that the first thing is *impact.*

The glamour and impact of such daredevilry rubbed off on the public image of the business as a whole. Doctor and Alikhan, in an overview of the history of the Indian advertising industry, report:

MCM above all brought glamour into [Indian] advertising. It created a whole group of fast-living, high-spending professionals, derisively described . . . as the "Churchgate Set" because of their exclusively South Bombay orientation. "Kersy lived like a mogul, and he spent like one too," says [Bobby] Sista [elder statesman of Bombay advertising, whose father founded one of the very first Indian ad agencies]. "There was a time when—I'm not joking—clients vied with each other to give their business to MCM simply in order to be entertained by Kersy!" (Doctor and Alikhan 1997, 51)

MCM itself crashed spectacularly as a result of bad debts in 1975. But the image of creativity hypostasized in the person of Katrak became incorporated into the industry mainstream and thereby domesticated, even as Katrak himself retreated for several years to an ashram in the foothills of the Himalayas. A house brochure put out in the early-to-mid 1970s by that most stolid of agencies, Hindustan Thompson Associates, shows the institutionalization—within the wider parameters of "solid business practices"—of the bohemian creative mythos: "The Creative Dept. is possibly the most attractive, informal part of any agency. Go towards it and the clothes get trendier. You might walk into a brain-storming session and hear the hum of new ideas. Or see a copywriter strumming his guitar while other writers and a secretary pilot a jingle through its early melody."[11]

By the early 1980s, however, as the advertising business geared up for the rise of commercial television, thesis made way for antithesis as the creative discourse of the 1960s and 1970s was comprehensively rejected.[12] There were two main reasons. First, the metropolitan and socially exclusive image enjoyed by the practitioners of the Indian creative revolution sat badly with the industry's new attempts to profile itself as socially engaged and inclusive. Second, as we have seen, the claim of inclusiveness required that the industry posit a whole new social ontology based on commodity images. The intuitive inspirations of an English-medium, educated, aspiring poet or novelist could not match the discursive blandishments of "science" for transcendent legitimation. As one of the rising new breed of GOMBAS (Grossly Overpaid MBAS) put it: "Advertising is no longer a string of beautiful pictures and smart headlines produced by long-haired, pot-smoking, *kurta*-wearing pseudo-intellectuals. Now the chap who handles your account at the agency side is more likely than not to have been your colleague at business school" (P. Mehta 1981). Concocting a spoof job ad, one partisan commentator contrasted the 1970s stereotype with the new rationalized venture:

Multinational agency requires go-getter with imagination and flair. Job involves glamour, travel, unending perks, and generous salary. No particular professional qualifications required, but the person must have sophistication, *elan,* and a *creative* bent of mind. The person must have the ability to talk well, get along with people, and sell ideas. . . . This, like it or not, is the ugly image of advertising. . . . The truth is that advertising has come a very long way from the days when this image was first formed. . . . Like a precise military campaign, it means setting clear objectives, defining the target, understanding and anticipating the response, and then, working out the detailed steps required to succeed. Before any new campaign is launched, extensive market surveys are conducted, the product's positioning carefully tested, and the market segments correctly identified, long before the artists and copywriters are even called in. . . . Long planning sessions with an emphasis on rigorous analysis are the inevitable foundation of any successful campaign. . . . Like in any other profession, advertising requires hard work, attention to detail, and an objective, professional approach. . . . Most people do not appreciate that an agency — like any other business — must be properly managed. They must be reasonably capitalized, have adequate staff, proper working procedures, and deliver on time. It is simply not enough to have great ideas. (Vasuki 1985)

The new "MBA-ized" advertising sought and found its legitimation as a form of mass address in the "objectivity" of scientific rationality. Ostensibly, the new paradigm was about creating an efficient mechanism for "taking marketing to the grass roots." The cosmopolitan stylings of the Churchgate writers receded into the past, to be recalled with a mixture of nostalgia and condescension by a new generation of ad professionals. Yet insofar as the new marketing paradigm stressed systems rationality, it also threatened to relegate advertising to a purely informational function. And as I showed in chapter 3, such a positioning was necessarily intolerable to the industry because it was unable to legitimate the "persuasive" or "value-adding" operation of the commodity image. Just as thesis had been opposed by antithesis, so a new synthesis was soon required. The mass basis of advertising needed to be reconciled with the industry's insistence that it was uniquely equipped to realize this mass potential through the medium of images. In the internal terms of the advertising business, the dilemma was one of finding the correct integration between creative inspiration and market research. In a slightly different register, one might say that the problem was one of maintaining the professional aesthetic authority of the advertising business. The name of the solution, when it came, was "the Big Idea."

The Big Idea, a concept adapted from international advertising theory, shared a certain superficial affinity with memories of the Churchgate Set's preoccupation with "impact" — the concrete potential of the image figured prominently in both. But it was nevertheless a rather different beast, insofar as its apologists were careful to stress its close, but highly ambiguous, connection to the rationalized apparatus of market research. The votaries of the Big Idea — particularly on the creative side of the internal agency divide — were often scornful of their account executive colleagues' reliance on systems. But many of them were no less critical of what they perceived to be the lack of a Big Idea in the advertising of the Churchgate period. Mohammed Khan reflected:

> If you look at MCM advertising today, I think this whole thing of positioning, in terms of strategic thinking, it wasn't really happening . . . the account planning function wasn't really there. It was just kind of gut feel. There was no process that resulted in great advertising. All the *trappings* were there [laughs] but I don't think it was functioning. . . . They may have been *influenced* by [DDB], but I don't think it had the kind of crispness or the power of the Idea. . . With MCM work . . . there were no headlines. I can't think of a single great headline that came out of MCM. There were long-winded lines that told you about, you know, mumblemumblemumble. They were not *ads*, you know? I think MCM advertising produced a great deal of impact through size and visual. But it didn't create impact through the power of the Idea, like Bernbach [of DDB] did.[13]

A younger copywriter, when shown some ads from the Churchgate Set era, remarked: "Well, I can see how these when they came out in the 60s or 70s must have created quite a hangama. But it just seems like garnish. Where's the *idea*? It's just too easy to write ads like this." On another occasion, an up and coming art director implied that precisely this ability to come up with the transubstantiating Idea was what distinguished "advertising people" proper from the metropolitan fripperies of the past: "See in the 60s and 70s, the ad world was very copy-led. It was full of all these Cuffe Parade guys, clever writers, guys like Frank Simoes, Kersy Katrak, and the rest of them. They were great writers, but they lived in their own little world, and they really were not what you would call great *advertising* people."

Ostensibly, the role of the Big Idea was to bridge creative intuition — manifested as startling images — and the "facts" of the market, as expressed in market research. Writes advertising legend David Ogilvy: "Big ideas come from the unconscious. This is true in art, in science, and in advertising. But your unconscious has to be *well informed,* or your idea will be irrelevant. Stuff your conscious mind with information, then unhook your rational thought process. You can help this process by going for a long walk, or taking a hot bath, or drinking half a pint of claret. Suddenly, if the telephone line from your unconscious is open, a big idea wells up within you" (Ogilvy 1983, 16).

Time Past
Time Present
Time Future

How the Taj Mahal Inter-Continental captures the fugitive hour from dawn to dawn, matching your mood of the minute, the hour, the day, the season...

For 70 years the Taj has borne witness to a colourful, tumultuous history. Flag bearer to the finest traditions of the past, creating the excitement of the present, and informed with a vision of the future...it has not been possible to think of Bombay without the Taj, or the Taj without its city.

Together the Taj Mahal and the Taj Inter-Continental create an unsurpassed welcome that lasts from dawn to dawn. The Shamiana beguiles you with a magnificent harbour sunrise and a royal choice of breakfasts. A cool pool called Aquarius sparkles with life from

morn till midnight. The Tanjore, the Golden Dragon, the Rendezvous span the epicurean world at luncheon or supper. The pursuit of after-sundown pleasures may find you lost in the rhythm of the Blow-Up discotheque or feasting your eyes and your inclinations in the glittering late-night shopping arcade.

The Taj is more than a place to live in, it is a way of life. Our guests are our friends. The welcome that comes from our heart is tempered to your mood of the moment and the time of day. Between friends nothing less will do.

THE **TAJ MAHAL** INTER-CONTINENTAL

7. Urbanely loquacious Churchgate Set advertising. With the massification of Indian advertising in the 1980s, the Anglocentric, quasi-literary style of the Bombay copywriters of the 1970s was immediately anathematized (and, at the same time, looked upon with nostalgia). This example, an ad for the Taj Mahal Inter-Continental hotel in Bombay, is both typically loquacious and typically lacking what a subsequent generation of Indian ad professionals would refer to as the Big Idea.

The discourse of the Big Idea brought advertising creativity—the persuasion necessary for added value—into line with the now necessary populist claims of the industry. The potential for added value introduced by the discourse of aspiration was socially legitimized through the mediation of the Big Idea, since it suggested a direct connection between the creative leap and the "facts on the ground." Furthermore, the Big Idea reclaimed a specifically *aesthetic* basis for good advertising from the increasingly prevalent emphasis on systems. Market research was still both strategically and rhetorically important. But the legitimacy of the Big Idea rested first and foremost upon the claim that effective advertising addressed its audience in two ways: as universally constituted *and* as culturally situated consumers. Piyush Pandey, who offered me a vision of the democratizing force of consumer aspiration ("So everyone wants to get the sun and the moon and the stars. It's not that people dream in segments—that I will only dream this much because I am here;" see page 89), explained:

My first objective every time I write an ad is that it should be able to run anywhere in the world. As an Idea. And once [I] have done that, then I layer it with the Indian cultural sense, or people's sensibility, level of understanding, or the kind of language that they use. . . . Culture in itself cannot be an Idea. That's another mistake we make. . . . [People] think that "Okay, you take ten rituals and put them together, and put a nice emotional song to it, and you have an Idea there." No—that's not so true. . . . Why do some people stand out and some people don't? Because some people actually have an Idea as the core, and culture only as a layer.

In part 3, I will have occasion to investigate the practical dynamics of this claim regarding "culture" vis-à-vis the Idea more closely. For now, however, let me note that the conceptual centrality and universality granted to the Idea here serves to render execution—the particular images, idioms, and inflections used in an ad—merely instrumental to, rather than really constitutive of, its operation. Aspirational images and the aesthetics of distinction are mere devices through which to reach an underlying human commonality. These were precisely the rhetorical devices deployed on behalf of KamaSutra (although Pandey himself was, I should note, dismissive of the KamaSutra campaign as elitist). In chapter 3, I recounted how Alyque Padamsee and Adi Pocha both narrated the moment of creative insight, and how Jayant Bakshi extended the "unconventional wisdom" embodied by this insight into a more generalized discourse on advertising communications, indeed on human nature. This aspect of the KamaSutra Idea linked the strategic importance of market research with a concomitant dismissal of the *creative* value of this research. It heralded the now legitimate return of the glamour and hubris that had been banished from the industry's self-image at the start of the 1980s by linking it, however shakily, with a discourse of social service.[14] The aesthetic politics of KamaSutra qua commodity image were not, however, only oriented toward providing a social justification for aspirational consumerism. Rather—and this was at least as important—the aesthetic idiom of aspirational consumerism, which had already been given a universal grounding, was figured as an index of social progress.

Progress of, and through, Pleasure

On a global level, the mass extension of aspirational consumerism— with its linkage of personal pleasure and collective social progress— was radical indeed. Kant, in the *Critique of Judgment*, had insisted that the judgment of the beautiful was necessarily an objective matter and, furthermore, that this aesthetic capacity was the true foundation of the Good Society. But for Kant this judgment must have nothing to do with personal pleasure or interest, since only if it was disinterested could it fulfill the requirement of objectivity and thus provide a universal basis for human coexistence (Behler 1999). In fact pleasure, as he noted in the section of his *Anthropology* titled "On Opulence," encouraged people to switch off their naturally endowed critical faculty of reason and therefore made them easy prey to the manipulations of politicians and churchmen alike (Kant 1978, 154).

Hegel's *Phenomenology* reintroduced desire as a motive force in history, but only at the cost of ascribing this desire to the quasi-mystical totalizing force that he termed Spirit rather than to particular individuals (see pages 39–40). Moreover, as his later lectures on aesthetics were to make clear, for Hegel the concretion and specificity of images necessarily relegated them to a relatively lowly position ("below" religion and, at the apex, philosophy) in the constantly generalizing progress of truth. Nevertheless, Spirit's desire was a kind of consuming desire; it subsumed all particulars in its restless quest for self-realization (Houlgate 1998, 45–123). Mass consumerism would need, at least rhetorically, to return the historical agency of desire to individuals. And it would also require the liberation of the aesthetic from the "primitive" position to which Hegel had assigned it. Much of the utopian resonance of the discourse of mass consumerism can be traced to these moves.[15] But as I have suggested in my analysis of the category of the aspirational, this liberatory promise was at the same time bound by a quasi-Hegelian pedagogical pledge updated for the age of electronic mass communications: namely, to route the spontaneous consuming energies of individuals through commodity images and thus on to their fulfillment in a "higher" aesthetic truth.

I confronted this equation the minute I started asking acquaintances in Bombay why they had been so struck by the KamaSutra campaign. Certain themes kept recurring: KamaSutra users understood that sex was "fun," also that it was "nothing to be ashamed of," and that the sex they were having, courtesy of KamaSutra, was sophisticated, premium quality sex. KamaSutra, I was told, spoke to a new class of consumer whose "attitudes" were more "evolved." Boldness felicitously coincided with sophistication, as a business journalist friend reflected one evening at the epicenter of Bombay yuppiedom, the bar of the Bombay Gymkhana: "I think what was so powerful about the campaign was that it managed to be extremely up front about sex — the baseline, after all, was 'for the pleasure of making love' — while at the same time making it *elegant*. That was very new in India. Previous campaigns had all been very coy — unlikely situations, giggling couples, with the product logo and descriptor virtually hidden. Or the imagery had been smutty, like the pictures on the boxes of the imported condoms that you buy on the roadside."

KamaSutra seemed immediately to offer itself as the accessory of choice for the sophisticated hedonist. Frank Simoes, former enfant terrible of the Bombay advertising scene in the 1960s and 1970s, wrote: "This was no quickie piece of plebeian latex for brief encounters of the furtive kind. This was the ultimate 'pleasure enhancer.' If no romantic evening was complete without the Jag, the champagne and roses, candlelight and violins, the perfumed suite with velvet drapes, making love would never be the same again once you slipped on a KamaSutra, or, noblesse oblige, 'let her put it on for you' " (Simoes 1993, 143).

KamaSutra was classically aspirational, suggesting a qualitative transformation that, furthermore, seemed to be moving Indian commodity aesthetics closer to "world-class" standards. "It just looked *classy,*" a copywriter remarked. "It was like something out of *Playboy.*" To the outside observer, KamaSutra appeared as a fait accompli; in this guise, it seemed a mere symptom of a deeper historical transformation. But perhaps the language of cause and effect is not really adequate here. As we will see in the following discussion, it might be more productive to think of KamaSutra as a medium, a zone in which certain key contradictions could be negotiated.

Factoid or Cultural Heritage: The Brand Name

Once the Big Idea of the sexy condom had been arrived at, the name KamaSutra seemed particularly fortuitous to the agency team because it instantly satisfied three crucial requirements: maximum reach/intelligibility, an erotic connotation, and cultural legitimacy. Alyque Padamsee remembers how it came about:

> One of the first names that had emerged was Tiger. It seemed apt. It had all the right connotations of virility and excitement, and seemed to lend itself to interesting visual imagery. But the drawback was it was too male-focused . . . then, during a brainstorming session, somebody came up with the name Khajuraho [the temple town where the (in)famous "erotic" carvings are located]. This led, naturally and immediately, to Kama Sutra. And the moment that happened, suddenly everybody sat up. Instinctively, we all knew that we'd got what we wanted. It was a winner. There was no need to search any further. The name Kama Sutra had everything. As a brand name it was universal. It telegraphed sex without actually mentioning the forbidden word. It was daring, yet culturally it was wholly acceptable. (Padamsee, n.d.)

The marketing possibilities seemed limitless. As Aniruddha Deshmukh, executive director of JKC (now JKC-Ansell) recalled: "See, the advantage of KamaSutra as a brand name, if you look at it simply as a brand name, is that it cuts across all language barriers. It's a brand name which is understood very clearly in south, in north, in east, in west. So that was a distinct advantage. It cuts across all income barriers . . . everyone in India was aware of *Kamasutra* as a cultural heritage."[16] The form of this awareness, moreover, was ideal. It was vague enough to permit a great deal of creative intervention. Kersy Katrak commented: "You see, *Kamasutra* is a book that very few people have read. They merely know of it as the old Sanskrit bible on sex. But that's all. Who has actually read Vatsyayana, even in the English translation? Very few people. It's arcane, William. It's common knowledge as a *factoid.*" Yet this "factoid" presented the possibility of a great deal of connotative play. Said Jayant Bakshi: "When we took *Kamasutra* within the Indian ethos and the Indian context, it was because we knew that in its expanded form mentally it would mean a lot more than we would ever say. That was the joy of it. We said less but we meant more."[17]

The third part of the equation, the cultural acceptability of the name, functioned as the perfect foil to its suggestive capacity, particularly when coupled with the startlingly bold images that came to define the campaign. Even beyond legitimation per se, the appropriation by JKC and Lintas of the name KamaSutra implied a kind of cultural restoration through consumption. Although strategically the name was above all useful as an "alibi," it also played perfectly into the critique of the alienating agency of centralized planning and enabled the impression that a more authentic, more sensuous Indian identity might be accessible through its mediation.[18] Adi Pocha explained:

> We thought that if we do something as radical as this, because in the Indian context that would be very radical, we'd need . . . something that would prevent people from jumping down our throats. So then we came up with the idea of using "KamaSutra" as the brand name, since that's part of Indian heritage and Indian culture. It legitimated it. See, Indians are very hypocritical about sex, okay? We have a population of some nine hundred million people; we must be knowing *something* about sex! But we don't like bringing it out in the open, we don't like talking about it. It's not considered good to be sexy. I think it's just a phase that our civilization is going through. Because at one time we were extremely sensual and erotic. I mean, if you look at the *Kamasutra*, it's as erotic and as advanced in sexual thinking as you can get. So all we said was "Let's just go back to the fact that that's what we genuinely are. Let's *use* that. Put the name KamaSutra on the condom, and then let the hypocrites try and attack us."

The sanctity of one reified collective (that of the "official" cultural heritage) was mined on behalf of another (that of aspirational consumer spectacle). As a result, bold images were legitimated, and it was this relation that most commentators focused upon. But the connection between the legitimation bestowed by the idea of a collective heritage and the fact that the *Kamasutra* itself was, after all, a text historically aimed at defining aristocratic behavior was just as important. This second connection contained, on the one hand, the populist implication that consumption might help restore to the masses an identity and a set of possibilities that had hitherto jealously been guarded by a national elite. On the other hand, it was important that the aristocratic connotations of the *Kamasutra* not be in any way "diluted," that they should become part of the aspirational identity of the brand, lending it, as Alyque Padamsee put it to me, "a touch of class": "You see, the *Kamasutra* is not a pornographic book. It's a sexual manual written, you know, hundreds and hundreds of years ago. And it talks about sex as an art and as a science. It doesn't talk about sex as, you know, the f-word, okay?"

Vatsyayana's text, then, combined aesthetic distinction with the idea of a collective heritage. Strategically, the effect of this combination was that it was not the direct means for the realization of the good life, but rather the "authentic" cultural basis for that aspiration, which was available to all. The brand profile, moreover, was coupled with a highly contemporary, visually oriented eroticization. Padamsee offered the following vignette as an illustration of this equation. To avoid point-of-sale embarrassment, "KamaSutra" had been given the alternate name "KS." Each ad bore joint baselines: the brand-conceptual "For the pleasure of making love," and the more practically oriented "Just ask for KS." "KS," it seemed, had become a kind of shorthand for desirability ("and if it's desirable, then it's buyable") among students in elite Bombay colleges: "We had tape recordings. We did a kind of vox populi in colleges, and we found that girls would describe a man as 'he's quite KS,' meaning 'he's quite sexy.'"

On one level it would seem that the campaign visuals simply brought an arresting contemporary execution into tension with the "high-cultural" and "traditional" backbone of the brand name. On another level, as we will see in the following section, the production of the KamaSutra images involved an entirely separate elaboration of the double field of the aesthetic, one that was brought into temporary alignment with the parallel elaboration already developed around the name.

Document and Provocation: The Image

As I have suggested, aesthetic politics always involve a double claim about the "natural": on the one hand, the "first nature" of visceral bodily response; on the other hand, the "second nature" of "good taste." In the story of the making of the images that would announce KamaSutra, we can follow this duality as it was mediated by the photographer's camera.

The campaign would be addressed, first and foremost, to heterosexual men; hence the client and the agency agreed that the weight of its erotic power would have to come from a striking female model.[19] Alyque Padamsee remembers his young client, Gautam Singhania, intoning a scopophiliac mantra during early meetings: "I want you to make my eyes dance with delight!" Eventually, and after extensive negotiations, an up-and-coming young actress/tabloid celebrity named Pooja Bedi (daughter of the prominent stage, film, and television actor Kabir Bedi, with whom Alyque Padamsee had professional connections) signed on to deliver the requisite hard-hitting sex appeal. In Padamsee's words, she was "quite a bit of a starlet, and something of a sex bomb." Jayant Bakshi remembered that the agency hoped to capitalize upon the "buzz" created by her tabloid notoriety: "She had a fairly amorous existence, and in fact one of the reasons when we took her as the right choice was to do with being able to get a rub-off from her personal life."[20] Having already established the charge attached to her image in the public sphere, the decisive test for the agency was to gauge Pooja's erotic efficacy in person. Adi Pocha was dispatched to meet her and was not disappointed. "I really liked her because she really kind of *exuded* sexuality. She's talking to you and, you know, you can *see* it and *feel* it."

After initially having agreed to work on the campaign, Pooja Bedi then abruptly pulled out, apparently on the advice of her father. Adi Pocha remembered: "We all agreed that she was a good bet, and we made her an offer, and she said 'Yes.' And everybody was really kicked about it. Then she came back and said, 'Sorry, but Papa says that I can't do it.'" An alternative model was quickly located, but four days before the shoot she called from Dubai to report that her boyfriend was refusing to countenance the idea of her appearing on a pack of condoms. "So we said 'Okay fine,' and then there were panic buttons and stuff, and then finally Gautam [Singhania] spoke to Pooja himself because they were friends, and something obviously transpired [laughs] between them, and she said 'Yes.' And she quoted a price which I think she expected we wouldn't accept, because it was about two and half times what she had quoted earlier. But [clicks fingers] we just accepted it and that was it."

Pooja Bedi, then, seemed ideally suited to fulfill the promise of the Big Idea: namely, to make something as lamentable as a condom seem desirable. The intensity of her physical presence promised to generate the kind of attention that the client and agency hoped would be convertible into exchange value. Nevertheless, the aesthetic calculus was not quite so straightforward. For purposes of legitimacy as well as market positioning, this visceral surge had to be regulated, made subordinate to the reproducible regularity of a brand narrative. This constraint was not simply a matter of *containing* an apparently wild current, but also of *sublimating* it into a more refined form. Adi Pocha remembered: "While we had borrowed from the book, the Indian book, our imagery was all very Western. . . . That was deliberate, because what we felt was that people at that stage looked up at Western imagery, okay? And we wanted to position the brand slightly higher. . . . Indian imagery was considered, you know, a little downmarket. For whatever reason."

Arvind Rajagopal (1999) argues that such a strongly sexualized series of advertisements would not have been acceptable had their visual components been more overtly "Indian." This is probably true, but it is also interesting to consider what the makers of the campaign actually rejected. Convention, as manifested in the countless coffeetable versions of the *Kamasutra* available in tourist bookshops, suggested that the name of the brand be allied with pictures of the erotic temple carvings at Khajuraho (or, alternatively, with miniature Mughal oils depicting turbaned princes at sexual play). Alyque Padamsee writes: "Now, with a brand name like KamaSutra, the immediate visual image that comes to mind is Khajuraho. So the original campaign had a whole lot of graphics of ancient Indian temple sculpture. But we discovered that the young thought this to be too traditional, too old-fashioned" (Padamsee 1999, 276).

Whatever the truth of this perception, a quick look at the public cultural career of Khajuraho reveals that, in at least one of its guises, it was far from being the "traditional" anti-type of the "Western-aspirational" imagery that KamaSutra was eventually given. In fact, one might speculate that some of the Lintas team's discomfort with Khajuraho may have stemmed from its embeddedness in another, contiguous, modern formation: the national imaginary of the post-Independence period. Ichaporia (1983) relates that the Khajuraho carvings became an important part of the Indian touristic itinerary under Nehru (whereas the Mahatma was, according to local — if apocryphal — lore, appalled by their potential for corrupting young minds). Indeed, according to Ichaporia, Khajuraho, like KamaSutra, provided a locally based justification for a controversially cosmopolitan practice: "Khajuraho offers the opportunity for a temporary suspension of customary prohibitions against overt prurient interest by providing ironclad alibis of patriotism and piety" (88), and "Candid contemplation of the erotic has [since the 1960s] become an important aspect of the educated Western mind, seeking to divest itself of the last vestiges of Victorian repression" (87). Temple-carvings are of course one thing; highly eroticized photographic images of human models quite another. But what I wish to underline here is the ambivalent contiguity — rather than the absolute opposition — between the kinds of imagery represented by Khajuraho and that chosen by KamaSutra.[21]

The project of refining the erotic energy embodied in Pooja Bedi was at once geared to the articulation of an up-market brand image and to the question of maintaining "good taste." This was a matter of legitimating the intensity of the images, or in Pocha's words, "how to make these pictures erotic, without crossing that line of accepted social decency." In one sense, this project was self-consciously artificial: the agency imposed an aesthetic boundary on the campaign. In another sense, it was crucial that this imposition appear to be guided by "objective" and "natural" parameters.

Lintas called in the man they thought would be ideal for the job: a Delhi photographer named Prabuddha Das Gupta, who was becoming well known in the industry for his monochrome work in a number of genres, including calendars, "art" photography, fashion, and advertising. Das Gupta's own recollections of his first meeting with the Lintas team suggest that the desired "Western-aspirational" styling of the campaign was conceived in a kind of verité mode:

> They had a brief and . . . they even had some pictures which they had pulled out of some Western magazines because there wasn't anything in India that was like that. They wanted this whole feeling

of . . . spontaneity and sensuality . . . not the carefully created, beautifully lit kind of thing, but more of a kind of shot-from-the-hip and caught-as-they're-doing-it kind of thing. . . . . Again you come back to "the blossoming middle classes" — that's where it was targeted. And for these guys, for this set of middle-class people, for aspiration they would immediately turn their heads Westwards. So that was decided, that "we are going to make it Western-aspirational," as in . . . what was happening at that time? Calvin Klein, maybe.[22]

Das Gupta himself contrasted the "spontaneous" styling that he was being hired for with the high level of artifice characteristic of most Indian commodity imaging at that time by recalling the context for his own entry into commercial photography in the late 1980s, a time when he was working as a copywriter in a Delhi agency.

Commercially to work as a photographer in those days, you would have to have a battery of assistants, a huge studio, you know. All the paraphernalia. Lights and large-format cameras and all that. And the people that we were using as an advertising agency, when I was working as a copywriter, *were* like that. I was more keen on black-and-white photography, which didn't really have any commercial application at that time. Everything was color. It was just, you know . . . everything *had* to be shot in full color. And the photographers had that image about them. I went for a couple of assignments; there were like six people setting up the lights, it was like a big industry. [Later,] I tried to dispense as much as I could with that kind of artificial, plasticized, highly cosmeticized look. . . . . I don't really have any understanding of fashion. I'm not a fashion person, I never studied fashion. I have no idea when hemlines are dropping or stripes are in or polka dots are out or anything like that. I guess . . . it's been more of an intuitive and instinctive response . . . I mean, I like photographing people, and people in clothes I guess naturally translates itself into fashion. Commercially.

Indeed, for Adi Pocha, choosing Prabuddha Das Gupta as the photographer for the KamaSutra campaign meant bringing in someone whose aesthetic talent seemed to be at once "natural" or "intuitive" and highly eroticized.

You know, the thing about Prabuddha is that he's not cluttered by technology. I remember when I came to the airport and he was there and I look around, you know, "Where's Prabuddha?" And I saw Prabuddha and I said, "Okay, have you got all your equipment together?" And he said, "Yeah, this is it." And all he had was one *battered* old light, which looked like it was a hospital light or something. That was it. That was his equipment. . . . I think what was great about Prabuddha was that he is a very sexual person himself. I think he enjoys sex! . . . More than that, he enjoys being a voyeur. I think that's what he brought to the whole thing. He was able to . . . er, really bring some amount of sexiness to the pictures. *Very* subtly. He'd just be waiting for the right moment . . . and *boom!* That was it. . . . So he was literally just a voyeur capturing things on film. . . . Like I remember when I saw the contact sheets, he shot very little. . . . Most other photographers would go through this motor-drive thing like *ta-ta-ta-ta-ta!* [mimes machine-gun camera shutter action]. No, he would just find an image, he let that image happen. He allowed the people to find their own image and then he'd just capture it.[23]

The "documentary" role of the solitary camera provided the physical means; Das Gupta's "natural" aesthetic sense — itself driven by a powerfully erotic gaze — provided a universalizing moral justification for a set of stylistic parameters that were at the same time consciously geared toward capturing the aspirations of a particular imagined audience, "the blossoming middle classes." In parallel, the "unmediated" quality of Das Gupta's photographic craft served as a kind of ontological guarantee for these same preferences.

Western feminist film theory has of course long explored the historical connections between the rise of mass consumerism, particularly in the United States, and the fetishization of the eroticized female body in the golden age of Hollywood cinema (Mulvey 1996). This conjuncture involved a reciprocal movement between the commodification of images of women and the eroticization of fetishized commodities. As consumers, women were offered a highly ambivalent status in the image of the "New Woman" of the 1920s and, again, of the 1950s: at once embodied/empowered agent and sex object.

In the light of this critique, KamaSutra, as envisioned by Prabuddha Das Gupta, was particularly interesting for the way in which it brought together elements of this Western history with a local critique of the sexual imaginary of the Hindi film, read as a pathological symptom of the repressions of the post-Independence period. A parallel was generated between the artificial, "plasticized" aesthetics of Indian commercial photography in the 1980s and this "vulgar," regressive, and provincial sexual idiom. Counterpoised to this formation was Kama-Sutra—at once natural, sophisticated, and cosmopolitan. And yet—crucially—it *wasn't* just a matter of opposing "down-market Indian" to "up-market Western," or "repressed past" to "liberated future." Rather, the supposed ur-Indianness of KamaSutra as a label and as a set of historically embedded connotations suggested that the aspirational, cosmopolitan Indian consumer of the future would enjoy, at one and the same time, a return to an ancient and authentic Indian self.[24] During the course of our conversation, Das Gupta spontaneously brought up the topic of Mira Nair's then-new feature film adaptation of Vatsyayana's *Kamasutra:*

> I think that it acts as a very good counterpoint to the kind of trash and the kind of obscenity that sex has been reduced to by the commercial Indian cinema. I don't know if you've seen many Indian films, where the whole idea of sex is . . . it's operating at two levels. . . . At one level, they won't show anything directly, okay? When two people are about to kiss, you cut from that to butterflies coming together or something like that. So there it's operating at a kind of strange pseudo-Puritanical level: "We don't want to show this because it's sex, after all." At another level, if you look at some of the lewd, vulgar dance movements or the kind of degradation that women are subjected to, the kind of rape scenes that are shown . . . maybe not actually shown, not the actual physical act itself, but things leading up to a kind of gang rape and things like that, which is dealing with the idea of sex purely at a kind of titillation level. But nobody has really explored sex purely for what it is, as . . . a very, very strong means of communication between the sexes, or, if you like, within the same sex. Whichever way you look at it.

When I suggested a parallel between his interpretation of Nair's film and his own work on the KamaSutra condom campaign, he reflected:

> Yeah, in a sense there is a parallel there. . . . You know, the other thing that has always been dominant subconsciously in our society is that, even in sex, it's always a sort of male-dominated activity. The woman is just a receptacle. The woman does not have any busi-

ness to demand her pleasure or participation in the sexual act. . . .
It's the man who makes the overture, it's the man who does the
seduction, it's the man who . . . the man is looking for his pleasure,
you know. And the woman is supposed to give that to him. And I
deliberately shot this [the KS campaign] in a way also that that
wouldn't be the case. I don't know whether it's been successful to
that extent, or whether it's actually penetrated anybody [*sic!*].

Provinciality, sexual repression, and aesthetic artifice: all these came
together as the opponent forces of the liberation promised by the commodity image that was KamaSutra.[25] Yet this, paradoxically, was a
sexual liberation that depended upon the strictest aesthetic discipline:
upholding the boundaries of "good taste." Here is the exact point at
which we can see the intersection of two tensions: first, the ambivalence of an aesthetic discourse that simultaneously appeals to nature
and refinement; second, the ambivalence of a commodity image that
relies on a visceral, visual concretion that its discursive elaboration can
never quite contain. For Das Gupta, the man who had been hired to
oversee the aesthetic parameters of the campaign, this double tension
manifested itself in the form of his initial concern that the images of
Pooja Bedi's body would introduce a dangerous element of *excess*,
overflowing the boundaries of good taste:

> I do remember at one point I wasn't particularly comfortable with
> the idea of Pooja Bedi. . . . Basically I think it was . . . well, Pooja
> Bedi is a very voluptuous sort of woman. Big breasts, wide hips. I
> mean, she, if anybody fits in more with the traditional notion of an
> "Indian woman." . . . It didn't have anything to do with personal
> preferences, but I just thought . . . at that point — maybe I was
> wrong, because the pictures worked —. . . that that sort of volup-
> tuousness might tend to lead it more towards a sort of vulgarity, you
> know? I wanted someone with a less obviously . . . voluptuous body,
> which would, to my mind, keep it well on this side of what would be
> called . . . I guess, "good taste" — for want of a better phrase.

"The pictures worked," it seems, in spite of — or, perhaps, because
of — this tension. The public life of KamaSutra, like that of any advertising campaign, was about the management of affect. Most obviously,
this management was intended to generate commercial value. But as I
have suggested, the possibility of controllable commercial value de-

pended upon the elaboration of a particular aesthetic idiom. Nor was *that* project confined to the internal machinations of the agency and the client. Rather, given the boldness of the campaign and the explosive publicity that it generated, the affect-managing effort was necessarily extended into wider public spaces. My discussion in the following section, then, picks up the thread of the theme with which I started the present chapter: the connections between citizenship, embodiment, and publicity. What I hope to demonstrate is that the various kinds of value-generating projects that comprise public culture — moral, political, aesthetic, commercial — are deeply implicated in each other. I do not think, however, that we can or should counter the Habermasian ideal of a "rational" discursive public sphere simply with calls to "acknowledge the body." Rather, I think that the proper task for a critical study of public culture must be to keep a vigilant watch on the ways in which value is generated out of the constant and multi-sited struggles to define and control the dialectical articulation of discursive truth-claims and embodied experience. As we will see, these struggles are typically carried out in the name of "progress," "decency," "morality," and other one-word slogans, each of them marking the points at which strategic positions seek transcendent legitimation.

Erotica or Pornography: The Public Field

As we have seen, most people I talked to in Bombay remembered KamaSutra as a virtuoso publicity stunt, a textbook example of the high contrast between the persuasive agility of the new marketing and the alienating rigidity of government regulation. Between the lines of this story of heroes and villains, however, I discerned a more complicated set of negotiations. Among the most obvious of these negotiations was the struggle over the acceptability of the campaign itself, a struggle that was of course a direct response to the brashness of its entry into the public arena. But as I gradually reconstructed the public cultural field of the "KamaSutra moment," I began to suspect that this debate was itself the visible face of a larger process. To be specific, if somewhat technical: what was at issue was the legitimate authority to manage, through a normative-aesthetic discourse, the extraction of commercial value from the public circulation of affect-intensive images.

Let me illustrate. First there was the matter of anticipation. Lintas —

the agency in charge of the KamaSutra account—keenly fanned the flames of controversy even before the campaign had been released. Teasing "leaks" were offered to the press; Pooja Bedi, apparently, had demanded a "no-nipple" clause in her contract. And, as Jayant Bakshi pointed out, a great deal of advance "buzz" had been generated through media circuits, the publicity industries:

> While the shooting was going on, people had started sort of talking about "oh, do you know, something like this is about to happen." Because models talk, photographers talk, and a large part of the fraternity that talks, which is the so-called advertising and . . . its associated professions, like photographers etc., are also the ones who write about it. So the common folk read what is written about this so-called, you know, glitzy people and then when it's about to come out, they want to catch up with what's happening, they don't want to get left behind. So that's the way it happens.

Nor was Lintas disappointed by the publicity generated by critics of the campaign. One of the first to strike was the Women and Media Committee of the Bombay Union of Journalists, who lodged a complaint with a subcommittee of the Advertising Standards Council of India (ASCI), the Consumer Complaints Council (CCC),[26] calling the campaign "highly irresponsible, voyeuristic, and sexist" (Pillai 1992).

Meanwhile, a member of Parliament in the Rajya Sabha (the "Council of States" or upper house) named Dinesh Trivedi complained about the campaign in a "special mention" to the minister of state for Social Welfare, Margaret Alva, requesting that she call for a ban.[27] Arguing that ads like those for KamaSutra involved the "portrayal of women as sex objects," Trivedi and his parliamentary associates also sent a complaint to the Press Council, which alleged that "the ads sought to promote 'sex itself' instead of family planning and prevention of sexually transmitted diseases" (A. Prakash 1993). Doordarshan (DD), the national television network, had provisionally approved the storyboards for two KamaSutra spots in September 1991, and, according to Jayant Bakshi, the finished films were given a "verbal nod" in November. But in the wake of the parliamentary stir, DD informed Lintas in early 1992 that permission to screen the spots had been withdrawn pending a review of all relevant materials by the Information and Broadcasting minister Mahesh Prasad (Koppikar 1992).

In March 1992, the ASCI/CCC issued a ruling, informing JKC and

Lintas by letter that the campaign was indeed both "objectionable and sexist," attempted to satisfy "voyeuristic sensibilities which exceed common decency," and offered material that served "more to titillate than to sell" (Pillai 1992). Apparently, it took the Press Council another year to reach a decision; in March 1993, it issued a statement decreeing that KamaSutra was guilty of "titillating the sex feelings of adolescents and adults. . . . The photographs of the models and the postures in which they have been shown are no doubt obscene, because these are vulgar and indecent in the context of an Indian morality." Finally, in April 1993 — a whole seventeen months after his complaint — Dinesh Trivedi received a letter from the Information and Broadcasting minister pleading helplessness because "the Department of Women and Child Development, which administers the Indecent Representation of Women (Prohibition) Act of 1986, had failed to respond" (A. Prakash 1993).

All the uproar amounted to very little in the way of action but a great deal of free publicity. The ASCI/CCC reprimand merely required that Lintas "amend" the existing advertising. This they did, rearranging the existing pictures, writing some new copy, and publishing them as a legally "new" ad, triumphantly entitled "The Complete Unabridged KamaSutra." The "alibi" function of the brand name effectively served to screen Lintas and JKC from accusations of violating *Indian* morality. The government's hapless and ineffectual response seemed only to prove everything that the free market ideologues had been arguing all along about bureaucratic inefficiency. And DD's ban was not much of a strategic blow (although it did cost Lintas a handsome percentage of the hefty national television advertising rates), since KamaSutra's intended consumers could in any case be more efficiently targeted through cable television and cinema.

Once again, then, the trundling machinery of government appeared outwitted by the nimble agility of the publicity industries. But this could not appear to be just a strategic contest; rather, the proponents of liberalization appealed to a higher truth. Kamlesh Pandey, creative director at Rediffusion Advertising, brought together the popular trope of liberation/repression with an allusion to the heroic struggle of Ram to free chaste Sita from her imprisonment and potential humiliation at the hands of Ravana, the demon-king of Lanka: "television in this country is like a beautiful princess in the clutches of a demon" (Kankanala 1991).[28]

The melodramatic and polarizing terms in which this high-profile polemic was conducted provided moral energy for a struggle that, in fact, involved a far subtler calculus. At issue, as I have suggested, was the acceptable formula for the conversion of affect into exchange value. The stakes become clearer as soon as we situate KamaSutra in a wider context of contiguous commodity images.

First, there were the imported Southeast Asian semi-pornographic roadside condoms, selling under brand names like Push Me, Sexy Girl, and Happy Hours. The most important fact about these condoms was the high prices that they could command on the basis of their explicit packaging. Although they were estimated to account for little more than 11 percent of the market by volume, these "pornodoms" represented as much as 22 percent of the market by value (Annuncio 1993). Vendors charged prices ranging from Rs 6 to as much as Rs 50 for a single pack, at a time when KamaSutra was entering the market — positioned as a *premium* product — at Rs 6 a pack. The added value offered by KamaSutra in comparison to cheaper brands — that is, the brand component that allowed it to charge a higher price for the product — was, of course, its aesthetic claim: its refined eroticism, its promise of a sophisticated and discerning sensual experience. For the Southeast Asian pornodoms to be succeeding in realizing astronomical levels of exchange value on the basis of flagrant, "unsophisticated" imagery was clearly, from JKC's point of view, both conceptually and strategically intolerable. On the one hand, KamaSutra was aesthetically constrained by its own brand discourse. On the other hand, the pricing of KamaSutra was constrained from below by the fact that the government was at the same time distributing Nirodh free or at nominal prices. As Aniruddha Deshmukh of JKC put it: "You can't price the product in isolation, so the moment our price goes beyond a certain level, then there are all these subsidized and cheap brands which are available, so people do switch."

The World Health Organization (WHO) had, in 1991, just passed stringent new quality regulations on the manufacture of condoms, and so the Indian industry was quick to use them as a weapon against the imported, "exploitative" brands. But the real issue was clearly the question of the aesthetic formula through which profit might legitimately be extracted from eroticized images. The KamaSutra brand idea had carefully sought to articulate the affective power of its sexualization (expressed most concretely in the body of Pooja Bedi) with an aesthetically elaborated set of positions and references. A compromise between spectacle and legitimacy had been reached, one that, unlike the surging and unpredictable affect/exchange-value ratios attached to the pornodoms, sought to establish, through the careful calibration of a given brand identity, a regularized and predictable source of exchange value. The emphatic manner in which the advertising industry sought to distance its own products from the imported brands perhaps belied a deeper recognition of kinship, specifically their mutual reliance upon the visceral resonances of sexualized imagery.[29] The spectacular profitability of the pornodoms functioned as a kind of illicit shadow Other to the licit added value of KamaSutra; in relation to the latter, it was therefore necessarily deemed "exploitative" and "pornographic."

As we have seen, KamaSutra's creators had intentionally positioned the brand as the sexy condom, "for the pleasure of making love." The indignant exclamation of an industry spokesman therefore unintentionally highlighted both the flimsiness of the categorical separation between acceptable and unacceptable commodity erotics and the social politics of distinction that lay at the heart of the desire to maintain this separation as far as legitimate profitability would allow: "Even in a village, a single [imported] condom may sell for Rs 10 as though it were an aphrodisiac!" (Rai 1992).

The aesthetic politics of profitability also took subtler forms than the demarcation between erotica and pornography, legitimate and illegitimate commodity imaging. KamaSutra provided the Indian advertising industry with a concrete yardstick with which to measure aesthetic legitimacy even *within* the realm of legitimately branded products, condoms and otherwise.

An early victim was Adam, a brand of condoms manufactured by Polar Latex, and launched mere weeks before KamaSutra in 1991. Adam's platform, devised by an agency called Contour, was humor, which at that time, in the condom category, was just as novel as sexiness. The angle was decidedly macho: alongside depictions of a cartoon caveman and his hapless female counterpart, the English-language ads featured headlines like "Show her who's the boss," "The freedom to love when and as you like," "Manpower," "Have a fling without a care in the world," "Put the zest back into life," and—for an added eroto-patriotic frisson—"Freedom at midnight." One of the illustrations, which appeared to show the caveman dragging his partner/victim off by her hair, caused immediate offense. (Contour, not exactly helping its cause, quickly pointed out that in fact the cartoon hero was holding on to the arm, not the hair, of his prehistoric paramour.) Questioned as to the tastefulness of his team's executions, the agency's creative director insisted that he saw no problem in promoting a condom with "a sense of fun about what's a part of life between husband and wife." Nevertheless, other advertising professionals were quick to slam the campaign. Gangadhar Menon, then creative director at Avenues Advertising, called it "badly conceived, badly executed, done without finesse, very crude and aesthetically vulgar." Kamlesh Pandey at Rediffusion offered a similar critique, and went on to emphasize the professional skill and judgment that was necessary to achieve a suitable balance between sheer spectacle and good taste: "There is a fine line between being bold and being rude. It takes a great amount of expertise to stay within that line. This campaign hasn't" ("Who Wants to Be Boss Man" 1991).

Not only did KamaSutra become a yardstick for aspirational commodity erotics, it also quickly spawned a host of imitators. One of the most closely indebted efforts was the campaign for MR Coffee, which appeared in late 1993 in the Bombay *Mid-Day* newspaper. Substituting models Malaika Arora and Arbad Khan (brother of movie star Salman Khan) for KamaSutra's Pooja Bedi and Marc Robinson, the ads duplicated the "passionate clinch" look of the KamaSutra series in order to suggest that filter coffee, while slower to make, provided greater satisfaction than instant coffee. "Real pleasure can't come in an instant," punned the headline. The outraged tone of the consequent critical response was familiar. But what had changed was that KamaSutra had now evidently managed to take legitimate possession of that particular aesthetic territory on behalf of condoms. Wrote a *Mid-Day* reader, one S. N. Kabra of Goregaon (W): "When I first saw it, I thought it was a condom ad." Kasim Pervez of Govandi added: "The advertisement was in an [*sic*] extremely bad taste. I doubt whether it was meant to popularize coffee or pornography. At first, I thought it was a condom ad" ("Shocking Advertisement" 1994).

The aesthetic politics of social distinction continued to be crucial to the advertising industry's reactions. Mohammed Khan, who had called KamaSutra "a watershed event in Indian advertising," panned the MR Coffee campaign as being "in *exceedingly* bad taste, I thought. It was just a vulgar ad. . . . I think the *copy* is very vulgar. . . . I don't think it's classy, and I would certainly not describe it as 'in good taste.' It is very low-brow humor. Downright vulgar, I mean there's no *class* to it."

A dizzyingly rapid historical dialectic was taking shape. The boldness of KamaSutra had been justified partly on a double basis: a simultaneous appeal to absolute aesthetic values and to the "progress" that such an appeal inaugurated. Now, only months later, apologists for these new campaigns were themselves appealing to a changed historical context, a context that KamaSutra had, in part, been responsible for bringing about. Suddenly, it seemed, sex in advertising had become not so much a controversial option as a necessity. "All the ad agencies use sex to sell their products," argued MR Coffee model Malaika Arora. "What's wrong in that? And besides, coffee is a stimulant." Indur Chowdhury of Art Advertising, the agency that had produced the campaign, argued, in a more serious vein, that it had been a matter of strategic positioning. "The human situation of a young couple making love" was used to make "this meaningful difference between filter coffee . . . and instant coffee . . . explicit."[30] Chowdhury also lent an interesting twist to the ongoing equation of political economy and aesthetic politics when he suggested that aggressive attention-grabbing tactics might be counted among the weapons of the weak. The need for making a striking visual statement was heightened "considering the fact that MR is a small swadeshi brand lacking the financial clout of the multinationals who dominate the instant coffee market." The Bombay-based managing director of MR Coffee, Rajesh Durgani, added a less elaborated rationale: "*Sex ke bina ad mein maja nahin hota hai*" [Without sex there's no fun in an ad] ("Shocking Advertisement" 1994).

Other notorious campaigns followed: Tuffs Shoes and Calida "innerwear," to mention only two (incidentally, Prabuddha Das Gupta was the photographer on both of these campaigns). Increasingly, particularly in the wake of the arrival of satellite television and the onslaught of advertising for global brands, the case for bold images was made in terms of "keeping up with globalization," a process whose dizzying dynamics could not be regulated on a national basis. And yet in some ways, precisely the constant escalation of the visual stakes may have been one of the reasons why, by the time of my fieldwork in 1997–98, KamaSutra — the brand that, more than any other, had inaugurated the bold commodity image in India — was thought by many in the advertising industry to have "lost the plot."

These critiques pointed precisely to the two central problems in the commercial management of affect: brand control and aesthetic legitimation. Like stamping an insignium on a herd of livestock, consumer-goods branding proclaims ownership of, and control over, a productive resource. But in the case of brand control, the productive resource comprises the evanescent symbolic and affective elements of public culture. On the one hand, this means that claims to brand ownership always entail a kind of "cultural enclosure," a private arrogation of a public resource (Coombe 1998; Mazzarella 2002). On the other hand, this work of enclosure is locked in a perpetual struggle with the ever-accelerating transformation of public cultural meanings. In a sense, branding is akin to a puppy chasing its own tail, since this perpetual acceleration is itself partly caused by the relentless drive for differentiation that competitive marketing brings about.[31] In short, the textbook example of a successful brand parries a dual command: keep abreast of changing times, but maintain a continuous identity.

The custodians of KamaSutra were quite forthright about the balancing act involved. The continuity of the brand was a matter of maintaining certain "key ingredients," as Aniruddha Deshmukh of JKC put it — visual markers and conceptual foundations. Its adaptability, conversely, depended upon Jayant Bakshi's ability to integrate a constant attention to changing public discourses on sex with the overall structure of the brand, to "freshen the expression" of its "core Idea." At the same time, this affect-managing project was not simply about maintaining a formal balance between structure and change. The transcendent legitimation of the "truth" of the brand had, from the beginning, been an aesthetic one. KamaSutra had to be *tastefully* erotic or it was nothing.

Adi Pocha and Alyque Padamsee had both once been close to the brand and had observed its development after their own respective departures. Interestingly, their critiques of latter-day installments of the campaign spoke precisely to the dual foundation — structural and aesthetic — that I have just described. Pocha, for his part, deployed a classic creative's critique of the executives' unimaginative preoccupation with structure over impact. "They're *suits*," he told me.

> You know what I mean? They're suits, they're gonna think that way, okay, because they're scared. . . . I still see the same kind of shots. Just because the original campaign had blue photographs

doesn't mean you continue with blue photographs, okay? There's a certain sameness, it's lost the surprise. It's lost the unpredictability of a good fuck [laughs]! Which is what sex is all about. . . . Nobody gets turned on by sameness. You see a woman nude once, twice, thrice, four, five times. After that you're not scrabbling over each other to take her clothes off anymore. You know what I mean? It's okay. You want to see something else. . . . What they've done is they've kept all the elements but forgotten what worked for them. I mean, who cares? Throw away the blue pictures! Who cares?! Throw away the little wiggly sperms and throw away the quotes from the *Kamasutra*. None of that is important! What is important is that when I see a KamaSutra ad, I should feel just a little bit sexier. . . . They've lost that.

Padamsee, for his part, felt that the all-important aspirational aesthetic positioning of the campaign — "its class" — had become confused:

[The campaign] went to HeartBeat and my good friend, who was looking after it anyway at Lintas, Jayant Bakshi, took over the account. I think then he went a little off the rails and thought that what we were doing was selling sex. We were not. We were selling sensuality, which is not the same as sex. . . . It was a bit too explicit. You know, the girl was half undressed, and big boobs, and you know the whole thing became a kind of . . . not even *Playboy* . . . I'll say *Hustler.* You know? . . . So I think it needs to get back a little of its class. It needs also a model who is today's epitome *not* of Monica Lewinsky,[32] but let's see . . . I wouldn't mind Sharon Stone, to tell you the truth, hm? Because from her . . . what was that movie? *Basic Instinct,* she's moved up the ladder a bit, you know. Just as Marilyn Monroe did. So I'd like that sort of image. Someone who's sex-u-al, but not cheapo-sexy. You know? Not someone you'd find in a porno palace.

My point here is not to evaluate the "truth" or otherwise of these judgments, but rather to indicate how important these two sets of considerations were to perceptions of the efficacy of the campaign: on the one hand, the tension between the need to formalize and "own" a particular image/identity relationship, and, on the other hand, the need to give this relationship — the brand — an aesthetic legitimation.

Looking back over the statements I have collected here, a particular

8. KamaSutra in 1996: Pornography or erotica?

discursive binary emerges with some regularity: a "classy" campaign versus a "vulgar" campaign. The way in which this terminology speaks to an aesthetically grounded politics of social distinction is obvious enough. Over the course of my discussion of KamaSutra, I have repeatedly stressed the importance, for the whole consumerist dispensation in India, of emphasizing its populist credentials. I have already shown how this was a matter of offering a mode of universal address that would be a credible alternative to citizenship in the developmentalist dispensation of the post-Independence Indian state. But it was also a response to the particular machinery of affect management that had been put into place during the Nehru years. Indian broadcasting and film censorship policies were based, quite overtly, on an aesthetic paternalism according to which male viewers with low incomes and little education were thought to be particularly susceptible to the unpredictable effects of affect-intensive images (see Shohini Ghosh 1999 and Vachani 1999). So if the consumerist dispensation promised to extend the healing properties of the mass-mediated image to each and every Indian, was there not something contradictory in using the word "vulgar" — which, after all, literally designates the "common" people — to dismiss unacceptable ads?

Perhaps it was nothing more than a matter of a professional elite habitually and unreflectingly perpetuating the aesthetic paternalism that it had inherited. But against the background of the argument concerning the category of the aesthetic that I have offered in this chapter, I think we might also explore some subtler connections. Recall that Kant suggested that aesthetic judgment might provide the true basis for the good society. In his *Anthropology*, Kant in fact defines the *vulgus*, or "rabble," as those who are separated or excluded from the civil union of the *gens*, or the "nation" (Kant 1978, 225). "Taste," or the ability to bring reasoned judgment into harmony with aesthetic experience, is the condition for entry into the fellowship of the gens. Once again, we may read Kant's terminological distinction simply as a justification for social distinction, a connection that may easily be traced down to the present-day cultural politics of globalizing consumerism. But such an interpretation would also miss a parallel, but this time generative, affinity: the promise of the aesthetically grounded realization of the fullness of the good social community. And it was in this register that KamaSutra, once more, provided a crucial means of transition.

Calling the product KamaSutra, as I have shown, offered both a means of legitimizing the bold content of the campaign *and* the promise that aspirational consumerism, more than simply providing a long-awaited outlet for pent-up libidinal energies, could channel those energies into a higher purpose: the future rediscovery of a more authentic "Indianness." A culturally specific sensus communis, then, but one that depended on a coordination with the global sweep of history rather than the specifically national time of development.

To be sure, the aesthetics of KamaSutra belonged to a moment immediately preceding the globalization of consumer goods markets in India. But insofar as the campaign pointed toward the possibility of the eroticization of cultural identity through aspirational consumerism, it also prefigured one of the most important problematics of the 1990s, namely the ambivalent commercial value of "Indianness" in advertising. Parts 2 and 3 engage this aspect of the cultural politics of globalization in relation to Indian as well as to foreign brands. But to conclude the present chapter, I would like to focus for a moment on the connection between KamaSutra and a subsequent advertising strategy that I have called "auto-orientalism": the use of globally recognized signifiers of Indian "tradition" to facilitate the aspirational consumption, by Indians, of a culturally marked self.

Auto-orientalism

Certain kinds of product categories, particularly those associated with luxury or sensual indulgence such as body care, upscale "ethnic chic" clothing (see Tarlo 1996), jewelery, and hotels, seemed to have a special affinity for auto-orientalist advertising strategies. And just as importantly, other product categories (as I will demonstrate in part 2) seemed more or less incompatible with such approaches. The reasons for these differences are themselves worth exploring for they can help us understand the ways in which advertising, as a cultural practice, draws on — and informs — a global political economy of images that comes with its own histories of circulation and connotation.

Let me illustrate the auto-orientalist genre with a couple of examples. A 1997 advertisement for the Rambagh Palace Hotel, formerly the palace of the Maharajah of Jaipur, reads (in part): "In the good old days, you needed an official invite to experience the grandeur of the Rambagh. Today all you have to do is call [number]. Or email [address]." In theory, access to luxury — which is distinctly marked as "Indian," yet mediated through the globally standardizing form of the hotel as commodity image — is here democratized by being made accessible through the apparent impartiality of money and technology. In practice, premium pricing maintains social distinction both by excluding those without adequate means and, more interestingly, by confirming the quality of the product ("reassuringly expensive," as the British commercials for Stella Artois lager once put it).[33]

Another advertisement from the same period, for Samara skin and hair products, starts with a pastiche of a quotation: "In India, beauty was born in the gardens where Radha and the Gopis spent hours oiling, perfuming, and costuming themselves to express their love for Lord Krishna." The mythical past is thus established both as specifically "Indian" and as a locus of languorous expertise and opulent pleasure. With the modicum of didacticism expected of aspirational branding, the copy goes on to explain that "Samara" is "a Sanskrit word that means 'to meet,' " and, further, that it is "a simple word that inspired Dabur Research scientists to create a complete range of 33 beauty therapies." Ancient Indian sensuality and modern science are granted a mutually legitimating affinity through the mediation of a transhistorical aesthetic sensibility; this affinity enables the scientists (for they must still be that) to appear in the guise of artisans rather than technicians, "inspired" to "create." It is, indeed, a "blending of our rich Shringar heritage with the spirit of sophisticated research. A fusion of the miracles of nature with the magic of science. The Samara range rejuvenates, replenishes, protects, complements and respects the Indian skin [sic] and hair." Once again, the distinguished quality of this magical fusion is assured: "Available at select outlets only."

Auto-orientalist advertising occupies a crucial mediating position in regard to the themes that I have been exploring in this chapter: the relationship between aspirational consumerism, aesthetic community, social distinction, and cultural identity. Recent writings have spawned a barrage of hyphenated orientalisms: "counter-orientalism" (Moeran 1996b), "ethno-orientalism" (Carrier 1992), "internal orientalism" (Schein 2000), "internalized orientalism" (Heng and Devan 1995), "self-orientalism" (Ching 2000), and "self-orientalization" (Ong 1993; Tang 1993), to name but a handful of variations on Edward Said's influential term (Said 1978). Two themes emerge with particular clarity.

First, there is the so-called "neo-Confucian" celebration of (East) "Asian values," according to which the success of the "Asian Tigers" proves not only that Western social scientists from Max Weber down to the present were wrong when they insisted that capitalism could only flourish in the West, but, furthermore, that the erstwhile "orientals" are, if anything, even better capitalists than their historical rivals. According to neo-Confucianism, Asian "discipline" (which the orientalizing West decried as despotic) and kin-mindedness (which was seen as a hurdle in the way of establishing a bourgeois civic culture) jointly ensure a form of capitalism that is both more efficient and more "caring" than that of the (decadent and excessively individualistic) liberal democracies of the West. This, then, involves the appropriation and refunctioning of previously pejorative orientalist stereotypes for affirmative ends.

Second, there is the projection of orientalist stereotypes onto internal minority groups, frequently the better to consume their "cultures" (in the shape of crafts, "traditional" performances, etc.) through domestic tourism. This second mode of orientalism is, in fact, internally constitutive of the first. Whereas Singaporean premier Lee Kwan Yew, according to the neo-Confucian formula, celebrates Chinese culture as uniquely consonant with capitalist modernity, the Indians within his borders are still figured — in unreconstructed orientalist fashion — as the feminine, excessively sensual other: "Indians, . . . Lee confidently proclaims, are 'naturally contentious;' like women, they are loquacious and theatrical, too indulgent and irresponsible ('soft') to be capable of the social discipline of 'hard' Confucian cultures which renders East Asian societies increasingly potent as political powers to challenge the West" (Heng and Devan 1995, 352fn).

Lee's discourse is a prime example of the middle register occupied by so much public speech: it mediates between grassroots stereotypes and long-standing formal scholarly categories. He is speaking in the name of a revitalized "Confucianism," but the historical agency that is being attributed to modern East Asia is simply that which Kant and Hegel articulated on behalf of Europe at the dawn of European industrial capitalism. From Kant, we recognize the figuring of sensual pleasure as a barrier in the way of realizing the universal; from Hegel, a vision of historical progress that involves a passive, feminized, sensual *object* of history — typified, as in Hegel, by India — that must be controlled and contained by an active, masculine, austere *subject* of history.

This is of course the conceptual foundation and the philosophical legitimation of a productivist history of world capitalism, expanding by virtue of its capacity to abstract exchange value out of concrete raw materials. By the same token, it is also the genealogy of the modern bourgeois citizen, shot through with the pathos of the struggle to overcome concrete sensual attachments in order to attain the "higher," general good. Taken together, these two narratives naturalized the connection between the world-historical triumph of capitalism and the ultimate self-realization of man as rational, enlightened citizen.

It was precisely against this background that the consumerist world view was so radical. Not only did it refuse the distinction between sensual pleasure and historical progress; it made the former a necessary condition of the latter. Likewise, the consumer-citizen's progress from the provinciality of self-interest to the universality of civic participation was based precisely on an *indulgence,* rather than a denial, of bodily desires. Routing the consumer-citizen's libidinal energy from the "first nature" of embodied inclination to the "second nature" of taste, commodity images provided the concrete means for the realization of the aesthetic community.[34]

Auto-orientalist advertising closed the circle. Consumerism had already made the realization of the universal community compatible with the particularity of embodied preference. Now, in an apparently paradoxical move that I will explore in some detail in the following chapters, the dynamics of globalization were making the realization of the universal community dependent upon the rearticulation of cultural identity. Western media critics pointed to the ambiguous way in which the eroticized images of women in advertising encourage female consumers to become at once subjects *and* objects of a desiring gaze — Robert Goldman describes this as "commodity feminism" (R. Goldman 1992). The globalization of mass consumerism extends this ambiguity from gender to cultural identity: consumers of auto-orientalist commodity images are at once subjects and objects of the cultural community that is being sold.

And yet the ambiguity persists in this extension from eroticized female images to eroticized cultural identity partly because the latter continues to depend on the former. Key to the liberatory promise of KamaSutra was its overt cosmopolitan insistence upon the importance of female sexual pleasure. Further, a large part of its rhetorical power derived from its capacity to link this insistence with an indisputably "Indian" heritage. Nevertheless, KamaSutra shifted neither the prevalent scopic gendering of advertising as a field of visual culture nor the discursive gendering of modernist narratives of progress.

Some of its devices were familiar from a century or more of nationalist experiments with representation. Woman as the privileged and sacrosanct locus of Indianness was of course a standard figure of nationalist visual art and literature from the late nineteenth century onward (Chatterjee 1993; although cf. Freitag 2001). The generative erotic force of the feminine principle was here, through a strenuous

sometimes firm
    sometimes soft

    sometimes distant
        sometimes warm

Don't you love being a woman?

Celebrate

the woman in you

with our timeless

collection of sarees,

lehengas, suits,

and shawls.

Love yourself

HERITAGE™

G XII HANDLOOM EMPORIUM
SOUTH EXTENSION PART ONE NEW DELHI 110049
TLFN 011- 462 3208 FAX 011- 469 7265
email he@heritageosho.com
www.heritageosho.com

3sixty©

9. Auto-orientalism: Woman mediates cultural self-discovery. This ad for Heritage clothing co-opts a feminized consumerist subjectivity, pampered and willful, into the service of auto-orientalist branding. "Woman" has of course long served as an ideological location of Indian cultural difference; the baseline of this campaign, "Love yourself," cleverly brings together the sensuous narcissism of the upscale consumer with the cultural self-respect offered by "ethnic chic" design. The ad also implies that precisely a woman's willfulness will allow her to negotiate the contradictory demands of public expectation: steadfast and "timeless" as a bearer of tradition, yet fickle and indulgent as a modern consumer.

game of sublimation, at once asserted and denied by its masculine-positioned citizen-custodians. KamaSutra, proudly proclaiming a sexual revolution, would at first sight seem radically opposed to this tradition. And yet, as this chapter has argued, its erotics were equally subject to a strict regime of controls, only this time the idiom of sublimation was a cosmopolitan, aspirational consumerist aesthetic.

Within the cultural politics of globalization, the KamaSutra moment was structurally ambivalent. The coupling of sensuous pleasure to historical progress appeared, from one perspective, as a radical critique of the feminizing discourse that first the Europeans and then the East Asians had applied to India. Nevertheless, the terms of its realization demanded a subordination of all excessive ("vulgar") elements in this pleasure to an aesthetic calculus that was both exclusivist in its cosmopolitan desire and perhaps excessively dependent on precisely the orientalist tropes that had framed India as a perpetual nonstarter in the race of progress. As we will see in part 2, this dependence upon a globally authorized set of images became more problematic when the product to be advertised was not as closely tied to the blandishments of sensuous indulgence. Consumer electronics, for instance, evoked embarrassment among many of my informants over India's feminized status as a mere "recipient" of East Asian innovations and productive excellence.

Then again, for that very reason, the ability of consumerist globalization to make the extraction of exchange value from cultural identity appear as a reassertion of civilizational pride becomes all the more compelling. Hegel's Spirit of history—bent on subordinating all concrete otherness to an abstract (European) universal—appears to be getting its just deserts as (some) local cultural preferences are no longer seen as something to be overcome. This is why globalizing consumerism can appear as the very *opposite* of the "McDonaldization" of the world, and rather more like a long overdue liberation from cultural alienation. As the C.E.O. of one of the major Bombay advertising agencies put it:

> See, today a lot of Indians at my level, which means we have no complaints about life in terms of material things—I have a car, I have a house, I don't have to think about where my next meal is coming from—90 percent of such people that I meet are already talking about going back to a simpler life. The other thing which I think has happened . . . is that we really have grown independent of

British thought now. So we . . . suddenly rediscovered . . . our confidence and said, "Oh, it's *okay*." You know, it's *okay* not to be able to eat with three different kinds of forks. It's *okay* not to understand the difference between Strauss and Stravinsky. You know, it's *okay*. If I like the kind of music that I have liked since childhood, it's perfectly fine. My identity is not under any kind of crisis. [It's] almost like I was poor; I didn't know that I was in this culture. Now I am well-to-do, but I realize the value of this culture. And therefore we'll start going back into it. . . . So as a culture, after that two hundred years of British rule, the culture is not very self-respecting. Now we have begun to respect ourselves, saying "it's okay." So therefore you will find more and more of KamaSutras coming up. And saying "Hey! This is from your past! Now you believe it, right?! Now you know that this is correct."[35]

Under the sign of global consumerism, the double structure of the commodity image brought together that which in Hegel had to be kept separate on pain of death: the voluptuous sensuality of India, and the "progressive" agenda of modernity. For Indians like this c.e.o., this reconciliation seemed to spell an end to the postcolonial predicament: that "unhappy consciousness," the split between self-identity and world modernity that colonialism had inaugurated.[36]

And yet, in the guise of the new form of expertise required to make culture marketable, the totalizing Hegelian spirit still animated at the least the *effort* to subordinate all particularity under a general formula: the formula of the commodity image. "Realizing the value of this culture," in practical terms, meant realizing the potential for exchange value embedded in marketable signs of cultural identity. Just as the official legitimacy of Vatsyayana's *Kamasutra* depended upon its canonization by professional orientalists, so the self-realization offered by the culturally marked commodity image depended upon a type of authoritative self-reflexivity that necessarily separated a cosmopolitan educated elite from the masses. Once again, we can see the ideological duality of the aesthetic in operation: liberation from the postcolonial predicament was figured as collective insofar as the markers of "Indian tradition" were part of a shared heritage. But the capacity to *understand* this heritage fully, to consume it discerningly (not to mention expensively) resided only with a minority. "You will see it," continued my interlocutor:

If you put on the television you will see the middle class going back to tradition without being aware of it. Without reflecting upon it. Saying that "oh, those days were the good old days." So let me now go back to this rich mythology which my grandmother used to tell me. The airwaves are plastered with mythologicals. But I am talking about the next level where it's not just mythology. My grandmother *has* told me the mythology, but I have also read Joseph Campbell. So I know where mythology falls into this entire place — what is at the root, what is subterranean, what is below that mythology I know. What is the truth before that. I know my grandmother used to teach me Sanskrit *shlokas,* but now I know what the meaning of that shloka is. Now that is a different thing, which is not tradition for tradition's sake, as a habit. I would definitely make that difference. . . . Self-reflectiveness is a symptom of a mind which is literate, which has read everything and is being asked to rediscover what it already had. But if I were to sell a condom called KamaSutra to a villager, I don't think this would work. . . . If I were to use *Kama-sutra* and try and sell it to the "other" Indian, who is not in a reflective mode, who doesn't have a distance between him and the tradition that he's living out . . . it's an invisible script as far as he's concerned. I don't think it will sell.

Conclusion

In part 1, through a discussion of the KamaSutra condom campaign, I have examined the manner in which consumerism, in the 1980s, was put forward by the Indian advertising business as an alternative social ontology. Chapter 3 focused on the general norms and forms of this dispensation, while chapter 4 analyzed the specific content and career of the KamaSutra campaign itself. In particular, I have tried to show how the notion of an aspirational community, which arrived in the 1980s as a model of a society united by distinction, depends upon the doubleness of the aesthetic, a doubleness that becomes mobilized through the form of the commodity image. By 1991, the aspirational community additionally had to parry the onslaught of globalization, and so the question of the exchange value of a suitably revalorized "Indianness" itself became part of the equation. Because of the way in which it sought social legitimation by means of reference to officially sanctioned "Indian tradition," KamaSutra prefigured the active deployment, in the post-1991 period, of "Indian tradition" as an aspirational set of signifiers for certain "auto-orientalist" products and brands.

My discussion of the KamaSutra campaign has largely been concerned with understanding the positions taken by clients and agencies vis-à-vis the forces of regulation. By the same token it has not, in any systematic way, examined the relationship *between* clients and agencies. This will be one of the main themes of part 2. In particular, I will focus upon the dialectic of the commodity image in the flow of practice. I will consider the relationship between affect-intensive image and its "capture" within brand narratives as a mode of performance through which the client-agency relationship is mediated. Finally, the narrative in part 2 offers a significant contrast to that of part 1 in that it highlights a situation in which the globalization of consumer markets *undermines* the commercial deployment of "Indianness."

PART TWO

5

Bombay Global:

Mobility and Locality I

In the final section of chapter 4, I suggested that KamaSutra prefigured an important claim: namely, that an aspirational mode of consumerism could, by way of a cosmopolitan aesthetic orientation, provide the foundation for a determinately Indian cultural revitalization. In part 3 of the book, I will show how this claim was extended into even more unlikely territory, when *foreign* brands were made to power national pride. In either case, these examples illustrate the important fact that consumerist globalization is as much about the cultural politics of producing the local as it is about contesting homogenization. To be sure, only certain kinds of locality turn out, in any given case, to be congruent with global dreams. This, of course, is precisely the complaint of those whose social agendas, for one reason or another, conflict with those of global capital. But as I will show in this chapter and the next, the search for acceptable forms of locality can become a dilemma *within* the marketing machine itself. Marketing discourse tells us that the problem for contemporary capitalism is how to reconcile the situated preferences of local consumers with the universalizing requirements of global brands. My argument, conversely, is that this appeal to the interests of consumers is frequently a legitimating device that obscures the fact that the contents of many advertising campaigns have far more to do with the politics of the relationship between an advertising agency and its client than with the relationship between the client and its customers.[1] Before a campaign ever hits the streets, it is here that the cultural contradictions of global capital are first played out.

Whatever the actual value of locality in specific advertising campaigns, globalization had irrevocably raised it as an issue to be confronted. Goutam Rakshit, managing director of the independent Bombay agency Avenues, reflected:

> What I *think* is happening is that because you have now non-Indian products, versus 1991, when all products were Indian . . . there becomes a marketing position available which says "this is Indian." So the environment has created a positioning opportunity. . . . And in that sense "Indian" has therefore become a differentiator in these three or four years. Now the question is whether that differentiator can be applied across the product segments and category segments. I think that also largely depends on what is the experiential quality of products that have chosen to be Indian, and what's been the customer experience of that Indianness.[2]

Any marketable definition of Indianness would also, however, have to be discerned against what was now a global field. On the one hand, writer Gita Mehta remarked: "As the pace of India's exchanges with the outside world accelerates there is a growing demand both inside India and abroad for some comprehensible definition of what India actually is" (G. Mehta 1998, 163). On the other hand, as corporate identity management guru Wally Olins put it: "Over the next decade or so, Indian companies will have to perform world-class, look world-class, behave world-class, and convince their customers, and above all themselves, that they are world-class" (Olins 1997).

As elsewhere, Indian apologists for liberalization argued that it would bring consumers unprecedented choice, quality, and value for money by means of a long-overdue liberation from the shoddy Indian goods churned out by flabby domestic industries, which for decades had enjoyed the market protections of the permit-license raj. What this vision ignored, however, was the ambivalence of the situation faced by many of these homegrown corporations, particularly those whose identity had been defined by offering Indian consumers access to sources of foreign technological excellence.

In the narrative that follows, then, I examine the impasse encountered by an Indian company torn between the benefits and the drawbacks of an Indian identity. I tell the story from the perspective of the

RIDE WITH THE MOB IN MILAN. IN BREEZY PASTEL CO-ORDINATES FROM THE URBAN NOMAD COLLECTION. BELONG. *Park Avenue*

Awarded the most admired mens wear brand at IFA 2000.   The Urban Nomad Collection is available at all Raymond Shops and select garment stores.

10. World-class Indianness? This ad for Park Avenue "suitings" by Raymond assertively projects an Indian brand into a Western context specifically chosen for the way it indexes the height of global achievement in fashion. The juxtaposition of the name of the line (Urban Nomad) with the baseline ("Belong") succinctly catches the dual promise of aspirational consumerism: liberation from mere locality, yet membership in a transcendent commodity ecumene. (To American ears, the phrase "Ride with the mob in Milan" may not, however, carry quite the intended resonance.)

11. Globalization as wishful thinking. When foreign brands started flooding the Indian market in the wake of the reforms of 1991, many Indian brands found it necessary to redefine their position within a newly globalized repertoire of products and images. Some, like the Raymond ad (Figure 10) and this campaign for Vicco Vajradanti toothpaste, attempted, quite simply, to assert their place in a global scheme. Here, Indian "tradition"—in this case "the time-honoured formulae of Ayurveda"—powers the ambitious orbit of Vicco. Claims to world-class status, however, always had to run the gauntlet of a subtle calculus of distinction. The same commentators who swooned over the "sophistication" of upscale auto-orientalist branding strategies were routinely dismissive of efforts such as this. In reply to Vicco's baseline, "Popular the world over," one journalist sniffed, "Of course, that depends on how small your world is" (Sen 1995).

advertising agency team that found itself charged with producing concrete images designed to appeal to its client's aspirations as well as discursive solutions designed to resolve its identity crisis. In the process, I will show that the dialectical structure of the commodity image cannot simply be "read off" from finished advertising. Rather, what emerges is a view of the dialectical dynamic of the *production* of commodity images, a process of commodity production that takes the form of a series of interactions and negotiations both within the agency and between the agency and the client. This account of the production of commodity images sets the scene for the discussion in Chapter 6, where I explore the concept of the brand as at once the discursive centerpiece of marketing theory, as a complex metaphor built around gift exchange, and as a practical means of regulating the relationship between agency and client. By way of a conclusion, I point to some of the means by which an ethnographic examination of the cultural politics of branding brings us to the contradictions at the heart of consumerist globalization.

The Figure of Telecommunications

Telecommunications have a unique role to play in both the practice and the rhetoric of contemporary global capitalism. They are at once the crucial means and the privileged sign of globalization, at once the "infrastructure of infrastructures" and the spectacular image of universal progress.[3] In the shape of consumer goods, most paradigmatically the cellular phone (and most particularly in the "developing" world), they are at once the visible index of upward mobility and the perceived solution to government inefficiency. During the time of my Bombay fieldwork, no business meeting or, for that matter, informal gathering over beer, was complete without the participants establishing a gleaming and mutually covetous circle of handsets on the table. At the same time, cellular telephony was being touted as a tool of empowerment for the rural poor, through schemes that would "leapfrog" the cumbersome state-managed terrestrial networks.

Telecommunications lend cutthroat market competition a benign face by evoking the universal foundation of enlightened sociality: "communication." But, as a set of figures, they also partake of the more abstracted type of universality associated with "science." The impartiality that is accorded to scientific truth allows technology to appear as a non-ideological engine of historical change. In fact the liberalizers shared this assumption with the Nehruvian dispensation that they sought to replace. Precisely the notion of technology as "value free," as a "tool," was what most radically set Nehru's vision of science apart from that of Gandhi, who believed, on the contrary, that the truth of science was not separable from the social conditions of its implementation.[4] Under Nehru, it was the role of the Planning Commission to mediate between the supposed placelessness of technological knowledge and local needs; the planning mode of governmentality was concerned, in large part, with formalizing apparently objective "information" about Indian conditions in such a way as to enable the optimal application of scientific knowledge to social problems. The spectacular repertoire of this period — against which the consumerist dispensation, except in certain overtly "patriotic" modes, would dig in its heels[5] — was industrial, monumental, and progressivist: steel mills, hydroelectric dams.

The beginnings of consumerist liberalization under Nehru's grandson Rajiv Gandhi coincided with the rise of telecommunications technology as a central figure in official imaginings of Indian society. From the beginning "Computerji," as some of his aides referred to him, was identified not only with televisual spectacle (see pages 72–76), but also with the magic of "communication" and deregulated consumer markets as mechanisms for overcoming the stalemates of Indian national development or, as Rajiv's signature slogan had it, "taking India into the twenty-first century."[6]

During the 1980s, a number of Indian companies — such as the one that I am about to discuss — benefited tremendously from the boom in consumer electronics and telecommunications equipment that was brought about under Rajiv. In the main, these companies occupied a position vis-à-vis consumer technology that mimed the paternalistic stance taken by the Planning Commission vis-à-vis development technology. Through exclusive joint ventures with foreign, usually Southeast Asian technology suppliers, they built up their own corporate profiles on the premise that, through a locally based understanding of Indian consumer needs, they were able to provide their customers access to the best of what foreign markets had to offer. Post-globalization, as an increasing number of foreign brands began to operate in India under their own, global brand names, these Indian companies found themselves in a difficult position. No longer the exclusive sources of

12. Valorizing screwdriver technology. Part of EMW's ambivalence about its Indian iden-
tity had to do with the fact that the parts from which its products were assembled
were, in any case, of foreign origin. This ad for Zenith computers tries to turn the
dilemma of screwdriver technology into a Unique Selling Proposition (USP) by offering its customers the best of both worlds: "MNC Quality" at "Indian Prices."

foreign excellence, their only inalienable advantage over their foreign competitors was their Indian identities, their "understanding of Indian consumers." As the entry of global brands created a situation in which Indian companies had to think long and hard about their own potential positioning strategies, many of them were advised by advertising and marketing professionals not to relinquish the strong familiarity or "equity" that their company names had generated over the past few decades in the minds of Indian consumers.

In part, this was sound pragmatic advice: as competition intensified, it made sense to play to your established strengths. The problem was that excellence in high-tech, as a category, was so strongly identified precisely with global transcendence, with "world standards." In this matter, I was to find, market research proved all but unnecessary, since many client and agency executives had already internalized a sense of the inferiority of Indian consumer technologies. As the copywriter in charge of the account that I found myself working on during my agency fieldwork put it: "It's not that we don't *have* the technology. Even when *Terminator 2* was made, we had the technology here. It's more a question of attitude and expertise. Look at the States. There, neither the agency nor the client would be satisfied with anything but the most perfect execution. Here, the whole attitude is *chalta hai*, 'it's good enough.'" Chuckling, he continued, "Right from politicians down to manufacturers and everyone—the one phrase you need to know is chalta hai. That needs to go in your thesis! And dedicate the chapter to me." One of the art directors, who had been listening to the conversation, grunted his agreement: "This is why Indian goods are always *okay*. They operate, but they're always average."

As a product category and a set of image connotations, cellular phones stood exactly at the intersection of the local and the global, the intimate and the impersonal, the utilitarian and the ostentatious. It was therefore fortuitous that, right at the beginning of my agency fieldwork, I found myself assigned to following the advertising account of a Bombay cellular phone service provider. It was doubly fortuitous, for my purposes, that this service provider belonged to an overarching Indian corporate brand, which I will call EMW Group, that was struggling to reconcile precisely these antinomies.

Indianness without "*Mera Bharat Mahan*":
The Corporate Campaign

EMW Group, today a top Indian consumer electronics company, was founded in the early 1960s. Company lore portrays its founder as a valiant entrepreneurial underdog, emerging victorious over the chafing restrictions and entrenched privileges of the permit-license raj. To that extent, the EMW story is one of the more spectacular examples of the kind of entrepreneurialism encouraged by Indira Gandhi in the late 1960s and 1970s (see pages 71–72). The company's really decisive growth period, however, came with the consumer appliance boom of the 1980s, when, under Rajiv's selective relaxation of import duties in the middle of that decade, foreign components became more affordable.

Prior to the entry of foreign brands as direct competitors, EMW had not really required a unified corporate identity. Structurally, the company was divided into separate units, each comprising a series of product divisions. Each of these was managed as an individual profit center with its own ambitious sales targets. Generally, each division also made its own advertising and marketing arrangements; hence there was little "synergy" to EMW advertising viewed as a whole. The structural divisions persisted, but in the mid-1990s, EMW's corporate leadership decided to employ a Delhi advertising agency to develop a coherent and cohesive brand identity for the corporate "motherbrand."

The brief that EMW gave to the advertising agency required that both the sharpening of the corporate brand and the vexed issue of Indianness be addressed at the same time. The directive was to develop "a corporate campaign to lend EMW a cohesive identity across all brands and portray it as a true blue Indian multinational." If KamaSutra's Big Idea had been to turn a universally reviled object into an aphrodisiac, then the conjuring trick that EMW required was to "positivize" Indianness itself. According to a spokesman for the agency, the idea was to "place EMW on the 'trust Indian' plank. Not that patriotism is a last resort, but because Indian stuff need not always be inferior." The Indianness that was being portrayed in the ads was rigorously dissociated from any concrete geographical markers. According to the copywriter at the agency: "We've cut the bullshit out of nationalism. . . . It's Indianness without *Mera Bharat mahan*" (I. Singh 1996). The expression used by the copywriter was telling; it was the phrase emblazoned in rainbow lettering on the back of every diesel-belching heavy goods truck on the rutted network of national highways: "my great India." These crowded roads marked the physical extent of India as a territorial nation and of the developmentalist project of the independent Indian state. From the perspective of the ideologists of consumerist liberalization, however, it was a space of lumbering imperfect communications, the very opposite of the cosmopolitan technological sublime.

The agency selected Amitabh Bachchan, hero of Hindi cinema since the 1970s, family friend of the Nehru-Gandhis, and latter-day laptop-wielding corporate warrior, as the face of the new campaign. On paper, the choice of Bachchan as a celebrity endorser was inspired: he had established himself as a Bollywood icon by playing angry-young-man roles in the 1970s, characters whose native wit and aggressive individualism had enabled them to buck the system in an era of government controls and bureaucratic corruption. By the 1990s, Bachchan's real-life reinvention as a sleek entertainment entrepreneur drew upon the rebellious resourcefulness of his erstwhile screen persona, now tempered by a certain paternal urbanity.[7] In the words of one EMW executive: "We used Amitabh Bachchan as an icon to say that we are not shy of our Indian origin and take pride in being a global Indian citizen" (quoted in N. Gupta 1998, 101).

"Global Indian citizen": the phrase was, in itself, a kind of précis of the cultural politics of globalization. In its consumerist register, it suggested that the reconciliation of the local and the global could be painlessly achieved through a practice of the imagination, both motivated and disciplined by the consumption of commodity images. Formally, the first of the advertisements in the series produced by the Delhi agency was constructed according to a key trope in the visual imagination of modernity: "the world as exhibition." Coming into its own in the Europe of the second half of the nineteenth century, this visual trope was central to staging the relationship between global (colonial) capitalism and national cultural difference in such spaces as nationalist museum displays and world expositions (Barthes 1972; Foster 1991; Karp and Lavine 1991; Pred 1995; Richards 1990; Rydell 1984). Typically, commodities on display served as the concrete embodiment of the connection between comparative advantage in an economic world system and the cultural differentiation of nationality in a global division of identity. The question posed by the first of the Amitabh Bachchan press ads for EMW was precisely that of the potential exchange value of "Indianness" within such a global repertoire. "I'd love to be an American," declared the headline.

> And enjoy the power my country holds. I'd love to be an English-man, watching my language spread through the world. I'd love to be a Frenchman, a native of the world's fashion capital. Art capital. Wine capital. I'd love to be Brazilian, whenever the World Cup is on. I'd love to be Italian, revelling in my country's inimitably styled sports cars. I'd love to be German. Thorough. Professional. Efficient. Punctual. . . . I'd love to be Japanese, proud of what my country has achieved in just a few decades. . . . I'd love to be Caribbean, teaching the world to reggae and relax. I'd love to march ahead with a billion countrymen, like the Chinese. I'd love to be an example-setting Singaporean. I'd love to be proud of my country. I'd love to make people envious just by saying I'm Indian. I'd love to make you believe it's possible. I'd love to make you believe in yourself.

In chapter 4, I previewed the way in which the globalization of consumerism in India was presented by some of its advocates as a means to a restoration of self-respect. I also suggested that part of the radical appeal of auto-orientalist branding was that it appeared to reject a Hegelian vision of history in which the sensuous particularity of "Indianness" would have to be sacrificed for the sake of a higher, more abstract universal: modernity, conceived as "progress." Never-theless, as my discussion of the aesthetic politics of the KamaSutra campaign showed, this cultural self-recognition was still premised on a global scheme of value; that is, for this "Indianness" to be acceptable, it also had to be certifiably "world-class." The Hegelian dialectic returns, after all: particularity is only legitimate insofar as it participates in a higher, universal truth. This ambiguity was evident in the EMW ads' direct evocation of a Hegelian politics of recognition. Where the first ad had conjured a global division of identity, the second positioned Indians in the subordinate position of the slave, dependent for their sense of self-worth on the approbation of another:

> We Indians. Why do we have a need to impress all foreigners? Why do we think fair skin is beautiful? Why do we think local means cheap? . . . Why do we never get mentioned for having the killer instinct? Why does it take us 16 years to get a medal at the Olym-

pics? . . . Why do we think anywhere "abroad" is a better place? Why do we feel so good when others say India has potential? Why do we act as if having potential is an achievement? Why are we so easily contented? Why do we blame our failures on fate? Why are we down here in the third world, when we all know we could easily be up there? Why don't we believe we could do it? Why don't we believe in ourselves?

This ignoble condition was certainly not the result of a lack of faith. If anything, Indians positively overflowed with belief: "We believe it's bad luck if a black cat crosses our path. . . . We believe an itchy left palm means we'll get money. And it's a jackal's wedding if it rains when it's sunny. . . . Putting a black dot on your baby's cheek wards off the evil eye. . . . When we believe all this may actually be possible, when we don't find such wisdom strange, then what is it that keeps us from also believing in ourselves, for a change?"

The point was not to "transcend" such native faith in favor of some singular, rationalized modernity. Rather, this energy had to be channeled away from its perpetual dissipation in "superstition" and toward a value-generating entrepreneurialism. EMW, by means of Amitabh Bachchan's face, offered itself as the conduit that would enable the slave to achieve self-recognition through his own work, his own power of belief. Drawing upon the embodied recombinational resourcefulness of the bricoleur and its formalization in indigenous scientific knowledge, the brand provided the mediation between self-respect and confidence on the world stage:

> Have you noticed how we think? We have discovered uses for every part of every coconut tree. We find washing machines perfect for making *lassi* [a yogurt drink particularly popular in North India]. We think of throwing in turmeric powder to plug leaking radiators (and it works!). . . . We have methods to predict how much rain the monsoons will bring. We can launch satellites on shoestring budgets. We can make supercomputers on our own. And we still don't think we're good enough. We still don't think we can surprise the world. We still don't think we can believe in ourselves.

Formally, then, the EMW ads presented the brand as the cosmopolitan custodian of Indian pride. Local and global were smoothly reconciled, and the new age of aspirational consumerism heralded a triumphant end to the indignities of a developmentalist history that had relegated India to a position "down here in the third world." What my agency fieldwork revealed to me, however, was that this alchemical appearance concealed a number of contradictions. These contradictions were not the result of any fault in the advertising or in the marketing plan. Rather, they pointed to much more fundamental tensions in the cultural politics of consumerist globalization.

In the nineteenth century, the cultures of the world, arrayed in their booths at the great world expositions, were generally given a concrete embodiment in the raw materials or manufactures (a division that itself illustrated the political economy of colonialism) associated with each area. By the late twentieth century, what was striking about a campaign like EMW — and in this it was quite representative of its genre — is that it dispensed as much as possible with references to concrete products. The *brand itself* was the basis of the identification that the campaign attempted to conjure.

As I suggested in chapter 2, this apparent disconnection between the circulation of commercial images and the circulation of concrete commodities has been interpreted by many as a mark of "postmodernity." Conversely, this disconnection animates the liberatory promise of marketing as well: if value can be generated through a play with images floating free of the political economy of old-fashioned commodities, then perhaps the work of the commercial imagination can shrug off the oppressive weight of history.[8] In this chapter, I aim to show why we would be mistaken to think that the commercial value of images now operates independently of more traditionally conceived commodity markets. But we will also see that it is precisely in the realm of the imagination that the persistence of history, of concrete local experience, makes itself manifest.

Seduction and Intimacy: The Problem of Being Indian

In the abstract, cellular telephony embodied precisely the dizzying globalizing reach suggested by the EMW Group brand ads. And in terms of the kinds of connotations that attached to the product category, this fact remained crucial. At the same time, like all brands, EMW mobile found itself faced with several concretely local constraints.

After having been granted licenses by the Indian government in 1992, cellular phone service providers had commenced operations in

Indian cities in 1995. Initially, cellular licenses were granted in the four major metropolitan centers only (Bombay/Mumbai, Delhi, Calcutta/Kolkata, and Madras/Chennai). By 1995, the remainder of the country was divided up into eighteen "circles," the boundaries of which in most cases roughly coincided with state lines. To create limited competition, licenses in each circle were granted to only two operators.[9] The Bombay circle was allotted to EMW mobile and a company I will call SamTech, both of them Indian-foreign joint ventures. Early subscriber projections were generally optimistic. EMW and SamTech jointly expected, according to one source, a total of 100,000 subscribers by the end of 1995 and as many as one million by the year 2000 (Raina 1995). Actual numbers were more modest; in the immediate aftermath of the launch, EMW had 4,000 subscribers in Bombay (Nadkarni 1995). A significant turning point came in July 1996, when the Deve Gowda government announced a cut in import duties on cellular phone handsets;[10] by August of that year SamTech's subscriptions had jumped to 29,000, EMW's to 25,600. By the time I started my fieldwork at the Bombay agency handling the advertising account for EMW mobile, in September 1997, the figures were as follows: SamTech had succeeded in enrolling 100,000, with EMW mobile trailing behind at 70,500.[11] As a client, then, EMW mobile was driven by two worries in addition to the issues of locality and globality that I have already outlined. The first was generic to the product category: low overall subscription figures. The second was specific to the brand: being left behind by its competitor. As the agency account executive assigned to EMW mobile remarked: "This is a *huge* weakness, perception-wise. It's one of the shames of this company."

These two problems were, in fact, interconnected. The Cellular Operators' Association of India (COAI) had gone as far as hiring an advertising agency to create a campaign that would promote the generic benefits of cellular telephony to Indian consumers. The agency had reasoned that the category's reliance on high-end metropolitan business executive imagery was limiting its perceived relevance. Their plan involved a kind of reverse-emulation principle. As one of the executives involved told me:

> We found that we couldn't just tap onto the corporate types, because beyond some cities — the top five, ten cities — there just *aren't* too many corporate types. . . . So the thought came up: suppose we

find . . . people you would least expect to have a cell phone, who are actually seen with cell phones in the advertising. . . . I mean, you could probably show a small kid having a cell phone, but then you would just say it's irrelevant. It's a pure gimmick. But if you brought into it some amount of reality. . . . So what we did was advertising focused on people like the vegetable sellers, who were moving around from one place to another with a cell phone . . . a *prosperous* vegetable seller, or a steel trader, or something like that. Not a very big businessman, a tycoon, or anything of that sort, but a trader who has a lot of money. And in India, a lot of these people have a lot of — especially unaccounted — money . . . but they aren't the very sophisticated type generally . . . that *provokes*. It provokes everyone into saying, yeah — maybe he needs one. One of the things we had thought of was the priest who does religious stuff.[12] He's a guy who travels from house to house. And if you're a successful priest, you're a fairly rich guy. . . . You were not sure whether the priest would buy it or not, but the guy who was a middle-level guy in some kind of a job, or was a small businessman, would then find a reason to purchase one.

While the campaign idea found favor with some of the cellular operators in provincial circles, the metropolitan brands were reluctant to risk "diluting" the aspirational tone established by their existing advertising. As my executive informant put it: "The operator who's running a corporate status kind of a campaign in any of the metros gets a bit worried. Because then the association of the category moves away from what he's been trying to project as an individual operator. He feels a bit threatened about it." This anxiety had complex foundations. Beyond serving a specific metropolitan agenda of social distinction, the figure of the "corporate man" also provided a licit visual shorthand that tacitly indexed an illicit — but very important — segment of the cellphone market: the criminal underworld.[13]

EMW, already trailing behind SamTech in subscriber numbers, was particularly prone to status anxiety for two reasons. The first was, paradoxically, the high level of dignified brand equity already enjoyed by the EMW motherbrand, some of which the corporation hoped would rub off onto EMW mobile. Connotations would, however, necessarily flow both ways, and so EMW mobile found itself unable to engage in any advertising strategies that might "dilute" the equity of the motherbrand. In this regard, SamTech, a brand with no history in India, was at greater liberty to market "scrappy" sub-brands beyond the aesthetic boundaries of the corporate image. The most that EMW mobile could do was to play with the copy of its ads, one of which deliberately juxtaposed the product's ability to satisfy both the aspirational consumer's status hunger and the criminal's need for anonymity. The headline read: "Everybody wants to be somebody. You want to be nobody," and was followed by copy designed to reassure even the shiftiest of potential customers: "You have your reasons. We don't want to know."

EMW mobile's second great problem was that SamTech had effectively positioned itself as the "global" or "international" brand, and thereby — by default — heightened the relative provinciality of EMW. Once again, EMW Group's long-standing presence in the Indian market was a mixed blessing; while it meant high levels of brand recognition and a sense of reliability and "warmth," it also tended to position EMW as the "Indian" brand in a product category where globality was an important value.

Consumer focus groups commissioned by the ad agency helped to clarify the relative connotations that the two brands embodied with what, for the client and agency alike, was depressing starkness.[14] SamTech scored well on both "brand personality" and perceived quality. Research respondents, prompted to describe what kind of person SamTech represented, perceived the brand as masculine-gendered, somewhere between twenty and thirty years of age, with a dynamic, aggressive personality and international connections. EMW mobile, in contrast, had an age perception of thirty to forty, a tendency toward feminine gendering, a completely "Indian" identity, and a general association with "solidity" and "family values."

EMW mobile's Indianness meant stability, closeness, and reliability. As one focus group participant reflected, "Because they are Indian, they will understand Indian needs." To that extent, its Indianness made it a "warm" and "approachable" brand. SamTech, however, was deemed "international and more efficient, but also cold and distant." But while the warmth associated with EMW mobile seemed an ideal basis for brand loyalty, it offered little in the way of spectacular potential and eroticization. As another research respondent offered: "EMW mobile is like my wife . . . SamTech is like a beautiful colleague in my office . . . we all know who we would choose."[15] The copywriter on the EMW mobile account was surprised at the overwhelmingly positive portrait of SamTech that the focus groups had generated (even though he himself—I should add—was a SamTech subscriber). "I'd always thought that it was a little tacky, that somehow it smacked of Hong Kong-returned Sindhis; you know: flashy, over-cologned, loud."

Finally, EMW mobile and SamTech were competing in a product category where any innovation introduced by one company could be duplicated by the other within days. All that remained was to build preference on the basis of brand image. Locked in a frenetic struggle for "mind-share," the two Bombay cell phone operators had little time for subtle appeals. For EMW mobile, the situation was only aggravated by its sense of inferiority vis-à-vis SamTech, which commanded both a more glamorous image and a higher number of subscribers. This, then, was the context out of which the new product emerged.

The Making of RightAway

RightAway was the perfect counterexample to the myth of marketing: namely, that products are created in response to the needs of consumers. RightAway, on the contrary, was custom-made to serve the short-term needs of the producer: arrest the attention of consumers and quickly boost subscription figures. It so happened that these requirements paralleled those of the agency, which—in the light of EMW mobile's comparatively disappointing performance—urgently needed to arrest the attention of its client.

In terms of components, RightAway contained nothing new. The only functional benefit that it offered was relative convenience: for the first time in Bombay, a cellular phone handset, a prepaid SIM card,[16] and a charger were to be made available in a single package. Its purpose was to make cellular telephony a retail product like any other, more or less to be tossed into the shopping basket along with the groceries.[17]

"Velocity" was an early contender for the product name, but ultimately members of the team working on the account felt that it overemphasized speed per se; it was fine for a bicycle or an intercity train, but not adequate for a communications accessory. "Impulse," a name that the copywriter had been pushing for some time, since he felt that it connoted both the immediacy of purchase and the "pulse" of communication, was "bounced" as soon as the team realized that there was already a brand of perfume with that name. Then someone came up with "Contact": it was short, it suggested connection, and — most importantly — it looked good on the packaging design that was being generated on a computer in the agency's art studio.

The packaging visuals were an interpretation of a concept line that the copywriter had come up with: "the Contact pack as your survival kit in a harsh urban environment." The copywriter gave this concept to one of the agency artists, who in turn leafed through one of the large glossy international Image Bank catalogs that agency creative rooms are generally littered with, along with American and British life-style magazines.[18] The artist finally decided upon an image that he felt to be appropriate: a young man with his hand outstretched toward the camera, fingers magnified by a dramatically receding perspective, ambiguously suggesting both a desire for connection and a fashionably slacker-ish gesture of refusal. Finally, the visual conceptualizers in the agency's studio proceeded to place this image against a bright swirling pattern of red and green, overlaid in turn with the EMW mobile logo. "Contact" itself was rendered in a deliberately futuristic typeface. The overall effect suggested MTV or video games: fast, high-tech, loud. The aim, as the copywriter explained to me, not without a certain self-irony, was to achieve "maximum shelf throw" to arrest attention quickly in a cluttered retail environment.

The copywriter, in his usual phlegmatic way, slumped into a chair at the computer terminal in the middle of the office floor and started tapping away, more or less at random. "Your mother needs to talk to you. Why don't you CONTACT her?" Wincing at his own words, he proceeded to try something more in line with the concept that he had devised earlier: "All you need in the city is a love and one CONTACT." The name Contact had generated support within the agency team because it carried a sense of intimacy and warmth that attractively modulated the high-tech feel of the product category. Perhaps, in this way, the perceived warmth of the EMW brand might be "leveraged" into the realm of human communication without sacrificing the excitement of the urban swirl.

Nevertheless, there was some concern that, given the "retail orientation" of the product, Contact would not adequately convey the "product promise." Perhaps a "product descriptor" would have to be added to the package. But what was the right word? "Kit" and "System" were both considered, but rejected on the grounds that they sounded too technical and complicated, too much like something that would have to be laboriously assembled at home. "Package" was another option, but this was too redolent of the various airtime schemes — Value Package, Talk Package — with which the operators were bombarding consumers in their frantic attempts to outdo each other with fresh offers. "Pack" was finally agreed upon; Contact was to be a "ready-to-use mobile phone pack."

Still, doubts about the name itself lingered, and one afternoon there was a call in the office from the art director on the account, who was presenting ideas and concepts at EMW mobile headquarters. Mulling over alternative possibilities the night before, he had come up with RightAway, which he felt was closer to the intended product promise. The copywriter readily agreed, reflecting that RightAway had more of a "retail feel," whereas Contact was more "philosophical." Whatever the relevance of this distinction, the greatest hurdle remained: the packaging and the concept still had to be sold to the client. In fact, as we will see, it was in this act of selling that the commodity image called RightAway came into being.

The Client in the Mirror

A commodity image, as it traverses the pathways of publicity, is, to be sure, *re*produced — re*worked* — every time it resonates with local projects and situated desires. But before it is launched on its journey, it is produced as the specific configuration of word and image that will enter into these encounters. This act of production takes place within the client-agency relationship. It goes without saying that it draws upon "raw materials" that are in fact never raw, just as the bricoleur's materials are never immaculate but rather the detritus of particular pasts. What is perhaps less obvious is that this act of bricolage takes the form of a restless dialectical movement between concrete images and discursive meanings, between seduction and "narrativization."

If advertisements are commodity images, then advertising practice is a kind of commodity production. But it is a mode of production that is highly dependent on rhetoric, staging, and interpretation. On a formal level, when an advertising agency sells a campaign idea to its client, it realizes the advertisement as a commodity by *performing* it. This performance dramatizes the dialectical movement between the integral force of the images in the ads and the narratives that are conjured rhetorically in the course of the meeting. The intensity of images is arresting and may sway the client in the short term. But without a set of brand narratives and meanings elaborated around this moment of intensity, the agency will not be able to extend this impression into a lasting and profitable relationship with its client.

The first moment of the process — seduction with images — is primarily a matter of dramatics. The elementary forms of an agency presentation to a client include the arrangement and decoration of the conference room, including strategically placed pieces of advertising and a particular order of seating; the magician's flick-of-the-wrist and the solemn silence of an expectant audience as each new design is unveiled by the agency art director; the tag-team, good cop/bad cop presentational dynamic between various members of the agency team, and the subtle modulation between creative and executive discourse achieved through the occasional interventions of the copywriter and the art director. All this is routine agency theater performed to captivate, to heighten the client's flow of adrenaline and sense of expectation.

Kersy Katrak, doyen of the Churchgate Set (see pages 106–10), was legendary for his bravura stagecraft. An old associate of his told me a story about a presentation during the glory days of Katrak's agency, MCM. The agency team on a particular account had stayed in the office till 1:30 A.M. rehearsing for a presentation the next day. The client duly appeared at the appointed time of 9:30 that morning. Katrak had instructed one of his account executives to engage the client with small talk and coffee for half an hour, during which time there was no sign of Katrak himself. Finally, the account executive, feigning concern, excused himself, apparently to search for his boss. After another few minutes, Katrak appeared in the conference room looking disheveled and befuddled, apologizing profusely for having "forgotten" the meeting, and for being completely unprepared — "so very, very sorry, where to start?" By an apparently superhuman effort of focused inspiration, he then seemed to pull himself together at a moment's notice, reeling off detailed facts and statistics, to all appearances spontaneously generating stunning creative solutions to his client's business needs.

Such apparently casual feats are, of course, intended to impress the client. But more than this, the specific elements of the performative spectacle are designed to offer the client a medium for his own libidinal self-identification. At this stage, the advertising images operate as a kind of Lacanian mirror in which the agency hopes that client executives will discern an appealingly coherent — albeit contingent — image of themselves.[19] Calculated flattery of the client is a routine part of agency strategy. During my time on the RightAway account, I came to recognize the inherent value of such considerations.

During the very first agency-client meeting that I attended, the copywriter surreptitiously passed me a scribbled note: "Number one client request: 'Make my logo bigger!'" As if to provide precisely for this need in such a way that it would not unduly interfere with actual campaign ideas, the agency had generated a series of large press ad/billboard mock-ups, which they usually referred to as the "theme campaign." The most notable, not to say overwhelming, feature of these images was a large, floodlit EMW logo on the pitch of a vast and darkened sports stadium. It gradually became clear to me that the agency team, who would wheel out these boards at strategic moments, cared less about whether these ads would ever in fact appear than about their markedly soothing effect on the client.[20]

The RightAway package — at this stage still called Contact — certainly seemed to achieve the first moment of the commodity image dialectic. At the meeting where the newly mocked-up package design was first presented to the client team, the EMW mobile executive[21] was suitably entranced. Turning the box over and over in his hands, gazing raptly at its bright, sleek surfaces, he exclaimed: "Can we keep *exactly* the same graphic look? Don't change *anything*." So enchanted was the EMW mobile executive by the box that the agency team literally had to wrest it from his grasp in order to be able to proceed with the more mundane details of marketing strategy and retail initiatives that constituted the rest of the day's agenda.

After the meeting, euphoria gripped the agency team. At the same time, its more seasoned members knew that only half the battle had been won; the second moment of the commodity image dialectic was, as yet, unfulfilled. For all that the client was excited by the new package, this excitement was going to have to be captured and harnessed within a more or less permanent set of product or brand narratives before it cooled and dissipated. In the midst of all the backslapping the copywriter looked uneasy. "He's a rational man," he reflected quietly, referring to the EMW mobile executive. "He's going to go back to head office and reason is going to triumph over his emotions."

In chapter 6, I offer a detailed exploration of the role played by the notion of "the brand" both in marketing discourse and in the client-agency relationship. For now, let me simply suggest that while the ostensible purpose of a coherent brand is to manage the client's relationship with its consumers, it is at least — if not more — important to the agency's capacity to manage its relationship with the client. This is because brand "identity" narratives provide a mutually accepted and apparently objective set of parameters within which the play of images may proceed. This "capturing" effect is, by the same token, worthless if it is not constantly reanimated by new images, new surges of excitement. "If an account is going to go, then it will go," the account executive on EMW mobile told the creative director when she expressed concerns about losing the account. "It's like divorce: if the spark's gone, then you're not going to be able to stand there and try to convince them to come back to you with rational arguments."

It was gradually becoming evident that the problem with Right-Away was that it was all sparks and no argument. In their attempts to conjure a coherent brand identity that would link RightAway to the larger EMW brand, the agency team kept coming up against the problem that the focus groups had already articulated: the only advantage that the EMW brand enjoyed vis-à-vis SamTech was just as likely, in this product category, to be perceived as a *dis*advantage — EMW's qualities of locality, warmth, and Indianness. What made the situation even more difficult for the agency team was that this predicament was confirmed by the spontaneous reactions of their client, who was, after all, the immediate embodied representative of the corporation itself.

Joyfully reunited, at the next agency-client meeting, with the Right-Away package, once more caressing its contours, the EMW mobile executive impatiently brushed aside the account executive's rather insubstantial attempt to introduce even the semblance of a product narrative and exclaimed with gusto: "Excellent! Exceptional! Brilliant! If this doesn't win the awards and get the customers nothing will! This wild look is *happening!!* Visually, this is extremely brilliant. It doesn't look Indian, actually."

Increasingly, the agency team's pleasure at their short-term success was clouded by anxiety over the emergent contradictions that threatened to sabotage their long-term plans. Their next move was to suggest that radio might be the ideal medium in which to achieve a connection between the local relevance of the EMW brand and the "happening" attractions of RightAway. To this end, the creative team had scripted a series of commercials, each of which was constructed around a specific Bombay consumer stereotype. The first featured the Marathi-inflected voice of a young street hustler — a self-made man, always on the move: "*Apun ka* philosophy, RightAway! [My philosophy is: RightAway!] *Khana chahiye* RightAway. *Rona chahiye* RightAway. [I/you want food RightAway; to cry RightAway.] *Sab kuch abheech karneka!* [Get everything done right now!] *Apna* time waste *nahi karneka. Kya?* [I don't waste my time, yeah?] *Kuch* decide *kiya na, to phata—phat se,* boss. [When something's been decided, then get on with it, man.] *Kya poora din khada rehkar mu dekhega, kya?* [Do you think I've got all day to stand here staring at your mug or what?]" A smooth announcer's voice cut in: "Start talking RightAway with EMW mobile. The mobile phone, the charger, and the SIM card. All in one ready-to-use mobile phone pack. Pick it off the shelf and start talking RightAway!" For the sign-off, the feisty *Bambaiyya* character returned: "*Dekha! Apun ka* philosophy *ko sunna!* [Look, people listen to my philosophy! (i.e., it produces results)]."

Without pausing for a reaction, the account executive proceeded to the next in the series. This one featured a character dubbed "Sandra from Bandra" — the stereotype being a young Catholic airhead forever gossiping in the idiosyncratic English that members of other Bombay communities frequently parody. "What you're saying, men? You didn't know that Peter left Nancy and is now seeing Susie? Tree [*sic*] days ago. That's old news, men. You must know things fast, no? If something happens, I know it RightAway. And I also tell RightAway. That's how I get gossip, fresh and hot. RightAway!" The announcer's voice once again delivered the product message before Sandra returned: "Aey! Tell no, you're going to the Navy ball or what?"

In rapid succession, two more scripts were performed. One featured the voice of a "typical" Gujarati gold trader (calling Antwerp for gold prices, finding out about share prices, calling "*Maharaj*," his prima donna Brahmin vegetarian cook, to instruct him to make *nashta*). The other was an Anglophone version of the first spot: an impatient, finger-snapping "where-it's-at" young man, this time with added fashion references: "I shaved my head, RightAway. I tattooed my arm. I pierced my lip, RightAway."

Throughout the reading of the scripts, the EMW executive had been looking increasingly perplexed. As the presentation ended, there was a moment of silence as the agency team sat back apprehensively. "What is the consistency here?" the EMW executive finally demanded. "Today I'm in shirt and sleeves? Tomorrow I've shaved my head and I'm wearing rings? Next day I come in a *lungi?* I'm the same person, but the perception of me keeps changing. . . ?" The account executive stepped in: "I'll explain it to you. If you look at our press communication, it's very design-led. On radio I cannot get the same funkiness. We were talking about the whole thing being layered. Even this is layered—to different consumers. . . ." But for the EMW mobile executive, this very specificity, this attempt at local relevance, threatened to bring the identity of the product down-market; it seemed that he wasn't so much haunted by incoherence per se as by the specter of provinciality. "No, but you don't need to get so *localized,*" he protested. "[In] all the other communications, you're ten notches above."

Before his young account executive could waste too much time and client goodwill on the relatively unlucrative medium of radio, the agency office manager interrupted, telling the former: "What he is saying is that the rest of it is very classy, very contemporary. It's a *cityscape.* In radio, why are we suddenly going *ethnic?*" The EMW mobile executive nodded: "Why are we localizing it so much if this is an international, hip thing?"

Sense and Sensibility:
The Account Executive and the Agency Manager

What, on the surface, might have appeared as a difference of opinion within the agency team had at least as much to do with the respective roles assumed by the agency office manager and his immediate subordinate, the account executive. The agency manager was, in a sense, the agency's salesman. In terms of corporate hierarchy, he was the EMW mobile executive's opposite number. And indeed the dynamics of his salesmanship depended upon evoking a shared aesthetic understanding—a sensus communis, a commonality of habitus—between himself and his client. This implication of a "natural" resonance between two senior executives provided the medium for a mode of persuasion based on a tacit appeal to embodied preference. The evidence of this resonance was the agency manager's apparently superior ability to divine the deepest desires of his client. Frequently, he would act as if he understood his client's needs before they had been articulated; at other times, as in the meeting I have just described, he would appear to contradict his own team for the sake of expressing a more profound intuition. Invariably, creative ideas and marketing strategy would be submitted for the agency manager's perusal and approval before a meeting; thus apprised, he would proceed to offer the client his agency's services as if doing him a personal favor ("Let me see what I can come up with for you").

If the agency manager was in charge of sensibility, then it fell to the account executive to make sense of it all. The agency manager largely occupied a "front" position; the account executive, in contrast, was very much a mediator. Account executives, who routinely act as middlemen between agency creative teams and the client, are generally hounded by both sides for their pains (see Brierley 1995, chapter 5; Moeran 1996a, chapter 1). These days, account executives are often business school graduates; in this, the executive on the EMW mobile account was no exception. Because of the pragmatic and problem-solving orientation of his job, he was generally impatient with creative pretension, "over-intellectualization," and "post-rationalization." Moreover, his training predisposed him to reach for marketing logic to supply him with both practical solutions and rhetorical strategies. While the creative team was concerned most of all with the impact of the images and the copy of the ads, and the agency manager attempted to achieve perfect resonance with his client, the account executive worried about long-term strategy, a problem that expressed itself concretely as the need to develop a coherent brand.

While he understood the relative roles they had to play, the account executive often found himself frustrated by the agency manager's readiness to comply with his client's most fickle whims. "I'd rather have a few boring, simple ideas that work than go ahead and start presenting all kinds of wild schemes that might look good, but which there is no money for, or which would never work," he complained to me one day. "But he [the agency manager] tends to have this 'we can do that' attitude." The way in which the EMW mobile account had come to lean so heavily on sheer spectacle in his view only aggravated the problem. His frustration ironically took the form of accusing the client of displaying an *advertising* rather than a *marketing* mindset — that is, leaning on show rather than strategy.

Frenetically pacing up and down the small cubicle that I had been given at the agency, the account executive drew impatiently upon a series of cigarettes.

EMW is spending ten to twelve crore rupees on advertising every year just in Bombay![22] *Ten to twelve crores!* That's more than a *national* campaign for a fucking soap would have been a few years ago, that has to be on TV *every day!* Why not stop bombarding the consumer with so much information, so much advertising, and start *selling* the thing instead?! That's the problem with EMW — they're not marketing people, they're more like advertising people. Advertising is a subset of marketing. And it's a subset of sales. Advertising can only *support* marketing. As an advertising man, I have no problem standing up [he fixes my eyes with theatrical sincerity] and telling them "Cut back! Relax! Go and talk to the customer, one-to-one. Stop thinking so hard about the segment of consumers that the other guy has and start thinking about how to tap into the five hundred thousand potential customers that are there. Spend two crores on your image advertising, and spend five crores on some *direct selling.*"

The account executive was getting increasingly animated, enthused by his own plan: "Get 250 good salesmen to talk to 10 or 12 people every day, for half an hour each, and explain to them — in terms that make sense to them — why they *need* a mobile phone. Get them to work Monday to Friday . . . no, maybe they should work Saturday and Sunday too. You're talking to 2,500 people a day! 17,500 people a week! In any direct sales exercise a ten percent conversion rate is respectable. At that rate you could be getting over 90,000 subscribers *in one year!!*"

In practice, the account executive was of course not going to discourage his client's hunger for more advertising. And despite his talk of directly explaining the benefits of cellular telephony to potential customers, he knew that RightAway was not in itself going to sway the undecided. Focus group respondents had reacted with skepticism to the product's promise of instantaneous connection. As one of them remarked (giving a whole new twist to the notion of a "white elephant"): "Even if someone gives me an elephant free, I still have to feed it!" The account executive assumed that the only type of potential customer who might be swayed by RightAway was someone who had already been sold on the benefits of the product. "Let's look at which consumer you're talking to," he appealed to the agency team, brandishing a marker and whiteboard.

There are four broad categories: the already mobile, the fence sitters who are about to make a decision, the undecided, and those who are never going mobile. Out of these, the *only* guy who can be influenced by this is the fence sitter. For instance, Arijit [the agency manager] has a friend who wanted to buy a laser disc [player]. He told me about this the other day. The guy spends two months talking about it with three or four friends, debating, turning over the options. Then, out of the blue, one Sunday morning he calls and says, "I've decided, I want to buy it *right now!*" Arijit says, "*Baba!* It's a bloody laser disc, *yaar!* Can't it wait until Monday?" "No, I have to have it right now!"

Not only was the account executive skeptical of the persuasive powers of the product; in fact, he was doubtful that cellular telephony was, in the final analysis, relevant to most Indians. "We're stuck in a category that's not relevant to people," he told me. "Indians are not very interested in time management. Nor do they want to be available all the time, unless they're doctors. I don't *want* my boss to be able to call me all the time — he's only going to give me more work. And what does it matter if I'm twenty minutes late? The job will get done, I will be there. I'm committed to the job." Rational or functional appeals were not going to work. On the other hand, the account executive surmised that the warmth and intimacy established around the EMW Group brand might well help to create an *affective* basis for its insertion into the everyday lives of Indian consumers. But so far all the agency team's attempts to add some of this local resonance to the "happening" profile of RightAway had misfired. By now, several members of the agency team were extremely reluctant to hold up a mirror marked "local" to their client's face. What was needed was an answer to the question already posed by the Amitabh Bachchan ads: what might Indianness, conceived as an avatara of the global, look like?

"Very Bombay": A Possible Mediation?

A provisional answer to this question emerged within the agency through an improvisational attempt to find a connection between the aesthetic medium that affectively attracted the client to the agency's visual ideas and the need for a discursive definition that might harness this attraction in the long term.

Lounging around the creative room, having received their brief from the account executive, the copywriter and the art executive tried to bring the product into conceptual focus. "We need to come up with a *profile* for RightAway," the art director began, swiveling in his chair, tapping the ash off the end of his cigarette. "Bitchy? Status? Business? These kinds of things give different perspectives to the product." Trying to picture different segments of the target audience, the copywriter ventured: "Do it perhaps profession-wise? Have a line for doctors, for businessmen, etc?" "That can be stage three," retorted the art director. "For the launch we need brand specifics." The copywriter had assigned a junior copy trainee to come up with some ideas. She read out her latest effort: "Worried about success? Buy a ladder. RightAway." The art director nodded, pleased: "It's perfect to have the *symbol*, like the ladder, in there." Reviving his copywriting partner's original concept for Contact, he added: "Another approach might be 'things you need to survive in the city.' 'Gifting' might be another theme." Silence descended as the creative team gazed out of the office window, lost in thought, idly contemplating the ragged people and scrawny animals straggling around the warehouses and hospital buildings next door. The art director and copywriter both puffed pensively on cigarettes.

After some time, the office manager was called in, along with the executives working on the account. A number of phrases were batted back and forth. Furrowing his brow, the manager leaned forward against the back of a swivel chair and wondered "Yes, but how do we *lift* it?" What would enable the copy and the general product identity to capture, within a discursively articulated framework, the same excitement suggested by the design?

The copywriter motioned the copy trainee to read out her "ladder" line to the assembled team. The manager was baffled. " 'Ladder?' What does it mean?" The copywriter explained: the ladder was a metaphor for aspiration and social mobility. The manager looked irritated: "That's in your head. I didn't get that at *all*." In a standard move, he proceeded to contrast the fanciful wordplay and associations of the creative team with the "realities" of the market, conjuring a gestalt of an imagined consumer. "We have to look at the target audience. The more I speak to dealers—I don't necessarily agree with them—but they say that the upwardly mobile, the bulk of them already have acquired mobile. But those who are on the cusp"—the account executive's fence-sitters—"they are the traders or whoever. So don't make it *down*-market, but take out the ambiguity." The account executive, still wedded to the orienting device of visually concretized market segments, suggested: "You can show different people in different situations. Even a Gujju [Gujarati] guy with his printed shirt and white trousers." The manager, however, looked pained at this vision of what he clearly perceived as *desi* imagery (literally, "of the land"; in this context, "indian" or "local") and responded, "But take the stereotypes of the young modern guy." "Does it have to be *one?*" the account executive wondered quietly, almost to himself.

The generalizing feature of the office manager's imagined target audience was attitude rather than appearance.[23] Turning to the copywriter, and combining a remembered phrase with his "learnings" from the radio spot debacle, he urged: "Go with the 'survival' thing that you had for Contact. That had *Bombay* language, the *city* language." This was not the vernacular Bambaiyya caricatures of the ill-fated radio spots; rather, it was "Bombay" imagined as a collective space of aspiration and transformation. The art director was still perplexed, trying to imagine concrete consumers to whom he might direct his images: "Who *is* the target audience now? There is no one single target audience." The manager, however, had already converted the rather approximate referent "traders" into an even more generalized notion of urban entrepreneurial energies translated into consumer aspiration. "If you need to go blanket, focus it on the product itself, but give it added value: 'Today, this is the *latest way* to go mobile.' 'The newest, the *gizmo* way to go mobile.' 'The most *happening* way to go mobile.' Not necessarily to harp on the product, but focus on the package." He raised his voice: " 'The easiest, the best, the latest.' It's Bombay! It's happening! It's *now!*" By now he was on the edge of his seat, riffing, almost shouting with excitement: "*Give* me the latest way! *I need trappings!!* To feel the latest way the world moves!!!" Breathing in, he sat back, lowering his voice. "I'm giving you *that*. The latest hip thing is very 'Bombay.' " He looked around the room. "Let us not intellectualize it. This is *the latest way*. When you get to that kind of flavor then you have the news value. The line should be *in your face. On* your face. No beating around the bush. It's almost as if someone were telling me 'Get moving!' " Clicking his fingers impatiently: " 'Get your butt out!' He's always at the action point. 'If it's happening — I'm *there*.' " " 'Now become the cool-hunter,' " murmured the account executive, trying to pick up on his boss's improvisation.[24]

A pause followed, as the assembled appeared to be trying to imagine the concrete applications of the attitude that the manager had just performed for them. Someone handed him the latest proofs of the RightAway packaging. Instinctively miming his client's tactile attraction, he caressed them for a moment, appraisingly. Finally he looked up with a new earnest tone in his voice, as if humbled by the sight of the design. "This is a very contemporary, happening look. What are the things we can say in attitude terms? 'It's the latest.' If you were to launch a revolutionary concept you wouldn't hide the fact, would you? So give it a larger-than-life canvas of the whole thing in itself. Make it the ultimate toy: 'You haven't got it? How are you *living?*' It's like, 'You got it, but you got it the *dull* way. I got it the exciting way.' It's like that song on MTV—how does it go?" He hummed some half-remembered lines: " 'I know what I want . . . and I want it now.' " The entire team closed their eyes, straining to capture the thread of the tune. Finally someone cracked the name of the number: "Mr. Vain." "That's it!" exclaimed the manager. " 'I know what I want and I want it now. I want you, 'cause I'm Mr. Vain.' In fact, *that* is the selling point for creative here. . . . Get simple. Get hard-hitting. You need the here-and-nowness."

As a sign, this notion of "very Bombay" had the advantage of combining a reference to locality with an aspirational and transcendent connotation. It was also usefully inclusive. It was Bombay as contemporary urban jungle, a setting in which the cellular phone was a weapon of survival. This image of the city brought together, under a single name, the basic struggle for survival and the consumer's infinite aspirations. It connected the strivings of the most wretched inhabitants of the city's burgeoning slums, the government employee squeezing his way through the crunching mass of bodies on the suburban commuter train, all the way up to the figure of the city as business center, a node of transnational corporate warfare.

Beyond the physical boundaries of the city itself, the signifier "Bombay" also drew upon a complex set of public cultural connotations. For the last century or so, Bombay has been the hub of big business and finance in India (a position that is now gradually being eroded as many companies move to the relatively cheaper environs of Delhi and Bangalore). Money weds spectacle: Bombay is also the home of the most prolific commercial cinema industry in the world. "Bollywood" product enjoys a near-universal popularity in India—although it does have significant regional competitors, most notably the commercial Tamil cinema. "Bombay" hypostatizes in one signifier the transformative allure of modernity, both material (a new life in the city, the possibility of making a living—however precarious—on one's own terms) and phantasmic (the spectacular imaginaries of Bollywood, which increasingly play with the place of Indianness within a globalizing world).

A visitor to India will frequently be given apparently contradictory characterizations of Bombay. Bombay is a dazzling microcosm of the diversity of the nation. But Bombay is also nothing like "the real India," the India of half a million villages. In India, Bombay is everywhere and nowhere. Writes Amrit Gangar: "Bombay is often called Mayapuri, the city of *maya* — of illusion. . . . It is a generic city that exists everywhere in India in various forms" (Gangar 1996, 210). And yet Bombay can be sickeningly concrete in its uncompromising juxtaposition of extremes: the fingerless hand of a beggar brushing imploringly against the tinted window of an imported car; skyscrapers reaching into space with rickety slum shacks clustering around their foundations.

The all-India meanings of "Bombay" prefigure, on a national level, the imaginary imbrication of the local by the global. And the signifier "Bombay," in both its material and phantasmic dimensions, prefigures the restless mediation of concretion through generality that is the mark of the commodity image. Like the commodity image, furthermore, "Bombay," even within India, extends its connotations beyond India itself and into an imagined global field of modernity, of transactions, identities, and physical forms, into "the limitless space of the foreign" (Kelsky 1999, 232). Christopher Pinney describes the use of "cityscape" backdrops and vintage motorcycles in the prop-repertoire of the traveling studios of provincial Indian portrait photographers:

> The travelling studios that frequently used to come to Nagda always had an Enfield or a Yezdi, almost always positioned in front of a dramatic urban scene of bridges, high-rise buildings and a sky filled with planes inscribing dramatic vapour trails. It is against such a backdrop that Guman Singh of Bhatisuda sits astride his bike in front of a hybridized cityscape more suggestive (to me) of New York or Chicago than anywhere else, but which Bhatisuda villagers and Nagdarites will unequivocally identify as Bombay, the city which for them symbolized all that is most dramatically good and bad in the modern. (Pinney 1997, 183)

As a set of connotations "Bombay" thus indicated a recognizably Indian space of meaning, while at the same time opening onto a transcendently global vista; as Pinney puts it in a later essay, "The metropolitan effect that Indian popular culture invokes . . . is one that operates independently of America and of a particular version of capitalism" (Pinney 2001, 13). It was fitting, then, that the RightAway product launch should be held inside the futuristic monolith of the Centaur Hotel, situated in the heart of the *filmi*-identified Bombay suburb of Juhu, not far from Sahar International Airport. A triumph of spectacle, the launch pushed RightAway as far as it would go. After that, it was time to pick up the pieces.

Staging the Technological Sublime: The Launch

In a glittering Centaur ballroom, a couple of hundred Bombay EMW mobile dealers, dressed in suits and collectively moving toward a state of advanced refreshment, were treated to a show. The first half would introduce the product; the second was given over to the coaxings and coquetries of pop singer Sunita Rao. A lavish Mughlai banquet had been laid out on tables down the left side of the hall and a bar stocked with scotch and beer did brisk business in an adjoining room. The odd celebrity, among them *tabla* maestro Zakir Hussain, could be spotted in the throng.

The lights dimmed and a sprightly young female video jockey (VJ), recognizable from Channel V broadcasts, bounced onto the stage. Bantering lightly, she congratulated the crowd on being the kind of brave and rugged souls who would suffer the vicissitudes of a rush-hour Bombay traffic jam for EMW mobile. Suddenly adopting a serious tone, as if speaking of grave strategic matters to an audience of select dignitaries, she listed a few of EMW's past innovations before concluding: "Today EMW is going to make our lives even easier. But first: EMW believes in the best. And since you are all part of this great company, you *are* the best." Thus reassured of their excellence, yet reminded of its corporate source, the assembled dealers were shown two company audiovisuals.

The first of these moved further in elucidating the chain of EMW's excellence: against a backdrop of the history of human tool use and technological innovation, EMW appeared as the embodiment, the distillation, of a universal history of human self-improvement. Backed by crashing, momentous chords, a gravely voice-over intoned: "In the beginning . . ." as the abstraction of collective human progress was anthropomorphically manifested as an animated, bare-breasted super-man, flexing his biceps and torso with each startling leap of civilizational evolution. Landscapes and oceans of possibility gave birth to a generic prehistory, while history itself, somewhat oddly, began only in 1969, with the first manned mission to the moon. This moment was itself, however, presented as the culmination of millennia spent gazing at a mysterious disc in the heavens: "One day, man thought, he would set foot there." Seated in the midst of the audience, the agency team exchanged puzzled glances. Images of great men were now flashing across the screens, beginning with perhaps the very first Indian mass brand, Mahatma Gandhi, followed in superimposed succession by Martin Luther King Jr. and Nelson Mandela. Meanwhile, the narrator explained that what brought them all together was that they "believed in possibility." Such faith, finally, bound all aspiring humanity together in a generalized (male) figure: "All he needs to do is believe . . . believe in the best." The camera pulled back for the final clincher: the entire epic narrative subsumed under the corporate identity as the earth, receding, morphed into the blue circle of the EMW logo.

Amid scattered applause, the screens came alive once more, this time filled with a crunching rendition of a song in American hard-rock style, purpose-built around the company slogan. More images of soaring and sweeping met the eyes of the dealers, as a passionate, gut-wrenching voice bellowed: "We will fly to the sun, find a place in the sun, because we believe in the best." A chorus chanted: "We believe in the best, we believe . . ." The strangulated voice continued: "We will reach above, be the eagle not the dove," as, once again, images of great men materialized, this time at a finer level of cultural resolution; these faces were all key figures of modern Indian entertainment: Amitabh Bachchan (included in an otherwise rather "high cultural" selection by dint of his brand-representative role), Ravi Shankar, Satyajit Ray, and others.

The adrenaline-stirring sequence of videos was followed by a series of dealer pep talks from leading EMW executives; afterward, the product-launch portion of the evening reached its climax with the literal unveiling of the new product. The moment itself was again framed by audiovisual clips, this time commissioned by the agency from a local directorial duo. A frenetic montage of images ensued, suggesting executive strivings mediated by high-tech equipment, all enacted against a generic office-cum-cityscape backdrop. E-mail scrolled down computer terminal screens, executives with granite profiles spoke assertively into cell phones, and jumbo jets roared into the sunset over "Bombay" figured as global metropolitan power grid. Moments were seized, opportunities taken — RightAway.

Suddenly the public address system came to life with a loud fanfare as searchlights swiveled frantically around the auditorium. The assembled crowd craned their necks curiously. Black curtains at the rear of the stage parted automatically to reveal a massive RightAway mural. Just as it seemed as if all this buildup had been in the service of nothing more exciting than being confronted by yet another poster, the mural itself silently split down the middle, and out lurched a gigantic duplicate RightAway pack, photorealistically constructed in three dimensions, accompanied by deafening pyrotechnics, billowing dry ice, and showers of confetti. Shuddering to a halt, the monstrous pack came to rest in the middle of the stage.

As I watched, my own thoughts ("talk about commodity fetishism" giving way to a sensation of being like one of the perplexed anthropoid apes confronted by the inscrutable monolith in Stanley Kubrick's *2001: A Space Odyssey*) were abruptly interrupted by the thunderous reactivation of the video screens. I soon realized that my intimations of quasi divinity were not simply the product of academic transference, as we were shown the image of a man, dressed in a business suit, walking toward a gateway through which light of a blinding brilliance was streaming. Beyond this gateway, rolling fields of fire could dimly be surmised. Striding closer to this ambiguous point of no return, this threshold of transcendence, the hero was suddenly engulfed in a dramatic (but harmless) deluge of EMW appliances raining down on all sides. Finally, with inevitable bathos, the sublime hereafter was revealed in all its concrete detail as an EMW retail outlet. Slapping his credit card onto the counter, the hero was liberated, becoming mobile RightAway. From the beginning of time, through a spectacular encounter with a gigantic box, now sitting inertly amid settled confetti, we had been taken to a vision of the hereafter: an EMW mobile gallery masquerading as the technological sublime.

The agency team working on RightAway had, on one level, managed to reconcile the divergent requirements of the product by constructing an image of locality that was at the same time nowhere in particular. This solution, evolved by trial and error through a "feeling-out" process between the agency's ideas and internal dynamics on the one hand, and the client's responses on the other, was all the more credible in that it drew upon an already established set of affective connotations for which "Bombay" was the generic name. The product launch had, by all accounts, gone down well with the dealers. EMW mobile's sales manager, in a subsequent meeting, all but slapped the agency manager on the back: "A *racy* film, *yaar!* Can we do something more like that? Something very *techno,* you know?"

And yet, for all its sound and fury, this solution was an imperfect sleight of hand, a short-term quick fix. Having removed all specific representations of locality from the advertising images, RightAway was unable in itself to fulfill EMW and the agency's joint long-term requirement, namely the transformation of the affective surge of an arresting set of images into a brand identity that would enable an extendable connection, ostensibly between consumer and company, but equally between client and agency. Market research, as we have seen, equated the EMW brand with warmth and locality, and prevailing marketing wisdom suggested that existing connotations were the compulsory point of departure for any project of reinvention. In Randall Rothenberg's words:

> To succeed, advertising cannot seek to invent a new soul. Instead, it must reinforce and redirect the existing image. It must serve as a form of mythology, providing the corporation's various and often competing constituencies — of which consumers are only one of many — heroes, villains, principles, rules of conduct and stories with which they can rally the faithful to remain true to the cause. Only then, with luck and effort can they win new converts. (Rothenberg 1995, 427)

How long could the agency go on relying on sheer spectacle, on inchoate excitement? And what was to be the point of connection between the work it had already done on RightAway and the existing "soul" of the corporation?

Conclusion

This chapter has been the first half of my consideration of an Indian high-tech brand struggling with the politics of locality raised by the globalization of consumer markets. I have argued that telecommunications technologies occupy a unique position vis-à-vis such markets, as both signs and means. Telecommunications signify ambiguously: they suggest, at once, a technological transcendence of concrete locality and a means for reconstituting locality through the intimacy of human communication. As signs, they underwrite two ideological visions of the cultural politics of globalization: on the one hand, the idea of the global market that supersedes all local particularity; on the other, the neo-Hegelian vision that the Amitabh Bachchan corporate ads expressed — cultural difference confirmed and redeemed in a higher global unity. Both of these visions represent a desire to transcend the inequities of the past. But as my account in this chapter suggests, even at the heart of the commodity imaging project, the legacy of the past continues to inform imagined futures by way of embodied responses and preferences.

To be sure, the horror that several of the people working on the EMW mobile account felt at concrete references to locality could not, and should not, be understood apart from a cultural politics of distinction, which helped to define them as members of a postcolonial elite. And yet, however much such impulses served to reproduce an exclusive social agenda, their very spontaneity demonstrated that none of the liberatory claims made on behalf of consumerist globalization could afford to dispense with the actuality of historical experience.

My focus in chapter 6 will be on the notion of *the brand* — its role in marketing discourse and its central part in the management of the client-agency relationship. It was through the agency's continuing attempts to reconcile the spectacular monster that they had created — RightAway — with their need for a coherent brand narrative that they finally came to confront the contradictions at the heart of the utopian ideal of the "global Indian citizen."

6

Bombay Local:

Mobility and Locality II

In chapter 5, I told the story of how a persistent structural problem—an Indian-identified brand in a globally identified product category—was temporarily ameliorated by recourse to spectacle. Even as the launch party confetti was settling, however, the agency team was aware that a longer-term solution needed to be found. What they required was a brand narrative that would serve two purposes at once: first, to capture and harness the energy and excitement generated by the RightAway visuals; and second, to align the "international" and "hip" tone of RightAway with the "warm" and "Indian" qualities of the motherbrand.

This chapter is, in part, an account of the steps that the agency team took to achieve these goals. But it is also a more general meditation on the peculiar cultural politics of a conceptual entity that exists at the core of contemporary marketing discourse—the brand. Brands are a conceptual extension of trademarks. Historically, trademarks enabled manufacturers to establish a "relationship" with customers that potentially bypassed the personalized authority of local retailers (Coombe 1998; Strasser 1989). Ostensibly a guarantee of quality, trademarks also enabled corporations to establish a legal right to a certain "identity," which was embodied in particular visual symbols (logos) and advertising images. Brands take this claim to control over publicly circulated signs much further, insofar as they attempt to establish—through advertising, promotions, and the strategic saturation of our everyday physical environments—virtual *worlds* into which consumers are encouraged to enter, as if by privileged identification.

In the discussion that follows, I examine several aspects of the cultural politics of the creation of these brand worlds—the way they attach an element of gift exchange to mass-produced commodities, or, seen from a slightly different perspective, the way they attempt to attach intimacy and concretion to exchange relationships that are increasingly anonymous and abstract. Of course it goes without saying that, in the rounds of everyday life, consumers—individually and collectively—construct all kinds of intimate and idiosyncratic relationships with the products they consume. What I am arguing is that branding is the way that manufacturers, and the advertising agencies that serve them, attempt to appropriate or preempt this intimacy so as to realize higher levels of profit.

Marketing theorists tend to uphold a kind of utopian ideal in which expertly managed, perfectly positioned brands enable a kind of alchemical transformation of consumer loyalty, based on experiential satisfaction, into corporate profits. For now, I would prefer to leave open the question regarding the relationship between corporate branding and consumer experience. Anthropological studies of consumption indicate that the affective surges provided by stark commodity images circulate in far less predictable ways than the best-laid marketing plans would have us believe. Nevertheless, the norms and forms of marketing discourse should be taken seriously insofar as they provide an orientation for marketing practice, a conceptual framework through which marketing and advertising professionals navigate their world.

Like any would-be science, the professional legitimacy of marketing discourse depends in part upon the apparent correspondence of its categories to those of the "objective world"—in this case, to the world of consumers. Like other positivistically inclined disciplines, marketing tends to downplay the degree to which its procedures help to mold the categories that it claims merely to discover (I will give a concrete example of this in chapter 7). The analogy starts to fall apart, however, when we attend more closely to the everyday *practice* of marketing. Suddenly it starts to look more like charismatic prophecy clothed in a scientific idiom. Marketing practitioners and theorists do not lie when they offer their science as a tool with which to manage consumers. But the promise does contain a deceptive displacement, because the consumers that are managed are not so much the ones who purchase the branded goods but above all the corporate client executives who "buy into" the categories of marketing discourse. This displacement, furthermore, serves a key legitimating function in that it enables all kinds of hunches, preferences, and tactical devices to be given an "objective" foundation in the name of the needs of "the" consumer. This became clear to me as I watched my agency informants use this discourse, and in particular the idea of the brand, first to make sense of their own activities and then to attempt to regulate their relationship with the client.

The agency's immediate problem, as I have shown, was the need to come up with a credible solution to the EMW Group/RightAway relationship. But this particular task was never entirely separable from the agency's own ongoing, more speculative plans to carve out larger chunks of the EMW business for itself. To this end, solving the Right-Away problem was only the first step in a larger project of constructing a compelling vision of the EMW brand as a whole. In the words of the creative director, the aim was "to make ourselves indispensable" to the client. In relation to this goal, the spectacular prominence of Right-Away was beginning to look like an eyesore.

The Brand as Prosthetic Personality

The pressure to develop a coherent brand narrative was coming from all quarters. Despite the EMW mobile executive's enchantment with RightAway, his superiors — more removed from the agency's magic show — soon complained that there seemed to be no sense of connection between the stark imagery of RightAway and the profile of the EMW brand as a whole. Having spent vast sums of money on advertising to build up their brand as a dignified, but also warm Indian alternative to the multinationals, the corporation was reluctant to spend more money on advertising that contradicted or diluted this image. In a meeting with the agency team, members of the EMW top brass expressed their concerns about the need to "synergize the retail segment."

All the market surveys continued to suggest that if EMW had a single strength vis-à-vis its competitors, then it was its intimacy and warmth. And when I asked an account planner from a different agency what he thought EMW needed to do, he framed it in similar terms:

I'll give you my personal view. I've always felt that you cannot be what you aren't. You know? And I think one of the things where

EMW has not realized it consistently is the fact that they are . . . as a company, they are *not about technology*. They're not about high-tech. That's not their core competency, you know? Inventions don't come out of EMW. It's all screwdriver technology. It's all borrowed stuff. So it's very difficult for them to get onto that platform, I believe, and sustain it in the long run. Just because that market is in a nascent stage, and therefore you want to jump on the bandwagon and be seen as the high-tech innovators, and so on and so forth, sort of smacks of opportunism. And, in fact, in the process they are ignoring their biggest strength, which is their relationship with the Indian public. I think EMW's point of difference lies not so much in its technology but in its personality. It's a far more *vibrant* company. . . . They're always into events. They are touching you in your life in various ways. It's very difficult for a Sony or a Panasonic or a Sharp or anyone to come and match them on that.

This external criticism resonated, in fact, with internal concerns. An account planner from the agency's Delhi office was visiting Bombay and was given the chance to peruse the proofs of the RightAway package. With the creative team and the account executive eagerly clustered around him, he reflected: "The graphic, the artwork is there. But I think that there's an overall idea, in terms of the writing, that you need to bind it into. It needs to be a unity of form, a *tonal* thing. There's a *voice* that needs to cut across all these." The art director objected that this would be hard to achieve given the highly various profiles of the products and events that EMW put its name to. The planner shook his head. "I'm not saying you should take this as an example, but if it were Nike, you'd see it in Nike language. Do you see what I mean? It's not necessarily a question of content, but of *voice*. The danger here is that each campaign will end up reflecting only the product offer and not the voice of the brand."

Finding the brand's "voice" would allow it to "touch" consumers "in their lives," that is to address them *intimately*. For this to be possible, the "voice" itself would first have to be solidly established. In client-agency meetings, the agency manager spoke to his opposite number about the need to create the impression that the concrete particulars of the various product offerings would indicate a recognizably shared point of origin: "They should look like they belong to the same family. Family resemblance, yet keeping [their] distinctiveness in place.

More than a look and feel, will it look like they come from what I call the same *source identity?*" Often leaning on the metaphor of personality, such a "source identity" would provide the basis of the "voice" that could then speak with credible intimacy to consumers. Crucially, the desired demonstration of the effectively articulated brand was the consumer's sense of being singled out — or, in Althusserian terms, interpellated. "Now that the physical product has happened," the agency manager told his client, "the aim is to create in the consumer a sense of 'it talks to *me!*' "

Taken together, then, the construction of the brand required the imagining of a brand *personality* and the articulation of a distinctive voice on the basis of this personality. These metaphors are basic to the contemporary marketing imagination. David Aaker, preeminent among U.S. marketing theorists, writes: "A *brand personality* can be defined as the set of human characteristics associated with a given brand. Thus it includes such characteristics as gender, age, and socioeconomic class, as well as such classic human personality traits as warmth, concern, and sentimentality" (Aaker 1995, 141). In what Aaker calls "the self-expression model," a brand may be offered to the consumer as a medium for self-identification: "The premise of the self-expression model is that for certain groups of customers, some brands become vehicles to express a part of their self-identity. This self-identity can be their actual identity or an ideal self to which they might aspire" (153).

From this perspective the relatively dowdy connotations of the EMW brand were clearly a potential problem. Yet Aaker goes on to suggest that some brands work precisely by having personalities that consumers do not necessarily *identify* with, but which they can *trust*. This is "the relationship basis model." "Some people may never aspire to have the personality of a competent leader but would like to have a relationship with one, especially if they need a bank or a lawyer. A trustworthy, dependable, conservative personality might be boring but might nevertheless reflect characteristics valued in a financial advisor, a lawn service, or even a car — consider the Volvo personality" (159).

Above all, argues Aaker, the brand should not be conceived as a static entity but rather as an "active partner" in the relationship.

When considering brand personality, the natural tendency is to consider the brand to be a passive element in the relationship. The focus is upon consumer perceptions, attitudes, and behaviour *toward* the brand; attitudes and perceptions of the brand itself are hidden behind the closed doors of the organization. Yet your relationship with another person is deeply affected by not only who that person is but what that person thinks of you. Similarly, a brand-customer relationship will have an active partner at each end, the brand as well as the customer. (161)

Aaker's prescriptions should be understood as something more than formalized commodity fetishism. The notion of the active, personalized brand is a fundamental component of the manner in which a consumer goods corporation is encouraged, within marketing discourse, to imagine its intervention into the public realm through the medium of a kind of prosthetic personality.[1] The tactile concreteness of the images that make much advertising so attention-grabbing is matched by the peculiar intimacy with which it hails its audience. David Ogilvy, British-born legend of the American advertising business, advises: "Do not . . . address your readers as though they were gathered together in a stadium. When people read your copy, they are *alone*. Pretend you are writing each of them a letter on behalf of your client. One human being to another, second person *singular*. Queen Victoria complained that Gladstone talked to her as if he were addressing a public meeting. She preferred Disraeli, who talked to her like a human being. When you write copy, follow Disraeli's example" (Ogilvy 1983, 80).[2]

Indra Sinha, a copywriter of Indian origin who has lived and worked in the U.K. for a number of years, expresses both ethical and aesthetic doubts about this tone:

It is . . . an interesting fact that the second person narrative (i.e. where the narrator addresses the listener/reader as "you"), is most commonly found in pornographic fantasy, advertising and interactive text-based computer games. In each case the word "you" is used to create an illusion of a human interaction, but the narrator is actually manipulating the "you" character, who has no real power to affect the exchange. This is the situation that the copywriter finds him or herself in. It is a rather bleak moral position — an impossible one for a novelist. But struggles to justify, aggrandize or rectify it are doomed to be ridiculous. (Thakraney 1998)

Both the eroticized solicitude of commercial publicity and its apparently fraudulent appropriation of an ideal of reciprocal exchange have been at the heart of critical analyses of "consumer culture." With his customary acuteness, Marx recognized this opportunistic intimacy at the very dawn of mass marketing: "[The producer] puts himself at the service of the [customer's] most depraved fantasies, plays the pimp between him and his need, excites in him morbid appetites, lies in wait for each of his weaknesses—all so that he can then demand the cash for this service of love" (Tucker 1978, 94). Over a century later, in a social world now profoundly mediated by new forms of mass publicity, Jean Baudrillard noted that consumer goods, by means of their eroticization, simulate a relationship in which the identity of the consumer is at once affirmed and constructed. By means of advertising, products "submit themselves to us, they seek us out, surround us, and prove their existence to us by virtue of the profusion of ways in which they appear, by virtue of their effusiveness. We are taken as the object's aims, and the object *loves* us. And because we are loved, we feel that we exist: we are 'personalized' " (Baudrillard 1996, 171).

What David Aaker presents as ideal-typical alternatives—"self-expression" or "relationship basis"—may perhaps better be read dialectically as the simultaneous tasks of the successful brand. Insofar as it is a coherently structured set of connotations, it can be offered to consumers as a virtual world, into which it is both their human right and their social privilege to be invited. In W. F. Haug's words: "The commodities are surrounded by imaginary spaces which individuals are supposed to enter and to fill in with certain acts. If an individual acts within them, these spaces organize his/her way of experiencing these acts and personal identity" (Haug 1987, 123). Yet at the same time, it is crucial that these "spaces" do not appear to be artificially *imposed* by corporate interests; rather, their content and meaning—while necessarily remaining the product and property of the corporation—should appear simply as a means by which consumers' existing identities and aspirations may be expressed and enacted.

Brands consequently take on an attitude that is simultaneously paternalistic and servile. From one perspective, their visual signs (logos, trademarks) operate like nothing so much as medieval royal insignia: consumers who wear these signs on their bodies are thus literally incorporated as loyal vassals, and Habermas's pessimistic diagnosis of the "refeudalization" of the public sphere by commercial interests rings true: "In the measure that it is shaped by public relations, the public sphere of civil society again takes on feudal features. The 'suppliers' display a showy pomp before customers ready to follow. Publicity imitates the kind of aura proper to the personal prestige and super-natural authority [once associated with divinely sanctioned kingship]" (Habermas 1989, 195). And indeed, one of the EMW mobile focus group respondents, as the account executive was quick to point out to the client, had explained that he expected to be looked after by EMW "as a father looks after a child."

From another perspective, however, this seemingly anachronistic mode of legitimacy is justified precisely in terms of its apparent op-posite: democratic populism. It is by faithfully serving the sovereign will and desire of the individual consumer that a brand may flourish. Seen from this angle, no customer wish should be judged too trivial to qualify as the corporation's command. For all its lordly and spectacu-lar stature, the mighty global brand is merely the humble servant of the least of its customers.[3] The brand must be at once intimate and awe-inspiring, nestled into the folds of our everyday domestic routines while at the same time flexing its muscles on the battlefields of the global market. In this, the brand recapitulates the duality of bour-geois (consumer) citizenship, at once a chest-thumping concentration of ruthless economic prowess and a genteel patron of the arts. How is this balancing act negotiated?

Keeping-While-Giving the Brand

While the structure of the brand depends upon a metaphor of person-ality, the practice of branding is built upon a metaphor of gift exchange. Branding effectively presents itself as an attempt to re-enchant a disen-chanted set of market relationships. My propositions here lean on the august tradition of anthropological writing on gift exchange. But by transposing the themes of this literature into the world of the mass-produced commodity, my hypothesis also requires that some deeply embedded conceptual distinctions be reconsidered.

It was of course Marcel Mauss who brought together a range of ethnological evidence in the service of a theory of social life that took the circulation of gifts as its foundation. Gift exchange brought to-gether in a single idiom the possibility of egalitarian reciprocity and the potential—as in the Kwakiutl potlatch—for agonistic status competition. Most crucially, "the spirit of the gift"—the mysterious element that cried out for the gift to be returned—linked the constitution of individual social identity to the perpetuation of the social whole: "If one gives *oneself*, it is because one 'owes' oneself—one's person and one's goods—to others" (Mauss 1990, 46, emphasis in original). The influence of Mauss's formulation, not only on the structuralist anthropology of Lévi-Strauss, but, through it, on French postwar thought in general, can hardly be overstated.

The Maussian emphasis on reciprocity and circulation was called into question by a subsequent generation of anthropologists, many of them working in and around the Melanesian island groups that had provided, through Malinowski (1922), Mauss's "kula ring" material. Despite differences of local detail, the work of these researchers converged upon the proposition that the management of social identity—the whole calculus of rank and reciprocity—had at least as much to do with *keeping* valuable objects as with giving them (Damon 1980; Godelier 1999; Munn 1992; Weiner 1985, 1992, 1994). Or rather, as Annette Weiner's influential formulation has put it, the problem was one of "keeping-while-giving." Keeping while giving, she argues, "is essential if one is to retain some of one's social identity in the face of potential loss and the constant need to give away what is most valued" (Weiner 1985, 211). If one's social standing is powerfully embodied in one's ownership of particular valuable objects, and yet such objects must be exchanged in order to cement social relations of alliance and patronage, then something that will continue inalienably to link the giver with the gift that has been exchanged becomes necessary. For Weiner this something is the mysterious and much-debated "force" that the Maori called *hau,* and which Mauss glossed as the "spirit of the gift," the element that demands a return (but also recognition) on pain of death or injury.[4] Whereas the Maussian reading of hau stressed its role in maintaining reciprocity, Weiner and her contemporaries were equally if not more concerned with hau as a vehicle for the prestigious name, or in Nancy Munn's terms, the "fame," of the giver. Some latter-day readers of Mauss have pointed out that, taken in conjunction with his political writings, the essay on the gift was in part intended as an exploration of the possibility of establishing an ethically binding system of reciprocity in modern industrial societies (Graeber 2001; Hart 2000). But in general, anthropologists have unfortunately persisted in contrasting societies organized around large-scale commodity markets with those in which the exchange of singular valuables plays a socially constitutive role.[5]

What I am suggesting is that the practice of branding is a game of keeping-while-giving, but one that is played on precisely the terrain where mainstream economic anthropology suggests it should not be possible: the market in mass-produced commodities.

Branded consumer goods combine the two categories that in Maori terminology are opposed: *taonga,* or valuables, and *oloa,* objects exchanged primarily on the basis of their functional utility. In themselves, marketing writers argue, mass-produced goods are "merely" commodities, akin to the Maori oloa, functional items humiliatingly forced to compete upon price. In the words of one Indian commentator: "You can't call yourself a brand if the market dictates your price. You're a commodity, sometimes a distress-sale commodity."[6] At the same time, Harvard professor of marketing Theodore Levitt insists that no product is irrevocably doomed to "commodity" status: "There is no such thing as a commodity. All goods and services are differentiable" (Ogilvy 1983, 140). Brands, one might say, are the hau that lends an aspect of taonga to what are otherwise merely oloa. They are the inalienable source of value that enables a corporation to keep its identity while simultaneously appearing to give of itself every time one of its products is sold.[7] Just as, in Weiner's account, part of the value and power of the ideally inalienable object comes from the risk of its loss, so corporations are constantly battling the threat of piracy, counterfeiting, and parody (Betting 1996; Coombe 1998).[8]

One might object that the brand cannot really be a gift since consumers agree to pay a premium for it. Does not a cash payment cancel any obligation that a gift exchange might impose? The branded good is certainly ambiguous in this regard. But I would argue that corporations, insofar as they subscribe to the discourse of branding, try to have it both ways. Premium brands certainly do enable producers to charge a premium price. And yet at the same time, the gift of the brand cannot really be repaid in kind, but is instead envisioned as the basis and justification for the customer's emotional loyalty to the corporation. Baudrillard writes: "To understand properly the term *response,* one must appreciate in it a meaning at once strong, symbolic, and primitive: power belongs to him who gives and to whom no return can be made. To give, and to do it in such a way that no return can be made, is to break exchange to one's profit and to institute a monopoly: the social process is out of balance" (Poster 1988, 208). It is, one might conclude, crucial for the functioning of the brand that it both can and cannot be repaid. Branding attempts to impose onto the impersonality of commodity exchange the appearance of a unique, emotionally textured relationship. At the same time, while ceaselessly referring to the interests of consumers, it nevertheless in the final instance depends upon asserting total corporate authority over this process.

Bearing all this in mind, it is perhaps not surprising that a temporary solution to the EMW/RightAway alignment crisis should have appeared precisely in the literal guise of gift exchange.[9]

A Season of Gifting

I do not mean to suggest that the discourse of branding is merely a cynical ploy. With Walter Benjamin, I believe that mass-circulated images—including those in advertising—hold the potential for tapping deeply resonant (and potentially "subversive") registers of affect and recollection. My account would certainly not be complete if I failed to mention the extent to which many of my informants felt themselves, quite sincerely, to be emotionally tied to the brands they handled. One executive, who had spent a couple of years "servicing"[10] Coca-Cola, told me: "Coke was my first wife." Even his second (human) wife had, in the lead-up to the decline that would eventually culminate in her husband's agency's humiliating loss of the account, insisted: "You *are* Coke—they can't take it away from you and give it to someone else!" This (Christian) executive also recalled being new on the Coke account and far from home at Christmas when a video featuring the new Coke Christmas ads appeared in the office. Watching this tape, which concluded with a scene featuring Santa Claus handing the gift of Coke (and thereby the brand) to a young boy, the executive was in his turn overcome with emotion—and comforted—by this corporate gift. (Incidentally, we might consider in this connection the fact that Baudrillard likens our attitude toward advertised goods to children's belief in Santa Claus [Baudrillard 1996]).

The EMW/Rightaway crisis was, as it happened, deepening precisely at the dawn of a season in which gift exchange, locality, and sentiment could be connected. The EMW mobile executive was, as we have seen, personally entranced by the RightAway package. But he was also acutely conscious of his superiors' concerns about the coherence of the brand, as well as his sales force's demands for some advertising that would exploit the approach of Divali — the "festival of lights," which also marked the beginning of the wedding season.

Each year, Divali is the occasion for a slew of heavily sentimental advertising tie-ins, combining, as it does, gift exchange with themes of family ties, patriotism, and material success. Insofar as it inaugurates the wedding season, it also brings to mind a very particular gift: *kanyadan*, the gift of a Hindu daughter (literally, "the gift of a virgin") to the groom's family. In the rush to "emotionalize" EMW mobile, all these strains came together. In an agency-client meeting, the EMW mobile executive stressed the need to capitalize upon the sentimental currency of "gifting": "This has to be gifting with emotion," he explained. "Gifting *is* emotion. Don't say 'EMW — now we can gift.' Work on the emotion. I don't want a tear-jerker, but I want . . . moist eyes. I want a kick-ass film that will not be a tear-jerker but will make me feel warm." Then he brought out his inspiration, a press ad mock-up generated by the agency's Bangalore office. Linking together the wedding theme with the aspect of "communication" that the cellular phone provided, the ad literalized the larger aim of the brand: keeping-while-giving. It featured a tearful but stoical father presenting his daughter, elaborately dressed in wedding finery and about to depart with her new husband, with a package. The line read: "How do you assure that someone who is going away doesn't go away?" Elaborated the EMW executive: "We need to dwell on the emotion of gifting rather than the emotion of separation."

The members of the agency creative team were appalled at what they saw as the banal sentimentality of the project, but their boss was keen to secure the large billings that television spots would generate. Moreover, the EMW mobile executive had effectively bought the creative team's commitment to the wedding spot by waxing unexpectedly enthusiastic about a proposed future series of high-tech animated RightAway spots, tentatively to be produced at Industrial Light and Magic (ILM) in California. The creative team tried their best to bring some stylistic "edginess" to the wedding spot, but their worst fears were confirmed at a pre-production meeting, when the director recommended by the EMW mobile executive produced his own alternate version of the script, entitled "Cry Film."

The commercial that eventually emerged combined what the entire agency team felt to be grotesquely overwrought sentimentality with spectacular components that were both locally resonant and carefully "aspirational": all the visual paraphernalia of an affluent Hindu wedding (elaborate jewelry and *mehendi* tracings on the hands and feet of the bride) set against the backdrop of a conspicuously luxurious bungalow in the Bombay suburb of Bandra. The product itself—the Right-Away pack—appeared rather incongruously in a zoom shot as the father handed it to the bride, an act soon capped by the baseline: "Keep your dear ones near you."

Troubled as they initially were by the aesthetic parameters of the finished spot, a subtle process of post-rationalization soon provided the requisite justifications. Having cut his teeth in the commercial Hindi film industry, the spot's director would brook no argument on popular tastes. The question was one of appealing to the masses, but also specifically to the *Indian* masses. In the discussion that erupted following the unveiling of his lachrymosely rewritten script, he insisted—successfully—that subtlety was out: "Indian audiences demand full-scale emotion" (see Ganti 2000 for an elaboration of this point vis-à-vis Hindi film). Conversely, and this worried the creative team, who had developed such a deliberately nonlocalized product image for RightAway, emotion also seemed to demand full-scale Indianness. In the course of recording the soundtrack for the spot, which combined synthesized strings with the mournful tones of a *shehnai* and a few phrases from a female Indian classical singer added on at the emotional climax, someone remarked that the version of the ad with a Hindi voice-over appeared to be working better than its English-language counterpart. "Of course," shrugged the director. "It's a Hindi emotion."

The EMW mobile executive had demanded an emotional spot. But back at the agency, the creative director had laughed in the creative team's faces when shown a video of the commercial. Accordingly, the account executive took on board the director's rationalization of its content. Preparing to present the video to his client, he briefed me: "I'll tell him we've gone right down the middle with this one. This is not left or right of center, but very clichéd." Like the director, he reached for the ostensibly objective affirmation of "the Indian consumer": "And that's because, when you're talking about weddings, the Indian consumer will *relate* to that kind of clichéd emotion. . . . I'm not saying this is the best ad film ever done. I'm not saying it's the worst. The question is: does it work? I'm not interested in producing advertising if I don't also know that the ad is working for me. We're not talking to each other when we're making advertising, we're talking to the bloody consumer. And he *relates* to cheese."

In the event, the account executive need not have worried; his client was as enthralled by the emotional charge of the wedding film as he had been captivated by the high-tech glamour of RightAway. Still, however, the basic structural problem of the account remained unresolved. For all that the wedding spot forcibly shoehorned the Right-Away pack into the affect-heavy context of multiple gift transactions, the connection was purely visual. There was still no *thematic* link between the "warmth" of the EMW brand, now given full voice, and the "happening" image of RightAway. The dramatic idiom of the gift had been the perfect vehicle for bringing out the affective resonances of the brand. But it had little to do with the specific appeal of the product. The agency account executive himself was quite clear on this. "Even if it's a seasonal thing," he asked me, "how many people do you know who would gift a cellular phone? And who would they gift it to? Either themselves or their wife. And even then, they're essentially buying it for themselves. And what about the bills? Do you agree to pay the bills as well? And if you gift a cellular phone, will you gift the top-end model? Then you're taking about forty grand [Rs 40,000, around U.S. $950 at the time]."

The desperate need for competitive spectacle had produced Right-Away, and the concern with "emotionalizing" the brand had generated the wedding spots. Both of these motives were real concerns for EMW mobile. In attempting to satisfy its client's desires, in both cases with little time to elaborate a coherent strategy, the agency's advertising had swung from pole to pole. And now, with EMW mobile's top brass skeptically arrayed on the opposite side of a large conference table, the agency team and the EMW mobile executive—this time seated together—were about to unveil the wedding spot. The biggest problem was to combine a justification for the extreme sentimentality of the commercial with the appearance of an overall strategic plan.

"When we made this film we wanted to attack the gifting segment," began the EMW mobile executive. "We felt that this segment could best be harnessed when using the *emotion* of gifting rather than the *process* of gifting. That's why we've taken a very emotional route that aims to stress EMW mobile as a gifting idea. Something you can gift to your near and dear ones." But what, wondered one of the corporate man-agers, was the connection between this theme and the overall image of RightAway? Quickly, the EMW mobile executive replied: "This is our reasoning on how we're going to bring together the happening, con-temporary image of RightAway as a whole with this gifting idea: we're using different mediums and different occasions now to highlight dif-ferent aspects of the product."

Conscious that his client's statement conveyed little in the way of discernible strategy, the agency office manager deftly intervened, intro-ducing a distinction between short-term tactics and long-term strategy: "Just to add — we're also working on the premise that we can capitalize on the timing here, with the marriage season just starting. Also we have scripted what we call theme ads. These are much more in line with the packaging of the product, and are being produced by ILM in Califor-nia. It's stuff that's hard to do here. They're going to be much more fun-oriented than this and represent our thinking on the *strategic* direction of the product. The gifting thing is one of the more *tactical* ways of selling it that we have taken. But you're very right — we're not going to *segment* it as a gifting item."

In fact, it was quite clear by this time to everyone on the agency team that the ILM spots were never going to be made. The EMW mobile executive had, in effect, used them as bait in order to hook the agency creative team into a commitment to do the wedding film. The agency had its "theme campaign" (see page 169), with which it assuaged its client's hunger for public grandeur. The much-mooted ILM spots had effectively become a similar device, only this time wielded by the client. Nevertheless, it was the agency manager — who, in relation to the cre-ative team frequently found himself situated on the client's side — who now saw fit rhetorically to resuscitate them.

Casting around for a suitable analogy from within the established system of brands, the agency manager alighted on the one Indian brand that was perhaps most strongly associated with gift-themed ad-vertising, Titan watches. "I think the example to learn from here is Titan. What they did was to first position the product and then present it as a gifting choice." Almost as soon as he had drawn the analogy, however, he appeared to realize that this was precisely what Right-Away, which had only just been launched, ran the risk of *not* doing. He rallied impressively: "What we're doing is we've collapsed the time between the two stages." Recovering his advantage, he proceeded to suggest that this approach was in fact in itself innovative rather than simply opportunistic: "Think of Titan. The difference is that Titan took an item [watches] that was already a gifting item. For us, we're dealing with a category [cellular phones] that's so new that we can take the opportunity of the timing to *introduce* it as a gifting item. But yes, the racy stuff, the fingers clicking, getting-off-the-train-or-the-plane-in-Bombay-and-getting-mobile, that will happen." Temporarily mollified, the EMW brass, most of them exuding an air of being pressed by more important issues, acquiesced to the film, eventually requiring only that the bride's mother's face, which the company director had apparently found "too garish," be blurred.

As always, the agency team left EMW mobile headquarters with the sense that cosmetic interventions were substituting for structural repairs. And so the next crisis to befall them was all the more unexpected: it seemed that the ads were actually working.

Unexpected Efficacy

Harshad Mehta, a man described by the agency copywriter as "the Michael Milken of India," published a column in the daily newspaper *Asian Age* in which he waxed enthusiastic about the prominence of the EMW brand. Particularly in the color television category, he argued, EMW was outdoing the multinationals without having to resort to the desperate tactic of the weaker brand: price competition. Mehta attributed much of its success to a close understanding of Indian consumers, manifested in the company's timely introduction of relevant models, and its excellent relations with dealers. Moreover, it seemed to Mehta that the brand itself had achieved a certain "critical mass" and, ironically, in view of the agency and client's perpetual worries, "synergy":

> [EMW] has excellent brand synergy in consumer durables in India. . . . Have you noticed that EMW doesn't sell EMW colour TVs or that it doesn't sell EMW washing machines? It simply sells EMW. So when EMW advertises for mobile phones in Mumbai, sales of colour TVs also rise. When EMW advertises for washing machines, refrigerators also sell. My reading is that EMW's power of advertising voice as a group has finally reached that critical mass where it is able to outsell Indian and international competition because it is a highly visible brand. (H. Mehta 1997)

When I showed Mehta's article to the copywriter, he snorted derisively: "Must be that he thinks it's synergy because all the ads have the same logo." The copywriter had himself just returned from a meeting at EMW mobile headquarters, where the company mood had been jubilant. The latest in-house "brand tracking" research had shown that, image-wise, EMW mobile was rapidly closing the gap on SamTech; respondents were increasingly calling it as hip, upscale, and sophisticated as its competitor. Amidst all the backslapping ("even I was clapping my hands"), the copywriter had nevertheless felt uneasy. Right-Away had been released only a few weeks earlier, and could therefore not have had any significant impact on the research results. Sheer visibility, it seemed, was having an effect that had nothing to do with carefully honed product image. And this, more or less, was also what Mehta's article was saying. "EMW's power of advertising voice" had created "a highly visible brand"; this *visibility*, rather than any *coherence*, had brought about a sense of "synergy."

Then the second bomb fell. Rumors started circulating that *Advertising & Marketing* magazine was about to name EMW the number one Indian brand. As it turned out, EMW's position in the survey was in fact somewhat less exalted than this; in a range of categories ("products are market leaders," "products offer value for money," "company has good relations with retailers/customers," "company's advertising is consistently superior," and so on), EMW routinely figured in the top six, but only came out on top in a single category, "company keeps in touch with the market constantly."

The result of all this apparently good news was, curiously, that the agency team was more apprehensive than ever. The ideal of the coherent brand served both as a powerful legitimating tool for the agency vis-à-vis its clients and as a practical guide for action. The implication that sheer spectacle might be just as effective as careful planning in the commercial public sphere was therefore highly unsettling. The orienting principle of the agency's work was that there should be a strategically intelligible relationship of cause and effect between its productive activities and events out there in the marketplace. *Failure* could always be blamed on imperfections or mistakes beyond the agency's control. One of the account executive's mantras was "advertising is only a subset of marketing"; in other words, the agency could not be held accountable for blunders of pricing, distribution, product design, and so on. The legendary Bill Bernbach was often cited by several of my informants to the same effect: "Nothing kills a bad product faster than good advertising." Unaccountable *success* was, however, a far more complicated beast. The agency team found itself in an ambiguous position. On the one hand, it seemed that the advertising was succeeding despite the lack of a coherent strategy. On the other hand, the agency's future on the account — and, even more, its chances of carving out larger chunks of the EMW business — depended on offering its client precisely such a strategy.

In part, this was a matter of performative credibility: did the agency look like it knew what it was doing? But the importance of the coherent brand discourse also extended to the agency team's own sense of being able to manage its relationship with the client. In chapter 5, I described the process of commodity image production as a constant dialectical movement between image and narrative. This movement was the basis of the apparently stable brand. In this chapter, I have argued that the discourse of branding rests upon a metaphor of keeping-while-giving. What I would like to suggest now is that while marketing theory requires that the exchange be figured as one between corporation and consumer, the really constitutive relationship of keeping-while-giving is the one that is elaborated between marketing and advertising professionals and their corporate clients.

Well-maintained brand narratives enable an advertising agency to perpetuate the impression of an agency-client relationship run according to mutual, rational, and measurable parameters. Ultimately, a coherently developed brand discourse becomes a kind of consensually maintained mutual fetish between agency and client, expressed in the form of a shared idiom. Executives pride themselves upon their exclusive understanding of the precise parameters of a particular brand. A brand thus appears as a shared substrate of image and meaning, which the corporation will then be able to extend into the public sphere. As a predictable semantic "environment," a space of meaning, the brand crucially *stabilizes* the seductive but unstable surges of affect that the agency's images introduce into their relationship with the client. Without such a stabilizing framework, the agency might do well in the short term but will be unable to formalize its success.

This is why the account executive was feeling squeezed on both sides. Over dinner one night at a Bandra restaurant specializing in "sizzlers" — grilled mounds of meat slathered with a heaped combination of grilled vegetables, cheese, rice and/or french fries — he expressed the ambivalence of the situation. From one perspective, the lack of clear strategy was the client's problem, and arose out of a frantic obsession with short-term predicaments.

If they would just relax and start thinking ahead a little bit, and give me some clearly stated objectives for at least one year in the future, I would be able to give them a brand plan. "Here is where we need to get to on sales." "This is what we need to do to build the theme campaign." I could give them a carefully planned approach on each of these levels. I could tell them, "Boss, so the numbers swing to their side a bit. *Relax* about the numbers — we're in this together for the long haul." If the client can give me a clear set of strategic objectives, then it's my job, as the agency representative, to come back with some solutions to their problems. If they can come up with a rational argument as to why the ideas don't work, in terms of the strategic objectives that they're trying to achieve, then fine. But don't give me comments like "I don't like it." They have no vision of where they're trying to go.

Ostensibly, the client's reluctance or inability to provide such a vision was a boon to the agency while it short-changed long-suffering consumers.

Like they call me up and they're shouting "Sales are demanding an ad!" What am I going to say? Am I going to say, "Boss, since when have sales dictated your marketing and communications strategy?" But of course I need the money. If you are a fool and you want to give me your money for another ad, sure I'll take it. And go laughing to the bank. How many times do you want me to go laughing to the bank? Do you know who has *really* been the beneficiary of the two phone companies put together? It's not been the consumer. It's been the support services providers: the agencies, the hoardings [billboard] operators, the mass media. We're laughing all the way to the bank!

For all his rhetorical bravado, the account executive also knew that the agency team was the most vulnerable link in the chain. If the client could not or would not come up with a clear strategy, the task would fall to the agency. And if the agency were not up to it, the account would, in all probability, soon be changing hands. In a quieter voice, the account executive continued: "The truth is that we're a mediocre,

small-sized agency, with mediocre employees. And I don't exclude myself from that description. By mediocre, I don't mean people's intelligence. I'm talking about the way work gets handled in the organization. We're like this," he illustrated, putting his hands in front of his
face, and then pulling them away as if in a sequence of layers, " 'here's a
job to do. Okay, that's done! What's next? And next? And next? And
then suddenly you're standing there wondering what the fuck happened. How do all the pieces fit together?"

The account executive's lament clearly expressed the stakes involved in the organizational failure of the agency-client relationship.
But this impasse was also a symptom of a far larger set of problems. It
would not, in fact, be an exaggeration to say that it expressed the
contradictions that lay at the very heart of the project of consumerist
globalization.

"Very Bombay": Reprise

I asked an account planner from another agency what he thought of
EMW Group's attempts to position itself as "globally Indian." His response was skeptical precisely in terms of the two problems besetting
the brand: the ratio of spectacle to meaning, and the vexed issue of
"Indianness."

> To me, even the Bachchan campaign was a combination of—these
> are probably harsh words to make a point—but I think it was a
> combination of being defensive and being irrelevant. And incredi-
> ble, all at the same time. Defensive, because you're wearing a chip
> on your shoulder about . . . the fact that "I'm an Indian and I'm
> having to compete." "I'm having to defend myself," you know. "It
> doesn't matter if I'm an Indian—I'm as good." So it smacks of
> defensiveness, and I'm not sure that it befits a leader, because EMW
> in a way had a bit of a leadership status. Incredible because Ami-
> tabh Bachchan is . . . I'm not sure how much weight his endorse-
> ment carries, in terms of actually getting people to believe that this
> is actually a better product, a better brand. You know? And if that
> doesn't happen, then it simply stops at being something that raises
> very quick top-of-mind awareness. Because Bachchan is a well-
> known figure and you ride on that, and you haven't seen him in ads
> ever. You've certainly sat up and noticed those ads and so you get

top-of-mind awareness. But I'm not sure whether EMW required top-of-mind awareness to begin with. I think they were an extremely top-of-mind brand. And after the Bachchan campaign, was I beginning to believe even one single thing about EMW which made it *my* brand, or made it a *preferred* brand? We've seen that, I think, in most countries including here, people aren't very nationalistic when it comes to purchase. . . . The consumer is saying that "I need the best value for money that I am spending. If you're giving it to me, and I'm buying it, it's a bit of a non-issue where you come from. I'm not going to buy you just because you're Indian." . . . People are still discovering the joys of choice. And they're discovering the joys of having all those glorious brand names within reach. So it's not good enough to tell them that "I'm Indian, therefore feel good about me, and buy me." Nobody's buying that logic in India. Therefore you've *got* to go out and tell them, either at a rational level or at an emotional level, something that brings them closer to the brand. Or something that tells them "why I'd rather be with EMW."

The globalization of brands was touted precisely on the basis that it would *liberate* both producers and consumers from the constraints of locality. In an equal field, all market players could now compete on the same terms.

Of course, on an economic level the claim was preposterous. But much of its appeal, I think, lay in its promise to liberate identity from history. Globalization represented, as I argued in chapter 4, the promise of finally transcending second-class citizenship status in the global ecumene. As such, it was the latest installment of a sequence of rhetorical gifts made in the name of universalism: bourgeois citizenship, nationalism, developmentalism. But it was also unique by virtue of the way in which it assigned to the figure of the consumer, with his or her incontrovertible desires, a decisive position of radical agency. In each case, however, the gift of universalism also came with a hidden and impossible price: the transcendence of history. As Immanuel Wallerstein puts it:

> In a historical system that is built on hierarchy and inequality, universalism is a "gift" of the powerful to the weak which confronts the latter with a double bind: to refuse the gift is to lose; to accept the gift is to lose. The only plausible reaction of the weak is neither to refuse nor to accept, or both to refuse and to accept — in short, the

path of the seemingly irrational zigzags (both cultural and political) of the weak that has characterized most of nineteenth and especially twentieth century history. (Tang 1993, 409)

The "gift" of globalization, which carries a universalist promise, implies a profound ambivalence vis-à-vis the value of the concrete, the locally embedded. Marcel Mauss argued that there is a deep-rooted tendency to assign value to that which is locally embedded. Taonga, or valuables, he writes, are generally "a class of goods that are more closely linked to the soil" (Mauss 1990, 10). The universalist gifts that have been the central offerings of the rhetoric of modernity — from the white man's burden to the disembodiment of cyberspace — challenge this equation on utopian grounds. Specific locations and particular modes of embodiment, insofar as they turn out to be barriers to this utopian transcendence, appear as historical ballast, but also — in a subaltern register, as it were — as a sensory key to a different way of being in the world. The politics of global consumer marketing are played out precisely at the intersection of the world-system of mass production and the political economy of local identity. In the words of a Singaporean entrepreneur: "We produce the Levi's, the computers and the spare parts, but we never have the brand" (Slater 2000, 58).[11]

Globalized consumerism appears, at first sight, to offer liberation from this unhappy consciousness. Since the desires of the sovereign consumer are always locally embedded, "cultural difference" becomes an officially legitimate parameter in global marketing, as well as a growth industry as a domain of professional expertise (as we will see in part 3). But this market multiculturalism imposes its own restrictions on membership. In some ways, these restrictions can be mapped "objectively": only those cultural identities at once globally recognizable and compatible with the existing global division of identity are admissible — think of the space designated "Indian" but yet left open in the original Amitabh Bachchan ads. But in another sense, this historical reproduction is always played out on a subjective level. We have seen one example of this process in the EMW mobile executive's strongly affective responses to the agency's ideas. And in chapter 8, I will show how the production of "the Indian consumer" as a culturally specific marketing category arose out of a combination of strategic necessity and executive aesthetic inclination.

In chapter 1, I suggested that there were striking parallels between the new swadeshi discourse of the ascendant BJP and the sense of cultural revitalization that the heralds of globalized consumerism identified. Both included critiques of the abstraction and alienation of previous regimes, and the liberatory promise of reconciling embodied local identity with global processes. And both were in some sense concerned with the reconstruction of India as a consumable brand. Christiane Brosius quotes G. Bharat Bala of Bharatbala Productions, Bombay: " 'Nation-building is the *basic brand* that is required today, India *needs* that' " (Brosius 1999, 109). Just as Asians had, in the Singaporean entrepreneur's words, long been denied control of the brand, so the politics of Hindu nationalism were quite self-consciously oriented toward claiming the long-overdue right to be *producers* rather than merely consumers of modernity.[12]

The EMW mobile impasse was particularly instructive in this regard since it literalized the connection between the structural constraints of the global division of commercial identity and the politics of the new swadeshi. The account executive reasoned that EMW was never going to be able to compete with its multinational rivals on status: "The guy who can afford to go out and buy a Sony is going to go out and buy a Sony. That's still there." What EMW could do to "leverage" its connotations of warmth was to address the *next* tier of consumers; not the narrow band of an elite with cosmopolitan identifications, but rather an upwardly mobile but culturally "Indian" middle class: "These guys are looking for a good brand, a brand that delivers great quality. Basically we're saying that EMW is a *modern Indian brand*. First-class technology with family values."[13]

"Who is the target audience?" the account executive demanded rhetorically, once again pacing up and down my cubicle, once again smoking voraciously. "The typical guy will be living in Andheri or Jogeshwari." The reference was to two solidly middle-class Bombay suburbs, neither elite nor *infra dig*. "This is a middle-class family, upwardly mobile. They're not living on Carmichael Road," he added, naming a particularly exclusive South Bombay location.

For all the reasons I have described — his own strategic needs, the objective features of the client's brand dilemma, as well as the client executive's subjective responses — the account executive was trying to reconcile a strategically viable marketing plan with a pragmatic acceptance of the cultural politics of global branding. But several members of the creative team insisted, with the planner I quoted above, that this was aesthetic defeatism: why should EMW be saddled with an undesirable Indian image?

At the next internal agency meeting, these differences flared up. Like a good dialectician, the account executive — in a final gambit — attempted to turn a deadlock into a defiant statement of national pride. "Mobile telephony is definitely a male category," he began. "And EMW *is* Indian. We can never get away from that. It *should* be modern. Young." The copywriter lifted his gaze: "I don't buy this idea that we can't get away from our Indianness." "Yes, okay," responded the account executive swiftly. "You *can* get away from the Indianness, but then you'll become parity. I'm saying we take the *strength* of the Indianness. The *philosophy*, not the nationality." The copywriter challenged the account executive to explain exactly what this "philosophy" entailed; the reply came in the form of a familiar signifier: "Bombay." This time around, "Bombay" was still a kind of virtual geographical marker. But now, rather than suggesting a *transcendence* of concrete place, or a subsumption of the local into the global, "Bombay" returned, reworked, as resistance to an alienated postcolonial repertoire of identities. "Can we say that this is for the 'new Indian'? It's a very *Bombay*-based concept," he improvised. "It's saying 'I no longer have to go to the U.S., or look to the U.S. I can now be successful right here in Bombay.' Yeah! Fuck 'India'! This whole thing is *very Bombay*. This guy might be saying 'I'm going to vote for the BJP because I want some stability finally. We're Indian, fuck it! We don't want some bloody multinational to come and bail us out.' "

The discussion had come full circle, all the way back to the Amitabh Bachchan ads. But in tracing this path, it had also made visible the ambiguities that underlay the smooth reconciliation between local and global that those ads had suggested. The medium of this attempted reconciliation was the "nation-brand," the profitable expression of local identity that was at the same time fully compatible with a universal field of equivalence. And it was EMW's historical fate to find itself in precisely the position where the impasses of this equation became visible. The dream of consumerist globalization aligns two utopian impulses side by side: the universalizing equivalence of all human beings qua consumers, and the absolute priority of each individual's particular, locally embodied desires and needs. It is therefore no accident that marketing and advertising reaches for the categories "cultural identity" and "cultural difference" because — when expressed through

13. Global dominance on Mama's terms. This ad for OCM suitings could serve as a stand-alone summary of the cultural politics of globalizing corporate capitalism. In the foreground, an embodiment of the GOMBA (the Grossly Overpaid MBA) ecstatically spans the breadth of the world with his unquenchable ambition. The first two-thirds of the copy sketch his persona in generic strokes as the very antithesis of the obstructionist, complacent bureaucrat of the "permit-license raj." But "Asian values" nevertheless complete the equation as a doting mother, again figured as a bastion of proud tradition, is revealed as the ultimate source of the fire in our hero's belly.

branded commodity images — these categories offer, at one and the same time, manageable conceptual distinction and powerful affective resonance: French fashion, Italian sports cars, Indian exotica.[14]

Nevertheless, the culture concept is dangerous to the best-laid plans of marketing precisely for the same reasons that it is such a serviceable tool. In a global field, culture is a "positioning opportunity," one that promises to resonate with consumer preferences at the intersection of thought and embodiment. But for that very reason, it also involves marketing and advertising practitioners with problems that they cannot hope to resolve: it obliges them to engage with the whole tangled cultural politics of postcolonial experience. This impossible obligation arises out of the inherent ambivalence of the consumerist dispensation.

As we have seen, the burden of history also interrupted the agency team's work by means of a calculus of Indian social distinction, most viscerally in the way that the cosmopolitan corporate imagery desired by the client was constantly haunted by the distasteful hexis of pro-vinciality. Globalizing consumerism confirms postcolonial elites as culture-brokers, now in the idiom of marketing. But in the calculus of branding, the expansive logic of the market continues to struggle with the exclusive logic of social distinction.

Generically, marketing makes a double claim. On the one hand, its practitioners like to say that they speak their customers' language, that they mirror consumers' desires. On the other hand, consumerism is offered as a unique means of self-transformation, even of liberation from quotidian constraints and imperfections, from the world that is. The globalization of consumerism leads to the entanglement of this double claim with the concepts of cultural identity and cultural differ-ence. The gift of the now (would-be) global brand promises to affirm the cultural particularity of consumers while at the same time liberat-ing them from *mere* particularity; it promises, in short, to solve the key problem of modern public life: the tension between embodiment and universality.

Conclusion

These are, to be sure, grand — not to say grandiose — claims. Few mar-keting or advertising professionals would make them explicitly or use this kind of terminology. But in a sense this is precisely my point. In chapter 3, I showed how the Indian advertising industry, as the social ontology of consumerism gradually moved to the center of mainstream public discourse, found itself saddled with expectations that it could not hope to fulfill. This predicament is equally characteristic of the globalization of consumerism. The end of the Cold War and the "tri-umph" of neoliberalism heralded an ideological vacuum into which the figure of the global consumer was pushed, virtually by default. The global commercial mass media apparatus that had become available over the preceding decade made possible an alliance between a world-coordinating marketing bureaucracy and a locally responsive imaging practice.

And it is to the complex internal articulations of this alliance that I wish to turn in part 3. In part 1, I offered a local account of a global phenomenon: the gradual and ambivalent forging of an Indian mass consumerist dispensation. In part 2, this global phenomenon became something called "globalization," and the commercial value of "Indianness" itself, as a brand constituent, was called into question. Part 3 extends this consideration of the cultural politics of globalizing consumerism, but shifts the focus onto the category of "the consumer." How was the cultural particularity of Indian consumers understood by Indian advertising and marketing professionals in the years following 1991? And how was this cultural particularity balanced with the transcendent promise of globalized markets?

PART THREE

7

Indian Fun: Constructing
"the Indian Consumer" I

In the early days of my fieldwork in Bombay, when I told advertising and marketing people that I was interested in studying "advertising and globalization," I would very often be greeted with a patient smile, an expression appropriate for a naïve Westerner who was convinced that "his" civilization was remaking the world in its own image. Had I not heard that Coca-Cola, veteran flagship of cultural imperialism, had stumbled badly in India, that it was trailing behind its worldwide rival Pepsi? And what about the ignominious failure of MTV, which in the autumn of 1997 had hastily "Indianized" its programming after an upstart rival on Rupert Murdoch's Hong Kong-based STAR network, Channel V, had demonstrated that locally relevant, not globally standardized, content was the way forward? India, my interlocutors insisted, was simply too complex, too ancient, too resilient, and too different to be subsumed under some worldwide umbrella of uniformity.

Of course, I would reply, I had read the countless articles in the business and current affairs periodicals of the time, which, almost obsessively, were focused on the theme of the apparent "failure of the MNCs." Corporate consumer goods giants, lured in the early 1990s by the promise of the mythical 250 million-strong Indian middle class, had set up shop in India following the 1991 reforms of the Narasimha Rao government. Many, if not most, of them had found that early sales projections had proved chimerical. Much of the commentary on this phenomenon, after an initial phase of bewilderment, had taken on a triumphalist tone; it was as if the trials of the multinationals were being interpreted as a kind of recapitulation of the colonial encounter, in which Indians, approached this time as sovereign consumers rather than imperial subjects, were proving resistant to the best laid plans that the finest marketing minds of the West had to offer.[1]

To my interlocutors I would protest that I did not equate "globalization" with "homogenization" and that my understanding of the term in fact highlighted precisely the kind of dynamics that they were describing. But it seemed that my objections simply did not register. It was only gradually that I came to understand the reasons why many of my informants insisted upon upholding the cultural imperialism thesis as a straw figure. These reasons may be summarized briefly as follows. First, their insistence upon the necessity of paying attention to the cultural specificities of Indian consumers allowed Indian advertising and marketing professionals to make themselves indispensable as consultants, interpreters, and local experts vis-à-vis their multinational clients. Second, it allowed Indian advertising and marketing professionals to present their involvement with multinational clients as beneficial to Indian consumers. All the market research projects that were at that time busy codifying and contesting taxonomies of the multiple avataras of "the Indian consumer" could thus be framed not only as commercially necessary (that is, sets of knowledge designed to facilitate selling more people more things) but also morally noble (respecting and even nourishing the cultural differences apparently embodied in Indian consumers).

What the advertising and marketing people who were now trumpeting the need to be sensitive to local cultural differences usually neglected to mention, however, was that only a few years earlier, in 1991–92, it was they who had held out to the MNCs the enchanting mirage of hundreds of millions of Indian middle-class consumers, willing and able to devour consumer goods on much the same scale and terms as their equivalents elsewhere in the world. Let me emphasize again that I am *not* arguing that local differences in people's consuming preferences are nothing more than inventions of the advertising and marketing industries. Obviously, such a claim would be insupportable. Rather, what I am suggesting is that the Indian advertising and marketing industries, in the mid-1990s, found themselves in a position where an insistence upon the cultural difference of Indian consumers was strategically and ideologically necessary to them. Moreover, the specific forms taken by this Indian cultural difference in advertising and marketing discourse had, as I will show, more to do with the professional requirements of reconciling global brand narratives with very particular understandings of "Indianness" than with any empirically objective description of Indian consumers. In the process, however, we will also see that the internal logic of globalizing consumerism calls into question — even if it doesn't overturn — the parallel alignment of global and local, form and content, subject and object.

In the present chapter, I use the specific example of the contested "Indianization" of a global soft drink brand that I will call Sparka to examine the shift from a global consumer market imagined as relatively homogenous to one in which cultural difference became an indispensable commodity in its own right. The ghost of Coca-Cola's relative failure in India informed strategic thinking on Sparka from the beginning, and helped to sensitize the multinational company's head office to the problem of cultural differences. We will see how the idea of culture gradually entered into the negotiation between agency and client on the brand, and — most importantly — how it shifted the terms of their interaction in a way that provided the local agency with a great deal more leverage vis-à-vis the client.

The Global Teen, the Cola Wars, and the Uses of Cultural Difference

Coca-Cola's difficulties in India were important to marketing thought not only because of the supposedly universal appeal of the brand,[2] but also because of the supposed universality of the category of consumer at which it was aimed: teenagers. Teenagers held a very particular place in the discourse of consumerist globalization for historical, demographic, and generic reasons. Historically, the global cohort of teenagers of the mid-1990s represented the first generation of consumers to come of age in an era of globalized telecommunications and free-market ideological hegemony. Demographically, it looked like marketers were in for a boom. "Barring widespread plague or other catastrophe," business writer Peter Schwartz ruminated (1996), "there will be over 2 billion teenagers in the world in the year 2001. . . . What will be the interplay between this new global adolescent community and the evolution of the new electronic media?" The fact that the vast majority of these teenagers would be in the less privileged zones of Latin America, Asia, and Africa mattered not a bit, it was argued, since new telecommunications media such as satellite television and the Internet would make such distinctions unimportant, establishing a kind of global teenage public sphere: "The distribution of new types of communication devices . . . is taking place so fast that by the time most of the global teenagers are teenagers, they will literally be in constant contact with each other. . . . The next wave of telecommunications will flow in two directions, it will encourage active intelligence; people won't be able to take part any more simply by sitting back and letting images flow over them. They'll be talking, selecting, ordering, criticizing, and (in some cases) creating" (Schwartz 1996).

To those who might object that connection alone — even if it were made available to this degree — does not guarantee intelligibility or community, Schwartz and other theorists of the teen ecumene responded that it was in the very nature of teenagers to combine a search for belonging with a rejection of established authorities and conventions. This made them ideal consumers of relatively standardized global brands, since they would "naturally" let the search for a connection with their peers elsewhere in the world be routed through the narratives and images of advertising. These narratives and images would, by the same token, take precedence over their commitments to older and more localized idioms of belonging represented by elders and "tradition." "We know what adolescents are like," wrote Schwartz. "The years when people come of age involve exuberance, exploration, confusion and rebellion against old structures. That's as true of teenagers in Bangkok, Nairobi, or Caracas as it is of teenagers in Los Angeles or Paris. . . . Adolescents tend to identify with each other, set apart by and from other age groups" (ibid.).[3]

This was the kind of premise upon which Coca-Cola launched its return to Indian markets in the early 1990s. The approach it adopted, which revolved around the sentiment "Share my Coke," sought precisely to construct the kind of one-world feel-good idiom that marketing and business writers like Schwartz were recommending for teen consumers. (Indeed, the Indian launch campaign subsequently become known in Bombay advertising circles as "the caring-sharing shit.") The problem was that it did not seem to have worked. Pepsi, on the other hand, launched a little earlier, adopted a completely different advertising strategy and did very well. In direct contrast to Coke's gentle global

Next to better vision, the most important thing for your eyes is better comfort and health.
Johnson & Johnson's Acuvue disposable contact lenses are specially designed to allow optimum
oxygen for your eyes to breathe, reducing tiredness, redness and irritation. Which is why,
eye doctors the world over, recommend Acuvue more than any other lens. And that's not all!
Acuvue lenses are so thin and soft, you can hardly feel them! No wonder millions of users
the world over say "Acuvue is the most comfortable contact lens that I have ever worn.
Well, it's almost as comfortable as wearing nothing at all."

Introducing
Acuvue Disposable Contact lenses

Acuvue. The No.1 selling contact lens in the world.

Contact your eye care practitioner today to find out if Acuvue is right for you and take home a free trial pair. Professional charges extra.   Lintas Acu 21 2618.

14. Modernity as perspicacity. In the early 1990s, international marketing discourse
was fixated on the notion of an emerging global generation of teenage consumers.
Their defining mark was their curiosity (translatable into a willingness to try new
products) and their contempt for the ways of their parents (translatable into a more-
or-less homogenous market for teen brands). This ad for Acuvue contact lenses
from Johnson and Johnson literalizes a young person's shrugging off the dead
weight of the past and attaining the (gently risqué) perspicacity of being "with it."

message, Pepsi opted for maximum spectacle and relied heavily on Indian celebrity endorsers. The general feeling in the Bombay advertising industry was that while Coke's communications seemed "arty" and "obscure," Pepsi came across as "direct," "cheeky," and "hard-hitting."

The locus classicus of this confrontation was the two cola giants' contest over the sponsorship of the 1996 cricket World Cup. Coke had apparently used sheer financial muscle to secure it, being willing and able to pay $4 million as opposed to Pepsi's $2.5 million (Pande 1996). Coke began its advertising onslaught months before the actual games, in November 1995, while Pepsi waited in the wings, apparently mulling over its strategy. The moment of truth came at the games themselves, when Coke's elaborate and ponderous "official sponsor" campaign was overshadowed by a ragtag banner suspended from some trees overlooking the stadium, upon which Pepsi mocked Coke's pretensions by insisting that there was "nothing official about it."

As far as the Indian advertising business was concerned, the cola wars had become a kind of morality play about the perils of multinational marketing. Certainly it was argued that any number of non-advertising factors probably played into Coke's relative lack of success—distribution problems, pricing issues, and so forth. This, of course, was an argument particularly close at hand for the agency executives who had worked on the Coke campaign. One member of that team recalled his discussions with the client: "I told them, 'You've got to take a look at the rest of the picture. Look at your product, your price, and your place. What's not working?' Advertising is there to create an emotional bond between the consumer and the brand. It cannot make you go out and buy something. But it can make your decision to buy this brand or that brand more likely. If you go out and you can't *get* it because it's not available, then that's a problem. But that's not the fault of advertising."

And yet at the same time, it was in the industry's interests to argue precisely that the one-world, delocalized approach that Coke had used in its advertising was not going to "create an emotional bond between the [Indian] consumer and the brand." From this standpoint, Pepsi's scrappy, localized approach appeared to have got the equation right. The same executive who had struggled with Coke told me that he thought Pepsi had succeeded by understanding a deeply rooted Indian predilection for uproarious spectacle, for *tamasha*, preferably couched in quasi-mythological terms as a battle between two mighty contenders.

> In India, if two guys start fighting on the street, two million people will gather around to watch the fight. They'll be craning their necks and shoving their heads in like this — *Kya hua?* [What's going on?] They won't intervene, they'll just be standing there offering comments and talking about it. This is an important thing to understand about Indian psychology: they love fights, like in the movies. And another thing in Indian psychology: everything has to be mega-mega this-thing [i.e., staged with maximum spectacle].

To underline his point, the executive related that, while traveling around India on behalf of various clients, he would regularly be approached by youngsters with ideas for Coke commercials. In one case, a young man had requested a Coke commercial set in a Gulf War scenario, featuring a Pepsi-glugging Saddam Hussein "having the shit bombed out of him" by a handsome Coke-sipping U.S. fighter pilot. (Unsurprisingly, I need hardly add, the executive did not attempt to submit this concept to Coke's U.S. headquarters for evaluation.)

One of the most striking aspects of the opinions offered by Indian commentators on the missteps and miscalculations of the multinationals was that they were only marginally patriotic. It was not that these commentators necessarily wanted Indian brands to thrive. Rather, they wanted to make sure that multinationals took into account and respected "Indian culture" in their marketing and advertising approaches. A good illustration of this was the story of the fate of a popular Indian cola brand called Thums [*sic*] Up. In the vacuum created by the departure from India of Coke and other multinational companies after 1977, many local brands like Thums Up had thrived. And yet such was the generalized conviction that the return of the multinationals in the early 1990s would sweep everything in its paths that Parle, the manufacturers of Thums Up and other local brands like Limca, had simply sold out to Coke rather than be trampled underfoot. Coke, according to its usual practice, intended to bury the local brand and take over its bottling and distribution networks for its own products. It was, therefore, unprepared for Thums Up's continued popularity. Thums Up's tenacious sales allowed local commentators to emphasize the importance of multinationals paying attention to the particularities of Indian tastes, and to reflect upon Coca-Cola's arrogance. But rarely, if ever, was the fact that Coca-Cola now controlled both the marketing of the "global" *and* the "local" brand raised as a matter of concern. If anything, it was the Chauhans, the family that ran Parle, who were ridiculed for buckling under so easily to the chimera of "globalization."[4]

From the point of view of the advertising and marketing industries, this position was easy to understand. On a practical level, dealing with local clients was in many ways easier and more straightforward, since important decisions could usually be made by the client executive sitting on the other side of the conference room table, as opposed to faceless "brandocrats" operating out of some regional headquarters on the other side of the world. But on the level of advertising content, as we have seen in part 2, globalization had created an important and potentially lucrative new niche for local advertising and marketing professionals, a niche that only made sense in relation to multinational clients: that of experts on, and guardians of, local cultural difference. In the following sections, I relate an advertising agency's attempts to carve out a zone of autonomy for itself vis-à-vis its multinational client, on the basis of the purported cultural difference of Indian teenagers.

The System

I became involved with the Sparka soft drink account at a time when client headquarters in the United States — "the Hub" — was attempting to reassert centralized control over the relationship between the global brand and the various advertising "executions" that were used for it in different countries. Only gradually, as I discussed the account with the various executives who worked on it, and read the voluminous documentation that the agency had accumulated on it over the previous three years, did I begin to see that this move was part of a much longer process of contestation between the Hub and its various local affiliates in "the field."

Dealing with an enormous multinational corporation like Sparka's parent company presented a set of challenges that were entirely different from those thrown up by a local client like EMW mobile. Two words, regularly used by agency team members, often accompanied by an exasperated rolling of the eyes, summed up this difference: "the System." With EMW mobile, the agency dealt directly with an executive who, although not at the top of the hierarchical structure of his corporation, was empowered to make important decisions on the spot. Hence, the agency was in a position at least to attempt to apply the dialectical technique of image and narrative directly to the client. With Sparka, such an approach was impossible. First of all, Sparka's parent company was an enormous multinational bureaucracy, based in the United States, with regional headquarters in several locations around the world. Any creative ideas submitted to the client would have to travel through all the various levels of the bureaucracy and be checked for their consistency with the global brand plan at central command in the United States before they could be approved for implementation back in India. Second, whereas with a client like EMW mobile, the agency was fully involved in at least contesting the outlines of the brand positioning and personality, Sparka's brand positioning was decided at the Hub and then handed down, *diktat*-style, to regional offices around the world.

For the agency, dealing with the System was frequently a complex and frustrating affair. Creatives — copywriters and art directors — would routinely gripe and complain about working on multinational accounts. On the one hand, they were forced to operate within tightly constrained boundaries; Sparka had issued a detailed and comprehensive set of manuals that established the precise limits of the variation that was deemed permissible in creative executions of the brand idea. On the other hand, they were deprived of the satisfaction and pleasure of witnessing the direct effect of their ideas on the client. Instead, their finely honed campaigns would disappear into the vast and inscrutable machinery of the System, first to Asia-Pacific regional headquarters in Thailand, then up to the Hub in the United States, where they would be adjusted to the point of unrecognizability by global strategy mavens.

As usual the account executives were more pragmatic. Finding themselves at the intersection between the local agency and the global client, their job was essentially to know and to understand the brand so well that they could intuitively predict whether an idea generated by their creative colleagues would survive the arcane twists and turns of the System. While on one level the fact that brand strategy was not open for discussion acted as a constraint on local advertising initiatives, on another level it meant that the local agency's liability was limited. Ostensibly, its responsibility was restricted to making sure that global brand strategy was implemented locally in appropriate ways.

At the agency one day, I had been perusing some Sparka brand documentation. I pointed out to the main executive on the account that although it was clear that a great deal of research effort had gone into understanding how Sparka's brand message should be expressed in Indian terms, there appeared to have been no inquiry into the appropriateness, in an Indian context, of the message itself. "You're right," he nodded. "It's global strategy. There's no point. It'd just get lost in Bangkok, the States, somewhere." He twirled his hand in the air, as if to suggest the churning, inexorable cogs of the System. The benefit of this predicament, I realized, was that if the strategy flopped, the agency could not be held accountable. "Correct," he nodded again. "It's their responsibility. But if we fuck up the execution, *that's* our responsibility."

On one level, then, it seemed as if dealing with a multinational client like Sparka simply meant a one-way process of translation: abstract global brand message into concrete local expression. And yet, as I was to find, the client-agency dynamic was, in a way, just as ambidirectional as it was on an account like EMW mobile. It was just that, in relation to multinational clients, the agency had to fight for control on a rather different kind of terrain. Most immediately, the difference became apparent in the far greater importance of market research to the handling of multinational accounts. An art director who worked on both the EMW mobile and the Sparka accounts put it succinctly, just before going into a client meeting in which the agency team would, as it happened, successfully convince Sparka's Bombay office to support the localized campaign that it had developed: "I'm not going to go in and *argue* with them about this. These are very *logical* guys. They're not like [the EMW executive] who will take a decision on gut feel. I respect his decisions — he's a consumer himself, so he knows what they want. But with these [Sparka] guys, if you don't do your homework, then it's gone."

The importance of market research to negotiations between client and agency opened up a new opportunity for the local agency. Briefly the logic of the situation was as follows: as long as the agency simply worked within the pre-established structure of the Sparka commodity image itself, it was bound to find itself in a subordinate negotiating position vis-à-vis its client. Since global brand strategy was in the hands of the Hub, the agency would always be at the mercy of the Hub's decisions as to what kind of executions were relevant to this strategy. The agency's way out of this trap was to bring its own *counter*-commodity into the equation: the Indian consumer. This counter-commodity had several advantages, from the local agency's point of view. First, the client had no say over its needs and requirements. Second, it existed independently of any single account, and could therefore be developed as an all-round idiom through which relations with the whole range of multinational clients might be managed. Third, the Indian consumer, qua counter-commodity, was itself merely a local instantiation of a larger global entity — consumers worldwide — and therefore allowed the local agency to draw upon the authority and resources of its own global network in such a way as to match, and to counter, the global ambitions of its clients' brands.

Intrinsics and Extrinsics: Sell or Tell?

The lesson that Sparka initially drew from the cola wars in India involved a kind of evolutionary scheme: "emerging" soft drink markets like India would have to be convinced to buy soft drink brands on the basis of solid "reason-why" appeals rather than on the basis of stylistically sophisticated campaigns.[5]

Sparka's parent company began in late 1994 by commissioning research in the four Indian "metros" — Delhi, Bombay, Calcutta, and Madras. The research was conducted by a Southeast Asian market research company during the first half of 1995. Its stated aim was to depict the Indian "beverage" market in its totality — from carbonated soft drinks to plain water. What were the factors motivating people's choice of beverage? What might make them switch — what were the key "conversion drivers"? What was more important to Indian consumers in their relationship to their favored type of beverage — brand "intrinsics" (that is, the physical qualities of the product) or "extrinsics" (that is, the imagery and connotations from which the brand image was constructed)? Was localization of the brand going to be necessary, and, if so, what *kind* of localization would be suitable? All these questions were inflected by Pepsi's unexpected advantage over Coke in India. The study found that urban populations in all four metros chose water as their preferred beverage. Tea came in as a strong second in Delhi, Bombay, and Calcutta, while Madrasis preferred coffee. Carbonated soft drink brand preferences were marked by strongly regional biases: only in Madras did Coke appear in first place, followed by Pepsi, and, in third place, the indigenous (but now Coke-owned) lemon-flavored Limca. The continuing strength of the indigenous brands was particularly noticeable in Bombay and Calcutta, where the cola brand Thums Up still occupied the top spot. Interestingly, however, a stated preference for a particular brand did not necessarily mean that people *bought* it; despite the apparent loyalty to Thums Up, consumers in Bombay and Calcutta both actually consumed more Pepsi and Coke, respectively.

Then things got complicated. While the study found that most consumers "evaluated" and had "good associations" to brands based on *extrinsic* features of the brand, the likelihood of converting them from one brand to another — in terms of actual consumption — appeared to be based squarely on *intrinsic* features of the product. Attributes driving choice, the study suggested, "are very clear: in order of importance, the attribute drivers of consumption are: preferred taste, refreshment (in the broad rejuvenating sense), and more narrowly, 'thirst quenching.'" At this point, the intrinsic/extrinsic pair was somewhat uneasily mapped into another binary: rational/emotional reasons for choosing a particular brand. And it was here that Pepsi seemed to have played the winning hand. Where my executive informant had opined that Pepsi had triumphed through an understanding of an Indian love of spectacle, the research report commissioned by Sparka's parent company suggested that Pepsi's advantage had been secured through fusing the Indian-focused emotional content of their communications with a clear "reason why":

> Pepsi's image-building campaigns are easy to understand [as opposed to the oblique montage spots by Coke], rely heavily on indigenous advertising [as opposed to the one-world pieties of Coke], and speak directly to the benefits of the brand. They give consumers *rational and emotional* reasons to drink Pepsi. . . . Pepsi's positioning is an indigenous implementation of their approach world-wide, i.e., to dimensionalize "refreshment" in terms of energy ("helps when you're tired"); and to place it in a mass-appeal, teen context.[6]

The next step was to translate these "learnings" into a more generally applicable formula, and it was here that the implicit evolutionism became explicit: "An emerging market like India needs to be treated with respect for its indigenous characteristics. There isn't enough of a foundation in collective consumer memory for an approach which floats the logo and bottle across the screen in entertaining ways." This apparently pluralistic evaluation then sailed perilously close to an essentializing diagnosis: "In India the brand is the product in the bottle. While it is essential to locate the brand in the right extrinsic consumer context, it is even more *essential* to begin to communicate about the refreshing characteristics of the product."

This evolutionary model rested on an ontological hierarchy. It wasn't so much that Indian consumers weren't ready to be sold relatively "nonessential" goods like carbonated soft drinks. Rather, the market research analysis implied that their comparatively limited experience with sophisticated advertising techniques meant that they would most easily be convinced to consume Sparka on the basis of appeals to the intrinsic features of the product itself rather than whatever extrinsic imagery might be associated with it. On the one hand, Pepsi's success over Coke had demonstrated the importance of emotionally resonant local imagery. On the other hand, this localized imagery was firmly *subordinated* to the intrinsic qualities of the product itself — the benefits of the "drink in the bottle" — that were understood to be global. For Sparka in India, the report concluded, local cultural particularity should be treated as an *epiphenomenal language* — a relatively superficial expression of an underlying, objective, and universal product characteristic: "superior orange taste."[7] As far as local advertising input went, then, the model that Sparka was propounding at this point consigned it to a relatively subservient role: local translations of a universal idea, which was in turn squarely focused upon the product itself.

Indeed, it was as if the product existed in immaculate isolation; in India, it had no history and no identity. All it had was its orange taste; that was the good news to be communicated. This immaculate state could, of course, not last since Sparka would have to be positioned in relation to an actually existing set of competing products and the various narratives and connotations that they had established within the general product category. In fact, as soon as Sparka was placed in the context of its immediate Indian rivals, it inevitably began to take on the social connotations that were found to adhere to the general category of orange-flavored carbonated soft drinks.

Liberating the Inner Child

The first problem that Sparka ran into was generic to the category: orange-flavored carbonated soft drinks were strongly associated with children. At the time of the Sparka launch, the category was over-whelmingly dominated by a Parle (and therefore now a Coca-Cola) brand, Gold Spot, which had appeared in 1971 and gone on to control 47 percent of the national market. Mirinda, a brand operated by Pepsi, had been available in India since 1991, but had managed to grab only 10 percent. (The remaining 43 percent was divided between a profusion of smaller regional brands, like Torino and Duke.) Research showed that orange soft drinks, as compared to other kinds of soft drinks like colas, were relatively popular in the Indian market (15 percent of the overall carbonated soft drink market, as opposed to 12 percent in Thailand and 9 percent in Japan).

The infantile image of the category was problematic for two main reasons. First, as we have seen, teenagers were fast becoming an increasingly attractive global market segment. Second, all available research suggested that children themselves generally did not make purchasing decisions, particularly not in India. If Sparka was going to appeal to teenagers, then, there might be a risk that the childish connotations of the product category would create a kind of cognitive dissonance. The potential upshot of all this, as far as the Hub was concerned, was that Sparka consumers would suffer from "low brand morale": a lacking sense of identification with, and incorporation within, the brand, which would make them more likely to be "brand-promiscuous."

Initially, in line with its conviction that Indian customers were going to have to be convinced on the basis of appeals to product intrinsics, Sparka had aimed to set itself off from Gold Spot and Mirinda—both of whom had played heavily on *extrinsics*—by focusing on "the drink in the bottle." But the childish connotations of the category were now forcing a shift in emphasis. Whereas the focus on intrinsics had relegated extrinsics to the more or less subordinate role of getting local celebrity endorsers to propound the intrinsic benefits of the product, it seemed as if the *extrinsics* were now going to have to do some more fundamental image-adjusting work.

The ontological hierarchy between global intrinsics and local extrinsics was, then, subtly beginning to change. As a result, the Hub now sought to intervene directly in the management of the extrinsics that had previously been a subordinate, local concern. Was there a way of imagining the desired consumer (the teen) that could include "the child?" The way around the problem might be to acknowledge that "the child" remained an emotionally important part of the psychological makeup of "the teen." Positioned as an innocent pleasure, Sparka would allow teenagers, faced with ever-increasing responsibilities, to get back in touch with their "inner children."

The key mediating concept was "fun." The child that Sparka promised to liberate in all its consumers was "fun-loving, playful, warm, and sensitive. . . . Although we grow up, there are moments in life when that little child inside of us comes out. These moments can be a lot of fun." Aware that "fun" was at the core of the product benefit of both Gold Spot and Mirinda, the Hub then attempted to specify a more exact understanding of Sparka fun. "What does 'letting the child inside come out' mean? Liberation—breaking away from the constraints of an everyday situation; fun-loving—making the most of an everyday situation by acting funny/childish but not slapstick/stupid."[8]

A crucial projection was taking place: in order to "positivize" the childish connotations of the product category, the Hub was now proposing an imagined generic consumer whose psychological makeup justified the positioning of the product itself. This was important, first of all, because it created a situation in which the meaning of Sparka depended upon an imagined construct that was external to the product itself. But more than this, because the usefulness of this construct depended upon its being presented in a *human* form, because it referred to allegedly "natural" and universal human proclivities, Sparka had effectively opened the window to an entirely different plane of contestation vis-à-vis its advertising agencies and local marketing associates.

Consequently, it was all the more important for the Hub to try to exercise the same kind of control over the definition of this imagined consumer as it had previously asserted over the intrinsic aspects of the drink. The manner in which this was done was to suggest that, in the final analysis, Sparka fun was about "authenticity," about accessing a level of universal human "reality" that transcended local or contingent expressions of enjoyment. Consequently, the agency was told that the playful "child in everybody" should be about "real values" and "real self": "Sparka is the real orange taste—the child in you is the part you enjoy most about your real self."

Initially, then, "fun" served not only as an identifying feature of Sparka's brand identity, but also as a way of conceptualizing the relation between intrinsics and extrinsics within the brand. The universalizing psychology fitted the globalizing ambitions of the corporation;

the teenager's search for an identity based on an inner authenticity seemed the perfect double for the claim of an intrinsic taste superiority that was being made on behalf of the drink.

Dimensionalizing Fun

Sparka's new emphasis on fun, although still appealing to supposedly essential qualities, had moved the negotiation of the brand away from the product itself and toward a relationship with an imagined consumer, understood in terms of a generic human psychology. Like the perfect social isolation in which the drink itself had originally been suspended, Sparka's imagined consumer was, at this stage, entirely abstracted away from local particularities. This state of affairs, however, was not to last.

The Hub quickly realized that if one of the defining characteristics of teens around the world was the importance of peer-group sociality, then Sparka fun, as portrayed in advertising, would have to involve images of social situations that might manifest such fun. Such a "socialization" of the brand would also help to rid Sparka of what the Hub termed "the brown bag syndrome," that is, its association with in-home consumption. The need of the hour, then, was to bring Sparka out of the home and into a more public realm. To do this, suitable "teen moments" would have to be identified.

On one level, then, Sparka was moving from an emphasis on an inner, individual quest for authenticity (the "real self") to grappling with questions of belonging and connection. By the same token, however, the need for the brand to be inclusive dictated that the teen sociality it appealed to had to exclude any references to the thornier, more antisocial aspects of adolescence. As I have suggested, the new emphasis on sociality had crucially transformed the terms of the interaction between the Hub and its various advertising agencies. Brand intrinsics, although formally still the bedrock of the product's positioning, had in practice been pushed to the margins. Instead, extrinsics — the level of representations and images, that is, advertising — had assumed a center-stage position. Whereas the intrinsic properties of the product had previously served as the Hub's centralized point of control over the marketing of Sparka worldwide (even at the point when a generic imagined consumer entered the picture), continued control now required creating a global/local hierarchy *within the extrinsic dimen-*

sion of the brand. The experience of Coke and other struggling MNCs had helped to establish the idea that advertising should be adapted to local markets. Nevertheless, it remained important for the executives at the Hub to constrain this local variation within a framework that could be centrally monitored and regulated.

The solution was for Sparka to commission a series of local studies aimed at "dimensionalizing fun" in a manner that would allow local preferences to be balanced with global brand objectives. By way of orientation, the Bombay agency was supplied with the tabulated results of a comparative study that had already been conducted to understand the meaning of fun among teenagers in six countries: China, Thailand, Germany, Italy, Mexico, and Brazil. In themselves, the research results were not particularly earthshaking; leisure activities like sports, shopping, and partying featured strongly all around.[9] On a structural level, however, the study was more interesting in that it sought to reproduce the hierarchical relation previously mapped onto the intrinsic/extrinsic binary *within* the extrinsic dimension of the brand. The rationale behind "dimensionalizing fun" was not simply to understand what constituted fun in each of Sparka's markets. It was also a way of creating a conceptual scheme that might isolate a level of deep and universal mental states from a surface level of localized expressions and activities. Values and emotions surrounding fun were deemed to be universal; specific attitudes and occasions, in contrast, were understood to be local.

Underlining the hierarchical relationship between these two levels, the Hub followed up this conceptual division with a series of unilateral and nonnegotiable assertions concerning the universal meaning of fun. This claim to global relevance was couched in terms of a universalizing psychology, in which peer relationships (as opposed to parental relationships) were the basis for the sense of belonging that teenagers everywhere purportedly craved. And fun activities among friends supported and fueled this sense of belonging. Sparka fun was necessarily both inclusive and conformist. The Hub defined it as, "Inclusive not individualistic; optimistic/positive not sarcastic/cynical; curious yet safe, not risky and dangerous; spontaneous/flexible, not rigid/unyielding; friendly/approachable, not separatist/distant; mainstream not edgy."

These, then, were the guidelines that the Bombay Sparka office and the advertising agency it employed had to bear in mind when attempting to "dimensionalize fun" for India. As I have shown, the Hub had decreed that the category "activities" was the acceptable container for localized expressions of fun (as opposed to the apparently deeper and more universal categories of "values, emotions, and attitudes"). It was striking, then, that in the research commissioned by the agency and Sparka Bombay, precisely this category should have generated a portrait of Indian fun that seemed distinctly "off brand."

Fun activities for Indian teens, it transpired, included "teasing, fighting, screaming/shouting, pranks, doing the forbidden" alongside the more placid "games/playing." The researcher had represented the "dimensionalization" of fun graphically as a field of clusters around a central point representing fun as a layered composite; among these clusters he had included "group vs. individual," "freedom," and "break rules/ do the forbidden." This last category was further subdivided into "innocent/safe" and "dangerous/destructive." Despite its title, "innocent/ safe" included components that were guaranteed to make the Hub squirm: "loud music, wild dance, costumes, make up, cook, on the phone for long, TV/radio—loud, long hours, lying, cheating, stealing." "Dangerous/destructive" fun, in turn, was utterly beyond the pale (although the juxtaposition of some of its elements was in itself interesting): "break valuable glass, tear books, play with fire, 'murder someone and get away with it,' 'bike . . . 80 mph,' 'put hand into electrical plugs.'" As if to make sense of this sudden eruption of violence in marketing-psychological terms, the researcher explained these less wholesome manifestations of fun by arguing that "destructive thrills and pleasure" were seen by teens as "aspirational" and "turned them on."

It was at this time that the executive who became my main informant on Sparka joined the account. He was immediately frustrated by the results of the Indian research. Having earlier remarked to me that there was no point in a local advertising agency thinking too much about global brand strategy (see pages 222–25), the executive was just as capable of taking the opposite tack and seething about the limitations that the Hub's policy was imposing on him. "*Everything's* fun!" he grumbled, "Pepsi's fun. Mirinda's fun. McDonald's is fun. What's *not* fun?!"

The account executive's frustration was in fact driven not so much by any resentment over fuzzy global positioning as by the uselessness of the research results that the attempt to "dimensionalize" Indian fun had generated. According to the parameters of the Sparka brand, those aspects of Indian fun that would be acceptable to the Hub were more or less indistinguishable from their counterparts in other countries. At the same time, the "destructive thrills and pleasure" listed above were quite obviously inadmissible as instantiations of Sparka fun. The practical upshot of this predicament was that, on the basis of this research, the account executive and his agency team were unable to construct a basis for local leverage vis-à-vis the Hub.

In fact the solution to their problem was already latent in the history of the account, which itself, of course, expressed much broader trends in global marketing. As the executives at the Hub had moved increasingly away from the characteristics of the "product in the bottle" toward extrinsics, they had self-consciously sought to exercise their control over the global-local marketing relationship through a model that was designed to contain local cultural variation within an overarching framework of psychological universals.

This movement was part of a tendency that went far beyond the specifics of the Sparka account alone. Indeed, it represented the widespread modification of the model of simple consumer convergence that had prevailed in the early 1990s (see pages 217–18), within which the global teen had been the paradigmatic conceptual figure. The earlier convergence model had foundered upon the shoals of the failed sales projections of many initially optimistic multinational consumer goods companies. The explanation of the actual causes for these failures was itself a highly contested terrain; in chapter 8 I will explore some of the analyses generated by Indian marketing and advertising personnel. But the important point for the purposes of the present discussion is that the movement toward a model that allowed cultural difference an important (albeit subordinate) place also allowed advertising and marketing professionals everywhere to develop a new kind of countercommodity through which to manage their relations with their multinational corporate clients: the culturally specific consumer.

Market Research: "Different and Modern Desires"

As a commodity, "the Indian consumer" shared the structural doubleness that is characteristic of the commodity form in general. It was crucial to its producers — that is, Indian advertising and marketing professionals — that it should contain both a general level of equivalence (the Indian *consumer*) and a level of irreducible particularity (the *Indian* consumer). Only in this way could "the Indian consumer" serve both as an effective and profitable conduit between multinational brands and Indian markets on the one hand, and as a proprietary object of local expertise on the other. It was only in its guise as "Indian *consumer*" that this commodity could be sold to multinational clients. And yet it was only in its corollary form, "the *Indian* consumer," that Indian advertising and marketing professionals could claim more or less exclusive rights to its production and distribution.

This conceptual balancing act was visible in a number of documents and reports generated by Indian advertising agencies around the time of my Bombay fieldwork. One of these was a research presentation constructed by the South and Southeast Asian offices of a large trans-national agency network, whose purpose was to guide the agency's clients in marketing to "Asian teens." On the one hand, the authors of the presentation cautioned that excessive cultural particularism was counterproductive: "Danger! Ignoring universal truths about people restricts the scope of brand-consumer relationships." On the other hand, the input of local experts was nevertheless indispensable since "blind borrowing from Western imagery is often self defeating, because [the consumer] realizes the difference between values and trappings; it may send wrong signals regarding social acceptance and approval."

Advertising agencies have always, in effect, brokered audiences and attention to their clients. Whether construed quantitatively (as so and so many viewers of an ad), or qualitatively (as market segments with particularly desirable characteristics), the implied ultimate product of an advertising agency, which accompanies and justifies its advertising, is an attentive consumer. The particular "Indian" versions of this atten-tive consumer were designed to convince corporate clients, first, that Indian consumers *were* just as hungry for consumer goods as their counterparts anywhere else in the world and, second, that the only way corporations were going to be able to tap into this hunger would be by employing local professional specialists as cultural guides.

Transnational advertising agencies were, in effect, matching the global scope of their clients' consumer commodities with a counter-commodity of their own, and insisting that the key that would "open" Indian markets to foreign companies could only be found by forging the two commodities into one.[10] Multinational clients like Sparka were being sold an apparent tool of access, while local consumers were being sold images of themselves, images that were tied to the branded products that were being advertised. Let us take a closer look at how this commodity, "the Indian consumer," was constructed in practice.

The most important aspect of the new market research programs that were being run by the agency networks was that they were not tied to specific client brands. Rather, they sought to provide a comprehensive profile of specific consumer groups, their needs, preferences, inclinations, and general environment. In this manner, agencies generated a commodity that was independent of their clients' goods, while at the same time insisting that these goods could not be successfully sold without reference to it. Furthermore, the value of this globally articulable information commodity would never be depleted since social change — or in marketing discourse, "the evolving needs of the consumer" — would require multinational clients to establish a running subscription.

Ostensibly this market research was purely empirical. Indeed, an important part of its legitimation rested upon the proposition that advertising agencies and marketing consultants were merely involved in "tracking" the objective and preexisting trends embodied in "the consumer," the better to enable their clients to engage in company-customer "relationship management" through strategically articulated brands. However, the manner in which the data was collected and processed ensured a kind of filtering through which fairly standardized types of consumer personae invariably emerged.[11]

There was, first of all, a peculiar circularity to much of the research. For instance, a research program operated within one agency network took "media ethnology" to be one of its central methodological devices, along with focus groups and consultations with selected trend gurus and professionals. The idea was that the program coordinator in the agency would keep him- or herself continually immersed in current media reportage on life-style trends, consumption patterns, and social transformations. This was faithfully and assiduously done; the coordinator dutifully made notes on articles of interest, assembled compilation videos of local television shows, and then sent them on up the agency system hierarchy to the regional research coordinator in Southeast Asia. Here, and at several points further up the chain, this information was further reduced, redacted, and tabulated. The aim was to produce a synoptic and globally integrated reference guide to local cultures of consumption. But one of the great ironies of the media ethnology aspect of this exercise (as well as one of its sources of internal consistency) was that many of its raw materials, for example the lifestyle articles featured in the weekly current affairs magazines, were themselves based on empirical data generated by advertising and marketing agencies.

Some of the diagnostic exercises performed in focus groups displayed a similar kind of self-referentiality. For example, teenage respondents would be given a pile of magazines, scissors, and glue and be encouraged to express their perceptions of a range of brands in the form of impressionistic collages. The fact that the basic semiotic elements that were available, and indeed chosen, for these collages were themselves fragments of existing advertisements was not thought to be problematic. If anything, the research coordinator interpreted it as evidence of his target consumers' fluency in the contemporary commodity image vernacular.

Certainly the research coordinator in the agency where I did my fieldwork was conscientious about avoiding overly "artificial" focus group settings that might make the respondents self-conscious. Sessions would, for instance, never be conducted in the agency offices. Often the coordinator would dispatch younger members of the agency team to lead the focus groups on the principle that "the kids" would be more likely to respond openly to someone closer to their own age. The coordinator was himself at this time only twenty-nine, but whenever he was in charge of coordinating a focus group he would be sure to dress in clothes that he thought would not make him look like a "corporate" or an "executive" type. Instead, in a bid to fit in, he would don jeans, baseball caps, and college sweatshirts—in short, the kind of Americanized global teenager uniform that had, in fact, been adopted by many of the participants in these focus groups. The coordinator's aim, of course, was to appear neutral; however, I gradually began to suspect that this uniform, in conjunction with the respondents' inevitable consciousness of the kind of exercise that they were engaged in, ended up encouraging responses along fairly standardized lines: a happy-go-lucky, consumption-friendly, self-consciously "modern" teen persona, frequently articulated in the sentimentally optimistic idiom of advertising itself.

This reproductive effect was particularly evident in one of the coordinator's favorite exercises, which was deliberately designed to move the data-collection process as far away as possible from being tied to specific products: encouraging his respondents to write short free-associative autobiographical essays. I have provided a mosaic of extracts here from male respondents in their late teens:

I am shy when I find a hi-fi crowd, but I handle myself well to carry on with them.

Well I like to be a little fashionable & I regularly hang out in discs [Bombay term for discos] like Razzberry, Madness, Waves.

My hobbies are: playing cricket, listening to music (English), roaming with friends, watching movies. I like to wear western clothes, and I am very much fond of foreign cars. I also like to visit historical places. I love to move with beautiful girls. I watch Channel V, MTV, Zee TV and Star Sports. I dislike: cigarettes, tobacco, drugs etc. Number of friends (boys): many uncountable. Number of friends (girls): seven (7). Names of girl friends: Meenal, Trishula, Meenakshi etc etc etc etc. Ambition: to become of Great Men [sic] or to become a Marine/Production Engineer.

Basically I am a kind of person who always likes to freak out [the phrase most often used by these respondents to denote having fun], and I have a dirty habit of never taking things seriously. I always want to do something new and obviously very unusual. Whenever I have any kind of problems, I always try to solve it by myself or something I ask my Dad about it [sic]. According to me my best friend is my Dad and no one else, as he always gives me the right decisions. . . . I also don't like to sit at one place — that's why my friends call me "WATER" as it is always flowing from one place to another.

I am cute+chubby, as my cousins+friends say. I am plump. I prefer going out at night with my cousins than sitting at home. I love late night parties. I am basically a freak out person. . . . I love talking on the phone. I love different types of watches. I love to be different from others. I am very frank. I hate arrogant people. I am very aggressive but also jolly.

From childhood to teenager, a funny, jolly boy, looking like a Parsi boy, that's why my friends and teacher call me "Bawa" [vernacular term for "Parsi"]. I like that my friends call me "Bawa." I like to be very close to my teacher because it has helped me in my studies and to increase my own potential. . . . I basically like wearing pants and shirt or T-shirt & rarely I wear jeans. I like making new friends whether a girl or a boy and like talking to them. I can ensure my friends that if they are with me in my company ie group, they will never ever feel lonely and bored. I like to help my parents and also friends to the best possible way that I can.

Basically, I'm a cool freaky person bobbling with enthusiasm. I would like to fool around and play pranks on others. . . . I like to dress smoothly/decently and am usually in jeans and T-shirts. I *love* to talk on the phone which I do everyday.

Before the way of spending my day was very simply and with outing with my friends and spending money. But now it is changed totally now I keep myself whole day busy, by playing, attending and bunking college, roaming with friends and girlfriends, spend money on different and modern desires.

I love to go to parties to freak out with the friends. To go for camps, to read. I don't know how to talk to the girl whenever a girl comes to talk I get very nervous.

Music is in my heart. . . . I am currently doing my computer animation and multimedia course with my college studies and planning to make advertisements which are good and catchy. I like to enjoy life to the fullest and dislike being tied down. I don't have any girlfriend in particular, I am a freelancer. I love women. They are my turn ons, and body odour my turnoff. My pals call me BOBBY. Evening I hang around at Pali Hill, Carter Rd, etc [fashionable Bandra (suburban Bombay) locations]. I am my papa's darling and my mummy's cherished pet. I like beautiful women and specially those burningly sexy eyes which turn igloos aflame. Well I like to end here and hope so you would like to know more about me. Tomorrow is mine. Keep smiling.

I'm basically a fun-loving guy. You come to know about it not from me but from the people around me. Whenever you have time, spend it to the fullest. And Enjoy. . . . I like to listen to MLTR [the Danish soft-rock group Michael Learns to Rock], Michael Bolton, Bon Jovi etc. My favourite numbers these days are "If ever you're in my arms again" & "Why did you break my heart?" With this you should get the hint that I'm heartbroken. My girl ditched me. But this is not the end of the world. We live . . . I'm not at all wise but I seek wisdom. It's like he who seeks wisdom is a wise man. He who thinks he has found it is *foolish*. This is what I think I am. Now it's up to you to decide what I am or how I am. But I enjoy my life. I love my life. I remember a song to end my biography. "This is the life, I don't want to let the feeling go. This is the life takes me where I want to go. As if living in Paradise. I'm living in Paradise."

In order to collate useful/usable information, the agency research coordinator would scan materials like the essays that I have excerpted here for recurrent themes and telling details. These themes included the importance of family and being perceived as an upbeat, sociable, and enthusiastic person;[12] the centrality of "freaking out" and "roaming" with friends; the popularity of television, music (both "English" and Hindi), talking on the telephone, and the opposite sex; the perpetual restlessness of teenage life ("my friends call me WATER").

At the same time, many of the responses showed a marked self-consciousness about the purpose of the exercise ("Now it's up to you to decide what I am or how I am"). One of the respondents — the one who was "planning to make advertisements which are good and catchy" — even appeared to see the essay as a promotional opportunity for himself, going so far as to embed his self-reflections in actual advertising slogans ("Tomorrow is mine" was at that time the baseline for Reebok sneakers in India). Others used phrases that directly echoed the tone and style of advertising copy, whether they were lifted from actual ads or not: "I love to be different from others"; "Music is in my heart"; "I love my life"; "Keep smiling"; "Enjoy." In this regard, the fact that the essays were written in English was important. The respondents were all recruited from elite or semi-elite Bombay "English-medium" colleges and educational institutions, and were therefore more or less fluent English-speakers.[13] Nevertheless, many of them would not have used English as their primary vernacular idiom outside of school hours. This may be one of the reasons why the expressions and idioms used by the respondents so often seemed to recapitulate and even quote advertising, television, and pop music, since these would be the source of a great many of the "modern" and "aspirational" English phrases with which these youngsters would regularly engage.

Where there's energy, there's HP

Propelling airplanes, mechanizing agriculture, energizing industries, igniting stoves, lighting lanterns ...
HP is synonymous with energy in India.

For the last 25 years and more, Hindustan Petroleum has been meeting India's energy needs in many ways. It's been powering the nation ahead with an inexhaustible supply of petrol, diesel, LPG, lubricants, kerosene and other petroleum products. In the new millennium HP is all set to unveil an exciting new phase in its growth. Diversifying into oil exploration and production, power generation, renewable energy ventures and much more. Confident of creating a future full of energy. Confident of enriching the lives of millions.

Future full of energy

• PETROL • DIESEL • LPG • KEROSENE • AVIATION FUEL • NAPHTHA • FURNACE OIL • BITUMEN • LOW SULPHUR HEAVY STOCK • LUBES & GREASES • SOLVENTS • INDUSTRIAL SPECIALTIES

15. Indian fun. Even the anti-erotics of an industrial wasteland can be injected with some innocent sex appeal by superimposing an image of an almost maniacally upbeat group of teens. This ad for Hindustan Petroleum plays on the juxtaposition to promise a "Future full of energy"; I have included it here to illustrate the insistently happy-go-lucky profile of the Indian teen as manifested in a great deal of mid-to-late-1990s advertising. The clean-cut gaiety of this image — complete with guitar, the obligatory index of "teen fun" — is strongly reminiscent of American beach-blanket movies of the early 1960s. The ad is a product of the theory, current in the marketing discourse of its time, that there is no such thing as a "GenerAsian X."

On this level, the focus groups, far from capturing a neutral snapshot of these young people's self-images, encouraged them actively to produce or construct themselves *as* consumers, whether in relation to specific products or not. No matter how "informal" a setting the agency attempted to contrive for its focus groups, the respondents would inevitably at the very least be conscious of speaking to peers who represented a world of glamour and fashion, a world of which they were conscious primarily through the messages and images of the commercial mass media. Thus the respondents were already, by the very nature of the interaction, interpellated as consumers.

This effect was endemic to the enterprise. The research coordinator's attempts to dress like "one of the kids" of course involved its own circularity, since his notions of how kids dressed were based upon the kinds of composite aspirational images that he distilled from his own research. Moreover, the teenagers with which he was interacting belonged to the first generation of young urban Indians for whom commercial satellite television and a profusion of multinational brands were a basic fact of life. Crucially, this point was constantly being underscored in the life-style features and editorial columns of the mass media. Whatever the actual relations of these teenagers to these new media (and that would be the subject of another study), this was a generation that was constantly being *told* that they belonged to a new global class whose collective identity — that which set them apart from their parents — resided in the commodity images and discourses relayed by these same media. Hence these images and discourses offered themselves as readily available and apparently suitable vehicles for self-expression in settings where these respondents were actively engaged qua consumers.

The very form of the market research exercise, then, actively helped respondents to objectify themselves through the deployment of commodity images. And if the process happened to throw up details that did not fit the requirements of the teen consumer persona, then these elements would swiftly be discarded as useless and even, in some cases, worthy of ridicule. For example, on one occasion the research coordinator came across a respondent essay that included the statement "I don't like to watch TV." Shaking his head in amazement, he exhaled, "What a loser!" and quickly disposed of the offending article. In this, his attitude was entirely ingenuous. While regularly offering me sophisticated and quite cynical commentaries on the advertising industry, he seemed at the same time to identify more or less completely with the "modernity" of the "aspirational" consumer personae constructed through the research over which he presided. Middle-class westerners who chose to reject the material comforts of their homes in order to live raggedly but righteously in Banaras were, to him, beneath contempt: "I have no respect for those guys. That they could just take a good career and chuck it . . . what about your family, you know?"[14] The research coordinator's reaction was telling in that, in the form of a personal reaction, it alighted precisely on one of the most important conceptual links between global consumer categories and their specifically Indian variants: the idea of the family.

A Family of Difference:
Dual Passports and the Value of Tradition

In the course of my discussion of the marketing category of "the global teen" (see pages 217–22), I pointed out that one of its most important distinguishing features was the promise of a transcendence of locality as a basis of identification, specifically of all the social institutions that most strongly embodied or represented locality, among them family (especially "the older generation") and "cultural tradition." It was notable, then, that "the Indian teen" involved a considerable modification — not to say a reversal — of this premise.

The cultural and moral centrality of family was a crucial marker of the cultural difference that, in the global marketing imagination, separated Indian teens — as a subspecies of the more generalized category "Asian teens" — from their Western counterparts.[15] This emphasis upon family involved two related themes: first, the authority of elders, which was itself read as an index of the persistent authority of Indian cultural "tradition";[16] second, the emphasis upon family in Indian life, which served to reproduce a binary scheme according to which Indians were contrasted with their more "individualistic" counterparts in the West. Sociologically speaking, there is undoubtedly some basis for suggesting that Indian teenagers, indeed Indians of any age, objectively depend on family connections more than their counterparts in the United States or in northwestern Europe do. However, that is not what concerns me here. Rather, I am interested in the way in which the emphasis that marketing professionals placed on the centrality of family to Indian and other Asian teenagers helped to construct a conceptual space within which "cultural tradition" could effectively coexist with an active participation in the globalizing dispensation of consumerism. As I have already suggested, in order to operate as an effective counter-commodity with which Indian advertising and marketing professionals could to some extent regulate their relations with MNC clients, the various manifestations of the Indian consumer had to take on this hybrid structure.

Let us return to the impasse at which the executive on the Sparka account found himself following his agency's attempt to "dimensionalize fun" for the Indian market (see pages 230–33). On the one hand, he was faced with a set of research results that could not, in any effective way, be used to gain any leverage for the Bombay agency vis-à-vis the Sparka system. All the unique manifestations of "Indian fun" that the research had generated were quite simply incommensurable with the Hub's guidelines for Sparka fun. On the other hand, as I have shown, the implicit drift of the account had been toward the elaboration of a universalist model of consumer psychology, within which cultural difference might be subsumed, much like a series of brand extensions. Precisely this transition toward a two-tiered model of consumer psychology and away from the specific positioning of the brand created the possibility for local marketing and advertising professionals to insist upon the right to define their own mediating— and indispensable—counter-commodity, the culturally differentiated consumer.

A research document generated by one Bombay consumer marketer around this time illustrates my point. First of all, the desires and aspirations of Indian teenagers had to be identified as fully congruent with consumerism: "Teenagers in India are success-oriented (success defined in material not spiritual terms)." On this level, their "key values and attitudes" were enumerated as follows: "Materialism: aspire for [sic] a comfortable life-style, material goods and live in a world of 'I, Me and Mine'; practicality: realists not idealists. They accept the status quo and have no desire/drive to change the system. . . . Friends provide the route to fun and freedom (group activity, belonging, approval). . . . Having fun/enjoyment provides them with a break from routine and is associated with friends (particularly within a group)."

Thus far, then, the Indian teen was entirely and necessarily generic. Nevertheless, this was only half the story, since these "modern values" were themselves subject to an "Indian expression": "Teenagers in India carry a dual cultural passport—that of Indian culture and global cultural popular culture. The modernisation of Indian teenagers manifests itself in their desire to adopt Western life-styles (materialism), their need for independence and their acknowledgement of the need for self-reliance. . . . These modern values, however, exist and are expressed within the Indian cultural context."

"Culture" was, first of all, not simply a matter of content for Indian teenagers, the authors of the document argued, but also of commitment. According to the authors, the bonds of culture were simply a *stronger* force for Indian teenagers than for their "Western" counterparts. The most direct instantiation of these bonds was the centrality of family:

> "Nativity" or the feeling of bonding with the social and cultural environment plays a pre-eminent role. The nativity factor works at two levels. 1) *values:* while teenagers feel the need for independence and self-reliance, these modern values exist within the framework of deep-rooted Indian values pertaining to *the family*. As opposed to teenagers from other countries ["other countries" here implies "Western countries," since the preeminence of family was also acknowledged as a more general "Asian" cultural characteristic[17]] the family plays a very important (acknowledged) role for them. Parents serve as role models, they respect/obey elders, look toward parents for guidance in important matters, are comfortable with arranged marriage. 2) *culture:* [Indian] teenagers have adopted global popular culture—junk food, preoccupation with fashion, importance of music, television—but they have been interpreted in an Indian cultural context.

The importance for marketers of paying heed to this "Indian cultural context" was then, once again, underlined with reference to the satellite music television wars: "The success of Channel V bears witness to the importance of adapting to the needs of the Indian teenager. Its rival MTV failed to capture a toehold in the market primarily because they offered global fare to the Indian teenager, failing to make allowances for the cultural context within which these teenagers operate."

One of the most notable features of "the Indian teen" was the overt conservatism of both its "global" and "local" components. On the global side, the Sparka document had coupled a "modern" materialism with the assertion that Indian teenagers "have no desire/drive to change the system." Similarly, a 1998 article in *Outlook* magazine (a news/current affairs publication that competes with *India Today*) featured the imagined voice of the contemporary Indian teenager as follows: "You know, *yaar,* we're not really into any cause-shause, conscience-shoncence, and all that *lafda.* Basically, Dropping Out, Revolution, Creative Expression is for the old guys, *yaar,* all that '60s *hungama* is a load of shit. Dylan and all are totally *khatam.* Better just to *sambhalo* your own life, *na?*" (Ghose and Jahagirdar 1998, 61).

By the same token, because the "global" side of the equation had already been defined as modern, the "Indian" side of this humanoid commodity — which was its necessary badge of difference — had to be defined as "traditional," and therefore also essentially conservative: the persistence of family values, the continued relevance of "traditional" practices like arranged marriage, and so forth. Some, like *Femina* editor Sathya Saran, unwittingly extended Partha Chatterjee's discussion in "The Nation and Its Women" (Chatterjee 1993), by suggesting that the maintenance of "Indianness" within the larger framework of a globalizing consumerist dispensation was both the privilege and the responsibility of women (see Mankekar 1999 for parallel reflections on the social ideology of Indian television vis-à-vis womanhood and national identity).[18] Saran explained to me that since Indian men tended to have "gone in for globalization headfirst,"[19] it was part of her duty, as the editor of India's premier women's magazine, gently to remind her readership that their consumerist/careerist aspirations should not let them forget their pivotal social position as the moral anchors of the domestic sphere.

Here, once again, Indian difference from the West was understood as rooted in the cultural-moral bedrock of family life. Saran saw *Femina* itself as a source of advice, a medium through which women faced with the confusing onrush of choices brought by modern life and consumption might be offered "some guidance." On the one hand, she understood her readers as motivated by eminently "modern" appetites: "Our target reader is the working woman, a professional, aged twenty to forty, married, with one to two children, or thinking of having one to two children. It's the woman who wants to better her world. But the target reader is not necessarily the same as the *actual* reader. The actual reader includes all women in India who can read English, who have an aspirational mindset."[20] On the other hand, Saran was concerned to remind her readers not to discard too quickly what she understood as their unique role within Indian family life, a role that fused moral authority with a quiet social conservatism. By avoiding the "confrontational" methods of their more atomized sisters in the West, Saran was suggesting, Indian women might seek to combine their participation in all that was new with a careful maintenance of the local social fabric. "We keep underlining to the Indian woman that she is part of a *society*—unlike in the West, where they seem to think that [people] function in a vacuum. Somewhere the Indian woman holds onto persuasion, patience, and taking a stand, rather than confrontation. It's a very quiet social mission. We tell the Indian woman not to let herself be subjugated, but not to walk out either."

As I have shown, the maintenance of "Indian culture" was not in every case understood to be the province of women. Womanhood, however, operated as a unique construct through which to highlight the moral *priority* of the observance of "traditional" values in a changing world. At the same time, the figure of the Indian teenager, as another modern/traditional hybrid Indian consumer-type, served to exemplify the *persistence* of "tradition," even at the demographic cutting edge. A theme that I will explore in greater depth in the next chapter was the way in which many Bombay culture industry professionals drew upon the claim that Indians, as colonial and then postcolonial subjects, were well practiced at the art of forging composite identities out of culturally disparate materials. Invariably, however, the figure of the family operated as a convenient shorthand for the continuing importance of "tradition" and "Indian cultural values" in the lives of Indian teenagers, thus distinguishing their lives from the presumed anomie and excessive individualism of their imagined western counterparts. The distinction frequently manifested itself, for example, as the assertion that there was no "GenerAsian X."

One effect of this increasingly standardized distinction was that India — along with several other imagined localities — was set up as the location of "authentic culture," in contradistinction to "the West," whose complementary identity rested upon individuation, universality, and "culturelessness." On the one hand, this relationship appeared, in a limited way, as a challenge to the perceived universalizing ambitions of Western-made (a.k.a. "global") popular culture. On the other hand, Indian consumers were still understood to have "aspirational mindsets," to want to participate in a global repertoire of images, goods, and services. Consequently, the ways in which they could acceptably be marked as "Indian" were rather restricted and inevitably stereotypical.

This is not to say that the semiotic repertoire of Indian difference, as staged through commodity images, was necessarily either finite or unchangeable. Nevertheless, because so much of the legitimacy of the consumerist dispensation depended upon its promise to articulate Indianness with "aspirational" standards that were themselves imagined as global, that Indianness would inevitably have to be recognized as congruent with a well-established and internationally acknowledged system of significations.

In parts 1 and 2 of this study, we have seen how this dynamic played itself out in the marketing and advertising of two Indian brands. In the context of the present chapter, which describes a relationship between Indian advertising and marketing professionals and a global client, the question of marketable Indianness has additional ramifications. On the most basic level, I have shown that the insistence upon the difference of the Indian consumer allowed these Indian professionals a certain amount of leverage, a zone of relative autonomy, vis-à-vis their multinational clients. More generally, and here I am prefiguring the arguments of the next chapter, the construction of "the Indian consumer" allowed the Indian marketing and advertising industries to legitimate their own roles in the overall project of consumerist globalization.

In the first section of this chapter, I described the way in which many of my industry informants in Bombay seemed bent on identifying the term "globalization" with an older narrative of cultural imperialism. In the light of the material discussed in this chapter, we are now in a position to see why this was a strategic move. The deployment of the hybrid "Indian consumer" allowed these professionals to situate themselves as the guardians and defenders of Indian cultural specificity and national pride. John Hutnyk has remarked, in a different context, that the figure of hybridity, which for some time has claimed radical potential in postcolonial studies and elsewhere, is in fact quite congruent with consumer capitalism, since "the place for the articulation of hybridity is also a space that already seems all too easily articulated with the market. Hybridity and difference sell; the market remains intact" (Hutnyk 2000, 36).

From the standpoint of the Indian marketing and advertising industries, the particular hybrid formation that was "the Indian consumer" had the distinct advantage of displaying the apparently beneficent capacity of globalizing consumer capitalism to support and even revive cultural specificity. By the same token, the supposedly inherent and traditional cultural difference of "the Indian consumer" — duly supported by consumerism — served to limit the potential social disruptions of the global expansion of capital. The journalists who had offered the insouciant yet quietist voice of the imagined contemporary Indian teen were thus led to reflect that Indian teens possessed "conservative values, but also perhaps values that have helped India avoid some of the uglier pathologies of Mcmodernity" (Ghose and Jahagirdar 1998, 70). In this way, the invention and deployment of "the Indian consumer" used figures of cultural difference simultaneously to affirm and to deny globalization.[21]

Conclusion

In this chapter, I have considered the strategic basis for the creation, by Indian advertising and marketing professionals, of a culturally marked counter-commodity called "the Indian consumer." By examining a particular advertising account, the multinational soft drink brand Sparka, I have sought to demonstrate the way in which the increasing globalization of consumer markets in the 1990s necessitated a gradual shift away from a concentration on the specific ingredients of individual brands to a more general consideration of the place of cultural difference within a still-universalist model of consumer psychology. This shift was in turn a particular response to a more general change in the way that global consumer markets were conceptualized from the heyday of "the global teen" in the 1980s and early 1990s to the insistence upon cultural hybridity that followed.

From the perspective of local advertising agencies, dealing with a multinational client involves quite different kinds of strategies than dealing with local accounts like the ones I discussed in parts 1 and 2 of this study. Although the interpersonal dynamics between agency and local client representatives remain important, the complexity of decision-making processes in a global client system requires local advertising and marketing affiliates increasingly to stake their positions on the discursive terrain of market research. I described the way in which this market research, partly because its object is the production of a commodity that can be sold to multinational clients, in complex ways tends to reproduce certain quite standardized representations of consumer identity as well as of "Indian tradition."

In chapter 8, I will step back from the detailed consideration of individual advertising campaigns in order to situate the construction of the new "global Indian" consumer in relation to larger transformations in a postcolonial system of distinction and value. While my discussion in chapter 7 focused on the strategic relationship between the Indian advertising and marketing industries and their MNC clients, chapter 8 is more closely concerned with these industries' attempts to cope with the peculiar effects that the globalization of consumer brands had on their own professional terrain: the calculus of value and desire in metropolitan India. In chapter 7, I narrated the move toward an increased amount of local leverage vis-à-vis the MNCs as a victory of sorts for my Bombay informants. In chapter 8, we will see that the process of globalization that made this ostensibly empowering move possible was, in equal measure, perceived as a crisis by these very same informants. Even as I move away from the specifics of individual campaigns, the recurrent themes of the previous chapters move back to center stage: the affective force of the commodity image, the ambivalent effect of globalization on locality, and the simultaneously defensive and triumphant construction of "the Indian consumer."

8

Close Distance: Constructing "the Indian Consumer" II

In chapter 7 I showed how cultural difference could become a means by which local advertising and marketing professionals could deal with MNC clients. Quite deliberately, I emphasized the strategic aspect of this process, how it helped my informants to carve out a zone of relative executive autonomy for themselves. In the present chapter, by contrast, I want to take a step back from the specific details of individual campaigns in order to return to the "big picture." I will argue that the globalization of consumerism did not merely offer my informants an opportunity to create a proprietary commodity called the Indian consumer. Rather it also brought about a radical shift in the politics of value that structured the project of advertising in India, a shift that, for all the media boosterism, was in the first instance experienced as a crisis.

This crisis of value initially presented itself to me, during my fieldwork, as a puzzle. It seemed that my informants, as well as the media that expressed their collective vision, were presenting me with a double discourse on what to do about MNC brands. On the one hand, they loudly berated foreign corporations for what one marketing consultant called their "value arrogance": Did they not realize that Indian consumers needed to be addressed in ways that respected their essential cultural specificity? On the other hand, these same executives had nothing but scorn for the apparently condescending way in which many transnationals had tried to "Indianize" their advertising or their products: Did Indians not deserve the same quality as everyone else? Either way, the MNCs were trashed for their neo-imperialist assumptions. Now this double discourse prepared the ground for the kind of strategic maneuver that I described in chapter 7. But it also reflected a profound ambivalence on the part of my executive informants, an ambivalence that was experienced as personal and aesthetic as much as it was felt to be professional and strategic.[1]

In the last paragraph I spoke of the collective vision of the business. Certainly, I would not wish to imply that my informants' opinions were uniform. Far from it. But taken together, and understood in relation to the practices and political economy of their professional situation, they did reveal the kind of patterned intersections of objective possibility and embodied preference that Pierre Bourdieu calls a "field," or, in the case of particular professional groups, a "field of production" (Bourdieu 1993). As a participant observer, one aim of my *field*work was, precisely, to come to grips with the field of production in which my informants lived and worked. From such a vantage point, the advent of globalization — expressed in this case as "the coming of the MNCs" — was a bolt of lightning that, in its brief brilliance, illuminated constitutive connections between professional practice, cultural history, and personal preference.

Throughout my account, I have emphasized how the production of advertising is, in complex ways, inextricable from the aesthetic inclinations that structure its makers' positions and desires. Certain themes have recurred: the production of an "aspirational Indianness," the tension between populist claims and elitist aims, the dialectical movement between affect-intensive image and the articulation of narrative, the struggle between the consumerist dream of social transformation and the inescapable weight of history. My hope in the present chapter is to pull all these strands together by means of a meditation on a moment of crisis. But in order to make sense of this moment, we must first make sure that we understand the cultural formation whose passing it marked.

The Elementary Forms of Globalization

My informants' ambivalence about the localization of MNC brands arose out of a contradiction between the official narrative of globalizing markets and the cultural politics of a postcolonial world system of images. In chapter 7, I showed how an early universalizing vision of globalization was gradually adjusted to incorporate cultural difference, not least because it was in the interests of local executives to promote such a localization. In the present section, I suggest that this adjustment was not simply a matter of local strategy, but arose in part from fundamental gaps in the way that globalizing markets had been conceived in marketing theory.

There were two important problems. The first was a tendency to confuse the universal appeal associated with the functional advantages of goods with the global prominence of certain brands. The second problem was an elision of the way in which the value of global brands in many "developing" markets was structured by a postcolonial politics of distinction that, in turn, was based on what Orlove (1997) calls "the allure of the foreign." In both cases, the role played by advertising — by commodity images — was misunderstood.

In order to see how these misunderstandings (or omissions) were built into the classic theory of globalizing consumer markets, I will focus on an article that was both inaugural and paradigmatic in its field, Harvard Business School Professor Theodore Levitt's "The Globalization of Markets" (1983).[2] Levitt's first, and relatively uncontroversial, claim was that recent advances in telecommunications and transport technologies had created a global infrastructure that now demanded that marketers think in global terms in order to compete successfully. It was

> a new commercial reality — the emergence of global markets for standardized consumer products on a previously unimagined scale of magnitude. Corporations geared to this new reality benefit from enormous economies of scale[3] in production, distribution, marketing and management. By translating these benefits into reduced world prices, they can decimate competitors that still live in the disabling grip of old assumptions about how the world works. . . . The world's needs and desires have been irrevocably homogenized. (Levitt 1983, 92, 93)

It is important to emphasize that Levitt was *not* arguing that all consumers should or, indeed, would soon be consuming the same models of the same products everywhere. Rather, his argument was premised upon the same kind of logic that gave birth to the notion of "the global teen" (see pages 217–22). The idea was that market *segments* in one country — teenagers or professional women, for instance — were, because of the expansion of telecommunications technologies and all that went with that fact, tending to converge not with other segments in their own countries, but rather with their equivalent segments in *other* countries: "A market segment is seldom unique; it has close cousins everywhere precisely because technology has homogenized the globe" (ibid., 94).

The most fundamental part of Levitt's argument, however — and this was an insight for which he thanked the Japanese — was that a good product at a low price would have an unbeatable appeal. This appeal would be powerful enough to transcend "superficial" cultural differences, because it plumbed deeper levels of consumer motivation. It was at this stage in the argument that Levitt's appeal to the primacy of functionality entered the picture. Intelligent marketers, Levitt advised, would not let themselves get tangled up in pandering to the potentially endless levels of cultural variation that they might encounter in local markets (in fact, Levitt used Clifford Geertz's "turtles all the way down" anecdote about the quicksand of cultural interpretation to support his argument [ibid., 102]). Contrary to the gospel that held that a key aspect of the sovereignty of consumers was their right to have their cultural identities addressed by the products they consumed, Levitt stressed that

> the global competitor will seek constantly to standardize his offering everywhere. He will digress from this standardization only after exhausting all possibilities to retain it, and he will push for reinstatement of standardization whenever digression and divergence have occurred. He will never assume that the customer is a king who knows his own wishes. . . . Most executives in multinational corporations are thoughtlessly accommodating. They falsely presume that marketing means giving the consumer what he says he wants rather than trying to understand what exactly he'd like. So they persist with high-cost, customized multinational products and practices instead of pressing hard and pressing properly for global standardization. (94, 96, 97)

Now, as Armand Mattelart (1991) has pointed out, Levitt's pivotal article says next to nothing about advertising. At first sight, it might appear that it is precisely by ignoring the kinds of "intangible" value created by advertising that Levitt is able to maintain the impression that material functionality ultimately takes precedence over "cultural meaning." And yet at the same time, advertising implicitly sneaks into his argument as soon as he gets around to providing concrete examples of the kind of globalization that he is discussing.

Here, then, there is a tension: To illustrate his good product/low price theorem, Levitt uses a case study of the marketing of washing machines in Europe, arguing that simple functional efficiency will always triumph over complex (and expensive) regional adaptations. But when he wishes to evoke the globalization of consumer consciousness, he turns, for empirical support, to brands whose value rests largely on their dramatization through advertising: "Commercially, nothing confirms [globalization] as much as the success of McDonald's from the Champs Elysées to the Ginza, of Coca-Cola in Bahrain and Pepsi-Cola in Moscow, and of rock music, Greek salad, Hollywood movies, Revlon cosmetics, Sony televisions, and Levi jeans everywhere" (ibid., 93).

Not only does the argument now appear to have moved from function to image, but the very prominence of these brands would itself seem to contradict both sides of Levitt's good product/low price theory of globalization. First, price: one of the main rationales for a corporation to invest in brand-building advertising is precisely to avoid having to compete on price. Second, the good product: whereas Levitt's model assumes that products compete on the basis of functional superiority (and price), branding as an exercise assumes that markets have been saturated to an extent where there are few discernible material differences between competing products within a particular category. As one Bombay advertising agency's brochure put it: "Parity situations are going to be the order of the day" (Contract Strategic Planning Group 1995). In a context where any technical or functional innovation will immediately be duplicated by a company's rivals, competitive advantage cannot, for any length of time, be based on the functional properties of a particular company's product.

Levitt's model, then, elided the role played by advertising in its depiction of the globalization of consumer markets. Much like the evidentiary effect of advertising images themselves, the readily observable fact that people all over the world desired Coca-Cola, McDonald's, and the rest helped to lend a superficial kind of credence to the idea of homogenizing global markets. Initially, this fact in itself seemed like evidence enough; which particular groups were doing the desiring, which particular groups were doing the buying, and what their relative motivations were remained, at this stage, a minor concern.

Such questions may well have been downplayed in part because the vision of a globalizing consumer consciousness proved eminently marketable. I have already argued that Levitt's model implicitly suggested a contradiction between the promise of lower prices and the globalization of brands. This contradiction became all the more evident as soon as Levitt's gospel was taken up by the transnational advertising business. Saatchi and Saatchi Advertising's meteoric rise (and equally precipitous fall) in the 1980s was, in no small part, borne aloft by Levitt's globalization discourse; indeed, Levitt himself — in his capacity as guru of globalization — was a member of the board of directors. (See K. Goldman 1996 for a lively account of this relationship.)

Whereas for Levitt the beneficiaries of market globalization had been both corporations (economies of scale) and consumers (lower prices and better products), the Saatchis, whose business was, after all, promoting their clients' brands, could only maintain this fiction as long as "the consumer" was now understood to be the corporate client. Public space, like any other commodity, came cheaper in bulk. As the Saatchis' 1986 annual report put it: "Power of scale in advertising means increased flexibility of resources, the ability to attract, reward and retain the very best talent, superior media-buying clout and better media-buying systems. . . . And it means improved global information systems, increased technological resources and increased access to a broad range of communications and consulting experience . . ." (Mattelart 1991, 51).

Similarly, the apparently hegemonic profusion of global brand images offered clients a kind of *semiotic* economy of scale. In the words of the Saatchi report: "The time has come for transnational advertisers to *capitalize on universally recognized cultural symbols and references. . . .* Without TV and motion picture education about the virile, rugged character of the American West, the worldwide proliferation of the Marlboro brand would not have been possible" (Mattelart 1991, 53, Mattelart's emphasis).

The ability to "capitalize" on such symbols and references meant, for corporate clients, *not* having to compete on price — particularly not with markedly inexpensive local brands. (Indeed, the anxiety surrounding the purity of global brands in "Third World" markets often suggested a fear of cultural miscegenation.) End consumers — those who could afford the products — also stood to "capitalize" on these symbols and references, precisely insofar as they remained reliable indices of aspirational achievement.

In the West, the ubiquitous availability of the products that these global brands represented had made them bywords for mass consumerism, elements of a commodity-based collective consciousness on a par with the postwar narratives of Hollywood or network television. In India, however, the social role of the same brands had been defined precisely by their highly *limited* availability — they had been, as it were, tokens in a prestige economy.[4] Before the mid-1970s, when several global brands chose to or were forced to leave India, this limited availability had largely been a matter of high prices and limited distribution. Consequently, until 1991, stringent controls on the importation and promotion of foreign brands in India meant that many of them had been available only through smuggled, "gray-market" channels.

At the same time, *awareness* of these brands in India far outstripped their actual availability. This was a result both of the advertisements featured in foreign magazines and of a deliberate policy on the part of many of these companies of continuing, in a limited way, to advertise their products even though they were currently not available in stores. Of course, particularly before the expansion of commercial television in the 1980s, this awareness was still largely restricted to a segment of the population that was, in proportional terms, rather small. This segment would include such groups as businessmen traveling to the Persian Gulf or Singapore, Indians with family members in the diaspora, and readers of English-language print media.

The upshot of this was that major Western brands became important markers of social distinction for a small elite. But I want to note just how much of the mystique associated with these goods depended on their capacity to serve as physical embodiments of a source of value that was understood to reside *elsewhere*. This elsewhere might in shorthand be called "the West," but in fact it was conceived as at once concrete and abstract, as a real place *and* as a mythical location. The de facto magic of the goods was that they provided concrete, *present* evidence of this absent source, as conjured in advertising. Auratic in Walter Benjamin's sense, at hand, tactile, yet transcendently irradiated, these brands reverberated with what one might call a kind of "close distance."

Formally, the effect is typical of consumer goods advertising as a *genre,* and of course Benjamin himself took commercial photography to be one of the most important sites of the "reactionary" deployment of aura (Benjamin 1999a). Its basis, I would argue, may be found in the double structure of the commodity image. Advertising photography typically mobilizes the most banal details of everyday life in such a way as to bring them almost dizzyingly close and yet at the same time suffuse them with a sense of transcendent — not to say euphoric — perfection. "Light is used in conjunction with focus to create a hypertactile effect. Things look real; in fact, almost too real" (Rosenblum 1978 quoted in Schudson 1984, 217). At the same time, this busyness of detail is abstracted away from the contingencies of everyday situations and pressed into the service of generic, quasi-mythological categories. As Schudson illustrates: "An actress seeking a role in a television commercial is expected to have two wardrobes ready for auditions — standard and 'upscale.' She is to represent either the middle-American housewife or the affluent American housewife, but never a particular person" (212).

For all its play with close distance, advertising in the United States nevertheless refers to an imagined location that is supposed — at least *in potentia* — to be the consumer's own. In India, however, the formula of close distance was quite literally mapped onto spatial, geographical separation. The auratic efficacy of foreign brands, as conveyed through advertising, was all too evidently *not* rooted in the local environment of Indian consumers, even as the tantalizing evidence of the pictures insisted that it was within reach. Any understanding of the aesthetic politics of globalization must take into account this double displacement. On the postcolonial periphery, the advertisement's formal play with close distance became entangled with the imagined difference between "the West" and the rest. This entanglement structured the way in which the "objective" conjunctures of global consumer capitalism in the postwar period became sedimented in the "subjective," embodied memory of a whole generation of urban, middle-class Indians. This historically distinctive experience was the background, I will argue, for the way in which my informants — come the mid-1990s — responded to the crisis of value that was "globalization."

Expressed in this formal manner, my argument allows us to move toward a critique of some of the key assumptions embedded in the marketing theory of globalization. Nevertheless, its abstraction fails to capture the dimension that, after all, provides the concrete basis from which the critique can be developed: what it was *like* to grow up at this time, in this place, amid these images. Therefore, I have devoted the following section to a series of personal accounts, each of which speaks to a distinctive aspect of this experience.

The View from Bombay: Remembering the Postcolonial Commodity Image

The memory of an imagined metropolis, distant yet always present, cherished in childhood or early adolescence, is a frequent trope in postcolonial writing. It is no coincidence that the media of such memories are frequently the forms through which Euro-American popular culture was diffused: magazines, advertisements, movies, fiction in all its forms.

Ardarshir Vakil's *Beach Boy,* a fictionalized memoir of growing up in the Bombay of the early 1970s, powerfully evokes this effect:

> Legally, foreign cigarettes, like other foreign products, were banned from sale in India. But there were paanwallahs and small cigarette shops everywhere that stocked smuggled goods. Mystique surrounded these imported items. They looked so bright, smelt so new. I used to peer at the cigarette advertisements in *Time, Newsweek* and *Life:* Marlboro men on their horses, women smoking Virginia Slims in Victorian underwear, with the logo [*sic*] "You've come a long way baby!" and Salem girls, dark-haired, blue-jeaned, healthy women, romping around with some tanned muscular jocks. The women laughed while training a hose-pipe on the men. These were clean, fresh, fun-loving, minty-breathed Americans. I stared intently at these modern gods, trying to catch every detail and motion of their bodies. White, foreign, but so within reach on the page. One day, I told myself, I would be there. In those green New England woods in the background of the picture. With my striped shirt and my coloured backpack, gambolling with that dark-haired girl who looks like Ali McGraw and smoking Salem cigarettes. In the meantime I honed my knowledge of which paanwallah in Bombay stocked the freshest brand of smuggled American fags. (Vakil 1998, 83–84)

Vakil's passage is powerful not least because it documents the tension that is formally constitutive of the commodity image while at the same time illustrating how, from a postcolonial standpoint, this tension additionally comes to describe the spatial gap between the postcolony and the metropolis. These remembered images characteristically fuse the quotidian with the transcendent in depicting cigarette-smoking "modern gods." Moreover, in Vakil's recollection, a relatively straightforward consumerist aspiration is inextricable from a much larger longing to participate in a metropolitan modernity ("foreign, but so within reach. . . . One day, I told myself, I would be there"). The most tangible focus of this desire is a product sexualized according to a semiotic repertoire that is on one level colonial and nostalgic ("women smoking Virginia Slims in Victorian underwear"), on another contemporary and banal ("clean, fresh, fun-loving, minty-breathed"). Indeed, much of the power behind the conventionally stylized details of the image appears to reside in the half-sincere belief that there is a "real" location, an elsewhere, where such a life is embodied and attainable ("in those green New England woods").

Arjun Appadurai, for his part, evokes the moment at which the imagined modernity conjured by earlier British popular cultural forms, inevitably bound up with the colonial experience, began to be supplanted by a more consumerist and more sexualized American variant:

> In my own early life in Bombay, the experience of modernity was notably synaesthesic and largely pretheoretical. I saw and smelled modernity reading *Life* and American college catalogs at the United States Information Service library, seeing B-grade films (and some A-grade ones) from Hollywood at the Eros Theatre, five hundred yards from my apartment building. I begged my brother at Stanford (in the early 1960s) to bring me back blue jeans and smelled America in his Right Guard when he returned. I gradually lost the England that I had previously imbibed in my Victorian schoolbooks, in rumors of Rhodes scholars from my college, and in Billy Bunter and Biggles books devoured indiscriminately with books by Richmal Crompton and Enid Blyton. Franny and Zooey, Holden Caulfield, and Rabbit Angstrom slowly eroded that part of me that had been, until then, forever England. Such are the little defeats that explain how England lost the Empire in postcolonial Bombay. (Appadurai 1996, 1–2)

Unwittingly echoing Appadurai, a Bombay journalist in 1997 described the relative seductiveness of this new "colonization" by U.S.

mass consumerism in terms of a proffered modernity to which full access was — at least ostensibly — not restricted by the colonial calculus of "not quite/not white" (Bhabha 1994):[5]

> Informal colonization, without administrative coherence, seemed hardly as threatening as 300 years of imperial shackles. The company *sarkar* [government] was back, only it wasn't bowler-hatted but disguised as a public limited caucus. Everyone could belong to America in a way they never could to Britain for all the Dickens one read and the John Donne one quoted and that too by the simple expedient of quaffing a Coke, eating a burger, or wearing blue jeans. Perhaps it was then that the Battle of Britain was truly lost. (R. Ahmed 1997)

Moving back another decade, Salman Rushdie, whose Bombay childhood took place in the 1950s, recalls a "dream-England," similar to the one that was supplanted in Appadurai's imagination by American commodity images only a few years later. Rushdie's breakthrough novel, *Midnight's Children*, teems with commodity images looming into view as concrete fragments of a remembered world.[6] Reflecting upon the writing process, Rushdie writes that the very fragmentation of the memories that offered themselves to his imagination two decades later made them all the more suggestive: "The shards of memory acquired greater status, greater resonance, because they were *remains;* fragmentation made trivial things seem like symbols, and the mundane acquired numinous qualities" (Rushdie 1991b, 12).

This numinous illumination of prosaic details suggests an intriguing and troubled kinship between childhood memory fragments and the representational devices of the commodity image. And indeed, Benjamin's notion of "aura" juxtaposes them. He speaks of advertising as a form of "photography that can endow any soup can with cosmic significance but cannot grasp a single one of the human connections in which it exists" (Benjamin 1999a, 526). And yet, precisely this same abstraction from the purposive and instrumental rounds of productive life makes a fragment of childhood memory so powerful, "at once as evanescent and as alluringly tormenting as half-forgotten dreams. For childhood, knowing no preconceived opinions, has none about life" (Benjamin 1999b, 613).[7]

Embedded in childhood memory, the auratic postcolonial commodity image anchors the "allure of the foreign" in a manner that is so resonant precisely *because* it is charged with an affective significance that goes far beyond the instrumental purpose of the advertisement. And this is perhaps also why the denouement of this imaginary investment is so traumatic. For many of these writers and their precursors, the moment of shock is their actual arrival in the metropolis that, close up, turns out to be grimy and disappointingly prosaic. As Benjamin at his most "Marxist" might have hoped, the encounter often leads to some form of radicalization, whether literary-philosophical, as in the case of Rushdie, or more traditionally political. But whatever its outcome, the moment is defined by a sense of disjuncture in which the longed-for elsewhere, in which personal ambitions and identifications have been so deeply invested, turns out to be nowhere (and yet inescapably "now-here").[8]

None illustrates this sense of (possibly salutary) estrangement better than the protagonist of V. S. Naipaul's *The Mimic Men* who, at a moment of personal distress, finds himself and his female companion at the physical heart of the global transmission of colonial imaginaries, the canteen of the BBC World Service:

> Her despair worked on me; we acted and reacted on one another, there in the canteen of a radio service which, when picked up in remote countries, was the very voice of metropolitan authority and romance, bringing to mind images, from the cinema and magazines, of canyons of concrete, brick and glass, motorcars in streams, lines of lights, busyness, crowded theatre foyers, the world where everything was possible; there now, at the heart of that metropolis, we sat, at a plastic-topped table, before thick cups of cooling tea and plates with yellow crumbs, each drawing out the frenzy from the other. (Naipaul 1969, 46)

Meanwhile, back in the Indian postcolonial periphery, the distance between the actuality of Bombay life and the commodity-colored perfection of the metropole remained a heightened source of commercial value.[9] A particular class of professionals, the relatively small group of Anglophone copywriters and advertising executives known as "the Churchgate Set" (see pages 106–15), were forging careers out of their self-consciously cosmopolitan identifications and their expert understanding of this imagined empire of signs. They were the producers of the very words and images that would etch themselves onto the young minds of the likes of Vakil and Appadurai.

Also coming of age at this time was the generation of advertising professionals that would take over from the Churchgate Set, who would grapple first with the massification of Indian advertising in the 1980s and then with the onslaught of globalization in the 1990s. As I argued in chapter 4, the unabashed Bombay-centric cosmopolitanism of the Churchgate Set rendered it both technically and ideologically unacceptable to the new mass consumerist dispensation. Nevertheless, its idiom was necessarily constitutive of the early experience of the next generation. And in fact for all that the extension of mass consumer markets in the 1980s required a new idiom to go with the new technology of television, the basic equation upon which the close distance of the older commodity image had been based remained unchanged. As we have seen, Indian corporations like EMW continued to position themselves as the conduits to a source of quality that was understood to be *foreign*.

It was not until the reforms of 1991, which brought about the sudden appearance of a host of "global" brands on Indian shop shelves, that the imagined *spatial* configuration of value that had underpinned the colonial and postcolonial commodity imaging project was decisively challenged. As in Levitt's foundational portrait, in the new dispensation, Indian consumers were supposedly no longer members of a merely national market; rather, they were graduating to membership of a globally interlinked series of segments. And the goods were, it seemed, meeting them halfway: longed-for brands and distant technologies were suddenly available over the counter, around the corner. Within just a couple of years, however, it was becoming clear that the Levittian utopia of lower prices and globally linked segments was not coming to pass. Foreign brands were generally priced far above equivalent local products and the much-hyped 250 million-strong Indian middle class was, in the event, simply not buying, at least not with the avidity upon which the "opening" of Indian markets had been premised.

Bombay advertising and marketing professionals consequently found themselves in a singularly ambivalent position. In 1991–92, as I will show, many of them had participated fully in painting the Levittian picture of hundreds of millions of "middle-class" Indians desperate to get their hands on global brands. At the same time, these same professionals could not help but be personally conscious of the postcolonial politics of distinction that, during the preceding decades, had structured the value of these brands in India. It was out of this double situation that the puzzle with which I was initially confronted emerged: the insistence upon "Indianization" and the simultaneous scorn for the forms that this "Indianization" had taken.

My industry informants understood that the sudden availability of many of these brands effectively demystified them, thus undermining the existing basis of their desirability for many of their potential consumers. The challenge, then, was to develop a *new* basis for brand aura, a new kind of close distance that would not depend on the immaculate "foreign."[10]

The New Triumphalism: Globalization as Cultural Revival

By the time of my fieldwork in 1997–98, deflating the much-hyped figure of the (at least) 250 million-strong Indian middle class had become something of a public pastime for commentators inside and outside the advertising and marketing industries. One of the most notable and interesting features of these commentaries was their markedly triumphalist tone. The failure of initial MNC sales projections was reworked as evidence of the resilient cultural difference of Indian consumers. Conversely, if these brands wanted to be successful, they would have to amend their arrogant ways and adapt to local needs. Thus consumerist globalization, far from bringing cultural imperialism, was being figured as the opportunity for a comprehensive revitalization of "Indianness."

The ideological implications of this position should not be underestimated. First, globalization per se, and therefore its brokers, the local advertising and marketing industries, were thereby rehabilitated as a force for cultural effervescence and Indian pride vis-à-vis the rest of the world. Second, globalization was given a populist face through a revival of the representation of consumerism as an unbeatable sensitive index to the innermost needs of the population at large. (See chapter 3 for an account of the earlier mobilization of this rhetoric.) Ironically, given the way that the value of foreign brands was embedded in a postcolonial politics of distinction, the globalizing moment was actually being figured by many commentators as an opportunity to *redress* the humiliations of the colonial experience. With some relish, one journalist wrote of the now-troubled MNCs:

They came to the Indian market with much fanfare. Ambitious projects, hefty capital investments, flashy launches, swank outlets and swankier packaging showed their confidence in victory. They dreamed of a cakewalk, lured as they were by the proposition of enticing the 200 million-plus seamless Indian middle class that they believed hankered after the elusive foreign label. But many of the multinationals that entered the country over the last decade were in for a shock. Years after their entry, dreams of a market takeover remain chimerical, with the vagaries of the Indian economy and consumer purchase patterns putting paid to what were once considered successful global marketing formulae. (Irani 1996)

There were countless other examples of this discourse, invariably rehearsing the trope of humbled pride. The evocation of colonialism was not merely implicit. As one columnist put it: "In the 8 years that India's markets have been thrown open to the global corporate superpowers, successive waves of transnationals have been unable to colonize the country's customers" (Skaria 1999). Another journalist, referring to the travails of Kellogg's, remarked: "A big Western breakfast cereal maker saying with much machismo [that] it would change Indian tastes in ten years dropped prices on one of its mainline products." And on the subject of a latter-day Mercedes ad: "Its servile tone also showed how humbling the Indian market could be for a proud automobile giant and how it had to bow" ("New Survey Puts Middle Class at 425 Million" 1997).

Despite the apparent cultural populism of this new critique, we should not forget that many of the same executives who were now triumphantly proclaiming the collapse of globally standardized marketing templates had, only a few years earlier, themselves eagerly hyped up the idea of a 250 million-strong Western-equivalent Indian consuming class. In the wake of the 1991 reforms, the head-on collision between Indian executives looking for Western joint ventures and Western corporations desperate to get a slice of a newly "opened" market with seemingly immense potential had produced what a business journalist informant — himself at that time an account executive at a leading Bombay ad agency — remembered as a "feeding frenzy." In an atmosphere of heightened expectations and unlimited ambitions, Indian executives — wining and dining foreign corporate guests — had pumped up the figures. And their guests, already primed on Levittian visions of globally converging consumer segments, had often been all too ready to buy in. In retrospect, some of these local executives presented the selling of these dubious figures as a strategic gambit on their part, intended to sort the MNC men from the boys. The managing director of one agency offered: "In part this was a deliberate decision on the part of some Indian businessmen to merchandise this 250 million-strong middle class to the outside world. The truth is that the definition of the middle class in India is radically different from that of the Western world. . . . Some of the MNCs asked 'What exactly *is* the middle class?' Others didn't. And perhaps they were disappointed." Another senior advertising executive put the matter more bluntly: "Are the MNCs really that *dumb?! Can't they check?*"[11] Still other executives acknowledged that India had come to the encounter with prospective MNC partners from a position of weakness. Looking back on the local industry's decision to push the inflated middle-class figures, an independent marketing consultant told me:

I think they were pushing [the 250 million middle-class figure] to attract, because the only thing India had to sell to foreign investors was people. And if you said, "Actually, listen guys — the kind of money cut-off that you have in mind, there are only 65 million people," it would have meant that no collaborator would have come to you. It's pretty tough going. I mean, the Arvind Mills [Indian denim giant] guys tell me that when they actually went with fabric samples to companies overseas, the companies said that "we refuse to believe that this has been produced in India." So the only incontrovertible fact was that you had people. . . . I think a lot of the reason that these middle-class figures were hyped up was because what did you ever say to a foreign investor? I mean, I've done millions of these presentations. All you can say is, you know, "We're huge, and while the rest of the world is stagnating and stabilizing, come to us and tie up with us."[12]

Between the inflated expectations of the first half of the 1990s and the triumphalist discourse of the second half of the decade lay the field in which my informants had to act. In either case, the overt promise had been populist — from the purported trickle-down benefits of the induction of a massive middle class into globalized consumerism to the new discourse of cultural self-respect that followed upon the deflation of these expectations. And in either case, the foremost concern of the

Indian advertising and marketing industries was to "merchandise the middle class" to foreign corporations in such a way that their own status as middlemen would be ensured. For all the scorn that many Indian executives were now pouring upon the standardizing arrogance of Western marketing templates, they were still obviously keen to remain on the MNC payroll. And the sine qua non for doing so was the ability to maintain and to "leverage" the heightened value that their clients' brands had enjoyed before they had attempted to expand into Indian markets. Price reductions were therefore often out of the question. As one executive asked me with some irritation: "do you think that I am going to go to an MNC and tell them their entire pricing policy sucks?! I'm also running a business here!"

As self-appointed mediators between the local and the global, my informants needed to connect the interests of two constituencies: on the one hand, MNC clients who wanted big profits, and, on the other, Indian consumers who were unwilling or unable to buy sufficient quantities of these clients' goods. The great advantage of the new triumphalist discourse was that it offered Indian advertising and marketing professionals, at one stroke, two kinds of solutions to this dilemma. The first of these was to insist to MNC premium-brand clients that early expectations on sales volume would have to be scaled down, but that by maintaining high prices and engaging in concerted upscale brand-building advertising campaigns, a gradual expansion of a small market could be achieved. This option served to maintain the exclusivity of an MNC brand while nevertheless ensuring plenty of lucrative work for local advertising agencies. The second path was to push for higher volume more quickly. Here, again, most advertising professionals advised against price reductions and suggested instead that the brand would have to be made more "relevant" to Indian consumers through a carefully calibrated process of "Indianization." Although this second option ostensibly seemed to undermine the "distance" that was so crucial to the value of these brands, we will see that the process of "Indianization" was managed in such a way as to ensure that the aspirational "gap" would remain intact.

"Foreign" as Equity

Levi's jeans were a good example of the first kind of strategy. To start, the official appearance of Levi's in India marked a crisis of value. As a young account executive at one of the large Bombay advertising agencies remarked:

> First, globalization has certainly brought about an increase in choice for the Indian consumer. . . .[But] the foreign players have come in at really high prices. They have found that beyond a certain point, the market is inelastic [meaning that people will not buy when prices are too high]. Take, as an example, Levi's. The brand has *enormous* equity. "Foreign" itself has an equity value, which is part of the brand, perhaps even half of it. But once it came into India, and started manufacturing jeans in India — although many of these brands were made of Indian denim anyway — the equity becomes significantly diluted.

One agency head, reproducing the standard triumphalist line, commented: "Lots of Western brands have failed because they have assumed that a Western brand will have superior equity in India." As I have suggested, the matter was more complicated: it was not so much that Levi's did not enjoy "superior equity," but rather that this "superior equity" depended upon the brand maintaining a certain degree of exclusivity and distance. Although there was much talk in the advertising industry of Levi's "not getting the numbers," the strategy that the corporation adopted in India was in fact guided precisely by a recognition of the importance of this distance.

There were important cautionary examples. Through special arrangements with Indian distributors, certain multinational jeans brands like Wrangler and Pepe had already been marketed in India before the reforms of 1991. In 1987, when Wrangler launched its products in India, preliminary market research suggested that Indian consumers were hungry both for jeans per se and for foreign "badge products" (i.e., status-marking products) specifically.[13] Market research also indicated that because Wrangler jeans had long been available through smuggled channels, the brand in fact enjoyed a high degree of brand awareness *and* brand equity. In other words, the brand was, apparently, both well known and highly valued.

Consequently, it seemed to make good business sense to capitalize on this felicitous situation by pricing Wrangler jeans at a level significantly higher than its Indian competitors — Rs 365 per pair as compared to only Rs 150 per pair for the popular indigenous brand Flying Machine. The distributor, Du Pont Sportswear, however, made the crucial mistake of shipping Wrangler jeans out to a comprehensive range of retail outlets, thereby evidently "diluting" the equity of the brand. Consumers, it seemed, were less willing to pay a higher price for a brand that was suddenly so widely available.

In 1994, when Levi's were about to launch, market research simi-larly showed that the brand enjoyed enormous awareness and equity. Indeed, although it was at that point only available through informal channels and in the form of counterfeits, the Levi's brand was, accord-ing to I. Gupta (1994), the single best-selling jeans brand in India.[14] But being conscious of the risks of brand equity dilution, Levi's opted to make their jeans available for purchase through only fifty-four retail outlets nationwide. These were a combination of single-brand Levi's outlets, so-called "shop-in-shops" (that is, sections of larger depart-ment stores devoted entirely to the brand), and a carefully selected handful of multi-brand stores. As of mid-1998, it was assumed that such a strategy of relative exclusivity would enable the company to stick with a range of prices that started at over Rs 1,000 per pair — in other words, far higher than even most of their MNC competitors.

Yet of course the problem of calibrating the close distance of a brand like Levi's was not just a matter of pricing or distribution. Rather, it was also a question of what kind of messages and images were being used in its advertising. Whereas Alyque Padamsee, the for-mer head of Lintas:India (see chapter 3), was now cutely insisting that MNC in fact stood for "Misreading National Culture" ("Key to Real-ity" 1997) and another informant complained that "it's not compelling enough, just sheer 'Levi's' and what it stands for," still others were convinced that attempts at "Indianization" would be the kiss of death for such a brand. One highly respected advertising executive — who, perhaps not coincidentally, was particularly known for his cosmopoli-tan connections — argued:

> See, the point [the MNCs] are missing is that the only value the brand has is because of what it is abroad. Right? Now if you change that, then you've *finished* that product, because what is there to buy? Coca-Cola doesn't have any intrinsic sort of goodness in it that I'm going to buy it any which way. I'm buying that image that it has. That is the only thing worth buying. If you take that away from the brand, then what are you selling? You're selling colored water, for God's sake. And nobody wants that. . . . Look at Levi's! What do

they do? There's a person who's familiar with Levi's and who is buying what Levi's stands for. Which is not just the fabric and that thing, it is *the magical aura around the brand*. That is what I am really paying the premium for. I mean, I can go and buy a pair of Indian jeans if all I really want is to wear denim. Then I'll buy an Indian pair of jeans for one tenth of the cost. But why I want the Levi's name, why I'm paying the premium, is for that little red tag that says 'Levi's' on it. That Levi's magic is what the brand stands for in America. All right? If you take that away, to the guy who *knows* the brand, okay, you've taken the magic away from the brand. To the guy who *doesn't* know the brand, it means nothing anyway.

What was particularly interesting in this informant's commentary was that his position at once affirmed and denied the elitist basis of Levi's global image in India. On the one hand, its relevance in India was specifically tied into the experience of a relatively restricted segment of consumers; on the other hand, the Indian consumer's interest in the brand was portrayed as an interest in "what it is abroad . . . what the brand stands for in America." As we have seen, however, this equation between the social profile of the brand in India and its profile in the United States was one of the basic miscalculations (or perhaps strategic elisions) of the Levittian model of globalization. The ideological advantages of this equation were obvious — it enabled the portrayal of consumer globalization as the creation of a kind of global village, a borderless world. But, in the light of the preceding discussion, I would argue that the actual value of a brand like Levi's in India was represented less by "what the brand stands for in America" than "the way in which the brand stands *for* America."

Indeed, in the course of my conversation with this executive, it became clear to me just how tightly linked the preservation of the brand's close distance was to a local scheme of social distinction, in which my informant's professional concerns were more or less inextricable from his personal responses. To put this another way, these personal aesthetic responses provided a basis for a more generalized recipe for the aspirational brand. I had asked him why he felt that so much MNC advertising was so bad. Note how his response blurs the difference between Indians in general and the aesthetic and social preferences of a highly select group of consumers:

The only way I can explain this is that I think the marketers who come and market their brands in this country probably believe that Indians are not capable of understanding the advertising that they do abroad.[15] Kellogg's was a classic example of how they came and blew an *enormous* amount of money saying "Good morning, Bombay!" I was *appalled*, and I think it was really a slap in the face. You know, the kind of people who eat corn flakes are English-speaking, very sophisticated English-speaking people. You can't come and down-talk to them like saying "Good morning Bombay!" I'm not an idiot, you know! . . . I felt offended when I saw those ads. Now large companies come with big budgets. I'm sure they've done their homework. I'm sure they're trying to explode the market. They're probably talking to the middle class or whatever. . . . Coca-Cola had an ad here, which was right outside my house in Warden Rd., which is one of the most affluent areas in a very affluent city, which said, "Sweaty bus ride? Have a Coke." I mean, *for God's sake!!* Tell me, is that what Coca-Cola is all about? About sweaty bus rides? In an Indian bus?? Have you been in an Indian bus?? Do you know how sweaty it is??? What are you *doing??!*

Here the all-important close distance of the MNC commodity image was being undermined in a different way. Whatever numinous capability it may have had was now being desecrated through an ill-advised attempt at "localization." The power of the original commodity image had resided in the tension between the concrete and profane details of its visual components and the transcendent referent of the meaning of the brand (the impression of "what it means in America"). This value-generating tension was now, however, being defused, as the attempt to connect the brand with a wider range of Indian consumers was defiling the very meaning of the brand itself. My informant perceived this as a "slap in the face," a personal affront that, to him, spoke of a more general disregard for the dignity of Indian consumers.

And yet this rejection of misguided "Indianization" was not, of course, the whole story. As we have seen, the suggestion that MNC brands would now have to adapt their strategies to Indian conditions was a crucial legitimating platform for the local advertising and marketing industries, both because it ensured them a professional position as cultural brokers and because it allowed them to present consumerist globalization as more generally beneficial to their consumer-constituents. On a more pragmatic level, the drive to "Indianize" MNC advertising was also driven by the fact that many MNC corporations certainly *did* expect to be able to boost sales volumes in the *short* term. In this context, many of my informants were deeply involved with generating explanations for why Indian consumers had disappointed their initially boosterish expectations and how Indian consumers might be approached more successfully in the future.

The discourses that were generated at this juncture were not only oriented toward their manifest function, that is to provide marketing solutions for foreign clients. Rather, they also served two very important additional purposes. As I showed in chapter 7, they attempted to ensure the professional indispensability of Indian advertising and marketing executives as guides to, and interpreters of, "Indian culture." But beyond this, they provided a much wider legitimation of the globalizing project per se. This legitimation, again, consisted of two main strands. The first was the suggestion that India was uniquely socioculturally suited to turn consumerist globalization to its own advantage. The second strand was a development of this first proposition, namely that consumerist globalization, far from imposing a standardized culture upon consumers around the world, implied a kind of "participatory resistance" — a wholly new revitalization of Indianness and Indian self-confidence. As a thematic thread, I have touched upon this second idea at several points throughout this study; we encountered it during my discussion of "auto-orientalism" (chapter 4), in the context of the RightAway account executive's groping for a "new Indian" identity that he was convinced globalization had made available (chapter 6), and finally in the Sparka team's insistence upon the resilient pertinence of cultural hybridity (chapter 7).

We are now in a position to see how the crisis of globalization brought together all these strands: the critique of MNC "value arrogance," the promise of cultural revitalization, and the creation of "the Indian consumer." The amalgam emerged at a moment of ostensible disillusionment: the collapse of the much-vaunted Indian middle class.

Spending Psyche, Price and Value

My informants' critiques of existing MNC branding strategies were important, not least for what they revealed about the politics of value that structured the moment of globalization in India. But, as I argued in chapter 7, it was only with the invention of their own counter-commodity, "the Indian consumer," that they were able to gain real leverage vis-à-vis their global clients. The Levittian model of globalization (see pages 251–58) rested upon the expectation that the Indian middle class was equivalent in its consuming power (and consuming needs, if not stated preferences) to its counterparts in other parts of the world. The conjuncture of the meeting between foreign corporate executives and Indian marketing and advertising professionals in the wake of the 1991 reforms (see pages 264–66) had not only perpetuated this fiction but encouraged vastly inflated estimates of the numerical size of this Indian middle class. Some felt that this had been a key mistake. The managing director of one agency remarked: "Despite all this talk of the '200 million middle class,' a truer assessment would be that there's a sharp division between a five million elite on the one side of a wide gulf, and the other 195 million on the other. This five million have the same buying attitudes and, more importantly, buying *capacity* as Western consumers."

For the kinds of generic reasons that I have discussed, lowering prices was always going to be an advertising agency's least likely recommendation. The transcultural predicament of these MNC brands, furthermore, made it far preferable to suggest that the real barriers to larger sales volumes were a misunderstanding of consumers' preferences, values, or habits.

One of the most popular explanations in this genre revolved around the thriftiness of the majority of Indian consumers, their concern with "value for money." This thriftiness was often in turn explained as an Indian sociocultural tendency to downplay material wealth that was both ancient and at the same time specifically embedded in post-Independence Indian public culture in the form of Gandhian asceticism and Nehruvian socialism. An agency planner remarked:

> If [a product is] purely seen as glamour, if it's purely seen as style, in this country where a lot of people—especially as you go down pop [population] strata—a lot of people are very diffident about projecting. . . . I mean, they *under*project themselves. There are chaps—even in Bombay you will find—[a chap] who probably wears a simple shirt or pant, and who carries Rs 50,000 in his pocket, who *doesn't* want to project. It's only among the younger crowd who's out to overproject. The mass of the country is all about under-

projecting themselves. It's actually a culture . . . I mean, apart from the sheer socialism which has been ingrained in the country for the past forty-fifty years, I think overall it's a culture which is saying "materialism is not the best thing." It's . . . saying "chasing money is not your goal in life." . . . So I might still be chasing money — I wouldn't want to project it. . . . Who's the most powerful person in Indian society is not always the richest guy. It's about the guy who knows a lot of people, who can get things done. . . . Chasing pure materialism, chasing money, is not something that I would want to *tell* the world. I might still be doing it — all of the country's doing it — but that's not seen as a . . . [trails off]. And that will have a residual effect on people.

Here, then, was on the one hand an acknowledgment of the situational advantages of social capital over financial capital (and by implication, the kinds of symbolic capital that could be bought with financial capital — that is, premium branded goods). On the other hand, however, my interlocutor was arguing that the deeply embedded reluctance to "overproject" gave rise to a kind of moral hypocrisy ("all of the country's doing it"), which might in fact be resolved by an acceptance of the advantages of consumerist display.

There was also an evolutionary assumption embedded in my informant's analysis: it was the younger generation that was more comfortable with "projecting" themselves through consumer goods. And this assumption of a historical trend was frequently allied with a normative evaluation; dawning consumerism meant both social progress and moral enlightenment. In the words of another (female) executive:

Out of our population of 900-plus million, it was often claimed that there is this middle class of 300 million people. What experience has told us, however, is that only about 50 million of these people have *the spending psyche*. Most women — the woman is *the influencer,* but the decision has to go through the man — would rather use a bit more elbow grease than spend a few more rupees on convenience. Thrift still dominates. It's only a small segment of the population where the women are evolved and enlightened enough to convince their husbands to part with the money for the brand they want.

Some might assume that this purportedly Indian thriftiness, this concern with value for money, would make the relatively insubstantial attractions of brand benefits a secondary concern. But of course my informants generally did not believe this was so. If the MNCs were guilty of "value arrogance," then their mistake was not to believe that Indians would be willing to pay more for a branded product. Rather, their greatest mistake had been to assume that what was valuable to a Western consumer would automatically be valuable in India. The question of value was of course related to the issue of price (as demonstrated by the prominence of the expression "value for money"), yet it was also analytically and discursively independent of it.[16] My account planner informant insisted that it was not a matter of available resources, since it was quite obvious that ordinary Indians were happy to spend vast amounts of money on apparently inessential goods as long as there was a psychological or cultural "context," a justification for it:

> It's not that people don't have money. They have money — I mean, if you were to go through the economics of it, there are people who . . . they *have* money. Marketing in this country requires some degree of justification — internally, and in the context of society — which makes me want to buy a product which is outlandishly priced. . . . I don't think price is the issue. I think if you find the *context,* there would be people who would pay for it. There are chaps, there are a fair amount of people in this country who splurge a few thousand rupees at Divali on [fire]crackers. A few tens of thousands. And they don't bother about it. Because [he's thinking] "Somewhere bursting crackers on Divali is something which is a part of my life and I do it, and then there are some stupid people who don't see any reason for it. That's a problem for them."[17] Well, the same guy is saying "I don't see any context for spending 1,200 on a pair of jeans." It's what they call a "jeans pant," and my local dealer can probably give me that pant at 500 bucks [i.e., rupees]. Or [Indian brand] Newport is giving me the same pant.

The account planner, then, was suggesting that successful marketing and advertising to Indian consumers meant "finding the right context"; that is, elaborating a combination of brand identity, product characteristics, and price that would convince consumers who tended toward frugality of the rationale for buying. At first sight, it appeared that the only thing that separated Indian consumers from their counterparts elsewhere in the world was their relatively lowly position on the grand evolutionary scheme of the globalizing spread of "the spending psyche." Indian difference was, on this level, understood as quantitative and relative — Indians were (so far) less willing to part with their money for consumer goods, but given time, things would "improve."

Yet the question of "finding the right context" was more complicated, for it included a qualitative and absolute dimension of distinction: cultural difference. "Finding the right context" also meant making a brand socioculturally "relevant" to Indian consumers. These two axes of difference were always in uneasy tension; indeed, this tension expressed the ambivalent position of the Indian advertising and marketing industries vis-à-vis their foreign clients. On the one hand, it behooved them to insist that the thriftiness of the majority of Indian consumers might gradually be "softened," making them more amenable to consumerism in the long term. On the other hand, it was equally important to these professionals that a zone of cultural difference should remain, a terrain over which they might credibly claim authoritative expertise. The upshot of this ambiguous situation was, as I argued in chapter 7, an insistence upon the desirability of hybridizing Western brands in order to appeal to the apparent aspirations of Indian consumers who were themselves located at the intersection of "local tradition" and "global modernity." In this way, MNC brands might be "assimilated" faster into the Indian cultural "context." The agency planner remarked:

> The kind of advertising that Levi's is doing has nothing to do with my life. Yeah, it's good stuff, it's interesting music, I watch it as entertaining, but it doesn't make a difference for me. It's not *connecting* with me, which is the whole thing. . . . There is an assimilation that happens. In due course of time, even Levi's will become a standard somewhere. But would you want to wait for ten years or fifteen years while that happens? You have to increase that pace, and you want to make it a more relevant product as soon as possible because that's when you get your numbers. . . . I mean, the sheer *presence* of Levi's or Reebok in the country will change views about these kinds of products among consumers over a period of time. But you need to do that faster. If you do it faster, you get your numbers faster. . . . A lot of [the MNC brands] come from the point of view that "see, the smuggled route had been selling so many pieces, so I

think there's a huge market [in India]. We'll just say we are there and people will rush and buy us." That doesn't happen. McDonald's is facing huge competition from [Delhi-based fast food chain] Nirula's. Because McDonald's thought that if they just said "McDonald's is here," people will queue up. They queued up for the first day, second day. Then you aren't interested. A lot of people are saying "McDonald's is tasteless food. It's a big experience to be eating McDonald's, but when I need good stuff I go to Nirula's next door and they make tandoori chicken which is the kind of thing I like." Or they make tandoori *pizzas*. That's another thing: you have this composite stuff which happens, and that really sells. So tandoori chicken pizza becomes [a] very big thing at Nirula's. And that's what's interesting.

On the one hand, then, the advertising and marketing challenge involved tracking the empirical permutations of these hybrid cultural preferences. On the other hand, this exercise fed the construction of an expert discourse, which required that its object — the Indian consumer — be at once familiar and strange. In this, the marketing imagination replicated the structure of an earlier colonial project of classification, which brought "together the exoticizing vision of orientalism with the familiarizing discourse of statistics. In the process, the body of the colonial subject is made simultaneously strange and docile" (Appadurai 1996, 133). Appadurai goes on to argue that the colonial classifying exercise found its "natural" counterpart in the Indian caste system, a preexisting (and yet colonially elaborated) system of differences. Interestingly, the much-discussed cultural complexity of India served this very same function in marketing discourse, although here it could never be expressed in the language of caste. Here, too, it was at once the empirical proof of the truth of its classifications *and* a kind of "organic" bulwark against the homogenizing impulse of any alien political or economic projects. Globalizing consumerism was not cultural imperialism, understood as a project of global homogenization. But in its concern with the comprehension and tabulation of Indian difference, the contemporary marketing imagination was more than a little indebted to its colonial forebears. The "Jewel in the Crown" of the British empire had been at once the showcase of the imperial project and its inscrutable heart. To the marketing imagination, India was similarly indispensable: both a stunning demonstration of the categorical

made Pizza
go Tandoori.

Ever heard of the Vegetable Hamburger? Or Masala Tea?
Or a Tandoori Pizza? All creations inspired by my refusal to eat
exactly like the rest of the world does. So the food chains
read the message on their wall (or on their cash registers) and
tailored a whole new menu to my taste. While we are on the
topic of tasteful tailoring, check out these look-formal,
feel-casual Crufte shirts - created for my comfort by
Indian Terrain. Topping aren't they?

INDIAN TERRAIN

16. Consumerism as bulwark of cultural difference. By the mid-1990s, globalizing consumerism was being presented by the advertising and marketing industries as a guarantor of Indian cultural integrity. Multinational corporations, having entered Indian markets with much fanfare, were now being forced to adapt to the situated particularity of Indian tastes. In this narrative, the embodied aesthetics of cultural identity — so long as they were translatable into corporate profits — finally guaranteed a reversal of the historical indignities of colonization. Hybrid figures like "tandoori pizza," at that time a favorite example among Indian marketing professionals, invoked the capacity of transnational brands to offer the best of both worlds: global form, local content. Ironically, the final line of the copy, "Topping aren't they," suggests nothing so much as the argot of late colonial-period British officers.

versatility of consumer capitalism and a living reassurance that it was powerless to homogenize the diversity of local lives.

Models of Indian Difference: Ganesha's Homepage

The explanations of Indian difference that I was offered by my informants in the Bombay advertising and marketing industries involved three interconnected propositions. First, that India as a whole was too complex and ancient for anyone to homogenize or control. Second, that Indian consumers were too "savvy" to be ruled by multinational propaganda. Third, that it was central to both the duty and the talent of Indian marketing and advertising professionals to understand and to capitalize upon the first two propositions. In the present section,

I explore the complex and sometimes contradictory interrelationships of these ideas.

An initial thematic division appeared between what might be called passive and active models of Indian difference. The basis of the passive model was the empirical geographical, linguistic, and cultural diversity of India, which, so I was told, formed a "natural" and a priori bulwark against "multinationalization." One old industry hand insisted, somewhat wearily:

> *Do* understand, William, that India is not a country like France is a country, or England is a country, or any of your European countries is a country. Or even in terms of the United States of America it is a subcontinent with fourteen principal languages and about 250 dialects. The cultural differences are vaster than they are between the American Deep South and the middle and Eastern seaboard. You go to the Indian Deep South and you go to Kashmir, and you're in two different continents. There's a *huge* diversity here, which can't be multinationalized in terms of idiom. You may have the same brands here, but . . . there are *very* few multinational campaigns that have come through and that have remained unchanged here. Look at Coke. Look at Pepsi. They all have highly Indian equivalents of their international campaigns. So . . . this is *not* an Indonesia. This is not a Philippines. It's another . . . it's a unique ball game.

This distinction between a complex India and apparently simpler, smaller Asian countries helped to position India as a uniquely equipped challenger to the forces of globalization. As one observer commented, "The long accepted law of globalization — One World, One Strategy — doesn't hold once India's borders are crossed" (Skaria 1999). A planner at another agency elaborated, linking the apparent cultural inviolability offered by India's cultural diversity with the complex expertise that was required in the Indian advertising and marketing game:

> I remember reading this article in *Advertising Age* [a weekly U.S. trade paper] once that some media planner in Canada had written about how media planning in Canada is just becoming impossible because of continuously having to juggle around with French and English. . . . And I was just thinking, we have twenty-one thousand publications and we have sixteen official languages. . . . These are not like English and French, where there's a strong commonality.

The script is different, the tone is different, the pronunciation . . . everything is radically different. . . . And as a nation I think we have lived with sixteen languages, six religions, twenty-three states . . . and each one of them has a very distinct dress code, a very distinct food code, a very distinct cultural code, you know, different forms of art. And I think that prevents us from getting overly preoccupied with this whole concept of homogenization. "What does India stand for?" and things like that. We are quite comfortable. . . . I imagine that with very tiny countries like Singapore, or even let's say Vietnam, which are much tinier and which have one culture, therefore when something is imposed, it's a clash of the titans and one of them may emerge stronger. Right? But over here, someone coming in . . . it's like a kaleidoscope. It's difficult to imagine one color coming in and taking over the kaleidoscope. It just becomes the eighteenth color! Or the fifty-third color in the kaleidoscope. And you become part of the pattern.[18]

First, India's very diversity insulated it from "homogenization" — the meaning spontaneously attributed by most of my informants to my questions about globalization. Second, this same diversity presented an enormous challenge to local marketing and advertising professionals. Here there was an ambiguity. On the one hand, my interlocutor was telling me that living with diversity had made Indians relatively immune to identity crises (" 'What does India stand for?' and things like that"), particularly when compared to apparently more homogenous smaller countries. India, then, was figured as uniquely equipped to emerge not merely unscathed but positively strengthened from its involvement with transnational consumer capital. On the other hand, my informant's own work, of course, perpetually involved him in developing generalized representations of Indian cultures and behaviors.

Indeed, one of things that India "stood for" — and in this, the marketing imagination drew upon far older romantic and orientalist models of Indian difference — was not simply empirical diversity, but a psychological tolerance for blurred boundaries, multiplicity, and apparent contradiction. There was a historical genealogy at work here: India's long history of repeated invasion had given it a contemporary resilience that was based not upon force of opposition but rather on a capacity to absorb and transform. Again the apparent weakness of India, so classically stereotyped by Europeans of the nineteenth century (see Inden 1990; A. Nandy 1983), had, after all, turned out to be a source of strength. For outsiders—as indeed Hegel had warned—adaptation to India could easily mean a loss of self.[19] One agency C.E.O. mused: "If we look at it historically . . . right from five thousand years, it's almost as if whatever influence has come has had an influence, and then has now become part of the mosaic. So if you take Islam as having come in, it has had an impact because what is Taj Mahal but an Islamic structure? Its architectural style is Islamic. . . . So it has come in but it has got sort of absorbed. And now you can't tell which is which. Whether is this Islamic or is it Indian? You don't know."

This insistence upon the uniquely absorptive capacity of Indian civilization—born of repeated invasion—was not simply a reappropriation of the Hegelian ideas that had formed the conceptual motive force of the colonial wish to introduce "history" to India. It was also, in effect, a rebuttal of Marx's claim that the encounter between India and Western capitalism was qualitatively different from the many invasions that had taken place in earlier centuries.[20] Indian cultural difference was, then, anciently equipped to withstand the onslaught of foreign pretenders—be they military, commercial, or some combination of the two. Moving from geopolitics to cultural psychology, the collective memory of millennia manifested itself in the mental habits of Indian consumers. The agency planner drew once again upon long-established orientalist binaries, this time refunctioned with the sweet ironies of reverse generalization:

> At a broader level, I think that being very comfortable with an ambiguous situation is a very oriental trait. I find that the Westerners—and sorry if I appear to be generalizing them—but I find them much more comfortable with cut and dried, you know, yes or no. So [in the Western mind] you have three ways of looking at things, and the idea is to keep on discussing them and you rule out two of them, and you say "this is it." Whereas in our part of the world, you find that people are quite comfortable with living with contradictions, and living with ambivalence, and living with ambiguity. And that—in this context of culture, food, language, dress—is already a reality.

This was not merely idle speculation; rather, the model had become the basis for the professional discourse through which many Bombay marketing professionals sought to mediate the impact of MNC consumer goods companies. One (female) consultant referred back precisely to the epic narratives of mainstream Hindu religious tradition to demonstrate the social and psychological basis for the hybridity that was now a necessity in consumer marketing:

> [We] have a pantheon of gods, right? And you will accept that Krishna was the ultimate playboy. [Krishna] and Ram, who is the ultimate good guy, are both incarnations of one and the same. Even if you look at the music . . . I mean, the Gitagovinda is about as erotic as it can possibly be, and that's semi-devotional too. But the Ram *bhajans* are all about what a good guy he was. I mean the Tulsi *Ramayan* keeps talking about how good he was. Similarly women: I mean, there is Kali, and there is Shakti, but there's also Parvati. And Parvati was the ultimate . . . from a feminist standpoint [chuckles], she was the ultimate wimp, right? In many ways. And you had a Draupadi. And [then] you had a Sita. You know, Sita, who said, "Mother Earth, swallow me up because I am being tested" [for her purity]. She was tough in her own way, but [she's] not Draupadi, who said, "I will not tie my hair unless you give me the blood of that guy." You know?![21]

The objective existence of this multiplicity and ambivalence in Indian society and culture, then, became the basis for an argument about the *agency* of Indian consumers, above all, their ability to turn the recombinational talent of the bricoleur into a kind of indigenously adapted technical know-how (see page 160 for the deployment of precisely this characterization in the EMW Amitabh Bachchan campaign). At this point, the "passive," absorptive quality of Indian culture was transformed into an "active" principle of consumer agency (again, this stress upon the agency of consumers everywhere was of course an important legitimating tactic for the marketing enterprise). This adaptive agency operated on a "grass-roots" technical level, as the agency planner illustrated:

> Washing machines. I don't know if somebody's told you this, but when they came to India first in the '70s, in Punjab, which is a state up north, one of the favorite drinks up there is what they call a lassi. And you have, you know, what they call *dhabas*. Dhabas are like roadside inns, where the truckers and all these guys stop. And there lassi is a very staple kind of thing. With every meal you must have

one big glass of lassi. The way it's made is by taking this thickset yogurt and churning it. Now if you're trying to produce it for fifty people, it's an awful lot of hard work. So the very first use to which India put washing machines was to take these top-loading types . . . and they would dump the yogurt into it [along with] sugar and it would churn. And it would produce lassi. . . . Indians have this amazing capacity to see what is most apt and right for them. And even to sit around and make something which, you know, nobody else would have even thought of. . . . It's a grass-roots savviness kind of a thing. And you'll find that . . . despite the 900 million people, they don't move blindly in hordes.

This "grass-roots savviness" was an important premise for two reasons. First, it located Indian creativity in the domain of everyday life. Second, in so doing, it provided a relatively uncontroversial mass basis for claims that were more specifically related to the consumerist project. The marketing consultant made the link between a long-standing tradition of the hybridization of Indian tradition and global modernity on the one hand, and the "Indianization" of global consumer technologies and forms on the other.

Our faith in astrology doesn't decrease, but in deference to the scientific temperament [a possibly ironic invocation of Nehru's cherished "scientific temper"] you move to computerized horoscope forecasting. Now that is pretty much the Hindu way of doing things. You don't have arranged marriages in that sense, but I hear now a lot of young people using the phrase "engineered marriages." . . . Lord Ganesha has his own [Internet] homepage, right? You now have videocassettes that have the *puja* [devotional ritual], so if you don't know what the *puja* looks like on *Ganeshottsav* [the annual Ganesh festival], you can have the videocassette and you're okay. . . .[22] Hinduism is great at finding new interpretations. In the days of the Brit, the clerk would have a tie and a shirt upwards but he would have a *dhoti* and *chappals* below.[23]

In passing, we should note the way in which the conceptual versatility of *Hinduism* (as opposed to any other Indian religion) is pulled into service as a kind of prophylactic against the potentially debilitating effects of globalizing consumerism. This equation is one among many instances of the elective affinity between the rise of consumerism and the contemporaneous "Hinduization" of Indian public life (Mankekar 1999; see also the debate between Rajagopal 1994, 1996, 2001 and Prasad 1995 on this theme).

This, then, was the territory that Indian marketing and advertising professionals had carved out for themselves, and in which they had to act. As my planner informant acknowledged, his practice necessarily required reduction or generalization:

> We have made an attempt to reconcile . . . this complexity of the Indian population, which makes it so difficult to actually segment them. You know, it's mind-boggling to imagine a market of 900 million. Or even 300 million. And it's very difficult to therefore start charting out a course or a strategy for your brand — whether it's in marketing terms, or product terms, or in communication terms — unless you have some kind of a fix. And from that point of view, segmentation often becomes necessary. And that's a contradiction that you're trying to manage.

Ostensibly, getting a "fix" on the Indian market meant "segmenting" Indian consumers internally. At the same time, the need to manage the relationship between Indian consumers and foreign corporations — which necessarily involved imagining the relationship and differences between Indian consumers and consumers elsewhere — was really the crux of the challenge of globalization. By speaking of a "contradiction" between the objective complexity of Indian markets and the work of "segmentation" involved in marketing, the planner rhetorically moved some way toward an acknowledgment of the reification involved in the transnational commodity imaging project. And yet presented as such, the work of market research appeared, with innocence fully intact, as a positivistic attempt to reduce processes of cultural hybridization *that were taking place independently* to a manageable level of generalization.

Certainly, it would be nonsensical for me to argue that Indian consumers did not in various ways behave differently than consumers elsewhere. Equally, it would be blatantly erroneous for me to claim that complex processes of adaptation and hybridization were not taking place as new commodities and technologies were articulated with the conditions of everyday life all over India. What I am arguing, however, is that the metropolitan Indian advertising and marketing industries were not in fact much interested in the actuality of most of these processes. It certainly served their interests to show that adaptation and hybridity were spontaneous Indian traits, operating, as it were, from the ground up. But the kind of hybridity that was professionally most important to them was of a rather restricted kind.

What my Bombay informants needed was a new variant of the close distance that had generated such a heightened sense of value for many foreign brands prior to the reforms of 1991. Now that foreignness itself could no longer automatically be relied upon to signify aspirational distance, a hybrid "Indianness"—that was nonetheless flagged as culturally authentic—had to be made to fit the bill. This is why for all that advertising executives might rhetorically celebrate the grassroots "savviness" of dhaba operators, they could only actually make commercial use of such imagery if it could first be aligned with the aspirations or identifications of an elite whose consuming energies were driven by a desire that was analogous to the hybrid structure of the transnational commodity image: a libidinal and imaginary investment in "world-class Indianness."[24]

Conclusion

The people I have discussed in this book are, in one sense, the latest representatives of a long line of Indian moderns; mediators between a self-consciously elaborated Indianness and a universalizing colonizing idiom, their cultural predecessors are the Indian nationalist intellectuals—literary, artistic, and scientific—of the nineteenth century (Chatterjee 1993, 1995; A. Nandy 1983, 1995). At the same time, their situation is marked by the peculiarity of the commodity image as a mediating idiom, in particular by its acute juxtaposition of the aesthetic and the instrumental.

In chapter 7, I highlighted the strategic dimension of my informants' struggle: the problem of carving out a zone of executive autonomy, an authentically marked space of cultural difference, within a universalizing system. In the present chapter, I have tried to push this analysis further in a quest for a historical understanding of the auratic potential that both powers and undermines the work of advertising. The ambivalence that I found both in textual materials and in conversations brings me back to the inaugural image of shoveling smoke. Vergil Reed's exasperated dismissal of India's potential for realizing a modern destiny (see pages 34–36) both does and does not live on in the

Bombay account planner's complaint about the "contradiction" involved in distilling workable generalizations out of the manifold of Indian life-worlds.

The differences between Reed and my Bombay informants are positional as well as historical. The account planner does not enjoy the dubious luxury of evaluating India and Indians from the outside. In fact, the credibility of his diagnosis depends upon juxtaposing a universalizing taxonomy (market research) with an insider's privileged understanding. Moreover, he is speaking in the late 1990s, a time when the consumerist dispensation has established a new variation on the modernist theme of progress. The realization of historical destiny no longer depends upon the obliteration of anachronistic cultural survivals; rather, these life-worlds are now being held up as the very substance of a new, multicultural market mechanism.

The commodity image is the vehicle of this mediation. But it is also its Achilles' heel. To be sure, the commodity image is the space in which a series of reified Indian identities are being tabulated, normalized, and offered up for consumption. Yet at the same time, it is the medium of an infinite profusion of potentialities. From a strategic point of view, all the talk about "getting a fix" on the endless complexity of Indian life-worlds may be understood as a matter of generalization, reification, stereotypy. But this generalizing work necessarily proceeds at the intersection of professional technique and aesthetic experience. A project that is necessarily built upon the work of the imagination — and as such is necessarily rooted in concrete conjunctures and memories — comes clothed in the trappings of a rational universality.

Both Theodore Levitt's strident proclamations on the globalization of markets (see pages 251–58) and the cultural triumphalism of the Indian advertising industry in the mid-1990s (see pages 263–66) are, from this standpoint, professionally necessary misrecognitions. In either case, a cultural politics in which global corporate actors — not least the advertising business — seek to make authoritative (and therefore profitable) interventions is presented in terms of universal logics and objective referents. Levitt appeals to the fraudulently neutral calculus of functional utility, my informants to the historical integrity of cultural difference.

And yet these strategic misrecognitions are not exactly symmetrical. Nor is this asymmetry merely a matter of political economy or geopolitical power relations. Rather, as postcolonial cultural producers, my informants are, with all the embodied resonance of a lifetime of personal experience, attuned to the close distance of the commodity image, to the auratic foundations of its value. For all that they might adopt the systematizing language of global market research, they never forget — in a way that their Western counterparts perhaps do — that it is a fiction.

In his *Negative Dialectics*, Theodor Adorno describes the error involved in imagining that the truth of an object or an image is attainable by moving closer to it:

> What is a metaphysical experience? If we disdain projecting it upon allegedly primal religious experiences, we are most likely to visualize it as Proust did, in the happiness, for instance, that is promised by village names like Applebachsville, Wind Gap, or Lords Valley. One thinks that going there would bring the fulfillment, as if there were such a thing. Being really there makes the promise recede like a rainbow. And yet one is not disappointed; the feeling now is one of being too close, rather, and not seeing it for that reason. (Adorno 1973, 373)

Adorno presents his example as a personal meditation and a critical intervention from within the heart of the modern European philosophical project. But I would suggest that his insight also, albeit unwittingly, describes the kind of postcolonial cultural politics that I have sketched in this chapter, and more generally in the book as a whole. Here, too, we might think that once the foreign dream — H. Rider Haggard's "empire of the imagination" (Haggard 1991) — has been exposed as merely contingent, we will, to adapt Marx and Engels's famous words once more, be "compelled to face with sober senses [our] real conditions of life and [our] relations with [our] kind" (Tucker 1978, 476). Behind the veil of ideology, we naïvely expect to encounter ourselves.

Certainly, we see this principle in operation as the culturally liberatory claims made on behalf of globalizing consumerism engender a revitalization of tired orientalist stereotypes. But I would like to think that my study also points the way to a rather different kind of conclusion. There can be no doubt that the advertising business has an interest in presenting its particular and interested juxtapositions of image and word, proximity and transcendence, as general and disinterested.

But in doing so, it does not draw an ideological veil over a world that would otherwise be readily intelligible to us.

Simply because commodity images do not show everything, we should not think that they obscure. In this book I have tried to demonstrate that situating commodity images in the concrete contexts of their production and circulation has the capacity to make visible the fault lines at which contemporary cultural politics suture materiality and meaning, affect and narrative. If the advertising business seems illegitimate, it is not primarily because it lies. Rather, it is because it reaches into the concrete foundations of our collective experience and, on that basis, performs an imaginative labor that cloaks its partiality in the vestments of the universal.

NOTES

Chapter One. Locations

1 For a convenient introduction to the study of consumption per se, see Miller 1995a. Other texts that grapple with the cultural politics of the consumption of media and goods in a variety of ways include L. Abu-Lughod 1993; Ang 1985, 1991, 1996; Appadurai 1996; Barker 1999; Breckenridge 1995; Caldarola 1994; Clammer 1987; Featherstone 1991; Foster 1995, 1996, 1999; Gewertz and Errington 1996; Hebdige 1987; Howes 1996; Kemper 2001; Lull 1991; Lury 1996; McCracken 1988; Miller 1987, 1994 1995b; Orlove 1997; Osella and Osella 1999; Sherry 1995; Skov and Moeran 1995; Sulkunen et al. 1997; Tobin 1992; Watson 1997; Wilk 1990, 1994.

2 The question of whether Fernandes actually forced Coke out or whether the company chose to leave is controversial. Fernandes decided to enforce the then-operative Foreign Exchange Regulation Act (FERA), which stipulated that multinational corporations could only have minority equity in their Indian operations. Under Indira Gandhi, Coke had de facto been allowed to maintain 100 percent equity. When faced with Fernandes's demand that they comply with FERA, Coke insisted that majority Indian equity was impossible since it would require the company to share the "secret" of its formula. Consequently, the company left.

3 The rationale for the reforms, however, was not officially consumer oriented. In fact, many (e.g., Das 2000) have argued that the government, to its detriment, lacked any clear vision at all. Nevertheless, the massive foreign exchange borrowing undertaken by Rajiv Gandhi's administration in the years 1984–89 was in part intended to subsidize middle-class consumerism. This borrowing also in large part precipitated the fiscal crisis that forced the more comprehensive reforms of 1991. And in practice, in the years that followed, the government, despite placing infrastructure projects at the top of its list of foreign investment priorities, continued to answer to the urban middle-class consumer lobby. As Sen et al. show:

> A breakdown of Foreign Collaboration Approvals reveals that the largest part went to core, priority sectors: telecommunications (25%), energy development (21%), transportation (6.5%), metallurgical industries (6.3%) and chemicals (6%). But while the pattern of industry-wise inflow of *approved* FDI [Foreign Direct Investment] indicates the importance of core sectors, the figures of industry-wise *actual* FDI reveal a different picture. The actual FDI into domestic appliances, finance, services, electronics and electrical equipment and food and dairy products combined accounted for 29.3% of the total actual FDI in 1992–93, 44.9% in 1993–94, 47.4% in 1994–95, and 41.2% in 1995–96. (Sen et al. 1997)

4   Bombay's name was officially changed to Mumbai in 1995, by the then BJP/Shiv Sena state government. Mumbai has long been the local Marathi-language name, and is therefore not inextricably or exclusively associated with the naming politics of the Hindu right. Nevertheless, I have chosen to use the older name throughout this book, not least because my informants almost invariably referred to the city that way. The cosmopolitan imaginary that the name "Bombay" signified to many of them is of course connected to their own status as a cultural elite.

5   The term had first come to prominence in national political life following a series of agitations in Bengal in 1905–1908 (see Sarkar 1973; Bayly 1986). Unlike Gandhi's later extension of the movement, this was predominantly an intervention of the urban intelligentsia. Its primary targets were British cotton cloth and other consumer goods, but it was also connected to a wider program of "self-strengthening" or *atmashakti,* which was associated with the Bengali literary figure Rabindranath Tagore. In this guise, the movement also expressed itself as administrative noncooperation and educational reform (Bose and Jalal 1998).

6   In Gandhi's words:

> *Swadeshi* carries a great and profound meaning. It does not mean merely the use of what is produced in one's own country. That meaning is certainly there in *swadeshi.* But there is another meaning implied in it which is far greater and much more important. *Swadeshi* means reliance on our own strength. We should also know what we mean by "reliance on our own strength." "Our strength" means the strength of our body, our mind and our soul. From among these, on which should we depend? The answer is brief. The soul is supreme, and therefore soul-force is the foundation on which man must build. (Gandhi 1997, 21 fn.)

7   It is important to note both the religious connotations of the term *sangha* and the fact that the word *parivar* is frequently used in such contexts to denote elective family, a network or set of relationships that are understood through the idiom of kinship. The centrality of the metaphor can be seen in the discourse of S. Gurumurthy (see note 9 below), as well as in my later discussion (chapter 7) of the importance, in marketing thought, of "family" as a marker of both "Asianness" in general and "Indianness" in particular. Thanks to Christian Novetzke for impressing this point on me.

8   The way in which the Hindu right in the last twenty years or so has appropriated the Gandhian philosophical heritage is discussed in R. Fox 1989, but see also Rajagopal 2001.

9   On the Nehruvian modernists of the post-Independence period, Gurumurthy had this to say: "The secular-socialist leadership systematically fragmented Indian society into majority and minority, rich and poor, forwards and backwards — and denied India of [*sic*] the deeper awareness of its intrinsic unity brought about by the Hindu values and civilization" (Gurumurthy 1998b).

10 The debate around the value and/or desirability of a "secularist" approach to public life in India is both heated and complicated. For useful interventions, see Bhargava 1994, Bharucha 1998, Madan 1995, and Mankekar 1999.

11 Gurumurthy himself acknowledged this accusation, complaining (with some justification) that: "anyone who dissents against globalization is being labeled as backward-looking and anti-modern" (Gurumurthy 1998b).

12 The Indian wing of McDonald's went to great pains to point out that their supplies were all domestically sourced. According to Ragvinder S. Rekhi, McDonald's local vice president: "Our burger buns are made by Cremica Industries of Punjab, the mutton patties are supplied by Al-Kabeer in Mumbai, cheese comes from Baramati in Maharashtra, pickles from Hyderabad and the iceberg lettuce from Ooty, Tamil Nadu and Dehradun. So what's *videshi* [foreign] about this?" (Jetley and Shastri 1998).

13 Gurumurthy offered a rather memorable riposte to one interviewer who wondered, apropos pragmatism, whether the English language was not "a must" in modern India: "A must is different from being worshipped. Toilet is very necessary, but will you do *pooja* [offer prayers] there?" ("India Has Never Had *Swadeshi* Economy" 1998).

14 Examples of this economic discrimination against Indian business that were cited around this time included the imbalances between Indian interest rates (18 percent) and international ones (anywhere from 2.5 percent to 6 percent), and a capital gains tax rate of 30 percent for Indian companies versus only 20 percent for multinationals (Jishnu et al. 1998). Another instance was sugar. Whereas foreign companies and importers were able to import sugar freely or under low import tariffs, domestic producers were subject to complex regulations and additionally obliged to provide a 40 percent quota at a negligible subsidy to the Public Distribution System (Jetley and Shastri 1998).

15 While many saw the evident differences between the BJP and the SJM on the

question of swadeshi as evidence of damaging dissension in the ranks, others detected a useful political mechanism. By having affiliates like the SJM publicly criticize policies of the BJP-led coalition, these affiliates could effectively ventriloquate the more radical or extreme aspects of the Sangh Parivar's agenda. If a policy succeeded, the BJP could of course take credit for it. If it failed, it could once again point to statements made by its own affiliates and then complain that its hands were forced by its coalition partners.

16 Measurements of the size of the advertising industry worldwide tend to be calculated in terms of capitalized billings, in other words, the amount of money that the agencies charge their clients. Since only a fraction of this money actually ends up with the agency, such figures give a rather inflated impression of financial clout.

Nevertheless, the expansion of the Indian ad business in the years 1980–2000 was nothing short of astonishing. (I have adjusted the following rupee amounts according to historically relevant exchange rates.) Sarna (1982a and b) suggests that the industry grew from 37.38 crores of rupees in 1975 ($44 million) to 89.11 crores in 1980 ($111.4 million). An OBM Media Bulletin from 1983 is more boosterish, figuring 236 crores for 1980 ($295 million) and 296.9 crores for 1982 ($312.5 million). Karlekar (1986) offers 200 crores for 1981 ($232.5 million) and 400 crores by 1986 ($317.5 million). Some impression of the exponential growth that followed can be gained from figures cited in Jeffrey (2000, 58), according to which the business grew from 930.9 crores in 1990–91 ($423 million) to 5,331 crores in 1997–98 ($1.4 billion), at an average rate of growth of 30 percent a year. Steven Kemper notes that there were ninety-three advertising agencies in Bombay 1960 and 425 by 1988 (Kemper 2001, 35).

17 In many cases, these joint ventures were formalized extensions of previously established affiliations. At the same time, many of the multinationals that had been "Indianized" in the 1960s and 1970s were trying to buy back controlling stakes in their Indian operations. While all this was going on, Indian agencies were themselves trying to establish regional networks of their own, in part to improve their leverage vis-à-vis multinational clients. So, for instance, in 1996 Trikaya Grey bought 60 percent equity shares in local agencies in Dhaka (Bangladesh) and Colombo (Sri Lanka) (Roy 1997).

18 One should of course not forget that "mass consumerism" is a relative term, nor that the nationalist movement was not always as austere as Gandhian swaraj would make it appear. An earlier Indian consumerist moment, much more restricted in scope, arose in the late nineteenth century as new audiovisual technologies joined forces with the cultural politics of the nationalist movement (Freitag 2001). And, again, the Hindi middle-class cinema of the late 1960s and early 1970s toyed with an urban consumerist ethos, while never reconciling it with the moral authority of the "traditional" family (Prasad 1998). Precisely this work of reconciliation becomes a major motif in the consumerist family dramas of the 1990s (Ganti 2000).

19   The characterization of the period stretching from roughly 1950 to 1980 as an era of "socialism" was a commonplace of the liberalizers' rhetoric. Although both Nehru and Indira Gandhi had, in very different ways, claimed to be pursuing socialist policies, the Indian economy was never run on a Soviet-style command basis. Rather, the system involved heavy subsidizing of public sector enterprises and strict licensing and regulation of private producers. Note the unexpected affinity between the liberalizers' position and Gurumurthy's critique of the impositions of socialism. The major difference lies in the SJM's concern for liberating the productive energies of domestic entrepreneurs, while the consumerist line is obviously more focused upon freeing consuming energies.

20   See Tomlinson 1991 for a thoughtful dissection of the concept.

21   See Sahlins 1993 for an exemplary statement.

22   The Comaroffs' discussion of the complex cultural economy of conversion in colonial South Africa is a salutary reminder that the utopian — and in many cases, overtly religious — ethical discourse attaching to participation in global markets has a long and venerable history (Comaroff and Comaroff 1997, chapter 4). This history continues today in the form of the tight connection between new global media, booming Christian evangelical movements, and the norms and forms of mass consumerism, starring "not a Jesus who saves, but one who pays dividends" (Comaroff and Comaroff 2000, 315).

23   Jacques Derrida succinctly expresses the way in which this ambiguity — here applied to discourse — is at once necessary and seductive: "If a speech could be purely present, unveiled, naked, offered up in person in its truth, without the detours of a signifier foreign to it, if at the limit an undeferred *logos* were possible, it would not seduce anyone" (Derrida 1981, 71).

24   My intention here is as much to find a way to think about the production of value from commercially circulated images as to counter the meaning of the word commodity in marketing discourse, where it has come to denote a "merely" generic item, unsanctified by the gift of a purposively constructed brand image.

25   Williams, in his widely read essay "Advertising, the Magic System," argued:

> If we were sensibly materialist, in that part of our living in which we use things, we should find most advertising to be of an insane irrelevance. Beer would be enough for us, without the additional promise that in drinking it we show ourselves to be manly, young in heart, or neighbourly. A washing-machine would be a useful machine to wash clothes, rather than an indication that we are forward-looking or an object of envy to our neighbours. . . . It is clear that we have a cultural pattern in which the objects are not enough but must be validated, if only in fantasy, by association with social and personal meanings which in a different cultural pattern might be more directly available. (Williams 1980, 185)

Williams was here writing in a vein that Marx himself had inaugurated. In the 1844 Manuscripts, Marx stated that

Under private property . . . each person speculates on creating a *new* need in
another, so as to drive him to fresh sacrifice, to place him in a new dependence and to seduce him into a new mode of *gratification* and therefore
economic ruin. Each tries to establish over the other an *alien* power, so as
thereby to find satisfaction of his own selfish need. . . . Excess and intem-
perance come to be [the modern economic system's] true norm. Subjectively,
this is even partly manifested in that the extension of products and needs
falls into *contriving* and ever-*calculating* subservience to the inhuman, refined, unnatural and *imaginary* appetites. (Tucker 1978, 93)

26 This ghost is, additionally, in Rousseauian fashion, identified with an imagined
archaic other, a social dispensation in which the relatively egalitarian ambiva-
lences of symbolic exchange prevail, as opposed to the reified tyrannies of the
modern sign. As Levin remarks, in an introduction to Baudrillard 1981: "Thus
symbolic exchange 'haunts' the authoritarian structures of the political economy of the sign, while *ambivalence* perpetually threatens to deconstruct the
reified process of signification" (Levin 1981, 22).

27 Schudson's (1984) work on advertising suggests that consumer goods advertising only has a rather tenuous relationship to sales (except in more clear-cut
cases like price advertising). If additional support for this contention is required from within the industry, the legendary adman David Ogilvy may be
quoted: "Many manufacturers secretly question whether advertising really
sells their product, but are vaguely afraid that their competitors might steal
a march on them if they stopped. Others — particularly in Great Britain —
advertise 'to keep their name before the public.' Others because it helps them
to get distribution. Only a minority of marketers advertise because they have
found that it *increases their profits*" (Ogilvy 1983, 171, emphasis in original).

28 Vance Packard's *The Hidden Persuaders* (1957) is paradigmatic in this genre.
It is worth noting that Packard's position was ultimately favorable toward the
industry; his strategy was to stir up paranoia on the basis of the suggestion that
certain "bad eggs" were using "motivational research" (a then fashionable
psychologistic idiom most closely associated with Ernest Dichter [see Brierley
1995]) in unscrupulous ways. The subliminal advertising scare, which erupted
shortly after Packard's book was published, extended the theme of sinister
unseen forces manipulating unsuspecting minds (see S. Fox 1990). According
to Fox, a 1958 case in which a consultant named James Vicary used quick-
flash messages urging the consumption of soft drinks and popcorn at a New
Jersey cinema remains the single documented deployment of subliminal advertising. The narrative has, predictably, persisted among conspiracy theorists
(Key 1972, 1976).

29 T. J. Lears (1994) and T. Frank (1997) both document the ways in which each
of the poles of the dialectic between managerial rationality and romantic transcendence, in addition to being built into the structure of the business, enjoy
alternate moments of emphasis in the industry's public image. Lears argues

that the advertising business itself reflects a particularly American oscillation between hedonism and asceticism. While his historical documentation for the American context is compelling, the thesis that this doubleness is peculiar to the United States cannot withstand comparative evidence. In Hinduism, for example, the tension between asceticism and worldly pleasure is inscribed in the distinction between the *yogi* and the *bhogi* (see for instance Burghart 1983; Doniger 1981; Dumont 1960; Flood 1996; Madan 1982, 1987). Subsequently, of course, the question of asceticism versus indulgence has animated key historical moments of transition, such as the swadeshi phase of Indian nationalism (Bayly 1986; Mukherjee and Mukherjee 1908; Sarkar 1973), the revival of the term in contemporary Indian politics in relation to globalization (M. Aiyar 1997, 1998), and of course the boosting of consumerism in the 1980s (see part 1).

30 It is certainly the case that research plays a greater role in agency dealings with some clients than with others. Companies like Procter and Gamble and Unilever (makers of a wider range of packaged goods — soaps, laundry detergents, shampoos, etc.) are notorious in the advertising world for the rigidity of their planning. This kind of client will quite often have a minutely articulated template for its advertising all over the world — scene-by-scene breakdowns, the composition of which have been thoroughly researched before implementation, are common. The advertising industry maintains an ambivalent relation to such clients. On the one hand, they are felt to stifle creative thinking and advertising execution — and to this extent both creatives and account executives often complain about working on such accounts. As one executive put it to me: "In frame six, what is the significance of the woman holding the cloth at this particular angle?" Or: "P&G have a book for everything. You'll be sitting there having a conversation, and they'll bring out the bible on that particular topic that they've already researched." On the other hand, they are tremendously lucrative business for the agencies (Procter and Gamble is widely supposed to be the largest advertiser in the world although this position may recently have been usurped by Philip Morris), and, for account executives, working on packaged goods accounts is one of the key stepping stones for career advancement. This is not just because of the large billings that such accounts bring, but also because they are considered to be particularly challenging — more market variables, more competition in each category, and the problem of selling to a market that straddles almost every conceivable segment. Finally, the fact that the advertising agencies, through these kinds of clients, can make claims about improving the quality of life of even the poorest consumers gives them a kind of ideological importance in the agency world.

31 The need for this kind of ideological legitimation appears to coincide with the rise of branding as a model of social life, and the corollary appearance of the anthropoid figure of the consumer-citizen. It was the case in the United States and Europe around the turn of the twentieth century (Buckley 1982; Curti 1967; Ohmann 1996) and — as I argue in this study — in India in the 1980s. By

the 1980s in the United States, in contrast, industry voices were actively engaged in attempting to dispel this image. There were complex reasons for this; in part, it was a response to the critique of the industry growing not only out of Packardian alarmism (see note 28) but also of the counter-culture/leftist attacks of the 1960s; in part, as Ohmann suggests, it may have been a response to a situation in which marketing failure was becoming much more commonplace, unlike the heady era around the turn of the century when entirely new product categories routinely triumphed. Against this background, it might be worth recalling that Appadurai (1986), after citing Schudson's work approvingly, goes on to suggest that the rapturous reception it received from the advertising business itself should give us pause for thought.

32 Perhaps the paradigmatic embodiment of the creative maverick in U.S. advertising is the legendary New York art director George Lois, who dismisses marketing "science" as follows: "The problem with pseudoscientists of 'positioning' is their deification of logic and linear thinking. The best 'positioning' ideas invariably derive from breakthrough advertising, from surprising, disarming *creative* solutions. A logical, rational methodology handcuffs any possibilities for a thrilling creative solution that can make miracles" (Lois and Pitts 1991, 41).

33 The reflections contained in this section are developed more extensively in Mazzarella (2003).

34 The agency component of my fieldwork involved attending the office on a daily basis, usually for the entire working day, which might extend from around 9 A.M. to somewhere in the region of 7 P.M. During office hours, I would participate in strategy sessions, creative meetings, and agency-client consultations. Frequently, I would accompany groups of agency personnel on trips to the main offices of various clients, to locations where commercials were being filmed or advertisements being photographed, and to meetings with directors. It is worth mentioning that although the agency was part of a transnational network, all its employees were Indians. The languages used in the course of the working day depending on the setting. In general, because higher-level personnel tended to have higher levels of education, but nevertheless came from all four corners of the subcontinent, their only shared language was English. Subsets of agency personnel would, of course, switch between English and other shared languages, generally Hindi, Marathi, Gujarati, and Kannada. The agency art studio, whose employees were largely drawn from local art schools, and had often not been educated in English, was Marathi-dominated. Kemper (2001, 24–25) makes an equivalent argument for Sri Lanka.

35 There was no significant relationship between such an "insider-outsider" location and particular job descriptions in the agency. However, I should mention that the father of one of my most consistently helpful informants had been an anthropologist at a provincial Maharashtrian university.

36 At the same time, there are obviously powerful commercial pressures at work

to collapse the distinction between businesses and research campuses, to the extent that corporate funding underwrites both research and infrastructure. Vis-à-vis this tendency, there is of course value in defending the partial autonomy — and therefore the critical potential — of the campuses.

37 Hartman Center Archives/Samuel W. Meek Papers/International Offices/ International Department/International Marketing/Box 4/Bombay: General, July–December 1949.

Chapter Two. Elaborations

1 I borrow this phrase from Michael Warner (1992).

2 I adapt this phrase from Rolph Trouillot (1995, 22).

3 The remarkable persistence, even in the most sophisticated quarters, of this binary can be seen in a recent comment by David Harvey: "The production of real (by which I mean affective and socially embedded) as opposed to commodified cultural divergence, for example, can . . . be posed as an aim of anticapitalist struggle" (Harvey 2000a, 83).

4 We can see this assumption operating in the more neo-Lukácsian moments of Robert Goldman's work on advertising: "Constructing signs that have market value exacts a societal cost, because when meaning systems are systematically abstracted and plundered as a resource for producing commodity-signs, the penetration of the commodity form has a 'dissolving' influence on culture" (Goldman 1992, 6).

5 Adorno does, in fact, appear to offer an acknowledgment that the process leaves a remainder. But this remainder is itself perverted in the service of a false sentimentality: "The result for the physiognomy of the culture industry is essentially a mixture of streamlining, photographic hardness and precision on the one hand, and individualistic residues, sentimentality and an already rationally disposed and adapted romanticism on the other" (Adorno 1991, 101).

6 In his Third Critique, *The Critique of Judgment,* Kant declares that "judgment in general is the faculty of thinking the particular as contained under the universal" (Behler 1999, 141).

7 Strictly speaking, it seems that Adorno is suggesting that two things are going on here. On the one hand, the culture industries appear to be usurping the faculty of judgment from the individual. On the other hand, this usurpation involves the substitution of one kind of judgment — what Kant called "determinant judgment," in which particulars are entirely subsumed under a concept — for another — what Kant called "reflective judgment," which was characteristic of aesthetic judgments and which did not involve the subordination of judgment to a determinate concept. In this light, the culture industrial usurpation of judgment is doubly violent: it alienates judgment from the individual *and* it violates the principle of aesthetic judgment.

8 "The Marxian vision recaptures the ancient theory of knowledge as *recollection:* 'science' as the *re*discovery of the true *Forms* of things, distorted and

denied in the established reality, the perpetual *materialistic core of idealism*" (Marcuse, quoted in Jay 1984, 227).

9 In fact, Massumi himself uses the term "commodity image," but in the context of a rather conventional diagnosis of the "postmodern" predicament: to denote the image that has become completely disconnected from concrete referents, that has become completely available for the realization of exchange value (see Massumi 1992; Yoshimoto 1996).

10 For important discussions of the political stakes of realism in both painting and photography in India, for both the British and the Indian nationalist movement, see Guha-Thakurta 1992, Kapur 1998, Pinney 1997, and Srivatsan 2000.

Chapter Three. Citizens Have Sex, Consumers Make Love

Parts of chapters 3 and 4 appeared in an earlier version as "Citizens Have Sex, Consumers Make Love: Marketing KamaSutra Condoms in Bombay," in *Asian Media Productions*, edited by Brian Moeran. Honolulu: University of Hawai'i Press, 2001.

1 The *Kamasutra* was originally compiled by the fourth-century scholar Vatsyayana, and has, like most major "Hindu" texts, since then spawned a vast supplementary literature of commentaries and interpretations. Its introduction into nineteenth-century European Victorian society through Richard Burton's selective English translation contributed to its popular and prurient reputation as an oriental sex manual, a reputation that still persists among contemporary Indian middle-class professionals, the intended audience of the KamaSutra ads. Although much of the text of the *Kamasutra* is indeed concerned with sexual practice, the refinement of sensual pleasure (*kama*) through sex is to be pursued in relation to the other major goals of life—*dharma* (a famously complex term that is often translated as righteous or ethical action, in relation to one's position in life) and *artha,* the management of material interests. Consequently, the *Kamasutra,* before launching into its famous sequence of sexual recommendations, dwells in detail on interior decoration, education, leisure, and care of the body.

2 Alain Danielou offers the following characterization of the nagaraka: "a wealthy, cultivated bourgeois male who is an art lover and either a merchant or civil servant living in a large city" (Danielou 1994, 7). See Doniger and Kakar 2002 for a superior translation of the text itself. In contemporary usage, as Chatterjee (1995, 102) reminds us, *nagarik* is in fact used to denote "citizen."

3 The juxtaposition of "high" literary content with "low" imagery was, from the beginning, a conscious move on the part of the founders of *Debonair,* and one of the ways in which the magazine sought to carve out a "progressive" aesthetic agenda. Without denying the tremendous differences between the two publications, both in terms of content and sociohistorical role, it should not be

forgotten that *Playboy*, at the time of its inception, involved a similarly novel combination.

4 J K Chemicals is one of the main companies of the J K Group, named after its founder, the late Juggilal Kamlapat Singhania. In 1988, The J K Group was divided into three separate corporate entities, each headed by one of J. K. Singhania's sons — Padampat, Kailashpat, and Lakshmipat — and *their* sons. The three family groupings were given control of, respectively, J K Synthetics along with cotton, jute, and iron companies; Raymond (leaders in high-end men's suitings and body-care products); and J K Industries, which included J K Chemicals.

5 This and all subsequent quotations from the launch ads are taken from the KamaSutra advertising supplement that appeared at the center of the October 1991 issue of *Debonair* magazine.

6 In April 1998, I attempted to schedule an interview with Mr. Singhania. His secretary, however, was of the opinion that since I had already spoken with Aniruddha Deshmukh, the executive director of JKC, I had "the whole story."

7 At the time of the KamaSutra launch there were two large-scale producers: Hindustan Latex (HL), a public sector company — and the largest manufacturer of condoms in the world — and TTK-LIG, a private operation, which had evolved out of the earlier London Rubber Co. The commercial market amounted to a total of around 400 million pieces annually, including the subsidized government brand Nirodh (which commanded 56 percent of the market by volume, primarily supplied by HL). There was only one substantial non-subsidized branded player, a TTK brand called Kohinoor (with 20 percent of the market at that time), which was being marketed on a relatively conservative family planning platform. Another TTK brand called Fiesta had acquired a 5 percent market share with a campaign that had been quite risqué for its time (the mid-1980s), in which the theme had been "different colours for different days of the week," thus to some extent preparing the ground for a more eroticized approach. These figures on market share are from Annuncio (1993) and Irani (1991).

8 Lobo (1991) estimates that the AIDS "scare" had caused a 12 percent per annum growth in the Indian commercial condom market in the late 1980s and early 1990s.

9 In fact, the launch campaign ended up wildly overshooting promotional budgets, although accounts of the original budget vary. Alyque Padamsee, then C.E.O. of Lintas:India, told me that it was Rs 3.3 million; in Doctor and Sen 1997 Jayant Bakshi, the executive in charge of the account, estimates it at Rs 6–7 million, and suggests that around Rs 11.9 million was actually spent.

10 Interview with Alyque Padamsee, Bombay, February 1998. All subsequent quotations from Padamsee, unless otherwise referenced, are from this conversation. The market research that Lintas conducted around this time confirmed their hunch: it showed that although awareness and even one-time trials of condoms among members of the target group (at the time of launch, defined as

urban middle-to-high income males, twenty-five to forty years old) were as high as 80 percent, continued use was a dismal 2 to 3 percent.

11 This other condom account, which Lintas did not win, was for a brand called Adam. See pages 131–32 for a brief discussion of the manner in which the subsequent aesthetic route taken by KamaSutra was compared and contrasted with that taken by Adam.

12 Interview with Adi Pocha, Bombay, February 1998. All subsequent quotations from Pocha are from this conversation.

13 Interview with Jayant Bakshi, Bombay, November 1997. All subsequent quotations from Bakshi, unless otherwise noted, are from this conversation.

14 Bakshi told me that this particular group of professionals went out and did field interviews in cities and towns with populations of more than fifty thousand people. At no point during this initiative, and the one that followed in 1979–80 (unlike earlier advertising industry involvement in government family planning initiatives; see pages 80–87), was there a serious move to engage the advertising industry in communicating with people in rural areas.

15 The frequent brutality of Emergency-period sterilization initiatives is widely discussed but thinly documented. A powerful fictionalized account appears in Mistry (1995). For relevant references, see those cited in Krishnaji (1998). While the sterilization camps came to be identified with the authoritarian excesses of the Emergency, the period was not without its own moments of tragicomedy, especially for those not directly affected by it. Raj Thapar remembers in her memoirs:

> Little decorated vasectomy plants sprang up on every street, adorned with tins of cooking oil as giveaways — this, which had disappeared from the market — and armed with loudspeakers throwing out suggestive film songs. . . . At the Irwin Road camp one evening there was a macho looking man at the mike singing a little ditty — in English, with a broad Punjabi accent: "Come have yourself vasectomised, make your family systematised," whatever that may mean. I realised that it could only be aimed at me — certainly none of the fruit-sellers around were familiar with English, so who else, thought I, as I looked up and down the street. No one. (Thapar 1991, 419)

16 Interview with Jayant Bakshi, Bombay, January 1998.

17 Ardashir Vakil, in his fictionalized memoir of a Bombay childhood in the early 1970s, describes the scenario: "I walked back to the corner of Carmichael Road, where the paanwallah on the corner still had his shop open. I had forty paise in my pocket. I thought I might find something to eat. In the front of his shop I saw a box of Nirodhs. I had no idea what they were though I had seen the advertisements saying, 'Hum do, Hamare do' (The two of us and our two children), with the round cartoon faces of mummy, daddy, smiling son and pigtailed daughter. The model family" (Vakil 1998, 124).

18 In the course of my November 1997 interview with him, Jayant Bakshi ex-

plained: "We launched 'For the pleasure of making love,' and the delightful part of it is that now when we do our attitude surveys, there is an actual position that comes through from the consumer, which says 'What do you use a condom for?' 'Birth prevention?' 'STD and AIDS prevention?' And then there is one for 'pleasure.' And every time we see that we're delighted because we say, 'KamaSutra will live for a few more years.' "

19 Interview with Jayant Bakshi, Bombay, January 1998.

20 Varma further illustrates the changes in government policy under Indira Gandhi with the following: "Between 1966 and 1978, almost half of all factories that started production were in the small-scale sector; the number of products exclusively reserved for the small-scale sector rose from 128 in 1971 to 844 by 1981" (Varma 1998, 91).

21 Wadhawan (1992) estimates that a government employee taking home Rs 400 per month in 1980 would have been making Rs 4,000 per month in 1990. Although half of this gain would be offset by inflation, it still represents a substantial increase.

22 The very first television broadcasts in India took place in 1959, but at that time there were only around 150 television sets in the country, most of them donated by UNESCO. Daily broadcasts in Delhi began in 1965; in 1972, transmission was extended to major cities and "sensitive" border areas. This last move was largely a response to the expansion of Pakistani TV, and the recognition on the part of the Indian government of its power as a propaganda tool (Shah 1997). Commercial television in India started, on a limited scale, in 1976, but at that time television was still transmitted in black and white, and commercial spots were restricted to still images.

From 1982 onward, when color transmission began, the government embarked upon a massive infrastructure expansion program. The high-point of this expansion was in 1984, which — not coincidentally — was also an election year. Whereas there had been 20 transmitters in the country in 1983, 1984 alone saw the addition of 172 new transmitters. By the end of the decade, there was a total of around 300 transmitters.

The same period saw a dramatic rise in television advertising revenue. From a measly 77 lakhs (Rs 7.7 million) in 1976–77, the year when television went commercial, revenues steadily rose to 9 crores [Rs 90 million] in 1980, 16.1 crores in 1982, and then exploded upward: 30 crores in 1984, 50 crores in 1985, 60 crores in 1986, and 135 crores in 1987 (Ahmed and Sen 1988; Karlekar 1986; Ninan and Singh 1982; *OBM Media Bulletin* 1983; Singhal and Rogers 2001; Vasuki 1986).

Today, Doordarshan competes with several satellite channels, and has accordingly further expanded both its infrastructure and its portfolio of channels. As of the time I am writing this (April 2002), DD has 21 channels relayed across the subcontinent by 1,244 transmitters, reaching (by its own estimate) 88.4 percent of the total population, as compared to a mere 25 percent in 1982 (www.ddindia.net; accessed 18 April 2002).

General overviews of the history and social politics of television in India may be found in N. Gupta (1998), Mankekar (1999), Rajagopal (1993), and Shah (1997).

23 Interview with Anand Varadarajan, Bombay, January 1997. All subsequent quotations from Varadarajan are taken from this conversation.

24 Interview with Mohammed Khan, Bombay, May 1998. All subsequent quotations from Khan, unless otherwise noted, are taken from this conversation. In some respects, one might argue that what Khan is describing here as a new social formation represents the generalization of conventions of conspicuous consumption/display that were previously restricted to certain ceremonial contexts, for instance weddings, particularly in the form of daughters' dowries. Thanks to Raminder Kaur for reminding me of this point.

25 The private sector's enthusiasm could be counted on particularly insofar as such reforms did not unduly threaten the positions of industrialists already well established under the permit-license raj. The protests of the so-called "Bombay Club" (see pages 9–10) at the inequities of the "globalizing" reforms of the 1990s can be read in this light.

26 There is at least anecdotal evidence that this perception succeeded in embedding itself in the perceptions of some viewers at a grass-roots level. Anjali Monteiro quotes a Goan shipyard fitter, speaking in the late 1980s: "Under [Rajiv Gandhi's] leadership, they (the Congress) have brought progress in the country by introducing the latest, modern things. India is a world leader sending up satellites and all" (Monteiro 1998, 195).

27 The advertising industry was, as ever, both sensitive to the prevailing public climate and keen to preempt criticism. The rubric under which the Asian Advertising Congress held its thirteenth annual meeting in Delhi in late 1982 (ADGRO '82) was therefore hardly coincidental: "Advertising: an essential input to economic growth." Incidentally, the major draw at ADGRO '82 was legendary adman David Ogilvy, who had appeared in advertisements for the conference stating that although he "loathed" flying he nevertheless thought the future of advertising in Asia so important that he was prepared to overcome his phobia for the cause. See Ogilvy 1983 (182–84) for reflections on his experiences in India; not surprisingly, population control figures prominently in his discussion.

28 See Chakrabarty (2000) for an effective critique of historicism, not least as it pertains to writing histories of capitalism from a South Asian perspective.

29 See Ganti 2000; Prasad 1998; and Thomas 1985, 1995.

30 In fact, the authority of centralized planning in India had already been politically undermined in the early 1970s by Indira Gandhi's version of authoritarian populism. Economist A. Vaidyanathan (1995) argues that by the late 1960s and early 1970s the decline of Congress "hegemony" meant that no straightforward consensus on planning goals was possible. Instead, Congress governments at the center sought to placate different interest groups with different kinds of programs, none of them economically sound in the long term.

31 Michael Schudson's (1984) characterization of consumer goods advertising as "capitalist realism" implies just this connection — one need look no further than the Soviet debates over the place of popular art in a revolutionary society to grasp the relationship.

32 Nehru, for his part, subscribed to the "false needs" theory of advertising that was fashionable in both leftist and liberal circles in the immediate postwar period. In *The Discovery of India,* he wrote: "With all its splendid manifestations and real achievements, we have created a civilization which has something counterfeit about it. We eat ersatz food produced with the help of ersatz fertilizers; we indulge in ersatz emotions, and our human relations seldom go below the superficial plane. The advertiser is one of the symbols of our age with his continuous and raucous attempts to delude us and dull our powers of perception and induce us to buy unnecessary and even harmful products" (Nehru 1948, 469).

33 Beyond this specific area, the relationship between government and advertising in India can be traced at least to the decade immediately preceding Independence. Already at this point, the advertising industry was attempting to prove the indispensability of its skills to the propaganda efforts of the colonial wartime government, and finding it a thorny client to work with. In 1942, Peter Fielden, legendary long-time head of J. Walter Thompson's Bombay office (1930–66), wrote to his colleague Don Foote, who was based at the head office in New York:

> As you know, we are doing a considerable amount of work for the Government of India. This, I think, is largely a result of representations we started making to Government early in 1939. For a year no one paid much attention and when the desirability of propaganda and advertising was finally accepted we were able to get our recommendations through only in small part. I wanted to see a Department created which would co-ordinate media for propaganda — radio, cinema, press, outdoor, village propagandists, etc — and direct a unified effort through all channels. (Hartman Center Archives/Treasurer's Office Records/International Offices/Box 6)

> Four of the principal agencies of that era formed an acronymically named consortium, KATS (Keymer, Adarts, Thompson, and Stronach), but were joined after 1942 by General Advertising of Calcutta and Press Syndicate. Together, these agencies formed what became known as the CPU (Creative Publicity Unit), a centrally located government propaganda unit that was disbanded after the war (Hartman Center Archives /E. G. Wilson Papers/International Series/Box 10/Bombay: The Future of JWT in India, March 1961–June 1962). It appears, however, that this small group of agencies was able to monopolize government accounts until well into the 1960s.

34 ICS stands for Indian Civil Service, which was the pre-Independence name for the bureaucratic administrative framework of the state. After Independence, it was renamed the Indian Administrative Service (also known as the "heaven-born service"), and continued to enjoy an unchallenged prestige up until the recent apotheosis of the corporate private sector in the 1980s and 1990s.

35 Interview with Subhas Ghosal, Bombay, April 1998. All subsequent quotations from Ghosal are from this conversation unless otherwise noted.

36 Public Law 480 laid out the conditions under which U.S. funds were to be deployed in "Third World" aid programs in the postwar period.

37 The origins of the DAVP can be traced to World War II. Soon after the war began, the government appointed a chief press advisor, one of whose duties was overseeing government-related advertising. In 1941, responsibility for advertising was delegated to a specially appointed advertising consultant, who reported directly to the chief press advisor. The following year, the office of the advertising consultant became the Advertising Branch of the Department of Information and Broadcasting. In 1955, as its scope and activities expanded, it was renamed the Directorate of Advertising and Visual Publicity and given the official rank of an Attached Office (with its own financial and administrative powers) of what had by then become the Ministry of Information and Broadcasting.

38 Interview with Sylvester da Cunha, Bombay, January 1998. All subsequent quotations from da Cunha are taken from this conversation.

39 Hartman Center Archives/E. G. Wilson Papers/International Series, Box 11/India: "Indianization" and Position of the Company, August 1970– February 1971. Despite appearing in this folder, I am assuming that these advertisements were in fact released in response to Krishnamachari's 1965 tax initiative.

40 Sylvester da Cunha (as did his brother Gerson) subsequently became involved more deeply in attempts to adapt his communicational expertise to social development programs. In the 1980s and early 1990s, he served as population and nutrition consultant on the Information, Education, and Communication Unit of the World Bank, a job that took him to Brazil, Turkey, and Zambia as well as various parts of India. Remembering his participation in a program intended to teach rural Indian mothers about the importance of regularly weighing their infants, he related:

> We worked out a plan by which we were going to try and get our message through. How? Through cycles. Instead of walking — *cycles!* Motivate you guys. Motorcycles. Lambrettas for them. Sometimes five villages could be something like thirty miles in circumference. . . . We put up little service stations. We were training the mechanics. We worked out simple kerosene projectors where they could teach the various people simple lessons. We worked out stuff where they themselves could in fact create their own messages. . . . Very simple. And then we worked out at every level down, down, down. At the district level it was film, cinemas. Tamil Nadu, we found, was riddled with village cinemas. *Riddled.* Very cinema-conscious. . . . They

come at night; the big shows are from nine to twelve. And a *lot* of women to see these films. . . . They bought all the jeeps, they bought all the projectors, they bought everything else, and were using it for all kinds of reasons. They did nothing of the software that had made this hardware justifiable. And it broke my heart! We produced little leaflets and things that didn't see the light of day.

On one level, this narrative conformed to the general pattern of resourceful communications professionals being thwarted by lumbering implementation systems. On another, da Cunha's recollections appeared to be shot through with a deep ambivalence about the ability of advertising communications to effect fundamental change. He capped his story thus: "They [the World Bank team] didn't know where it was going, who was using it, how is it being used, how is it being applied, what was the feedback, pre and post. . . . If an advertising agency had been doing it, we would have [snaps fingers] changed that state in five years!" Yet at the same time, da Cunha also told me that what he thought was really needed was "changes that have to be done at the microlevel where advertising doesn't and can't work."

41   The argument had already been made by no less a public figure than Winston Churchill: "Advertising nourishes the consuming power of men. It creates wants for a better standard of living. It sets up before man the goal of a better home, better clothing, better food for himself and his family. It spurs individual exertion and greater production" (S. Mitra 1987).

42   Hartman Center Archives/E. G. Wilson Papers/International Series, Box 11/ India: Restriction on Advertising Expenditure, March 1965–April 1965.

43   This and the following sections of the memo are from the Hartman Center Archives/E. G. Wilson Papers/International Series, Box 10/India: "Indianization" and Position of the Company, September 1966. Emphasis added.

The occasion for Swamy's 1966 memo was an initiative on the part of the government to "Indianize" foreign joint ventures. This put several advertising companies in India in a complex position. On the one hand, companies like Thompson's relied upon their transnational affiliations for both prestige and infrastructural support; on the other hand, there was by the mid-1960s a new generation of Indian executives in these companies who were keen to take over the reins of power from their expatriate bosses. In this regard, Swamy himself had drawn the connection between the possibility (which eventually materialized) of J. Walter Thompson New York divesting its majority stake in the Indian operation and the British decision to relinquish imperial control of India two decades earlier:

> If we could think of the decision the British Government had to take in proclaiming independence for India as something parallel with what JWT New York is now faced [with] on the inevitable situation created by Section 18A [the proposed "Indianization article"] all we can say is that, in retrospect, the British Government has done very well indeed in regenerating

itself into a loose federation in a cooperative Commonwealth from its earlier more grandiose position of an impregnable empire. The present Commonwealth has kept the essential features of the British Empire in that a large number of nations and countries continue to be under one family, the British Commonwealth of Nations. But, every unit has become autonomous in that it is attending to its own law and order problems, is shaping its economic policies based on its natural resources and drives its own bargains in world markets based on its peculiar local strengths and weaknesses.

44   Eventually, the government did partially relent on the tax deductibility issue. The ceiling for tax deductible advertising expenses was raised to 4 percent of gross turnover, which left only a few companies affected — those that dealt in goods that traditionally have required a high advertising-to-turnover ratio: cosmetics, toiletries, certain kinds of food products, and patent medicines. The new ruling was set to go into effect in October 1965 but war with Pakistan intervened.

45   Note that the 1978 bill did *not* include consumer goods advertisements; they would only be included in the 1983 version of the initiative, along with company cars and hotel bills. This may be taken as a changing index of what was actually being advertised at the time; Sarna (1982a and 1982b) indicates that the three biggest ad spending product categories in 1978–79 were electrical machinery, medicines and pharmaceuticals, "other chemical products," and cotton textiles.

46   In 1985, Procter and Gamble would effect a worldwide merger with Richardson Vicks, the upshot in India being the transformation of Richardson Hindustan into Procter and Gamble India.

47   Das's equation of the utility of added value with those of lower prices or product improvements obscures an important aspect of the working of advertising, particularly in relation to brands, namely the manner in which this added value is at once "given" to the consumer and "kept" by the producer (see pages 192–95 for a more detailed discussion of this dynamic).

48   Interview with Piyush Pandey, Bombay, May 1998.

49   Rajiv's liberalizing achievements, while seen as insufficient or timid by many free market boosters, did reduce corporate and income taxes (from a mid-1970s high of 97 percent) and simplify tax procedures in general. They also raised MRTP limits — that is, the asset limit at which companies fell under the jurisdiction of the laws on Monopolies and Restrictive Trade Practices — from 20 crore rupees to 100 crore rupees. He did away with capacity ceilings for industries, and in fact introduced the idea of *minimum* capacities. Moreover, he reduced restrictions on foreign joint ventures and technological collaborations. Import restrictions were reduced, although by no means to the extent that they would be post-1991; in many cases where there had been complete bans, there was now merely a high tariff — averaging at 146 percent for intermediaries and at 107 percent for capital goods. The industrial growth that occurred during his time in office was in large part financed by heavy international borrowing; many commercial banks were at this time more than happy to lend to India, since their Latin American and African clientele were undergoing debt crises. The budgetary deficit consequently rose from 3,745 crores in 1985–86 to 7,484 crores in 1988–89, while the total external debt nearly doubled to 69,000 crores in this same period (Aiyar 1991; Gaya and Ghiara 1991; M. Singh 1998).

Economist Kaushik Basu commented acidly on the business-friendly 1985 budget:

> The Union Budget, 1985–86, should make everybody happy. The highly paid company executive should be happy because he will have to pay less income tax, less wealth tax, and no estate duty. The industrialist should be happy because the corporate tax has been lowered by five per cent and there is assurance that it will be lowered further in the years to come. The rural capitalist should be happy because he will continue to be exempt from income tax and he can now have insurance against crop failures. Finally, the poor man should be happy seeing so much happiness all around! This seems to be the essential philosophy behind this year's budget. (Basu 1991, 108)

50 See Ganti 2000 for a discussion of the significance of the search for a universal appeal among the makers of the contemporary Hindi cinema. In this regard, and for reasons further developed by Prasad (1998), the Hindi cinema is more wholeheartedly inclusive in its orientation than consumer marketing could ever be.

51 It should be pointed out that one of the main reasons that Padamsee was being sought out by journalists for his comments on public service advertising around this time was precisely because work done by Lintas in this vein *had* been winning prizes.

52 The metaphor is old; Lears quotes a 1925 J. Walter Thompson new business presentation: "Advertising is a non-moral force, like electricity, which not only illuminates but electrocutes. Its worth to civilization depends upon how it is used" (Lears 1994, 224).

Mankekar notes how state developmental policy in India was already oriented around the dissemination of information rather than any more drastic interventions: "The state's communication policy rested on the axiom that information, rather than structural change, was the most essential ingredient required for India to modernize: disseminating development information would lead to a change in the attitudes of Indians, and this attitudinal change would, in turn, lead to a change in their practices" (Mankekar 1999, 58).

53 In fact one doctor interviewed at the time made it sound more like a problem of ballistics than of reproductive health: "Says Dr Narayan Reddy, Consultant in Sexual Medicine, 'Because people do not know how to use condoms, the failure rate is high through the tearing of a condom, because during ejaculation semen is expelled at 40 to 90 km/h' " (Bhagat 1993).

54 There was certainly a *perception* on the part of key players in the publicity game that the medium in which they were operating was increasingly becoming eroticized. For instance, the much-maligned DAVP was by the mid-1980s widely being portrayed in the media as having been sidelined by Rajiv Gandhi's enthusiastic adoption of private sphere communications outfits (particularly through his association with Arun Nanda of Rediffusion). N. Banerjee (1986) paints a sorry picture of the DAVP as a "sick" public sector undertaking, lying more or less idle with an "unflexibly" large capacity. One of their senior officials is quoted as complaining: "No secretary [from the Ministry of Information and Broadcasting] has ever visited our studio or held any discussion with creative artists on our work. And suddenly, they seem to be very concerned about the quality of work and bringing in outsiders as professionals. As if we are not professionals." A "young art room boy" adds plaintively, further strengthening the association with the offices of government bureaucracies: "Who will visit us over some *chhalu* [ordinary] tea served in stained cups?"

55 Alyque Padamsee, in his published account of the campaign, is even more forthright: "There was a very spirited defence put up [at Lintas] against going the sex route. And instead opting for the safe route. As protection against AIDS. But we found that it was the wrong button to press. If you scare the devil out of people for having unprotected sex, they get turned off. They don't read your advertisement. They don't want to think about AIDS. If you want to sell a condom, don't tell your target audience, 'Unless you wear a condom, you'll get AIDS and die' " (Padamsee 1999, 274).

56 Interview with Aniruddha Deshmukh, Bombay, January 1998. All subsequent quotations from Deshmukh are taken from this conversation.

Chapter Four. The Aesthetic Politics of Aspiration

Portions of chapters 3 and 4 appeared in an earlier version as "Citizens Have Sex, Consumers Make Love: Marketing KamaSutra Condoms in Bombay," in *Asian Media Productions*, edited by Brian Moeran. Honolulu: University of Hawai'i Press, 2001.

1 Critics of Habermas frequently draw connections between his distrust of publicity and the influence of his Frankfurt School teachers, particularly Adorno. And in fact Habermas himself has suggested that his early work had yet to emerge from the substantial shadow of his mentors. It is true that Adorno's stinging indictment of the culture industries certainly drew a connection between the proliferation of mass publicity and a decline in the ability of ordinary people to think for themselves. But we should not forget that Adorno's objection was not to the affective potential of images per se. Rather what he objected to was the bureaucratic or commercial rationalization of this affective potential, in short, its reification.

Habermas's emphasis on reasoned discourse over other forms of communication is sometimes attributed to the historical experience of being part of the first generation to come to political maturity in the wake of the horrifying political aestheticizations of the Third Reich (see Jay 1984, 467). But it seems to me that the historical explanation can equally well go the other way: consider Walter Benjamin, who, pursued to the end by the living actuality of the Reich, struggled to formulate a dialectical theory of the image.

2 The essays contained in Comaroff and Comaroff 2000 contain elucidations of this transition from a variety of contexts.

3 Gandhi's description of his own path to celibacy also posits the harnessing of one's sexual desire as metonymically standing for a relationship to the world in general. But for Gandhi, self-realization, and the "potentiality" that came with it, would only come through the renunciation (or perhaps sublimation) rather than the indulgence of one's desires. Consequently, for him, using contraceptives amounted to taking the easy way out, since it did not deal with the fundamental problem of mastering (rather than being mastered by) desire. As recounted in his autobiography, his internal debate started with the problem of how his relationship with his wife could be based on pure motives if it consisted "in making my wife the instrument of my lust? So long as I was the slave of my lust, my faithfulness was worth nothing." At the same time, he admits that he fell short at first because his motivation was selfish. "My main object was to escape having more children. Whilst in England I had read something about contraceptives. . . . If it had some temporary effect on me, Mr. Hill's opposition to those methods and his advocacy of internal efforts as opposed to outward means, in a word, of self-control, had a far greater effect, which in due time came to be abiding. Seeing, therefore, that I did not desire more children I began to strive after self-control. There was endless difficulty in the task" (Gandhi 1982, 195).

Gandhi, however, also expanded a personal and pragmatic economy of desire into a political and ideological project: the birth of an independent India. Hence the double meaning of the term *swaraj*, which connotes "self-governance" in both the personal and the geopolitical senses.

4 *Webster's Third New International Dictionary* (1961).

5 Ibid.

6 *Funk and Wagnalls New Standard Dictionary* (1963).

7 *Random House Dictionary,* second edition (1987).

8 Interview with Mohammed Khan, Bombay, May 1998. All subsequent quotations from Khan are from this conversation unless otherwise noted.

9 Interview with Frank Simoes, Bombay, May 1998. All subsequent quotations from Simoes are from this conversation unless otherwise noted.

10 Interview with Kersy Katrak, Bombay, May 1998. All subsequent quotations from Katrak are taken from this conversation unless otherwise noted.

11 HTA promotional brochure, filed at Hartman Center Archives/Information Center Records, Box 10/International: India, 1952–1987.

12 Piyush Pandey of Ogilvy and Mather (Bombay) told me:

> I think television suddenly made advertising a lot more mass-based. And therefore, the older drinking-club kind of advertising was exposed. You were talking to ten people and those ten people backslapped you and you backslapped them and you gave awards to each other and felt very good about it. With the advent of television came the opportunity for now talking to millions of people. And to talk to those millions of people, you had to talk the language of those people.... I think that turned it around. I was fortunate to be a part of that era, where all those things which have made us successful today could get the right outlet. I mean, if I was thinking the same way, and perhaps existed in the 70s, maybe I wouldn't even have discovered myself.

13 Khan went on to discuss a campaign that had recently made headlines where a Levers brand of toothpaste had claimed to be "102 percent" more effective than a competitor's brand. To his mind, an award jury's willingness to heap praise upon this campaign demonstrated the inability of many of his contemporaries to distinguish between the information given to the creative team in a brief and the advertising idea that should develop out of it.

> Now, the thing happened again with the toothpastes, you know, the Levers and the Colgate brands. Again, this kind of advertising war, where Lever's is 102 percent better. . . . I'd like to know what the results of that kind of campaign really were. *Huge* amounts of money had been spent. And it's an advertising story, but whether the story is advertising is another matter! If you know what I'm saying. There's no *advertising* there, you know. It's just a lab test. Where's the advertising? The ring of confidence is advertising. . . . Okay now, very often, I think, clients are not seeing this. I was on the jury in India. Some members of the jury wanted to give that campaign an award. For creativity. I said, "Listen, this is a lab test. Give it to the lab! Don't give it to the copywriter! What has the copywriter done? What has the agency done?" Oh, but the agency may have come up with the idea. "Fine," I said. "Terrific. Agencies get paid to think up ideas. But why *we* are sitting around this table is to reward creativity. Where is the creative? Where is the ad [laughs]??" So somebody picked it up and said, "But *this* is the ad!" And I said, "But this is not an ad, this is a brief! It's the result of a lab test, but where is the ad?" It took them ten minutes to figure out that there was no ad there. "Oh, we understand what you're saying now." And this is the discussion that happened between judges who are sitting. . . . Now that is the level of our understanding of advertising today, in *1998!* Now you tell me. You talk to me about the 60s and 70s, you can imagine what it was like [laughs]! Today we don't know the difference between a brief and advertising. That is an amorphous area.

14 It is thus all the more fitting that Kersy Katrak, reinstated by Alyque Padamsee at Lintas as executive creative director since 1987, should have been credited by his old friend Frank Simoes as the driving force behind the KamaSutra campaign. Katrak himself, however, when I interviewed him, tersely confirmed the decisive role played by Adi Pocha:

> WM: Can you recall the relative contributions of everyone who was involved at that time — Alyque Padamsee, Jayant Bakshi, Adi Pocha . . .
>
> KK: Alyque Padamsee had nothing to do with it, Jayant Bakshi had nothing to do with it, Adi Pocha had a great deal to do with it, I had something to do with it.
>
> WM: What was your relative . . .
>
> KK: Relative weight? Relative weight?
>
> WM: Who brought what to the table?
>
> KK: Most, most of the goodies came from Adi Pocha. And his team. I, to the extent that all major campaigns involved me, was involved in it. Alyque rode it once it became a success. So did Jayant. They had nothing to do with the creation of it.
>
> WM: But of course Jayant Bakshi has taken over the thing since then.
>
> KK: That's besides the point. He's a friend of this guy . . . Gautam Singhania, who's set him up with a product. And I don't know how he keeps that agency going on one brand, which hardly spends anything at all, but he does.

15 There are interesting comparisons to be explored between the "radical" potential in the reclaiming of individual agency in the rhetoric of mass consumerism and Marx's attempts to "take back history" from Hegel on behalf of concrete human actors. On the one hand, one would obviously have to weigh the populist claims of mass consumerism — without, for all that, *denying* them — against the specific aesthetic politics of particular marketing initiatives. On the other hand, as I suggested in chapter 2, Marx's "inversion" of Hegel's theory of history is perhaps not much more sensitive to the contingencies of concrete locations than the vision it ostensibly challenges. As we have seen, moreover, the Marxian ambivalence about the historical importance of specifically embodied experience, not to mention pleasure or desire as legitimate sources of motivation, resulted in the kinds of impasses that Adorno and Benjamin — together and apart — began to explore.

16 Interview with Aniruddha Deshmukh, Bombay, January 1998. All subsequent quotations from Deshmukh are taken from this conversation.

17 Interview with Jayant Bakshi, Bombay, January 1998.

18 In fact, one might argue that there are structural parallels between Vatsyayana's exhaustive enumeration of sensual possibilities and the multiplication of possibilities for high-end consumer gratification through the profusion of product variants offered under a brand umbrella: one of the KamaSutra ads from the 1996–97 phase of the campaign seemed explicitly to play on this correlation. The ad presented the range of products as a kind of mirror for sexual self-understanding. The layout showcased the entire KS range, which by that

point included eight different packages of variously textured and "scented" condoms. There was by now even a bumper pack of fifteen for the insatiable. Beneath a headline demanding "What kind of lover are you?" the viewer could follow arrows through a flowchart linking the various packs, thus arriving at the product that was perfectly matched to his predilection: "Are you the moody type? Do you keep it simple, stupid, flowing with the tide, or do you occasionally swim against it? Are you fussy? Are you flexible? Are you driven by wild fantasies? We believe your condom choice can help come up with an answer."

19 As it happens, the male model in the original campaign, Marc Robinson, at that time virtually unknown, has since become one of the leading male models in India, in addition to attempting a move into cinema. At the time, however, in Adi Pocha's words: "Very frankly, Marc was . . . at that stage, he was a prop." The photographer, Prabuddha Das Gupta, who recommended Robinson for the job, elaborated: "Marc was relatively unknown. Pooja was a star. Pooja was getting a huge amount of money. Marc was getting like a piddly . . . some Rs 20,000, whatever."

20 See Moeran 2001 for a discussion of such promotional synergies.

21 The cultural politics of the particular kind of "Indian body" that Pooja Bedi may or may not have represented should be evaluated in relation to the nationalist formation that brought together the aesthetics of the nation with representations of the demure Hindu female body.

22 Interview with Prabuddha Das Gupta, Bombay, April 1998. All subsequent quotations from Das Gupta, unless otherwise noted, are taken from this conversation.

23 Note that Ansel Adams defined the serious photographer on the basis of a rigorous avoidance precisely of such "machine-gun photography" (see Sontag 1989, 117).

24 As a protest against the temporal scheme of the developmentalist state, we can read mass consumerism in the postcolony in Benjaminian terms: against the empty, homogenous, and linear time of the modernist project of national development, the consumerist dispensation held out the vision of a blinding flash of simultaneity — past, present, and future redeemed in one great "now."

25 The contrast made here between the cosmopolitan idiom of upscale advertising and the aesthetics of the Hindi film is prefigured by the one made from the 1950s onward between the neorealist Indian cinema embodied by Satyajit Ray and "Bollywood's superfluity of corporeal affectivity (computed by critics as a deficit of aesthetic and imaginative worth)" (Pinney 2001, 20).

26 The ASCI and the CCC were set up in 1985 and conclusively incorporated in 1986. The CCC is a board of fourteen professionals, composed in such a way that the majority are drawn from non-advertising contexts. It meets to review offending advertisements and can demand the withdrawal or amendment of existing ads. The immediate impetus for the creation of the ASCI/CCC combine seems to have been a government initiative, in 1982, to set up a separate

ministry for consumer protection. As in other countries, the Indian advertising industry decided that it would be better to be "self-regulating" through an autonomous body like the ASCI than to be directly beholden to the government. The Ad Club of Bombay appointed a committee in 1982 to formulate the guidelines for such regulation; by 1984, they were in general circulation. More or less duplicated from similar codes in the West, these guidelines were supposed to set the acceptable parameters for the professional behavior of agencies, clients, and media alike.

The ASCI guidelines assume that advertising is primarily informational and that it is on a gauge of truth/falsity that abuses are most likely to occur. The basic commandments are as follows: 1) to maintain the honesty of advertising claims and not mislead consumers; 2) not to offend generally accepted standards of public decency; 3) to safeguard against excessive promotion of individually and socially hazardous products; and 4) to observe fairness in competition (product comparisons are allowed "provided the claims are backed by independent research").

This strategically naïve content/information orientation is typical of industry self-regulation efforts, in part because it coincides successfully with the vision of advertising that governments are pleased to maintain. As then Information and Broadcasting minister K. H. L. Bhagat declared to a 1983 meeting of the Public Relations Society of India: "Advertising communication has to be objective, result-oriented and should be free from distortions." Robert Goldman has indicated some of the shortcomings of this kind of an approach to advertising regulation in the U.S. context:

> The FTC [Federal Trade Commission] does not address the *form* of advertisements in their calculus of what constitutes false and misleading advertising. By limiting themselves to a mechanical, legalistic review of surface content, the FTC assists in maintaining the hegemony of corporate interests: preventing questions about tacit ideological agenda-setting in ads from being posed; and sanctifying the daily articulation of a commercial grammar of reification as innocent and natural. It is hardly innocent: the advertising apparatus ceaselessly transforms our meaning systems as well as our desires into commodities, with vast sociocultural repercussions beyond whether or not an immediate sale is realised. (Goldman 1992, 83)

27   The complaint was lodged on November 28, 1991. Trivedi, who belonged to the Janata Dal party, was supported in his mention by a broad coalition of members, including Deputy Chairperson Najma Heptullah, M. A. Baby, Bhubaneshwar Kalita, Mira Das, Murli Bhandare, and Mohammad Afzal.

28   In chapter 3, I suggested that the apparently oppositional positions of government and commercial interests on the question of advertising-led consumerism partly served as a cover for a partly symbiotic relationship (see pages 75–76). Similarly, the advertising industry's grandstanding assaults on government regulation of television hid an arrangement that was considerably more hand-

in-glove. Throughout the 1980s, as the agencies worked hard to sell their clients on the possibilities (both geographical and affective) of commercial television, the government kept jacking up its advertising rates; in 1987, for instance, DD almost doubled commercial airtime charges in one fell swoop (S. Mitra 1987). Agencies and the government both stood to gain from high rates, agencies because they earned a percentage of media costs. Indeed, by the middle of the decade, a significant proportion of the large agencies' billings were for DD spots. (In 1987, for instance, as much as 40 percent of Hindustan Thompson Associates' billings were coming from advertising on DD.) The agencies, however, found themselves caught between the need to be seen to be championing the interests of their clients against the "demonic" hand of the government, and the financial benefits accruing to them from television billings.

29   Just how close this kinship was might be gauged from the fact that JKC was in fact itself simultaneously marketing a range of pornodom-style condoms, collectively known as "Indian-made foreign condoms," with a globally oriented theme: French Feelings, Latin Lover, Pussy Cat, Swiss Kiss, Hawaiian Holiday, and Waikiki Warrior. The strategic advantage of these products, as Aniruddha Deshmukh explained it to me, was that their profitability, which itself was a result of their lurid packaging, allowed JKC to offer dealers higher retail margins: "Let's put it this way: actually KS is the known brand that we have. The known and the advertised brand that we have. We have a number of other . . . I wouldn't call them brands because we don't promote them in any media or even point of sale, but products having various brand names which we largely sell on the strength of the retail-level activities that we do, either window displays or high retail margins."

30   Such was the similarity between the MR Coffee and KS campaigns that Chowdhury was actually forced to add: "There is no truth in the report that Pooja Bhatt [a prominent film actress also associated with sexual frankness] or Pooja Bedi have been approached for the MR Coffee ad. There is no truth in this report."

31   Daniel Miller reflects: "Could it be that one of the major appeals of brands is that they represent a kind of bedrock stability in a world of rapidly changing social structures and social relationships?" (Miller 1997, 57). No doubt this is accurate on an experiential level. And nothing would please the professional advocates of marketing more than such a proposition. But we might also propose that the "stabilizing" effect of branding—quite apart from its political economic functions—represents a palliative response to anxieties brought about, in no small part, by the relentless pace of consumer marketing itself. There, in a nutshell, is the dialectical movement of the cultural politics of consumer capitalism.

32   My interview with Padamsee took place just as the Lewinsky-Clinton scandal had taken over the news media of the world.

33   See Ramusack 1995 for an overview of the role that the Indian princely states have played in Western colonial and subsequently touristic imaginaries.

Ramusack's discussion, however, does not venture into an examination of the *domestic* marketing of these facilities. See also Sonnabend 1996 for an industry point view on the management of locality and globality within an international chain of hotels.

34 The abstract citizen of the Habermasian public sphere and the embodied consumer-citizen are each other's doubles. Both contain a radical potential, whether reasoned critique or embodied transgression. And both may equally well point in a reactionary direction, whether the fraudulent "view from nowhere" of practical reason or the tyranny that so easily emerges from all claims to "common sense" or the "higher truth" of embodied experience. The task of critical analysis must be to unpack the claims that each makes in the name of the other in the course of public life.

35 Emphasis added. I have used the following strategy throughout the book: When quoting industry sources as commentators on particular campaigns with which they are publicly identified (such as in most of the material on KamaSutra in chapters 3 and 4), I have cited them by name. Elsewhere, when informants were speaking to me in general terms about aspects of the advertising and marketing industries, I have usually preferred to cite them anonymously.

36 Sudipta Kaviraj (1995) specifically appropriates Hegel's phrase (from the "Freedom of Self-consciousness" section of the *Phenomenology of Spirit*) to illuminate the Indian colonial predicament. Comaroff and Comaroff (1997, chapter 8) discuss the tension in terms of a relation between the ethnic subject and the modernist citizen.

Chapter Five. Bombay Global

This chapter is, as requested, dedicated to Sri Rajendra Mohoni. Parts of chapters 5 and 6 appeared in a shorter version as "Very Bombay: Contending with the Global in an Indian Advertising Agency." 2003. *Cultural Anthropology* 18 (1): 33–71.

1 I am aware that "the client" remains something of a reified category in the narrative that follows. My ethnographic locations allowed me to unpack the practices and dilemmas behind the category of "the agency" in a different way. Nevertheless, I hope that my material will show the important ways in which "the client" as a discursive category does important conceptual work for agency professionals.

2 Interview with Goutam Rakshit, Bombay, September 1997.

3 See Mattelart 1991, chapter 5 for an interesting reflection on the constitutive role of telecommunications deregulation in the discourse of the global market society.

4 See the exchange of letters between Nehru and Gandhi in Gandhi 1997 on this topic; Nair 1998, G. Prakash 1999, Sarai 2001, 2002, and Visvanathan 1997 also contain relevant discussions of the sociopolitical place of science and technology in independent India.

5 In an article on the former Indian princely states as tourist sites, Barbara Ramusack notes that those former states that became important sites of modernization were consequently struck off the tourist itinerary: "Hyderabad, Mysore, and Baroda have been eliminated from the category of princely state. Now tourists do not come to India seeking examples of modernization in the Third World; they do not want to tour the petrochemical complexes of Baroda-Vadodra or the electronic industry of Bangalore (Mysore)" (Ramusack 1995, 76).

6 Abid Hussain, vice-chairman of the Rajiv Gandhi Institute for Contemporary Studies (and formerly ambassador to the United States and member of the Planning Commission), demonstrates this perceived connection between rationality, communications, development, and consumerism in a summary of Rajiv's contribution that he offered at a symposium on the subject:

> Rajiv Gandhi popularised the idea that a society is as rational and in the end as cohesive as its capacity to process information and to communicate with itself and others. It must have the means to do both—it must have computers, telephones, television sets, faxes, and all the other devices of modern technological societies. These were not "gadgets," toys for leisured and playful adults, but indispensable elements of a new and better society which strives consciously to salve the pain of those who have suffered the slings and arrows of repeated misfortune. . . . A third key idea or theme was consumerism. This is a pejorative word even now, but to the extent that it is less so Rajiv Gandhi can take credit. By consumerism he did not mean a mindless and spiritually vacuous, indeed dangerous, attachment to buying consumer products, but to a feeling that the here and now is worthwhile, that to live and enjoy today and the near prospective future is understandable, that endless sacrifice for generations to come, while laudable, is not essential and can become the source of a deep malaise. Of course, buying consumer goods in the here and now is a part of consumerism, but consumerism is also an impatience with shoddiness now and [with] an endlessly receding golden age in the future. (Hussain 1998, 188)

Other commentators saw Rajiv's technophilia as evidence of his scanty understanding of social issues, indeed of history. Jad Adams and Phillip Whitehead write:

> He toured extensively to all parts of the country, and in 1987 even went on a pilgrimage to rural India, trying to improve his image with the poor. Though state television showed every speck of dirt on Rajiv's feet from walking the dusty streets of India, he never did look like a man of the people. One of his favourite slogans was, "A computer in every village school by the twenty-first century," apparently oblivious to the fact that many village schools did not have electricity, or even a blackboard. It was as if he were trying to replace the bullock cart with the mobile phone. (Adams and Whitehead 1997, 329)

At the same time, as I argued in chapter 3, this apparent obliviousness was also a positive mark of the consumerist dispensation, with its drive to *overcome* the historical sequences of developmentalism.

7 For intelligent discussions of Bachchan's film persona, see Chandrasekhar 1988, Kazmi 1998, Prasad 1998, and Vachani 1999.

8 Even mainstream political science has appropriated the free-floating signifier of postmodernist rhetoric; see Van Ham's (2001) article on the "brand state."

9 The participation of foreign companies was made necessary by the government requirement that only consortia with members who had previous experience in cellular telephony be eligible. Initially, the Foreign Investment Promotion Board (FIPB) allowed foreign partners to control up to 49 percent of these joint ventures.

10 The basic tariff rate was reduced from 72.5 percent to 51.8 percent, and handsets were moved from the Special Imports List to Open General License status. There was, of course, a thriving black market in smuggled handsets; to counter this, the service operators offered insurance—against "loss, theft, riot, strike or fire" (Nadkarni 1995).

11 In addition to the disappointing overall subscription figures, Indian cellular phone subscribers were also using their phones less than their counterparts elsewhere. The average airtime usage in Bombay (which had the highest usage figures in India despite the fact that Delhi had the highest subscription figures—a fact used by Bombay marketing professionals as proof of the stagy status-consciousness of North Indians) was a mere 160 minutes per month. This figure compared unfavorably even with other low-income markets like Pakistan, Sri Lanka, and Vietnam. At the time I write this (April 2002), the figures have increased substantially, although not quite to the level of initial predictions. EMW mobile and SamTech now report around 380,000 subscribers each.

12 In Hong Kong, apparently, one telecom advertisement featured a Tibetan Buddhist monk protagonist whose phone delivers the awe-inspiring message: "Hello—This is God!" (Brian Moeran, personal communication).

13 There was an uneasy awareness on the part of the service providers that their attempts to make cellular telephony more easily accessible and more hassle-free had also encouraged its adoption by the Bombay criminal underworld. Indeed, in 1997 it seemed that no media account of gangland assassination, intimidation, or extortion was complete without references to cellular phones. This association became particularly pervasive in the wake of the introduction of freestanding SIM cards (see note 16 below), and prompted the recently installed Bombay chief of police, Ronnie Mendonca, to push for a ban. Mendonca's initiative was, however, ultimately unsuccessful (although Singhal and Rogers [2001] note that in 1998 it became illegal to sell SIM cards without verification of name and address).

14 The research company commissioned by the agency to conduct focus groups

on the new product had assembled three groups of around ten people, each of them featuring a mixture of self-employed businessmen, "professionals," and corporate executives. Each of the three groups, in turn, represented a different relation to cellular telephony. One was made up of individuals who already had cellular phones, "owners." This group was further subdivided into Sam-Tech and EMW subscribers. The next comprised people who were seriously thinking about purchasing one, the "intenders." Finally, there was a group consisting entirely of "non-intenders," individuals who expressly believed that cellular phones were not a relevant product category to them. Each group was presented with the vital statistics of the intended product and the members were asked for their reactions. So as not to bias any feedback that they might produce concerning overall brand image perceptions, they were not told which company — EMW or SamTech — was intending to introduce the product. The focus groups were conducted by a female executive of the research company in the conference room of a hotel in midtown Bombay. The participants were told that they were being recorded on audio and videotape; they were not told, however, that members of the advertising agency team were simultaneously watching the proceedings on closed-circuit television in another room on the same corridor.

15 This respondent was unwittingly recapitulating a famous example of "motivational research" produced by Ernest Dichter in the 1950s, which applied the wife/mistress analogy to saloon/convertible cars.

16 Briefly, a SIM (Subscriber Identity Module) card is the personalized brain of a cellular phone; it carries the subscriber's telephone number, keeps track of airtime usage, and can be slotted into any handset that uses compatible technology.

17 EMW mobile executives were themselves, however, ambivalent about this image. While emphasizing to the agency that the convenience of the product was a crucial component, they "bounced" a line of copy prepared just before the product launch — "Along with the sweets and the clothes, pick up mobility. Really. It's that simple" — on the grounds that it "trivialized the product."

18 It may in passing be noted that these Image Bank catalogues, expensive, heavy, and glossy, are produced in the West and circulated to the rest of the world.

19 Brian Moeran makes a similar argument: "The Agency first has to persuade its *clients* that its approach to a particular problem is the best. In this respect, it is as concerned with selling a would-be advertiser an image of *itself* as it is [with] selling consumers an image of that advertiser's *products*" (Moeran 1996a, 96, emphasis in original). Peter Mayle, in the irreverent mode befitting an industry insider, notes: "We are often told that advertising reflects the face of society, which would be extremely depressing if it were wholly true. Nearer the truth is that advertising reflects the face of the client" (Mayle 1990, 58).

20 David Ogilvy offers the following piece of cautionary doggerel:

When the client moans and sighs,
Make his logo twice the size.
If he still should prove refractory,
Show a picture of his factory.
Only in the gravest cases,
Should you show the clients' faces.
(Ogilvy 1983, 80)

21 I am using this designation for the sake of simplicity. EMW mobile was generally represented by a team of between three and six executives of varying rank,
whom I will insert into the narrative as required.

22 At contemporary exchange rates, these sums would have been equivalent to
U.S. $2.4–2.9 million.

23 This penchant for attitude or edginess was certainly connected to the new audio-
visual idiom of satellite music television channels, in this case STAR-TV's Channel V
and MTV India. As such it indexed a certain notion of globalized youthfulness.

24 The expression "cool-hunter" actually refers to a job category that boomed in
the United States in the 1990s: marketing consultancies that specialized in
conveying an understanding of the latest fads in street-level youth culture to
consumer brands corporations (see, for instance, Klein 1999).

Chapter Six. Bombay Local

Parts of chapters 5 and 6 appeared in a shorter version as "Very Bombay:
Contending with the Global in an Indian Advertising Agency." 2003. *Cultural
Anthropology* 18 (1): 33–71.

1 Sergio Zyman, who is most identified for his work on marketing Coca-Cola
worldwide, similarly stresses the notion of an active relationship when he writes
of "the dialogue between the consumer and the brand" (Zyman 1999, xiv).

2 It is interesting to recall that although Disraeli, who conferred the PR-minded
title Empress of India upon Queen Victoria, may have addressed his queen as a
fellow human being, it was also he who, according to Hannah Arendt, conclusively introduced the notion of fundamental racial difference into British
imperial politics (Arendt 1968, 62–63).

3 In *White Noise*, Don DeLillo mordantly captures both the sensuous euphoria
and the absurd hubris of this imagined relationship:

People swarmed through the boutiques and gourmet shops. Organ music
rose from the great court. We smelled chocolate, popcorn, cologne; we
smelled rugs and furs, hanging salamis and deathly vinyl. My family gloried
in the event. I was one of them, shopping, at last. They gave me advice,
badgered clerks on my behalf. I kept seeing myself unexpectedly in some
reflecting surface. We moved from store to store, rejecting not only items in
certain departments, not only entire departments but whole stores, mam-

moth corporations that did not strike our fancy for one reason or another. (DeLillo 1985, 83)

4 Godelier 1999 contains a relatively comprehensive account of the long and tortured debate on the "true" meaning of *hau;* see also Graeber 2001.

5 Godelier, for instance, envisions charitable giving as the compensatory response to a world in which the abstraction of the market increasingly comes to stand in for more concrete social imaginaries. Weiner, for her part, attempts to track the movement of inalienability into market societies, but insists upon equating it with singular objects. Consequently, she focuses on those areas of exchange that—*unlike* the apparently anonymous mass market—construct "symbolic density" around individual objects: heirloom transfers, auctions, and so on (Weiner 1992, 1994). Parry (1986) also points to the dangers of reading gift exchange simply as a matter of reciprocity, specifically vis-à-vis the South Asian practice of *dan,* later ethnographically elaborated both by Parry (1994) and Raheja (1988).

6 This industry insider was anonymously cited in the cover story ("The Promotion Circus") of the August 16–31, 1997 issue of *Advertising and Marketing.*

7 This ability to establish an inalienable core becomes all the more important in the age of the Internet, where the product itself may be even more evanescent. In this connection, Nick Dyer-Witheford extends Marx's observation that there is a limit to the desirable acceleration of the circuit commodity→money→commodity: "If a product passes instantly, without barrier or impediment, from producer to consumer, it destroys the moment of exchange. A commodity must remain in the owner's hands long enough to be sold" (1999, 202).

8 Conversely, South Asian analyses of giving have frequently stressed the *inauspiciousness* of keeping as well as receiving; the ritual gift, dan, transfers the "poison" from the giver to the recipient (Parry 1986, 1994; Raheja 1988). In the realm of branding, corporate sponsorship of social causes carries some of the same implications of moral benefit for the giver and an ambivalent— sometimes even tainted—position for the needy recipient.

9 For accounts of how the imagined line between "gift" and "commodity" may be negotiated in various everyday contexts see Kopytoff 1986 and Carrier 1993, 1994.

10 Account executives, although they often resist this label, are frequently referred to as working on the "client servicing" or simply "servicing" side of the agency business.

11 Thanks to James Watson for bringing this reference to my attention. One might add that the rise of concerted branding in India in the early 1990s coincided more or less exactly with a severe crisis in branding in the United States. This was the moment marked by "Marlboro Monday" in 1993, when Philip Morris Inc. decided to slash prices on its Marlboro brand of cigarettes by 20 percent, thus appearing to acknowledge that competition was now going to be on the basis of price rather than image (see Klein 1999). There is a global political economy at work here: precisely those brands that increasingly find themselves competing on price in the saturated markets of the West find new opportunities for brand building in developing markets.

12 In Partha Chatterjee's words: "We must remember that in the world arena of modernity, we are outcastes, untouchables. Modernity for us is like a supermarket of foreign goods, displayed on the shelves: pay up and take away what you like. No one there believes that we could be producers of modernity. The bitter truth about our present is our subjection, our inability to be subjects in our own right. And yet, it is because we want to be modern that our desire to be independent and creative is transposed on to our past" (Chatterjee 1997, 281).

13 In chapter 7, we will see "family values" being used as a particular shorthand for "Asian values" — the family-mindedness that supposedly set off Asian consumers from their anomic, individualistic Western counterparts.

14 Roland Barthes's classic discussion of the "Italianicity" of a series of ads for Panzani pasta is the inaugural text here (Barthes 1977).

Chapter Seven. Indian Fun

1 I will examine this triumphalist discourse at greater length in chapter 8.

2 As Daniel Miller has pointed out, Coca-Cola is one of a handful of brands that "stand conspicuously for the idea of being global" (Miller 1997, 80).

3 Corporate portraits of teenage consumers around this time routinely and blithely extended U.S. statistics to the rest of the world. A document generated by the consumer electronics giant Siemens cited a 1997 Kurt Salmon Associates Annual Consumer Survey to support its contention of the generic importance of shopping to teenagers worldwide: "Only 55 percent of Americans ages 21 to 62 'enjoy shopping;' . . . In sharp contrast, 88 percent of girls [note the sudden shift to single-sex statistics] between 13 and 17 say they just 'love to shop' " (Siemens 1997).

4 Ghosh Roy (1998) comments on Ramesh Chauhan's decision to sell out to Coca-Cola:

> True, the 1994 deal fetched him a cool Rs 160 crore, but never in his wildest dreams did Chauhan think that his puny brands would turn out to be Coca-Cola's best-selling ones in the country one day. Today, for every bottle that Coke sells in India, Thums Up sells three. In fact, Coca-Cola India supremo Donald Short, while sipping Limca between meetings, is busy chalking out plans to export Thums Up and Limca to Singapore, Hong Kong, and the Middle East. . . . Unfortunately, . . . several companies with a strong brand portfolio . . . panicked out of a sheer inferiority complex.

George Fernandes, the man known for "throwing Coke out of India" in 1977, recalled encountering Chauhan in the immediate aftermath of the latter's deal with Coke: "When I ran into Chauhan, I asked him, 'What happened, why did you make this deal?' I said, 'The people of India made you. You gave them a soft drink but they bought it and made you what you are. And you sold everything for $60 million? You actually sold India for $60 million, do you realize that?' " ("Coke Returns from India Exile" 1995).

Later, Fernandes would add: "Even entrepreneurs like Ramesh Chauhan have come to me later after being bought out and repented." Whether Chauhan's new-found contrition was due to patriotic guilt or the sight of his old brands doing well under the Coke umbrella remains unclear.

5 Kalman Applbaum points to the foundations of this evolutionary model in Abraham Maslow's highly influential "Hierarchy of Needs." Maslow's model, Applbaum writes,

> specifies a psychologically-oriented progression that individual persons are said to experience as they attain security in creature-maintenance matters, and, thus freed from brute concerns, go on to pursue more abstract needs or pleasures. . . . In its application to the Third World, the assumed temporal dimension of the Maslow Hierarchy becomes most visible, as the hierarchy opportunely mutates to an evolutionary theory in which progressions take place along three dimensions: from traditional to western-modern, from group-oriented to individualist, and, with reverberations to the spatial dimension, from local to global. (Applbaum 1999, 14).

6 All quotations from brand documents in this chapter are reproduced with original emphases.

7 It is worth adding that the declared universality of this intrinsic dimension was not equivalent to any universality of the actual material constituents of the product: at this time, Sparka was in fact made according to more than twenty different recipes around the world.

8 Here, as elsewhere in this chapter, I am quoting from unpublished documents and reports generated by the Sparka "Hub," its Bombay office, and some of the research agencies that worked for the corporation in the mid-1990s.

9 The only notable exception to the general pattern was provided by young Chinese respondents, who rather touchingly listed "reading" as one of their most favored fun activities!

10 Steven Kemper characterizes this move thus:

> For their part, transnational agencies claim to be more local than they might appear by making a localizing promise: we can "think globally, execute locally" by exploiting our organizational advantage, while recognizing the need to approach local markets with the same sensitivity that local agencies claim for themselves. In their view, they replace the product-oriented thinking of local agencies — "here is a product, now let's see who will buy it" — with market research that can locate needs and preferences waiting to be addressed. (Kemper 2001, 32)

11 See Maxwell 1996 for an insightful discussion of the ways in which the market research process coordinates the responses of consumers in particular ways so as to make them amenable to the marketing project. As I will argue below, however, the very forms of the focus group exercises that were used by the agency where I did my fieldwork often encouraged respondents to "produce" themselves as consumers even before any active processing of research data had taken place. See Applbaum 1998 for a related series of reflections on market research.

12 The perceived importance of confidently "bobbling with enthusiasm" and being socially active was underscored in respondent essays by the extensive space devoted to explicating behavior or tendencies that did not fit this generic model:

> I think like why did I shouted [*sic*] at that boy or bashed him or why did I not answer in class.

> I am a bit reserved type of a guy, ie to say a shy guy but people mistake me for a snob. I am full at peace with myself and maybe that way I am happy.

> I'm soft-hearted. This is one of my weaknesses. I get carried away very fast. I'm emotionally sensitive but I don't cry — proves that I have a strong heart. I'm basically confused about myself, about what am I supposed to do. . . . Once I was asked what is life? It's time wasted before committing suicide. My other hobbies are playing cricket, badminton, chess, table-tennis, and going to the gym.

> Basically my nature is very short-tempered and I just don't like all wrong things. Basically I am of a very moody nature.

> I am very temperamental and very moody. I do have frequent changes in behaviour like I can get angry on anybody without reason. I do respect my elders but there are some who are not liked by me.

13 In India, the term college refers roughly to what in the United States would include both senior high school and college.

14 During one of my conversations with the research coordinator, confusion arose over the term "conservative." I had wondered whether he did not find the apparently materialistic orientation of the aspirations of many of his young respondents rather conservative. Quite the opposite, he replied. After some elaboration, it turned out that his usage of the term "conservative" located it in semantic opposition to "modern," thus making it refer implicitly to the kind of "tradition" that he identified with the perceived stasis and backwardness of village life. As we will see, however, another kind of "tradition" — a high-cultural textual version of Indianness/Hinduness — was quite compatible with commodity modernity.

15 As the composite figures of the "Indian teenager" and the "Asian teenager" were articulated in market research, the figure that had previously been called the "global teenager" now became increasingly defined as the "Western teenager."

16 Chakrabarty (2000, chapter 8) shows the way in which the centrality of parental authority has been a recurrent figure by which Indian modernity has been distinguished vis-à-vis its European counterpart, in which citizenship is modeled on the figure of the patricidal compact of brothers.

17 The ambiguous manner in which "Indian difference" was sometimes presented as sui generis, and sometimes as subordinate to a larger category of "Asian difference" was indicative of the complex politics of the relationship between the local advertising agency, the larger global system of which it was a part, and the equivalent divisions on the client side.

18 Mankekar notes: "Unlike the late nineteenth century, when the Woman Question was 'resolved' by demarcating the private sphere (of women) from the public sphere (of men), late twentieth-century constructions of the New Indian Woman *complicated* notions of women's agency by valorizing 'emancipated' women who dexterously straddled the 'home' and the 'world' " (Mankekar 1999, 137). I would only add to Mankekar's pertinent comments the observation that Chatterjee, upon whose argument about the nineteenth century she draws, is quite particular about *not* necessarily equating the outside/material domain of Indian men and the inside/spiritual domain of Indian women with the European-derived constructs of public and private.

19 Interview with Sathya Saran, Bombay, January 1997. All subsequent quotations from Saran are taken from this conversation.

20 Saran's two-tiered vision of her readership underlines a crucial conceptual point regarding consumerist dispensations in general, namely that "aspiration" itself depends upon a particular set of commodity images being made available to a much wider audience than the population that is being directly addressed by them.

21 A similar dynamic has been detected by Arif Dirlik in relation to the "Confucian revival" in East Asia: "Confucianism appears, on the one hand, as a dynamic ideological force in the development of capitalism [thus countering the Weberian assumptions of Western social science], and, on the other hand, as a value-system with which to counteract the disruptive effects of capitalist development" (Dirlik 1996, 115). Nevertheless, as I argue on pages 139–41, the neo-Confucian and the Indian version of auto-orientalism differ significantly in their relative emphasis on productivism and consumerism respectively.

Chapter Eight. Close Distance

1 My informants' ambivalence vis-à-vis the MNCs was, on one level, an extension of an older dilemma, one that Indian nationalist intellectuals had grappled with since the nineteenth century. As Partha Chatterjee puts it: "As to the pursuit of knowledge, there would emerge a curious ambivalence: on the one

hand, a persistent complaint at being excluded from or discriminated against in the matter of equal access to the supposedly universal institutions of knowledge; and on the other hand, an insistence on a distinctly Indian form of modern knowledge" (Chatterjee 1995, 14–15). As Tapati Guha-Thakurta (1992, 1995) demonstrates, this dilemma also infused the realm of the aesthetic in the work of such self-consciously "nationalist" painters as Abanindranath Tagore.

2   By making Levitt represent the field in its entirety, I do not of course mean to suggest that there were not other important interventions, particularly critiques of his position. Some examples may be found in Fields 1989, Kotler 1986, and Wind 1986. I am merely arguing that Levitt's piece was foundational in that it established the ontological framework for the debate.

3   Levitt in fact explicitly addresses the counter-argument concerning the possibilities of flexible "economies of scope" in his article: "I will not deny the power of these possibilities. But possibilities do not make probabilities. There is no conceivable way in which flexible factory automation can achieve the scale economies of a modernized plant dedicated to mass production of standardized lines" (Levitt 1983, 96).

There is significant evidence to suggest that technological developments since Levitt's influential article have made this opposition redundant — that is, it is precisely in the *articulation* of economies of scale and scope that contemporary consumer goods production thrives (Allan Pred, personal communication).

4   I am, I should clarify, not primarily speaking here of widely distributed foreign-branded products in the fast-moving consumer goods categories like detergents or soaps.

5   I would not want to *overstate* the break between the British and the U.S. commodity imaging dispensations. On the one hand, the British commodity imaging dispensation, for all its steadily diminishing importance, should not be understood apart from the British institutional bequest that continues to structure Indian life to this day. On the other hand, Hollywood movies introduced premonitions of the U.S. dispensation during the final years of the British period (although, as Prasad 1998 points out, the British routinely censored U.S. movies in India precisely because of their corporeal realism). Nevertheless, I think it is important to distinguish the politics of consumer goods advertising within the formal structure of British imperialism from its post-Independence variants (see Burke 1996; McClintock 1995; Richards 1990).

Although my examples in this chapter are drawn exclusively from the elite stratum of Bombay intelligentsia, Prakash Tandon's recollections of a provincial Punjabi childhood in the early twentieth century provide an example of a less metropolitan instantiation of commodity spectacle, this time during the colonial period itself:

> The goods were usually British or German, and many of the brands had become household names. . . . One could buy knives, scissors, buttons,

cotton and silk thread, mirrors, soaps, bottled hair oils, razors, socks, woollen and cotton knitwear, etc. These imported things always held more glamour for us than the local ones. We preferred the imported combs to the handmade wooden ones, the electroplated Sheffield and Solingen knives and scissors to the solid steel ones made by our local smiths, Pears and Vinolia soap to the home-boiled desi soap, and the shining coloured buttons to the simple cloth ones. (Deshpande 1993, 18)

In addition, Tandon recounts how foreign products brought the idea of a globality organized according to consumer goods marketing, and hence the incorporation of cultural difference within generalized exchange and universal needs:

The first mechanical contraption arrived in our house. It was the Singer sewing machine, shining black and chromium-plated, with a highly polished case in wood. Few homes as yet possessed one. With it came a colourful calendar showing Singer's popularity in different countries of the world. This was my first introduction to people of other races, if only in pictures. (ibid.)

6   "All too fast . . . we are at Kemp's Corner now, cars rushing around like bullets . . . but one thing is unchanged. On his billboard, the Kolynos Kid is grinning, the eternal pixie grin of the boy in the green chlorophyll cap, the lunatic grin of the timeless kid, who endlessly squeezes an inexhaustible tube of toothpaste on to a bright green brush: *Keep Teeth Kleen And Keep Teeth Brite, Keep Teeth Kolynos Super White!*" (Rushdie 1991a, 288).
   Rushdie himself would, of course, work as an advertising copywriter in London for some time before finding literary success. Allegedly he devised, for a brand of cream cakes, the popular slogan "Naughty but nice."

7   I should add that Benjamin does not actually use the term "aura" in this discussion of childhood memory. But I believe that, when read in the context of his other writings of the period, the connection can and should be made. See Buck-Morss (1989, chapter 8) for a related discussion of the relationships between commodity representations, childhood memory, and adult experience in Benjamin.

8   Author Nirad Chaudhuri embodied an interesting variation on the theme. Fiercely Anglophile at the peak of the struggle for Independence, his own disappointment with the actuality of England did not stop him from living out his exceptionally long life there. Chaudhuri's personal "dream-England" became a kind of critical vantage point from which he could lambast what was, to him, the contemporary "decadence" of both India and Britain.

9   In this sense, these advertising professionals occupied an interesting middle ground between the traumatically encountered West of "serious" literary producers and the serenely un-Western West of the popular Hindi film. In Christopher Pinney's words: "In Hindi films, the encounter with the West is in no sense

dialogic; those who go there deal only with other South Asians. This contrasts powerfully with the English 'art' novel in India where the engagement with the West is frequently of major importance" (2001, 13).

10 Pinney, again, notes the way in which the figure of the metropolitan can fulfill this function: "The metropolitan aspiration . . . is oriented to an outside, to a realm beyond the familiar: although the familiar is all around, it is recoded in the glamorous language of the outside" (2001, 12).

11 Although warning signals about the discrepancy between sales estimates and the actual figures began to appear early on, many commentators felt that an adequate response had in many cases been delayed because local managers in India often wanted to avoid confronting their superiors with the figures. "Nobody wants to be the bad-news guy," observed an independent market researcher; the business journalist added: "Those guys were all on two-year contracts anyway, so once the shit hit the fan they had already moved on, leaving their successors to pick up the pieces."

12 S. Gurumurthy of the Swadeshi Jagaran Manch was suitably scathing of Indian businesspeople who implored foreigners for investment: "We are crawling and standing at the airports with garlands to get foreign investment" ("India Has Never Had Swadeshi Economy" 1998 and "India Cannot Live in Cities" 1998).

13 My information on Wrangler's experience in India is largely taken from I. Gupta (1994).

14 I. Gupta estimates that out of a total Indian jeans market of around six million pairs per year, approximately 50 percent was accounted for by unbranded generic products. The *officially available* branded segment was dominated by desi brands: Flying Machine remained in the lead, followed by brands like Sunnex (marketed on a self-consciously anti-MNC platform: "Thankfully *not* made in the USA") and Killer. A market overview by giant Indian denim producer Arvind Mills from 1998 depicts a much larger overall market of thirty million pairs per year. Out of this total, the "premium segment," consisting largely of MNC brands, is the smallest: 20 percent by value but only 4 percent by volume (Arvind Mills 1998).

15 In fact, my informant was not wrong on this point. Witness the doubts voiced by the market research conducted for Sparka (see pages 225–27) about whether Indians would be able to relate to complex graphics rather than a more direct selling message.

16 Price was of course itself a contested issue, outside of the specific opposition to price lowering put up by the advertising industry. MNCs would often argue that the high start-up costs of installing themselves in a new market effectively precluded any significant price reductions. Critics would respond that if anyone had the accumulated resources to lower prices and take losses for a few years in order to establish their brands in local markets, then it was the MNCs. One account suggests:

With the myth of the enormous size of the Indian middle-class having been blown, bringing in global brands with dollar-parity price-tags will eliminate all but the top end from the target universe. The obvious answer is to pick price-points that are lower down so that larger sections of customers can afford the product—which is what Revlon did, symbolized famously by its Rs 99 lipstick. But transnationals are often hampered here by being unable to lower their costs sufficiently to sell at such prices and still make money. (Skaria 1999)

17 In fact, during my fieldwork in Bombay, people would frequently tell me that they thought that the level of the average person's spending on firecrackers and annual celebrations in general had gone down in recent years. Frequently this change was attributed to the rise of television and the new prominence of other aspects of the consumerist dispensation. Although some professed a certain melancholy about the apparent decline of festival expenditure, others saw it as all to the good, suggesting that people were now spending their money "more rationally."

18 Claude Lévi-Strauss, in *The Savage Mind,* uses precisely this kaleidoscope simile to illustrate the practice of bricolage, a notion that could well be applied to the process that my informant is describing here (1966, 36).

19 Hegel, in his lectures on the philosophy of history, suggested that the blurring of rational conceptual boundaries that was to be found in Indian civilization was damaging both to a European understanding of things and to the related senses of agency, self, and direction: "*Things* are as much stripped of rationality, of finite consistent stability of cause and effect, as *man* is of the steadfastness of free individuality, of personality, and freedom" (Hegel 1956, 141). In his lectures on *The Philosophy of Right,* delivered a decade earlier, Hegel equated a lack of determinate categorical boundaries with "Hindu fanaticism" (Houlgate 1998, 330). This pathology was both constitutive of Indian life and characteristic of what Hegel considered temporary aberrations in Western political history, for example the all-devouring fervor of the Jacobins.

20 In his article "On Imperialism in India," which was originally published in *The New York Daily Tribune* in 1853, Marx wrote:

There cannot . . . remain any doubt but that the misery inflicted by the British on Hindostan is of an essentially different and infinitely more intensive kind than all Hindostan had to suffer before. . . . All the civil wars, invasions, revolutions, conquests, famines, strangely complex, rapid and destructive as the successive action in Hindostan may appear, did not go deeper than its surface. England has broken down the entire framework of Indian society, without any symptoms of reconstitution yet appearing. (Tucker 1978, 654–55)

Marx went on to describe how the British intrusion had broken down the self-sufficient economic structure of the Indian village, but that damaging as this had been in the short term, Britain had at the same time, half-unwittingly, nevertheless brought history and progress to a historyless India. In the companion article, "The Future Results of British Rule in India," Marx — at his most Hegelian — wrote: "India . . . could not escape the fate of being conquered, and the whole of her past history, if it be anything, is the history of the successive conquests she has undergone. Indian society has no history at all, at least no known history. What we call its history, is but the history of the successive intruders who founded their empires on the passive basis of that unresisting and unchanging society" (659).

Conversely, the impact of British rule, for Marx, could not help but bring about the material conditions for progressive change in India, almost in spite of itself: "The political unity of India . . . imposed by the British sword, will now be strengthened and perpetuated by the electric telegraph. . . . Modern industry, resulting from the railway-system [brought in by the British], will dissolve the hereditary divisions of labour, upon which rest the Indian castes, those decisive impediments to Indian progress and Indian power" (660, 662).

Of course, it was precisely this vision of the West bringing agency, progress, and history to an otherwise passive subcontinent that motivated the scholars of the Subaltern Studies collective to attempt to formulate an alternative historical materialism, one which would begin to address the conceptual lacunae and elisions that an orthodox Marxist historiography brought to the study of colonial (and postcolonial) India (see Chakrabarty 2000; Prakash 1992; Spivak 1999).

21 My informant's references to characters from the *Ramayana* and the *Mahabharata* should be understood in the context of the wildly successful TV adaptations of the epics that were screened on Doordarshan in the late 1980s. As Mankekar (1999) argues, Sita and Draupadi represent opposing constructions of Indian womanhood; Sita, in the *Ramayana*, is the impeccably dutiful and subservient wife who prefers to be swallowed by the earth rather than have any doubts about her purity besmirch her *husband's* public standing. Draupadi, in the *Mahabharata*, is a more ambivalent character in that she both actively questions her husband's right to do with her as he will (he has gambled her away in a game of dice) *and* actively seeks revenge against those who have attempted to dishonor her. "Draupadi tells her husbands that she will leave her hair loose until she has washed it with the blood of Duryodhana and Dushasana [the victors in the dice game] brought from the battlefield" (Mankekar 1999, 234). For other discussions of the televised epics see Gillespie 1995, Lutgendorf 1995, Rajagopal 2001, and Tully 1992.

22 For an interesting account of the diasporic deployment of Hindu religious videos, see Little 1995; for the cultural politics of the historical and contemporary Ganapati celebrations in Bombay and Pune, see Kaur (forthcoming).

23 See Cohn 1996 and Tarlo 1996 for analyses of the politics of clothing during the colonial period.

24 Channel V was perhaps the most glaring apparent exception to this aesthetic

formula. As a medium, it seemed capable of transforming *anything*—no matter how apparently low-brow—into a signifier of "hep" young India. But here, too, a structure of close distance was achieved, by way of a different set of parameters. Melissa Butcher's discussion of the aesthetics of Channel V demonstrate its creators' self-consciousness about opposing established canons of "international style" with a new practice of transforming "raw" cultural material into aspirational commodity images:

> Its imagery, according to Creative Director, Shashanka Ghosh, began with "raw" television, depicting street scenes that were familiar but presented in very stylized ways. Caricatures of quotidian India became its trademark: *paan-wallahs* (betel leaf/tobacco vendors), *sabzi-wallahs* (vegetable sellers), Subhas Chandra Bose look-alikes wanting a date with Madonna, Tamil film icon "Quick Gun Murugan," and the latest, a Haryanvi election "entrepreneur," Uddham Singh. "The imagery is heavily reflective of Indian culture. We are not about fantastically created montages of international stuff. We start from the grass roots, presented in a cool, hip, fashion" (Sunita Rajan — [Director of Marketing and Promotions]). (Butcher 1999, 170)

While ostensibly populist and Indian in tone, "grass roots" material is made "cool" and "hip" by way of an adjustment to a left-of-mainstream, student-oriented Western pop-culture aesthetic. Adds Shashanka Ghosh: "Campus humour, stuff that India never really saw, tak[ing] a nice Indian look and do[ing] it influenced by *Pulp Fiction* or Godard. The content is incredibly India, . . . but with completely pumped colours" (Butcher 1999, 171). By the autumn of 1997, MTV India was adapting its own previously "global" programming to Channel V's new formula for close distance. Cyrus Oshidar, creative director, explained: "The trick was to Indianize, localize, take things that are downmarket and grungy and make them trendy and aspirational" (Rodrigues 1999).

Despite all the talk of the cultural inclusivity of their imagery, media like Channel V and MTV were clearly nowhere near as favored by advertisers concerned to reach a mass middle-class audience as other satellite channels like Zee or Sony. Nevertheless, many executives felt that the cultural importance of the video channels outstripped their relatively limited audiences. As an account planner at one agency told me:

> When Channel V does this East meets West kind of stuff, they may or may not get numbers. But that is affecting mainline programming. Today I find a lot of programming, a lot of Hindi movies, reflecting that kind of humor. Reflecting the East meets West kind of philosophy in their movies. It has an effect. Today the guy who's choreographing or shooting a Hindi music song is influenced by music videos on MTV and Channel V and is hence incorporating. So it is a process . . . I mean, this society is also all about assimilation. There is an assimilation that happens.

WORKS CITED

Aaker, David. 1995. *Building Strong Brands*. New York: Free Press.

Abu-Lughod, Janet. 1989. *Before European Hegemony: The World-System, A.D. 1250–1350*. New York: Oxford University Press.

Abu-Lughod, Lila. 1993. "Finding a Place for Islam: Egyptian Television Serials and the National Interest." *Public Culture* 5 (3): 493–513.

Adams, Jad, and Phillip Whitehead. 1997. *The Dynasty*. New Delhi: Penguin.

Adorno, Theodor. [1966] 1973. *Negative Dialectics*. New York: Continuum.

———. [1963] 1991. "Culture Industry Reconsidered." In *The Culture Industry: Selected Essays on Mass Culture*, edited by J. M. Bernstein. London: Routledge.

Ahmed, Feroz, and Prabir Sen. 1988. "After the Big Bang, a Whimper?" *Business Update*, May 21–June 3.

Ahmed, Rashmee. 1997. "Goodbye Audrey, Hello Julia." *Sunday Times*, August 24.

Aiyar, Mani Shankar. 1997. "Globalising Swadeshi." *India Today*, October 13.

———. 1998. "Saffron Swadeshi." *India Today*, April 20.

Aiyar, Swaminathan Anklesaria. 1991. "Requiem for a Half-Hearted Liberaliser." *Times of India*, May 23.

Alter, Joseph. 2000. *Gandhi's Body: Sex, Diet, and the Politics of Nationalism*. Philadelphia: University of Pennsylvania Press.

Ang, Ien. 1985. *Watching Dallas: Soap Opera and the Melodramatic Imagination*. London: Routledge.

———. 1991. *Desperately Seeking the Audience*. London: Routledge.

———. 1996. *Living Room Wars*. London: Routledge.

Annuncio, Charubala. 1993. "A Barren Market." *Advertising and Marketing*, November.

Appadurai, Arjun. 1986. "Introduction: Commodities and the Politics of Value." In *The Social Life of Things: Commodities in Cultural Perspective,* edited by Arjun Appadurai. Cambridge: Cambridge University Press.

——. 1996. *Modernity at Large: Cultural Dimensions of Globalization.* Minneapolis: University of Minnesota Press.

——. 2000. "Grassroots Globalization and the Research Imagination." In *Globalization,* edited by Arjun Appadurai. A special issue of *Public Culture* 12 (1): 1–19.

——, ed. 1986. *The Social Life of Things: Commodities in Cultural Perspective.* Cambridge: Cambridge University Press.

Applbaum, Kalman. 1998. "The Sweetness of Salvation: Consumer Marketing and the Liberal-Bourgeois Theory of Needs." *Current Anthropology* 39 (3): 323–49.

——. 1999. "Crossing Borders: Globalization as Myth and Charter in American Transnational Consumer Marketing." *American Ethnologist* 27 (2): 257–82.

Arathoon, Marion. 1996. "Think Indian in Global Terms." *Economic Times,* February 21.

Arendt, Hannah. [1948; 1951] 1968. *Imperialism: Part Two of the Origins of Totalitarianism.* New York: Harcourt Brace and Company.

Arvind Mills. 1998. "Market Overview." http://www.arvindmills.com/market.html.

"Atal*ji* Is Just a Public Face." 1997. *Asian Age,* October 24.

Banerjee, Biswajeet. 1995. "Birth Control Programme in Disarray: Condoms Being Used to Make Toys." *The Pioneer,* November 24.

Banerjee, Nantoo. 1986. "DAVP in Doldrums." *Business Standard,* April 20.

Barker, Adele Marie, ed. 1999. *Consuming Russia: Popular Culture, Sex, and Society since Gorbachev.* Durham, N.C.: Duke University Press.

Barthes, Roland. [1957] 1972. *Mythologies.* London: Paladin.

——. 1977. *Image, Music, Text.* London: Fontana.

——. [1980] 1981. *Camera Lucida.* New York: Noonday.

——. [1975] 1983. *The Fashion System.* New York: Hill and Wang.

Basu, Kaushik. 1991. *Economic Graffiti: Essays for Everyone.* New Delhi: Oxford University Press.

——. 1999. "Globalization and *Swadeshi.*" *India Today,* March 29.

Baudrillard, Jean. [1972] 1981. *For a Critique of the Political Economy of the Sign.* St. Louis, Mo.: Telos Press.

——. [1968] 1996. *The System of Objects.* London: Verso.

——. [1970] 1998. *The Consumer Society: Myths and Structures.* London: Sage.

Bayly, C. A. 1986. "The Origins of Swadeshi (Home Industry): Cloth and Indian Society, 1700–1930." In *The Social Life of Things: Commodities in Cultural Perspective,* edited by Arjun Appadurai. Cambridge: Cambridge University Press.

Bazin, Andre. [1945] 1967. "The Ontology of the Photographic Image." In *What Is Cinema?* Vol. 1. Berkeley: University of California Press.

Behler, Ernst, ed. [1986] 1999. *Immanuel Kant: Philosophical Writings*. New York: Continuum.

Benjamin, Walter. [1936] 1968a. "The Work of Art in the Age of Mechanical Reproduction." In *Illuminations: Essays and Reflections,* edited by Hannah Arendt. New York: Schocken.

———. [1939] 1968b. "On Some Motifs in Baudelaire." In *Illuminations: Essays and Reflections,* edited by Hannah Arendt. New York: Schocken.

———. [1931] 1999a. "Little History of Photography." In *Selected Writings, Volume 2: 1927–1934,* edited by Michael Jennings. Cambridge, Mass.: Harvard University Press.

———. [1932] 1999b. "A Berlin Chronicle." In *Selected Writings, Volume 2: 1927–1934,* edited by Michael Jennings. Cambridge, Mass.: Harvard University Press.

———. [1933] 1999c. "Experience and Poverty." In *Selected Writings, Volume 2: 1927–1934,* edited by Michael Jennings. Cambridge, Mass.: Harvard University Press.

Berger, John, and Jean Mohr. [1982] 1995. *Another Way of Telling*. New York: Vintage.

Betting, Ronald. 1996. *Copyrighting Culture: The Political Economy of Intellectual Property.* Boulder, Colo.: Westview.

Bhabha, Homi. 1994. *The Location of Culture*. New York: Routledge.

Bhagat, Rasheeda. 1993. "Where Condoms Are Buried in Ground." *Indian Express,* January 28.

Bhargava, Rajeev. 1994. "Giving Secularism Its Due." *Economic and Political Weekly* 29 (28): 1784–91.

Bharucha, Rustom. 1998. *In the Name of the Secular: Contemporary Cultural Activism in India*. New Delhi: Oxford University Press.

Bose, Sugata, and Ayesha Jalal. 1998. *Modern South Asia*. New Delhi: Oxford University Press.

Bourdieu, Pierre. [1979] 1984. *Distinction: A Social Critique of the Judgment of Taste*. Cambridge, Mass.: Harvard University Press.

———. 1993. *The Field of Cultural Production*. New York: Columbia University Press.

Brass, Paul. 1990. *The Politics of India Since Independence*. Cambridge: Cambridge University Press.

Breckenridge, Carol, ed. 1995. *Consuming Modernity: Public Culture in a South Asian World*. Minneapolis: University of Minnesota Press.

Brierley, Sean. 1995. *The Advertising Handbook*. London: Routledge.

Brosius, Christiane. 1999. "Is This the Real Thing? Packaging Cultural Nationalism." In *Image Journeys: Audio-Visual Media and Cultural Change in India,* edited by Christiane Brosius and Melissa Butcher. New Delhi: Sage.

Buckley, Kerry W. 1982. "The Selling of a Psychologist: John Broadus Watson and the Application of Behavioral Techniques to Advertising." *Journal of the History of the Behavioral Sciences* 18 (July): 207–21.

Buck-Morss, Susan. 1989. *The Dialectics of Seeing: Walter Benjamin and the Arcades Project*. Cambridge, Mass.: MIT Press.

——. 1992. "Aesthetics and Anaesthetics: Walter Benjamin's Artwork Essay Reconsidered." *October* 62 (fall): 3–41.

——. 1994. "The Cinema Screen as Prosthesis of Perception: A Historical Account." In *The Senses Still: The Anthropology of Perception and Material Experience in European Modernity*, edited by Nadia Seremetakis. Boulder, Colo.: Westview.

Burghart, Richard. 1983. "Renunciation in the Religious Traditions of South Asia." *Man* (n.s.), 18:635–53.

Burke, Timothy. 1996. *Lifebuoy Men, Lux Women: Commodification, Consumption, and Cleanliness in Modern Zimbabwe*. Durham, N.C.: Duke University Press.

Butcher, Melissa. 1999. "Parallel Texts: The Body and Television in India." In *Image Journeys: Audio-Visual Media and Cultural Change in India*, edited by Christiane Brosius and Melissa Butcher. New Delhi: Sage.

Caldarola, Victor. 1994. *Reception as Cultural Experience: Mass Media and Muslim Orthodoxy in Outer Indonesia*. East Brunswick, N.J.: Rutgers University Press.

Caldwell, J. C. 1976. "Toward a Restatement of Demographic Transition Theory: An Investigation of Conditions Before and at the Onset of Fertility Decline Employing Primarily African Experience and Data." *Population and Development Review* 2:321–66.

Carrier, James. 1992. "Occidentalism: The World Turned Upside Down." *American Ethnologist* 19 (2): 196–212.

——. 1993. "The Rituals of Christmas Giving." In *Unwrapping Christmas*, edited by Daniel Miller. Oxford: Clarendon.

——. 1994. *Gifts and Commodities: Exchange and Western Capitalism Since 1700*. London: Routledge.

Castoriadis, Cornelius. [1975] 1987. *The Imaginary Institution of Society*. Cambridge, Mass.: MIT Press.

Chakrabarty, Dipesh. n.d. Historical Difference and the Logic of Capital: Towards a Difference Marxism. Manuscript.

——. 2000. *Provincializing Europe: Postcolonial Thought and Historical Difference*. Princeton: Princeton University Press.

Chandrasekhar, K. 1988. "The Amitabh Persona: An Interpretation." *Deep Focus* 1 (3): 57.

Chatterjee, Partha. 1993. *The Nation and Its Fragments*. Princeton: Princeton University Press.

——. 1995. "The Disciplines in Colonial Bengal." In *Texts of Power: Emerging Disciplines in Colonial Bengal*, edited by Partha Chatterjee. Minneapolis: University of Minnesota Press.

——. [1996] 1997. "Talking About Modernity in Two Languages." In *A Possible India: Essays in Political Criticism*. New Delhi: Oxford University Press.

Chatterjee, Partha, and Arup Mallik. [1975] 1997. "Indian Democracy and Bourgeois Reaction." In *A Possible India: Essays in Political Criticism*, edited by Partha Chatterjee. New Delhi: Oxford University Press.

Chaudhuri, Debashis. 1998. " 'I Am Not Anti-MNC but Pro-*Swadeshi*,' Says George Fernandes." *The Financial Express*, March 9.

Ching, Leo. 2000. "Globalizing the Regional, Regionalizing the Global: Mass Culture and Asianism in the Age of Late Capital." In *Globalization*, edited by Arjun Appadurai. A special issue of *Public Culture* 12 (1): 233–57.

Clammer, John, ed. 1987. *Beyond the New Economic Anthropology*. London: Macmillan.

Clifford, James, and George Marcus, eds. 1986. *Writing Culture: The Poetics and Politics of Ethnography*. Berkeley: University of California Press.

Cohen, Lawrence. 1998. *No Aging in India: Alzheimer's, the Bad Family, and Other Modern Things*. Berkeley: University of California Press.

Cohn, Bernard. 1996. "Cloth, Clothes, and Colonialism: India in the Nineteenth Century." In *Colonialism and Its Forms of Knowledge: The British in India*. Princeton: Princeton University Press.

"Coke Returns from India Exile: An Interview with George Fernandes." 1995. *Multinational Monitor*. July/August.

Comaroff, John, and Jean Comaroff. 1997. *Of Revelation and Revolution: The Dialectics of Modernity on a South African Frontier, Volume Two*. Chicago: University of Chicago Press.

——, eds. 2000. *Millennial Capitalism and the Culture of Neoliberalism*. A special issue of *Public Culture* 12 (2).

Contract Strategic Planning Group. 1995. *Up Front: On Issues and Trends*. Bombay: Contract.

Coombe, Rosemary. 1998. *The Social Life of Intellectual Properties: Authorship, Alterity, and the Law*. Durham, N.C.: Duke University Press.

Curti, Merle. 1967. "The Changing Concept of 'Human Nature' in the Literature of American Advertising." *Business History Review* 41: 335–57.

Dabholkar, Bharat. 1997. "The Dream Merchants." *Debonair*, 25th Anniversary Issue.

Damon, Frederick. 1980. "The Problem of the Kula on Woodlark Island: Expansion, Accumulation, and Over-Production." *Ethnos* 3–4:176–201.

Danielou, Alain. 1994. *The Complete Kama Sutra*. Rochester, Vt.: Park Street Press.

Das, Gurcharan. 2000. *India Unbound*. New York: Viking.

Davis, Richard. 1997. *The Lives of Indian Images*. Princeton: Princeton University Press.

Debonair. 1991. KamaSutra Advertising Special. October issue.

Debord, Guy. [1967] 1977. *Society of the Spectacle*. Detroit: Black and Red.

Deleuze, Gilles. [1983] 1986. *Cinema 1: The Movement-Image*. Minneapolis: University of Minnesota Press.

DeLillo, Don. 1985. *White Noise*. New York: Viking.

Derrida, Jacques. [1972] 1981. *Dissemination*. Chicago: University of Chicago Press.

Deshpande, Satish. 1993. "Imagined Economies: Styles of Nation-Building in Twentieth Century India." *Journal of Arts and Ideas* 25–26 (December): 5–36.

Dirlik, Arif. 1996. "Chinese History and the Question of Orientalism." *History and Theory* 35:96–118.

Doctor, Vikram, and Anvar Alikhan. 1997. "*Kyon Na Aazmaye?* Part Two." *India Magazine,* January.

Doctor, Vikram, and Suishashini Sen. 1997. "A Tough, Rough and Risqué Market." *Business World,* September 7.

Doniger, Wendy. 1981. *Siva, the Erotic Ascetic*. New York: Oxford University Press.

Doniger, Wendy, and Sudhir Kakar. 2002. *Kamasutra*. Oxford: Oxford University Press.

Dumont, Louis. 1960. "Renunciation in Indian Religions." *Contributions to Indian Sociology* 4:33–62.

Dussel, Enrique. [1992] 1995. *The Invention of the Americas: Eclipse of the "Other" and Myth of Modernity*. New York: Continuum.

Dyer-Witheford, Nick. 1999. *Cyber-Marx: Cycles and Circuits of Struggle in High-Technology Capitalism*. Urbana: University of Illinois Press.

Eagleton, Terry. 1990. *The Ideology of the Aesthetic*. Oxford: Basil Blackwell.

Featherstone, Mike. 1991. *Consumer Culture and Postmodernism*. London: Sage.

Fields, George. 1989. *The Japanese Market Culture*. Tokyo: The Japan Times Ltd.

Flood, Gavin. 1996. *Introduction to Hinduism*. Cambridge: Cambridge University Press.

Foster, Robert. 1991. "Making National Culture in the Global Ecumene." *Annual Review of Anthropology* 20:235–60.

———. 1995. "Nation Making and Print Advertisements in Metropolitan Papua New Guinea." In *Nation Making: Emergent Identities in Postcolonial Melanesia,* edited by Robert Foster. Ann Arbor: University of Michigan Press.

———. 1996. "Commercial Mass Media in Papua New Guinea: Notes on Agency, Bodies, and Commodity Consumption." *Visual Anthropology Review* 12 (2): 1.

———. 1999. "The Commercial Construction of 'New Nations.'" *Journal of Material Culture* 4 (3).

Fox, Richard. 1989. *Gandhian Utopia: Experiments with Culture*. Boston: Beacon Press.

Fox, Stephen. [1984] 1990. *The Mirror Makers: A History of American Advertising*. London: Heinemann.

Frank, Andre Gunder, and Barry Gills, eds. 1993. *The World System: Five Hundred Years or Five Thousand?* London: Routledge.

Frank, Thomas. 1997. *The Conquest of Cool: Business Culture, Counterculture, and the Rise of Hip Consumerism*. Chicago: University of Chicago Press.

Freedberg, David. 1985. *Iconoclasts and Their Motives*. Maarssen, The Netherlands: G. Schwartz.

Freitag, Sandria. 2001. "Visions of the Nation: Theorizing the Nexus between Creation, Consumption, and Participation in the Public Sphere." In *Pleasure and the Nation: The History, Politics, and Consumption of Public Culture in India,* edited by Rachel Dwyer and Christopher Pinney. New Delhi: Oxford University Press.

Friedman, Jonathan. 1994. *Cultural Identity and Global Process.* London: Sage.

Fukuyama, Francis. 1992. *The End of History and the Last Man.* New York: Avon.

Galbraith, John Kenneth. 1958. *The Affluent Society.* London: H. Hamilton.

Gandhi, M. K. [1927; 1929] 1982. *An Autobiography, or the Story of My Experiments with Truth.* Delhi: Penguin.

———. 1997. *Hind Swaraj and Other Writings.* Edited by Anthony Parel. Cambridge: Cambridge University Press.

Gangar, Amrit. 1996. "Films from the City of Dreams." In *Bombay: Mosaic of Modern Culture,* edited by Sujata Patel and Alice Thorner. New Delhi: Oxford University Press.

Ganti, Tejaswini. 2000. Casting Culture: The Social Life of Hindi Film Production in Contemporary India. Ph.D. diss., New York University.

Gaya, Javed, and Naval Ghiara. 1991. "The Unfulfilled Vision." *Business India,* May 27–June 9.

Gewertz, Deborah, and Frederick Errington. 1996. "On PepsiCo and Piety in a Papua New Guinea 'Modernity.' " *American Ethnologist* 23 (3): 476–93.

Ghose, Sagarika, and Archana Jahagirdar. 1998. "Cool in Kaliyug." *Outlook,* December 14.

Ghosh, Shekhar. 1987. "Catching the Public Eye." *Imprint,* November.

Ghosh, Shohini. 1999. "The Troubled Existence of Sex and Sexuality: Feminists Engage with Censorship." In *Image Journeys: Audio-Visual Media and Cultural Change in India,* edited by Christiane Brosius and Melissa Butcher (eds). New Delhi: Sage.

Ghosh Roy, Mahasweta. 1997. "The Big Idea." *Business World,* January 22–31.

———. 1998. "The Day of the *Desi* Brand." *Business India,* May 18–31.

Gillespie, Marie. 1995. *Television, Ethnicity, and Cultural Change.* London: Routledge.

Godelier, Maurice. [1996] 1999. *The Enigma of the Gift.* Chicago: University of Chicago Press.

Goldman, Kevin. 1996. *Conflicting Accounts: The Creation and Crash of the Saatchi and Saatchi Advertising Empire.* New York: Simon and Schuster.

Goldman, Robert. 1992. *Reading Ads Socially.* London: Routledge.

Goody, Jack. 1997. *Representations and Contradictions: Ambivalence towards Images, Theatre, Fiction, Relics, and Sexuality.* Oxford: Blackwell.

Graeber, David. 2001. *Toward an Anthropological Theory of Value: The False Coin of Our Own Dreams.* New York: Palgrave.

Guha-Thakurta, Tapati. 1992. *The Making of a New "Indian" Art: Artists, Aesthetics, and Nationalism in Bengal, c. 1850–1920.* Cambridge: Cambridge University Press.

———. 1995. "Recovering the Nation's Art." In *Texts of Power: Emerging Disciplines in Colonial Bengal,* edited by Partha Chatterjee. Minneapolis: University of Minnesota Press.

Gupta, Akhil. 1998. *Postcolonial Developments: Agriculture in the Making of Modern India.* Durham, N.C.: Duke University Press.

Gupta, Indrajit. 1994. "The Wrong Fit." *Business Standard,* December 20.

Gupta, Kanchan. 1997. "I Dream of a Strong, Prosperous India: Interview with Atal Behari Vajpayee." *Times of India,* December 25.

Gupta, Nilanjana. 1998. *Switching Channels: Ideologies of Television in India.* New Delhi: Oxford University Press.

Gupta, Shalini. 1996. "And Now, for Cause Equity." *The Hindu,* February 14.

Gurumurthy, S. 1998a. "Indian Agenda in the 21st Century World." *The Observer,* August 15.

———. 1998b. "Looking to the Future: Making India an Economic Superpower." *The Tribune,* August 15.

———. 1998c. "From Swadeshi and Nationalism to Swadeshi and Nationalism." http://members.theglobe.com/athreya/swadeshi.htm.

Gwatkin, Davidson. 1979. "Political Will and Family Planning: Implications of India's Emergency Experience." *Population and Development Review* 5 (1): 29–60.

Habermas, Jürgen. [1962] 1989. *The Structural Transformation of the Public Sphere.* Cambridge, Mass.: MIT Press.

Haggard, H. Rider. 1991. *She.* 1887. Reprint, Bloomington: Indiana University Press.

Halbertal, Moshe, and Avishai Margalit. 1992. *Idolatry.* Cambridge, Mass.: Harvard University Press.

Hart, Keith. 2001. *The Memory Bank: Money in an Unequal World.* London: Profile.

Harvey, David. 1989. *The Condition of Postmodernity.* Oxford: Basil Blackwell.

———. 2000a. *Spaces of Hope.* Berkeley: University of California Press.

———. 2000b. "Cosmopolitanisms and the Banality of Geographical Evils." In *Millennial Capitalism and the Culture of Neoliberalism,* edited by John Comaroff and Jean Comaroff. A special issue of *Public Culture* 12 (2): 529–64.

Haug, Wolfgang Fritz. 1987. *Commodity Aesthetics, Ideology, and Culture.* New York: International General.

Hawkins, Sophie. 1999. "Bordering Realism: The Aesthetics of Sai Baba's Universe." In *Image Journeys: Audio-Visual Media and Cultural Change in India,* edited by Christiane Brosius and Melissa Butcher. New Delhi: Sage.

Hebdige, Dick. [1979] 1987. *Subculture: The Meaning of Style.* London: Routledge.

Hegel, G. W. F. 1956. *The Philosophy of History.* 1830–31. Reprint, New York: Dover.

Heng, Geraldine, and Janadas Devan. 1995. "State Fatherhood: The Politics of

Nationalism, Sexuality, and Race in Singapore." In *Nationalisms and Sex-
uualities,* edited by Andrew Parker et al. New York: Routledge.

Horkheimer, Max, and Theodor Adorno. [1944] 1972. *Dialectic of Enlightenment.* New York: Continuum.

Houlgate, Stephen, ed. 1998. *The Hegel Reader.* Oxford: Blackwell.

Howes, David, ed. 1996. *Cross-Cultural Consumption: Global Markets, Local
Realities.* London: Routledge.

Hussain, Abid. 1998. Remarks in "Towards Liberalisation and Globalisation." In
*Rajiv Gandhi's India: A Golden Jubilee Perspective. Economics: People in
Democracy and Development,Volumer 2,* edited by V. Ramachandran. New
Delhi: UBS Publishers' Distributors Ltd.

Hutnyk, John. 2000. *Critique of Exotica: Music, Politics, and the Culture Industry.* London: Pluto Press.

Huyssen, Andreas. 1975. "Introduction to Adorno." *New German Critique* 6
(fall): 3–11.

Ichaporia, Niloufer. 1983. "Tourism at Khajuraho: An Indian Enigma?" *Annals of
Tourism Research* 10 (1): 75–92.

Inden, Ronald. 1990. *Imagining India.* Oxford: Basil Blackwell.

"India Has Never Had *Swadeshi* Economy" and "India Cannot Live in Cities."
1998. *Rediff on the Net,* interview with S. Gurumurthy. http://www.rediff.com/
business/1998/apr/02guru.htm.

"Interview with John Hegarty." 1998. *Business India,* February 23–March 8.

Irani, Madhavi. 1991. "What Is Your Brand?" *Times of India* (Bombay), December 8.

———. 1996. "Reading the Market Wrong." *Economic Times,* April 3.

"I Won't Say That We Need a Strong Government for Economic Growth: Interview with Gurcharan Das." 1998. *Rediff on the Net,* December 31:
http://www.rediff.com/business/1998/dec/31inter1.htm.

Jacob, Rahul. 1985. "Advertising as Crusading." *Business Standard,* October 13.

Jameson, Fredric. 1991. *Postmodernism, or, the Cultural Logic of Late Capitalism.* Durham, N.C.: Duke University Press.

Jameson, Fredric, and Masao Miyoshi, eds. 1998. *The Cultures of Globalization.*
Durham, N.C.: Duke University Press.

Jay, Martin. 1984. *Marxism and Totality: The Adventures of a Concept from
Lukacs to Habermas.* Berkeley: University of California Press.

———. 1993. *Downcast Eyes: The Denigration of Vision in Twentieth-Century
French Thought.* Berkeley: University of California Press.

Jeffrey, Robin. 2000. *India's Newspaper Revolution: Capitalism, Politics, and the
Indian-Language Press 1977–1999.* New York: St. Martin's.

Jetley, Neerja Pawha, and Paromita Shastri. 1998. "Baby and the Bathwater." *Outlook,* April 13.

Jishnu, Lata, et al. 1998. "The True Colours of Swadeshi." *Business World,*
April 7.

Kankanala, Ram. 1991. "It's an Ad, Ad, Ad, Ad World." *Gentleman,* April 1.

Kant, Immanuel. 1978. *Anthropology from a Pragmatic Point of View.* 1798, Reprint, Carbondale: University of Southern Illinois Press.

Kapur, Geeta. 1998. *When Was Modernism? Essays on Contemporary Cultural Practice in India.* Delhi: Tulika.

Karkal, Malini. 1992. "Women's Rights in Population Control." *The Independent,* June 11.

Karlekar, Hiranmay. 1986. "The Great Advertising Boom." *Indian Express,* September 11.

Karp, Ivan, and Steven Lavine, eds. 1991. *Exhibiting Cultures: The Poetics and Politics of Museum Display.* Washington: Smithsonian Institute Press.

Kaur, Raminder. Forthcoming. *A Trunk Full of Tales: Performative Politics and Culture of the Spectacle in Western India.*

Kaviraj, Sudipta. 1990. "Capitalism and the Cultural Process." *Journal of Arts and Ideas* 19:61–75.

———. 1995. *The Unhappy Consciousness: Bankimchandra Chattopadhyay and the Formation of Nationalist Discourse in India.* New Delhi: Oxford University Press.

———. 1997. "Filth and the Public Sphere: Concepts and Practices about Space in Calcutta." *Public Culture* 10 (1): 113.

Kazmi, Fareeduddin. 1998. "How Angry Is the Angry Young Man? Rebellion in Conventional Hindi Films." In *The Secret Politics of Our Desires: Innocence, Culpability, and Indian Popular Cinema,* edited by Ashis Nandy. New Delhi: Oxford University Press.

Kelsky, Karen. 1999. "Gender, Modernity, and Eroticized Internationalism in Japan." *Cultural Anthropology* 14 (2): 229.

Kemper, Steven. 2001. *Buying and Believing: Sri Lankan Advertising and Consumers in a Transnational World.* Chicago: University of Chicago Press.

Keshavan, Narayan. 1998. "Swadeshi Goes Global." *Outlook,* April 27.

Key, Wilson Bryan. 1972. *Subliminal Seduction.* New York: Signet.

———. 1976. *Media Sexploitation.* New York: Signet.

"Key to Reality — Are Advertisers Thinking Hard Enough about Who Their Target Consumer Really Is?" 1997. *Advertising and Marketing.* August 16–31.

Klein, Naomi. 1999. *No Logo.* New York: Picador.

Koppikar, Smruti. 1992. "Lintas to Serve Notice to Doordarshan on Kama Sutra." *The Independent,* April 11.

Kopytoff, Igor. 1986. "The Cultural Biography of Thirst: Commoditization as Cultural Progress." In *The Social Life of Things: Commodities in Cultural Perspective,* edited by Arjun Appadurai. Cambridge: Cambridge University Press.

Kotler, Philip. 1986. "Global Standardization: Courting Danger." *Journal of Consumer Marketing* 3 (2): 13–19.

Krishnaji, N. 1998. "Population Policy." In *The Indian Economy,* edited by Terence Byres. New Delhi: Oxford University Press.

Krishnan, M. 1984. "The Anomalies in a Bad Law." *Business Standard,* February 21.

Kumar, Dinesh. 1996. "The Missed Objectives." *The Pioneer* (Delhi), September 21.

Kumar, K. G. 1993. "Coy Public Sector." *Business India,* June 21–July 4.

Kumar, T. 1984. "Gandhi's Ideological Clothing." *Media Development* 31 (4): 19–21.

Lankesh, Gauri, et al. 1992. "Not My Problem!" *Sunday,* January 19–25.

Lears, T. Jackson. 1994. *Fables of Abundance: A Cultural History of Advertising in America.* New York: Basic Books.

Lévi-Strauss, Claude. [1962] 1966. *The Savage Mind.* Chicago: University of Chicago Press.

Levin, Charles. 1981. Introduction to *For a Critique of the Political Economy of the Sign,* edited by Jean Baudrillard. St. Louis, Mo.: Telos Press.

Levin, David Michael, ed. 1993. *Modernity and the Hegemony of Vision.* Berkeley: University of California Press.

Levitt, Theodore. 1983. "The Globalization of Markets." *Harvard Business Review* 61 (May–June): 92–102.

Little, John. 1995. "Video *Vacana: Swadhyaya* and Sacred Tapes." In *Media and the Transformation of Religion in South Asia,* edited by Lawrence Babb and Susan Wadley. Philadelphia: University of Pennsylvania Press.

Lobo, Austin. 1991. "Marketplace: Condom Marketing Has Come a Long Way." *Times of India,* October 21.

Lois, George, and Bill Pitts. 1991. *What's the Big Idea? How to Win with Outrageous Ideas (That Sell!).* New York: Plume.

Lukács, Georg. [1923] 1971. *History and Class Consciousness: Studies in Marxist Dialectics.* Cambridge, Mass: MIT Press.

Lull, James. 1991. *China Turned On: Television, Reform, and Resistance.* London: Routledge.

Lury, Celia. 1996. *Consumer Culture.* Cambridge: Polity Press.

Lutgendorf, Philip. 1995. "All in the (Raghu) Family: A Video Epic in Cultural Context." In *Media and the Transformation of Religion in South Asia,* edited by Lawrence Babb and Susan Wadley. Philadelphia: University of Pennsylvania Press.

Lyotard, Jean-François. 1984. *The Postmodern Condition: A Report on Knowledge.* Minneapolis: University of Minnesota Press.

Madan, T. N. 1987. *Non-Renunciation.* New Delhi: Oxford University Press.

——. 1994. *Pathways.* New Delhi: Oxford University Press.

——. 1995. "Secularism in Its Place." In *Religion in India,* edited by T. N. Madan. New Delhi: Oxford University Press.

——, ed. 1982. *Way of Life: King, Householder, Renouncer.* New Delhi: Vikas.

Malinowski, Bronislaw. 1922. *Argonauts of the Western Pacific: An Account of Native Enterprise and Adventure in the Archipelagoes of Melanesian New Guinea.* London: G. Routledge and Sons.

———. [1935] 1965. *Coral Gardens and Their Magic.* Bloomington, Ind.: Indiana University Press.

Mankekar, Purnima. 1999. *Screening Culture, Viewing Politics: An Ethnography of Television, Womanhood, and Nation in Postcolonial India.* Durham, N.C.: Duke University Press.

Marcus, George. 1998. *Ethnography Through Thick and Thin.* Princeton: Princeton University Press.

Marx, Karl. 1976. *Capital, Volume One.* 1867. Reprint, New York: Vintage.

Massumi, Brian. 1992. *A User's Guide to Capitalism and Schizophrenia: Deviations from Deleuze and Guattari.* Cambridge, Mass.: MIT Press.

———. 1996. "The Autonomy of Affect." In *Deleuze: A Critical Reader,* edited by Paul Patton. Oxford: Basil Blackwell.

Mattelart, Armand. 1991. *Advertising International: The Privatization of Public Space.* London: Routledge.

Mauss, Marcel. [1923–24] 1990. *The Gift: The Form and Reason for Exchange in Archaic Societies.* New York: Norton.

Maxwell, Richard. 1996. "Out of Kindness and Into Difference: The Value of Global Market Research." *Media, Culture, and Society* 18:105–26.

Mayle, Peter. 1990. *Up the Agency: The Snakes and Ladders of the Advertising Business.* London: Pan.

Mazzarella, William. 2002. "Cindy at the Taj: Cultural Enclosure and Corporate Potentateship in an Era of Globalization." In *Everyday Life in South Asia,* edited by Diane Mines and Sarah Lamb. Bloomington: Indiana University Press.

———. 2003. "Critical Publicity/Public Criticism: Reflections on Fieldwork in the Bombay Ad World." In *Advertising Anthropology,* edited by Timothy Malefyt and Brian Moeran. Oxford: Berg.

McClintock, Anne. 1995. "Soft-Soaping Empire: Commodity Racism and Imperial Advertising." In *Imperial Leather: Race, Gender, and Sexuality in the Colonial Conquest.* New York: Routledge.

McCracken, Grant. 1988. *Culture and Consumption.* Bloomington: Indiana University Press.

McCreery, John. 1995. "Malinowski, Magic and Advertising: On Choosing Metaphors." In *Contemporary Marketing and Consumer Behavior: An Anthropological Sourcebook,* edited by John Sherry. Thousand Oaks, Calif.: Sage.

Mehta, Gita. [1997] 1998. *Snakes and Ladders: Glimpses of Modern India.* New York: Doubleday.

Mehta, Harshad. 1997. "A Shaft of Light, and EMW Shines." *Asian Age,* December 3.

Mehta, Prem. 1981. "Advertisers' Responsibilities." *Business World,* November 9–22.

Menon, Raji. 1991. "Condom Courage." *Island,* October.

Metz, Christian. 1985. "Photography and Fetish." *October* 34:81.

Miller, Daniel. 1987. *Material Culture and Mass Consumption*. Oxford: Blackwell.

———. 1994. *Modernity: An Ethnographic Approach*. Oxford: Berg.

———. 1997. *Capitalism: An Ethnographic Approach*. Oxford: Berg.

———, ed. 1995a. *Acknowledging Consumption: A Review of New Studies*. London: Routledge.

———. 1995b. *Worlds Apart: Modernity through the Prism of the Local*. London: Routledge.

Mintz, Sidney. 1985. *Sweetness and Power: The Place of Sugar in Modern History*. New York: Viking.

Mistry, Rohinton. 1995. *A Fine Balance*. Toronto: McLelland and Stewart.

Mitchell, W. J. T. 1986. *Iconology: Image, Text, Ideology*. Chicago: University of Chicago Press.

Mitra, Ashok. 1998. "BJP Will Kneel before World Bank, and Tout It as *Swadeshi*." *Rediff on the Net*, June 27, http://www.rediff.com/business/1998/jun/27mitra.htm.

Mitra, Sumit. 1987. "The Ten-Second Girls." *Sunday*, May 31–June 6.

Moeran, Brian. 1996a. *A Japanese Advertising Agency: An Anthropology of Media and Markets*. Honolulu: University of Hawai'i Press.

———. 1996b. "The Orient Strikes Back: Advertising and Imaging in Japan." *Theory, Culture, and Society* 13 (3): 77–112.

———. 2001. "Promoting Culture: The Work of a Japanese Advertising Agency." In *Asian Media Productions*, edited by Brian Moeran. London: Curzon.

Monteiro, Anjali. 1998. "Official Television and Unofficial Fabrications of the Self: The Spectator as Subject." In *The Secret Politics of Our Desires: Innocence, Culpability, and Indian Popular Cinema*, edited by Ashis Nandy. New Delhi: Oxford University Press.

Moreiras, Alberto. 1998. "Global Fragments: A Second Latinamericanism." In *The Cultures of Globalization*, edited by Fredric Jameson and Masao Miyoshi. Durham, N.C.: Duke University Press.

Mukherjee, Haridas, and Uma Mukherjee. 1908. *India's Fight for Freedom or the Swadeshi Movement, 1905–1906*. Calcutta.

Mulvey, Laura. 1996. *Fetishism and Curiosity*. London: British Film Institute.

Munn, Nancy. [1986] 1992. *The Fame of Gawa: A Symbolic Study of Value Transformation in a Massim (Papua New Guinea) Society*. Durham, N.C.: Duke University Press.

Nadkarni, Shirish. 1995. "Hefty Deposits, Lower Air Time Charges 'Preferable.'" *Pioneer*, October 4.

Naipaul, V. S. [1967] 1969. *The Mimic Men*. London: Penguin.

Nair, Rukmini Bhaya. 1998. *Technobrat: Culture in a Cybernetic Classroom*. New Delhi: Harper Collins.

Nanda, Prakash. 1998. "BJP Turns *Swadeshi* on Its Head." *Ballot '98*. http://www.indozone.com/election/puri10.htm.

Nandy, Ashis. 1983. *The Intimate Enemy: Loss and Recovery of Self under Colonialism*. New Delhi: Oxford University Press.

——. 1995. *The Savage Freud and Other Essays on Possible and Retrievable Selves*. Princeton, N.J.: Princeton University Press.

Nandy, Pritish. 1998. "This Bane of Swadeshi Politics." *Rediff on the Net*, March 30, http://www.rediff.com/news/1998/mar/30nandy.htm.

Nehru, Jawaharlal. [1945] 1948. *The Discovery of India*. Calcutta: Signet.

"New Survey Puts Middle Class at 425 million." 1997. *Rediff on the Net*, December 31, http://www.rediff.com/business/dec/31vant3.htm.

Ninan, T. N., and Chander Uday Singh. 1982. "Coming of Age." *India Today*, September 30.

OBM Media Bulletin. 1983. Bombay: Ogilvy, Benson, and Mather.

Ogilvy, David. 1983. *Ogilvy on Advertising*. New York: Vintage.

Ohmae, Kenichi. 1990. *The Borderless World: Power and Strategy in the Interlinked Economy*. New York: Harper Business.

Ohmann, Richard. 1996. "Knowing/Creating Wants." In *Making and Selling Culture*, edited by Richard Ohmann. Hanover and London: Wesleyan University Press.

Olins, Wally. 1997. "Crafting Corporate Personalities." *Financial Express* (Special Supplement), October.

Ong, Aihwa. 1993. "On the Edge of Empires: Flexible Citizenship among Chinese in Diaspora." *Positions* 1 (3): 745–78.

Orlove, Benjamin, ed. 1997. *The Allure of the Foreign: Imported Goods in Postcolonial Latin America*. Ann Arbor: University of Michigan Press.

Osella, Filippo, and Caroline Osella. 1999. "From Transience to Immanence: Consumption, Life-Cycle, and Social Mobility in Kerala, South India." *Modern Asian Studies* 33 (4): 989–1020.

Packard, Vance. 1957. *The Hidden Persuaders*. New York: D. McKay Co.

Padamsee, Alyque. 1999. *A Double Life: My Exciting Years in Theatre and Advertising*. New Delhi: Penguin.

——. n.d. Just Say KS. Manuscript.

"Padamsee: TV Needs a Creative Chief." 1988. *Telegraph*, February 14.

Pande, Anuja. 1996. "Cold War." *Sunday*, March 31–April 6.

Parry, Jonathan. 1986. "'The Gift, the Indian Gift, and the 'Indian Gift.'" *Man*, n.s., 21:453–73.

——. 1994. *Death in Banaras*. Cambridge: Cambridge University Press.

Pillai, Ajith. 1992. "KS Ad Found Objectionable." *The Pioneer*, April 10.

Pinney, Christopher. 1997. *Camera Indica: The Social Life of Indian Photographs*. Chicago: University of Chicago Press.

——. 2001. "Introduction: Public, Popular, and Other Cultures." In *Pleasure and the Nation: The History, Politics, and Consumption of Public Culture in India*, edited by Rachel Dwyer and Christopher Pinney. New Delhi: Oxford University Press.

Poster, Mark, ed. 1988. *Jean Baudrillard: Selected Writings.* Stanford, Calif.: Stanford University Press.

Povinelli, Elizabeth. 2000. "Consuming *Geist:* Popontology and the Spirit of Capital in Indigenous Australia." In *Millennial Capitalism and the Culture of Neoliberalism,* edited by John Comaroff and Jean Comaroff. A special issue of *Public Culture* 12 (2): 501–28.

Prakash, Amit. 1993. "Ignoring Strictures, Kama Sutra Ads Are Back with a Bang." *The Pioneer,* May 16.

Prakash, Gyan. 1992. "Postcolonial Criticism and Indian Historiography." *Social Text* 31/32: 8–19.

———. 1999. *Another Reason: Science and the Imagination of Modern India.* Princeton: Princeton University Press.

Prasad, M. Madhava. 1995. "Ideology as Contagion." *Economic and Political Weekly* 18 (March): 1020–22.

———. 1998. *Ideology of the Hindi Film: A Historical Construction.* New Delhi: Oxford University Press.

Pred, Allan. 1995. *Re-Cognizing European Modernities.* London: Routledge.

Rabinow, Paul. 1986. "Representations Are Social Facts: Modernity and Post-Modernity in Anthropology." In *Writing Culture: The Poetics and Politics of Ethnography,* edited by James Clifford and George Marcus. Berkeley: University of California Press.

Raheja, Gloria. 1988. *The Poison in the Gift: Ritual, Prestation, and the Dominant Caste in a North Indian Village.* Chicago: University of Chicago Press.

Rai, Usha. 1992. "Govt. to Ban Import of Condoms." *Indian Express,* March 6.

Raina, Monica. 1995. "Ringing in the Future." *India Today,* June 30.

Rajagopal, Arvind. 1993. "The Rise of National Programming: The Case of Indian Television." *Media, Culture, and Society* 15 (1): 91–112.

———. 1994. "Ram Janmabhoomi, Consumer Identity, and Image-Based Politics." *Economic and Political Weekly,* June 2: 1659–68.

———. 1996. "Communalism and the Consuming Subject." *Economic and Political Weekly,* February 10: 341–48.

———. 1999. Advertising, Politics, and the Sentimental Education of the Indian Consumer. Visual Anthropology Review 14 (2): 14–31.

———. 2001. *Politics after Television: Hindu Nationalism and the Reshaping of the Public in India.* Cambridge: Cambridge University Press.

Ramusack, Barbara. 1995. "The Indian Princes as Fantasy: Palace Hotels, Palace Museums, and Palaces on Wheels." In *Consuming Modernity: Public Culture in a South Asian World,* edited by Carol Breckenridge. Minneapolis: University of Minnesota Press.

Richards, Thomas. 1990. *The Commodity Culture of Victorian Britain: Advertising and Spectacle 1851–1914.* Stanford, Calif.: Stanford University Press.

Ries, Al, and Jack Trout. 1981. *Positioning: The Battle for Your Mind.* New York: McGraw-Hill.

Rodrigues, Malika. 1999. "MTV Is Like This Only." *Brand Equity*, December 1–6.
Rosenblum, Barbara. 1978. *Photographers at Work*. New York: Holmes and Meier.
Rothenberg, Randall. 1995. *Where the Suckers Moon: The Life and Death of an Advertising Campaign*. New York: Vintage.
Rudolph, Lloyd, and Susanne Hoeber Rudolph. 1987. *In Pursuit of Lakshmi: The Political Economy of the Indian State*. Chicago: University of Chicago Press.
Rushdie, Salman. [1980] 1991a. *Midnight's Children*. New York: Penguin.
———. 1991b. *Imaginary Homelands: Essays and Criticism, 1981–1991*. London: Granta.
Rydell, Robert. 1984. *All the World's a Fair: Visions of Empire at American International Expositions, 1876–1914*. Chicago: University of Chicago Press.
Sahlins, Marshall. 1976. *Culture and Practical Reason*. Chicago: University of Chicago Press.
———. 1993. "Goodbye to *Tristes Tropes:* Ethnography in the Context of Modern World History." *Journal of Modern History* 65 (March): 1–25.
Said, Edward. 1978. *Orientalism*. New York: Pantheon.
Sarai. 2001. *Sarai Reader 01: The Public Domain*. New Delhi: Sarai; Amsterdam: Society for Old and New Media.
———. 2002. *Sarai Reader 02: The Cities of Everyday Life*. New Delhi: Sarai; Amsterdam: Society for Old and New Media.
Sarkar, Sumit. 1973. *The Swadeshi Movement in Bengal, 1903–1908*. New Delhi: Peoples' Publishing House.
Sarna, S. R. 1982a. "A Study of Expenditure by Various Industries." *Business Standard*, August 24.
———. 1982b. "The Top Ten Spenders." *Business Standard*, August 25.
Schein, Louisa. 2000. *Minority Rules: The Miao and the Feminine in China's Cultural Politics*. Durham, N.C.: Duke University Press.
Schudson, Michael. 1984. *Advertising, the Uneasy Persuasion: Its Dubious Impact on American Society*. New York: Basic Books.
Schwartz, Peter. [1991] 1996. *The Art of the Long View*. Excerpted http://www.patois.com/global-teenager.html.
Sen, Anindya, et al. 1997. "Self-Reliance, Indian Style." *Rediff on the Net,* February 15–16. http://www.redifindia.com/business/feb/15idr5.htm.
Sen, Antara Dev. 1995. "Reaching for the World." *Indian Express,* April 2.
Sengupta, Ranjana. 1991. "Who's the Boss, Anyway?" *Indian Express,* September 15.
Shah, Amrita. 1997. *Hype, Hypocrisy, and Television in Urban India*. New Delhi: Vikas.
Shankar, Ravi. 1984. "Cutting the Press Down to Size?" *Update,* April 4–17.
Sherry, John, ed. 1995. *Contemporary Marketing and Consumer Behaviour: An Anthropological Sourcebook*. Thousand Oaks, Calif.: Sage.
Sheshadri, G. R. 1983. "A Retrograde Disallowance." *The Economic Scene,* July 16.
"Shocking Advertisement." 1994. Letters page, *Mid-Day.* January 3.

Sidhvi, Shiraz. 1984. "The Year That Was." *Business India,* January 2–15.

Siemens. 1997. "Society and Culture: Driving Forces." http://www.siemens.com/ public/uk'sys/future/sys/sys'us/society/forces/sc'force.htm

Simoes, Frank. 1993. "A Perfect Pair of Breasts." In *Uncertain Liaisons: Sex, Strife, and Togetherness in Urban India,* edited by Khushwant Singh and Shobha De. New Delhi: Viking.

Singh, Iqbal. 1996. "Man and Machine: EMW Takes on Foreign Competition with an Appeal from a Native Hero." *Advertising and Marketing,* October 15.

Singh, Manmohan. 1998. Remarks in "Towards Liberalisation and Globalisation." In *Rajiv Gandhi's India: A Golden Jubilee Perspective. Economics: People in Democracy and Development, Volume 2,* edited by V. Ramachandran. New Delhi: UBS Publishers' Distributors Ltd.

Singhal, Arvind, and Everett Rogers. 2001. *India's Communication Revolution: From Bullock Cartsto Cyber Marts.* New Delhi: Sage.

Skaria, George. 1999. "The Indianization of the Transnational." *Business Today,* July 7.

Skov, Lise, and Brian Moeran, eds. 1995. *Women, Media, and Consumption in Japan.* Honolulu: University of Hawai'i Press.

Slater, Joanna. 2000. "Name Game." *Far Eastern Economic Review,* May 25: 58.

Smith, Adam. 1981. *An Enquiry into the Nature and Causes of the Wealth of Nations.* 1776. Reprint, Indianapolis: Liberty Fund.

Sonnabend, Peter. 1996. "Sonesta International Hotels." In *Making and Selling Culture,* edited by Richard Ohmann. Hanover and London: Wesleyan University Press.

Sontag, Susan. [1977] 1989. *On Photography.* New York: Noonday Press.

Spivak, Gayatri Chakravorty. 1999. *A Critique of Postcolonial Reason: Toward a History of the Vanishing Present.* Cambridge, Mass.: Harvard University Press.

"Spotlight: It's an Ad World." 1983. *Economic Scene,* December 1.

Srivatsan, R. 1991. "Looking at Film Hoardings: Labour, Gender, Subjectivity, and Everyday Life in India." *Public Culture* 4 (1): 1–24.

———. 2000. *Conditions of Visibility: Writings on Photography in Contemporary India.* Calcutta: Stree.

Strasser, Susan. 1989. *Satisfaction Guaranteed: The Making of the American Mass Market.* New York: Pantheon.

Sulkunen, Pekka, et al., eds. 1997. *Constructing the New Consumer Society.* Basingstoke: Macmillan Press.

Swadeshi Jagaran Manch. n.d.a. "The Philosophy." http://www.swadeshi/org/ f11.htm.

———. n.d.b. "The Movement." http://www.swadeshi.org/f12.htm.

Swamy, R. K. 1984. "Is Government Attitude towards Advertising Unhelpful?" *Economic Times,* February 25.

Szerter, Simon. 1993. "The Idea of Demographic Transition and the Study of Fertility Change: A Critical Intellectual History." *Population and Development Review* 19 (4): 659–701.

Tagg, John. 1988. *The Burden of Representation: Essays on Photographies and Histories*. Minneapolis: University of Minnesota Press.

Tang, Xiaobing. 1993. "Orientalism and the Question of Universality: The Language of Contemporary Chinese Literary Theory." *Positions* 1 (2): 389–413.

Tarlo, Emma. 1996. *Clothing Matters: Dress and Identity in India*. Chicago: University of Chicago Press.

Thakraney, Anil. 1998. "Up Close and Personal: Indra Sinha." *The Advertising Brief*, May 21.

Thakur, Sankarshan. 1985. "1985: The Year of the Ad?" *Sunday*, April 14–20.

Thapar, Raj. 1991. *All These Years: A Memoir*. New Delhi: Penguin.

Thomas, Rosie. 1985. "Indian Cinema, Pleasures, and Popularity." *Screen* 26 (3–4): 116–32.

——. 1995. "Melodrama and the Negotiation of Morality in Mainstream Hindi Film." In *Consuming Modernity: Public Culture in a South Asian World*, edited by Carol Breckenridge. Minneapolis: University of Minnesota Press.

Tobin, Joseph, ed. 1992. *Re-Made in Japan: Everyday Life and Consumer Taste in a Changing Society*. New Haven: Yale University Press.

Tomlinson, John. 1991. *Cultural Imperialism*. Baltimore: Johns Hopkins Press.

Trouillot, Michel-Rolph. 1995. *Silencing the Past: Power and the Production of History*. Boston: Beacon Press.

Trout, Jack. 1995. *The New Positioning*. New York: McGraw-Hill.

Tucker, Robert, ed. 1978. *The Marx-Engels Reader.*, 2d edition. New York: Norton.

Tully, Mark. 1992. "Rewriting the Ramayan." In *The Defeat of a Congressman and Other Parables of Modern India*. New York: Knopf.

Vachani, Lalit. 1999. "Bachchan-alias: The Many Faces of a Film Icon." In *Image Journeys: Audio-Visual Media and Cultural Change in India*, edited by Christiane Brosius and Melissa Butcher. New Delhi: Sage.

Vaidyanathan, A. 1995. *The Indian Economy: Crisis, Response, and Prospects*. Delhi: Orient Longman.

Vakil, Ardarshir [1997] 1998. *Beach Boy: A Novel*. New York: Charles Scribner.

Van Ham, Peter. 2001. "The Rise of the Brand State: The Postmodern Politics of Image and Reputation." http://www.batf.org.uk/docs/brandstate.pdf.

Varma, Pavan. 1998. *The Great Indian Middle Class*. New Delhi: Viking.

Vasuki, S. R. 1985. "The Coming Boom in Advertising." *Business India*, July 1–14.

——. 1986. "Doordarshan Share Goes Up." *Business India*, March 10–23.

Visvanathan, Shiv. 1997. *A Carnival for Science*. New Delhi: Oxford University Press.

Wadhawan, Ravi. 1992. "Rise of the Middle Class." *Deccan Herald*, February 27.

Wallerstein, Immanuel. 1976. *The Modern World-System*. New York: Academic Press.

Warner, Michael. 1992. "The Mass Public and the Mass Subject." In *The Phantom*

Public Sphere, edited by Bruce Robbins. Minneapolis: University of Minnesota Press.

Watson, James, ed. 1997. *Golden Arches East: McDonald's in East Asia.* Stanford: Stanford University Press.

Weiner, Annette. 1985. "Inalienable Wealth." *American Ethnologist* 12: 52–65.

———. 1992. *Inalienable Possessions: The Paradox of Keeping-While-Giving.* Berkeley: University of California Press.

———. 1994. "Cultural Difference and the Density of Objects." *American Ethnologist* 21 (2): 391–403.

Wells, Melanie. 1998. "Some Foreign Ads Have a Distinct US Flavor." *USA Today,* June 23.

"Who Wants to Be Boss Man in a Coloured Condom?" 1991. *Sunday Observer,* September 15.

Wilk, Richard. 1990. "Consumer Goods as a Dialogue about Development." *Culture and History* 7: 79–100.

———. 1994. "Colonial Time and TV Time: Television and Temporality in Belize." *Visual Anthropology Review* 10 (1): 94.

Williams, Raymond. [1962] 1980. "Advertising, the Magic System." In *Problems in Materialism and Culture: Selected Essays.* London and New York: Verso.

Williamson, Judith. 1978. *Decoding Advertisements: Ideology and Meaning in Advertising.* London: Boyars.

Wind, Yoram. 1986. "The Myth of Globalization." *Journal of Consumer Marketing* 3 (2): 23–26.

Wolf, Eric. 1982. *Europe and the People without History.* Berkeley: University of California Press.

"Xenophobic Investor Statements Outdated in India: Analysts." 1998. *Indian Express,* March 7.

Yoshimoto, Mitsuhiro. 1996. "Real Virtuality." In *Global/Local: Cultural Production and the Transnational Imaginary,* edited by Rob Wilson and Wimal Dissanayake. Durham, N.C.: Duke University Press.

Zyman, Sergio. 1999. *The End of Marketing as We Know It.* New York: Harper Business.

INDEX

Aaker, David, 102, 189–90, 191
account executives vs. agency managers, 172–75, 176–77
Acuvue contact lenses, 219
Adam condoms, 131–32, 300 n.11
Adams, Ansel, 312 n.23
Adams, Jad, 316 n.6
Ad Club of Bombay, 313 n.26
ADGRO (Asian Advertising Congress), 302 n.27
adolescents. *See* teenagers
Adorno, Theodor, 41, 42, 45–46, 286, 297 nn.5, 7, 308 n.1
advertising, 3–36; ambiguous roles of, 78, 80; budgets for, 174, 319 n.22; creativity in, 28–29, 107–10, 296 n.32; and culture areas, 29–31; culture as mirrored by, 25–26; and eroticized public speech, 95–97, 100, 308 n.54; and essential vs. inessential goods, 83–84; ethnographic research on, 31–34, 296 nn.34–35; expenditures in, 86–87, 306 nn.44–45; freedom of choice as

ensured by, 88–89; global model of, 3–4; growth of, as an industry, 12, 292 n.16; history of, 12–13, 292 n.17; and information, 78, 80, 85; joint ventures in, 13, 292 n.17; legitimation of, 78, 84–86, 92, 98; and liberalization, 89, 306–7 n.49; vs. marketing, 27–29, 85, 115, 295 n.30, 296 n.32; and motivation, 93; and politics, 60, 67, 78–87, 303 nn.31, 33, 304–5 n.40, 305–6 nn.44–45; practice of, 26, 27–31, 294–96 nn.28–32; and production vs. consumption, 84, 87–88, 305 n.41; regulation of, 128–29, 312–13 n.26, 313–14 n.28; vs. sales, 294 n.27; and signification of goods, 21–22, 25, 26, 294 n.26; and social projects, 79–80, 303 n.31; structuralism in, 21–26, 293–95 nn.25–26; subliminal, 294 n.28; and true vs. false needs, 13, 21, 75, 293–94 n.25, 303 n.32. *See also* aspi-

advertising (*cont.*)
  ration; Big Idea; locality/mobil-
  ity; mass consumerism; public
  service advertising; swadeshi
Advertising & Marketing, 201
Advertising Standards Council of
  India. *See* ASCI/CCC
aesthetic judgment, 104–5, 115,
  137
affect/intensity, 48–49
agency managers vs. account
  executives, 172–75, 176–77
AIDS, 64, 96–97, 299 n.8, 308 n.55
Alikhan, Anvar, 109
allochronicity, 89–90
Amul Butter, 67
anthropology of globalization, 14–
  18
Appadurai, Arjun, 17, 30–31, 259,
  276, 296 n.31
Arendt, Hannah, 319 n.1
Aristotle, 47
Arora, Malaika, 132, 133
art, 41–42, 103–4, 303 n.31. *See
  also* commodity images
Art Advertising, 133
Arvind Mills, 327 n.14
asceticism vs. hedonism, 294–95
  n.29
ASCI/CCC (Advertising Standards
  Council of India/Consumer
  Complaints Council), 63–64,
  128–29, 312–13 n.26
Asian Advertising Congress
  (ADGRO), 302 n.27
Asian discipline/values, 139–40
Asian Games (Delhi, 1982), 76, 91,
  302 n.26
aspiration, aesthetic politics of, 99–
  146; and audience scope, 324
  n.19; and autonomy vs. instrumentality, 103–4; and auto-
  orientalism, 138–46, 315 n.34;
  and citizenship, 100–101, 141,

315 n.34; and development,
  100–101; and the KamaSutra
  brand name, 117–19, 311–12
  n.18; mass foundation of, 106–
  15, 310 nn.12–13; and particulars vs. universals, 101–3, 105–
  6; and progress through pleasure, 115–17, 311 n.15; and
  publicity, 99–100, 308 n.1; and
  self-discipline, 101, 309 n.3; and
  taste, aesthetic/politics of, 103–
  6. *See also* KamaSutra condoms
attitude, 177, 319 n.23
aura, 53–55, 256–57, 260–61
authenticity, 44, 246
autonomy vs. instrumentality,
  103–4
auto-orientalism, 138–46, 315
  n.34, 324 n.21

Bachchan, Amitabh, 158–59, 160,
  181, 184, 204–5
Bakshi, Jayant, 66–70, 118, 120,
  128, 299 n.9, 300 n.14, 300–301
  n.18
Banerjee, B., 95
Banerjee, N., 308 n.54
Barthes, Roland, 21, 51–52, 53,
  321 n.14
Barton, Brian, 69
Basu, Kaushik, 9, 307 n.49
Baudrillard, Jean, 22–23, 25, 42,
  105, 191, 194–95
Bazin, André, 51
Beach Boy (Vakil), 258–59
Bedi, Pooja, 120–21, 122, 126,
  128, 312 n.21
Benjamin, Walter, 41, 45, 195, 309
  n.1; on childhood memory, 260,
  326 n.7; on photography/aura,
  53–56, 256–57, 260–61
Benson's (S. H.), 107
Berger, John, 51, 52–53
Bernbach, Bill, 106, 201–2

Bhabha, Homi, 18–19
Bhagat, K. H. L., 313 n.26
Bhagwati, Jagdish, 8–9
Bharat Bala, G., 207
Bharatiya Janata Party. See BJP
Big Idea, 111–14, 310 n.13
BJP (Bharatiya Janata Party), 5, 6,
    10–12, 291–92 n.15
Board of Industrial and Financial
    Reconstruction, 64
Bollywood, 178–79. See also cin-
    ema; Hindi cinema
Bomas Ltd., 12
Bombay, 290 n.4; cellular phones
    in, 162, 317 nn.11, 13; as a com-
    mercial center, 178–79; conno-
    tations of, 175–80, 208
Bombay Club, 9–10, 302 n.25
Bourdieu, Pierre, 33–34, 103,
    251
brands, 185–211; and client-
    agency relationships, 169–70,
    202–4; control/ownership of vs.
    aesthetic legitimation, 134–37,
    314 n.31; and cultural identity
    vs. difference, 208–10; and dem-
    ocratic populism, 192, 319–20
    n.3; efficacy of, 200–204; as gift
    exchange, 186, 192–200, 320
    n.5, 320 nn.7–8; globalization
    of, 205–6, 320–21 n.11; intrin-
    sics vs. extrinsics of, 225–29,
    230–31, 322 n.7; and loyalty,
    194–95; and marketing prac-
    tices, 186–87; and nationalism,
    207, 208; as paternalistic/servile,
    191–92; as personalities/iden-
    tities, 185–92, 194, 319 n.1;
    profitability of, 186; and pub-
    licity, 191–92; RightAway, 186–
    87, 195–200; vs. trademarks,
    185; U.S. branding crisis, 320–
    21 n.11; and the "very Bombay"
    concept, 208–10; Western, 255,

269–70. See also MNCs; specific
    brands
bricolage, 328 n.18
Brooke and Bond, 80
Buck-Morss, Susan, 42, 103–4
budget deficit, 307 n.49
bullock capitalists, 71
Burton, Richard, 298 n.1
businesses vs. research campuses,
    296–97 n.36
Butcher, Melissa, 330 n.24

Calida "innerwear," 133
Capital (Marx), 23–24
capital gains taxes, 291 n.14
capitalism: and the commodity
    form, 19–21, 23, 294 n.26; con-
    sumerist vision of, 19, 23; vs. cul-
    ture, 14–18; and difference, 19–
    21; and exchange value, 24, 39,
    43; irrationality of, 43; and neo-
    Confucianism, 139–40, 324
    n.21; and particulars vs. univer-
    sals, 18; and use-value, 23–25,
    26. See also commodity images;
    globalization
Castoriadis, Cornelius, 40, 43
CCC. See ASCI/CCC
Cellular Operators' Association of
    India. See COAI
cellular phones, 153, 156, 161–65,
    317–18 nn.9–14, 16. See also
    RightAway
censorship, 137
Centaur Hotel, 180
Chakrabarty, Dipesh, 19–20, 23,
    38, 89–91
Channel V (STAR-TV), 215, 244,
    319 n.23, 329–30 n.24
charitable giving, 320 n.5
charkha (hand-operated spinning
    wheel), 5–6
Chatterjee, Partha, 245, 298 n.2,
    321 n.12, 324 n.18, 324–25 n.1

Chaudhuri, Nirad, 326 n.8
Chauhan, Ramesh, 222, 321–22 n.4
Cheater, Angela, 47
Chowdhury, Indur, 133, 314 n.30
Churchgate Set, 106–9, 111, 112–13, 261–62
Churchill, Winston, 305 n.41
cinema, 178–79, 312 n.25. *See also* Hindi cinema
citizenship: and the aesthetic politics of aspiration, 100–101, 141, 315 n.34; and commodity images, 100, 141
close distance, 257, 268–69, 284, 286, 329–30 n.24
COAI (Cellular Operators' Association of India), 162
Coca-Cola Company, 215; brand recognition of, 217, 321 n.2; Christmas ads for, 195; eviction from India, 4–5, 8, 12, 221, 289 n.2; vs. Pepsi, 219, 220–21, 225–27; teen market for, 217–18; vs. Thums Up, 221–22, 225–26, 321–22 n.4
Coca-Colonization, 16
cola wars, 219–22, 225, 321–22 n.4
colonialism: cultural politics of, 18–19
Comaroff, Jean, 293 n.22
Comaroff, John, 293 n.22
commodity feminism, 141
commodity form, 19–21, 23, 38, 45, 294 n.26
commodity images, 20–21, 37–56, 284–85, 293 n.24; audience for, 324 n.19; British vs. U.S., 325 n.5; and citizenship, 100, 141, 315 n.34; and client-agency relationships, 149, 167–72, 318–19 nn.19–20; close distance of, 257, 268–69, 284, 286, 329–30 n.24;

image vs. text, 47; photography's materiality vs. meaning, 49–56; and politics, 60, 67, 78–87, 303 nn.31, 33, 304–5 n.40, 305–6 nn.44–45; postcolonial, 258–63, 325–26 nn.5–6, 326–27 n.9; production of, 167–68; sensibility vs. intelligibility of, 45–49, 298 n.9; and the totalization narrative, 38–45, 46, 49, 55, 297 n.3; and utility, 87–92, 306 n.47, 306–7 n.49. *See also* KamaSutra condoms
computers. *See* telecommunications
condoms, 64, 95, 299 nn.7–8, 307 n.53; pornodom-style, 130–31, 314 n.29. *See also* Adam condoms; Fiesta condoms; KamaSutra condoms; Nirodh condoms
Confucianism, 139–40, 324 n.21
Congress Party, 72, 79, 302 n.30
Conrad, Michael, 102
conservatism vs. modernity, 323 n.14
Consumer Complaints Council. *See* ASCI/CCC
consumerism: elitism vs. populism of, 13; mass, 13–14, 292 n.18
consumer protection, 128, 312–13 n.26
consumption vs. production, 84, 87–88, 305 n.41
Contour agency, 131–32
cool-hunters, 177, 319 n.24
counter-orientalism, 139
CPU (Creative Publicity Unit), 303 n.33
creativity, 28–29, 107–10, 296 n.32. *See also* Big Idea
criminal underworld, cellular phones used by, 163, 317 n.13
cultural imperialism, 16, 216, 247
culture: authenticity of forms of, 44, 246; and auto-orientalism,

Right, 40; on historical progress, 140, 144; on Indian civilization, 280, 328 n.19; *Lectures on the Philosophy of History*, 39–40; on market/civil society, 78; vs. Marx, 40, 311 n.15; on spirit, 39–41, 115–16, 143; totalization narrative of, 41–42

Heng, Geraldine, 140

Hindi cinema, 77, 124–25, 292 n.18, 307 n.50, 312 n.25, 326–27 n.9

Hindu female body, 312 n.21

Hinduism/Hinduization, 282–83, 295 n.29

Hindustan Latex (HL), 96, 299 n.7

Hindustan Lever, 80

Hindustan Petroleum, 240

Hindustan Thompson Associates (HTA), 80–81, 109–10, 305 n.43

historical materialism, 23, 24, 40–41

historical progress vs. sensual pleasure, 140–41, 143–44

Horkheimer, Max, 42, 45, 46

Hussain, Abid, 316 n.6

Hussain, Zakir, 180

Hutnyk, John, 17, 247

hybridity, 247–48

Ichaporia, Niloufer, 122

identity, Indian. *See* Indianness

Image Bank, 166, 318 n.18

images. *See* commodity images

Indian Administrative Service, 303–4 n.34

Indian cinema, 178–79, 312 n.25. *See also* Hindi cinema

Indian Civil Service (ICS), 303–4 n.34

"Indian consumer," construction of, 233–42, 250–87; and cultural difference, 247–48; and elementary forms of globalization,
251–58, 262, 285, 325 nn.2–3; via focus groups, 235–42, 323 nn.11–12; and foreign investors, 264–66, 327 nn.11–12; and foreignness as equity, 266–71; and globalization as cultural revival, 263–66, 277; and Levi's, 266–69, 275, 327 n.14; and the metropolitan, 283–84, 327 n.10; and the middle class, 271–72, 328 n.16; and MNCS, 250–51, 324–25 n.1; models of Indian difference, 277–84, 328–29 nn.19–21; and postcolonial commodity images, 258–63, 325–26 nn.5–6, 326–27 n.9; and value politics/price/spending, 250–51, 271–77, 327–28 nn.16–17

Indian difference, models of, 277–84, 328–29 nn.19–21

Indianness: and auto-orientalism, 138–46, 315 n.34, 324 n.21; as a brand constituent, 208–10, 210–11; Indian vs. Asian difference, 324 n.17; and locality/mobility, 150–51, 154–56, 157–65; and MNCS, 216–17; and the "very Bombay" concept, 175–80, 208–10; women's roles in, 245–46, 324 n.18. *See also* "Indian consumer," construction of

Indian Tobacco Company (ITC), 80

Industrial Light and Magic (ILM), 196, 199

information, and developmental policy, 307 n.52

Information, Education, and Communication Unit (World Bank), 304–5 n.40

inner child, 227–30

instrumentality vs. autonomy, 103–4

interest rates, Indian vs. international, 291 n.14

internal/internalized orientalism, 139

Internet, 320 n.7

Irani, Madhavi, 263–64

Italian identity, 321 n.14

ivory tower, 34, 296–97 n.36

Jacob, Rahul, 92

Jameson, Fredric, 42–43, 45

Jatia, Amit, 8

JKC (J K Chemicals), 61, 64, 299 nn.4, 6, 314 n.29. *See also* KamaSutra condoms

J K Group, 64, 299 n.4

J K Industries, 299 n.4

J K Synthetics, 299 n.4

Johnson and Johnson, 219

joint ventures, foreign, 84, 305–6 n.43

Joshi, Murli Manohar, 11

judgment, 46, 297 nn.6–7; aesthetic, 104–5, 115, 137

Kabra, S. N., 132

Kali, 281, 329 n.21

Kamasutra (Vatsyayana): canonization of, 144; reputation as a sex manual, 298 n.1. *See also* KamaSutra condoms

KamaSutra condoms, 21, 59–98; and AIDS, 64, 96–97, 299 n.8, 308 n.55; and auto-orientalism, 138–46, 315 n.34; brand control/ownership by, 134–37; budget for campaign, 64–65, 299 n.9; criticism of campaign, 63–64, 128–29, 313 n.27; *Debonair* ads for, 61, 62–64, 298–99 n.3; eroticism/pornography of campaign for, 127–38, 313 n.27; and family planning, 67–70, 91, 93, 95, 100, 300 nn.14, 15, 17; and the *Kamasutra,* 59, 61–62, 117–19, 121, 125–26, 311–

12 n.18; launch of campaign, 59–60, 61–64, 99, 299 n.7; Lintas, 61, 64–71, 122–23, 127–28, 300 n.14, 300–301 n.18, 310–11 n.14; mass-consumerist context of, 71–78; models for, 120–21, 312 n.19; origins of, 64–65, 299–300 n.10; photographic images of, 120–27, 312 n.19; political context of, 60, 67, 78–87; pricing of, 130; as progress through pleasure, 101, 115–17; and public service advertising, 91–98; and utility, 87–92, 306 n.47, 306–7 n.49. *See also* aspiration, aesthetic politics of; Bedi, Pooja; mass consumerism

Kankanala, Ram, 65, 129

Kant, Immanuel: on aesthetic judgment, 104–5, 115, 137; on the Ding-an-sich (thing-in-itself), 44; on judgment, 46, 297 nn.6–7; on pleasure, 115; on sensibility vs. intelligibility, 49; on sensual pleasure, 140

kanyadan (gift of a Hindu daughter), 196

Karlekar, Hiranmay, 292 n.16

Katrak, Kersy, 106, 107–8, 109, 117–18, 168, 310–11 n.14

KATS (Keymer, Adarts, Thompson, and Stronach), 303 n.33

Kaviraj, Sudipta, 79

Kellogg's, 264, 270

Kemper, Steven, 292 n.16, 322 n.10

Khajuraho, 117, 121–22

Khan, Arbad, 132

Khan, Mohammed, 74–75, 106–7, 109, 112, 132–33, 302 n.24, 310 n.13

Killer jeans, 327 n.14

Kohinoor condoms, 69, 299 n.7

Krishna, 281, 329 n.21
Krishnamachari, T. T., 81
Kumar, D., 92
Kumar, K. G., 96

Lankesh, Gauri, 95
lassi, 281–82
Lears, T. J., 294–95 n.29
Le Corbusier, 54
Lee Kwan Yew, 140
Levers, 310 n.13
Levin, Charles, 294 n.26
Levi's jeans, 266–69, 275, 327 n.14
Lévi-Strauss, Claude, 193, 328 n.18
Levitt, Theodore, 194; "The Globalization of Markets," 252–55, 262, 285, 325 nn.2–3
liberalization, 89, 306–7 n.49
Lintas, 29, 307 n.51. *See also* KamaSutra condoms
Lipton, 80
Lobo, Austin, 299 n.8
locality/mobility, 149–84; and account executives vs. agency managers, 172–75, 176–77; of cellular phones, 153, 156, 161–65, 317–18 nn.9–14; and client-agency relationships, 149, 167–72, 318–19 nn.19–20; of EMW, 155, 156–61, 318 n.17, 319 n.21; and Indianness, 150–51, 154–56, 157–65; of RightAway, 165–67, 169–71, 174–76, 180–84, 318 n.17; of telecommunications, 153–56, 184, 316–17 n.6; of the "very Bombay" concept, 175–80. *See also* brands; MNCs
Lois, George, 106, 296 n.32
Loos, Adolf, 54
Lukács, Georg, 41, 43, 44

Mahabharata, 329 n.21
Malinowski, Bronislaw, 23, 193

Mankekar, Purnima, 76, 307 n.52, 324 n.18, 329 n.21
Maori, gift exchange among, 193, 194
Marcus, George, 17, 32
Marcuse, Herbert, 47–48, 297–98 n.8
marketing/market research: vs. advertising, 27–29, 85, 115, 295 n.30, 296 n.32; the Big Idea, 111–14, 310 n.13; focus groups in, 235–42, 323 nn.11–12; media ethnology in, 235–36; by MNCs, 216, 224–27, 233–42, 248–49, 322 n.10; opportunism in, 191; practices of, 186–87, 235–39, 323 nn.11–12; of washing machines (case study), 254, 281–82
Marlboro cigarettes, 320–21 n.11
Marx, Karl: *Capital,* 23–24; on commodity form, 19–20, 45; *The Communist Manifesto,* 16, 41; vs. Hegel, 40, 311 n.15; historical materialism of, 23, 24, 40–41; on India vs. Western capitalism, 280, 328–29 n.20; on opportunism in mass marketing, 191; on use-value/needs, 23–24, 26, 293–94 n.25
Marxism: on abstraction vs. the concrete, 41, 43–44; on potentialities, 47–48, 297–98 n.8
Mass Communications and Marketing (MCM), 107–10
mass consumerism, 13–14, 55, 292 n.18; and the aesthetic politics of aspiration, 106–15, 310 nn.12–13; as eroticized, 191; and the eroticized female body, 124; and the government, 71–72, 73–77, 301 nn.20, 22, 25; and the green revolution, 71; and guilt, 74, 301 n.24; and individual agency,

115–16, 311 n.15; and the middle classes, 72, 75–76, 301 n.21; and the planned economy, 76–77, 82–83, 85–86, 302 nn.27, 30; and television, 72–75, 76, 81–82, 98, 301 n.22, 302 n.26, 310 n.12, 313–14 n.28; and temporal linearity, 312 n.24. *See also* commodity images

Massumi, Brian, 48, 298 n.9

Mattelart, Armand, 253–54

Mauss, Marcel, 192–93, 206

Mayle, Peter, 318 n.19

McDonaldization, 16, 143–44

McDonald's, 8, 276, 291 n.12

MCM. *See* Mass Communications and Marketing

media ethnology, 235–36

Mehta, Gita, 150

Mehta, Harshad, 200–201

Mehta, P., 110

Mendonca, Ronnie, 317 n.13

Menon, Gangadhar, 132

Menon, Raji, 97

Mercedes, 264

Metz, Christian, 53

middle class, 271–72, 328 n.16

Miller, Daniel, 27–28, 30, 314 n.31, 321 n.2

Mirinda, 228, 229

Mitra, Ashok, 11–12

MNCs (multinational corporations), 215–49; ambivalence toward, 250–51, 324–25 n.1; and brand intrinsics vs. extrinsics, 225–29, 230–31, 322 n.7; bureaucracy of, 222–25; "fun" connotations used by, 227–33, 240, 243; Coca-Cola, 217–18, 220–22, 225–27; cultural imperialism by, 216, 247; early failures of, 215–16, 220–21, 233, 263–65, 327 n.11; and family's centrality, 242–48, 324 n.16; and Indian-

ness, 216–17; market research by, 216, 224–27, 233–42, 248–49, 322 n.10; Pepsi, 218, 220–21, 225–27; Sparka, 217, 222–33, 243, 322 n.7. *See also* "Indian consumer," construction of; Indianness; teenagers

mobility. *See* locality/mobility

modernity/modernism, 42–43; vs. conservatism, 323 n.14; India as a producer of, 207, 321 n.12; Indian vs. European, 324 n.16; sensual pleasure vs. historical progress, 140–41, 143–44; universalist categories of, 38. *See also* totalization narrative

modernization, 35–36; temporal lag in, 89–90; and tourism, 316 n.5

Moeran, Brian, 27–28, 318 n.19

Moreiras, Alberto, 42

motivation, 93, 294 n.28, 311 n.15, 318 n.15

MR Coffee, 132–33, 314 n.30

MRTP (Monopolies and Restrictive Trade Practices) limits, 306 n.49

MTV India, 215, 244, 319 n.23, 330 n.24

Mudra, 14

Mukherjee, Pranab, 76–77, 87

multinational corporations. *See* MNCs

Mumbai. *See* Bombay

Munn, Nancy, 193

Murdoch, Rupert, 215

nagaraka, 59, 298 n.2

Naipaul, V. S.: *The Mimic Men*, 261

Nair, Mira, 125–26

Nandy, Pritish, 9

nationalism, 207, 208. *See also* swadeshi

Nehru, Jawaharlal: on false needs, 303 n.32; on freedom at midnight, 7; planned economy of, 6, 13, 36, 291 n.9, 293 n.19; on the Planning Commission, 78–79, 154; scientific vision of, 154
neo-Confucianism, 139–40, 324 n.21
Nirodh condoms, 65, 69, 80, 95, 130, 299 n.7, 300 n.17

OCM suitings, 209
Ogilvy, David: at ADGRO '82, 302 n.27; on advertising vs. sales, 294 n.27; on big ideas, 112; on client-agency relationships, 318–19 n.20; on commodities, 194; on the personality of brands, 190
Ohmae, Kenichi, 79
Ohmann, Richard, 296 n.31
Olins, Wally, 150
orientalism. *See* auto-orientalism
Orlove, Benjamin, 252
Oshidar, Cyrus, 330 n.24

Packard, Vance, 294 n.28
Padamsee, Alyque: on AIDS, 308 n.55; on Bedi, 120; and Kama-Sutra condoms, 65, 66, 117, 119, 121, 135, 299 n.9; and Katrak, 310–11 n.14; on MNCs, 268; on public service advertising, 93, 307 n.51; on Singhania, 120
Pandey, Kamlesh, 132
Pandey, Piyush, 89, 114, 129, 310 n.12
Park Avenue suits, 151
Parle, 228
Parry, Jonathan, 320 n.5
particulars vs. universals, 38–45, 46, 49, 55, 297 n.3; and the aesthetic politics of aspiration, 101–3, 105–6; and capitalism, 18

Parvati, 281, 329 n.21
Patel, H. M., 86
Patton, K. L., 102
Pepe jeans, 267
Pepsi, 218, 220–21, 225–27
Pervez, Kasim, 132
Philip Morris Inc., 320–21 n.11
photography: Adams on, 312 n.23; and aura, 53–55, 256–57, 260–61; and close distance, 257; in KamaSutra ads, 120–27, 312 n.19; materiality vs. meaning of, 49–56
Pillai, Ajith, 128–29
Pinney, Christopher, 179–80, 312 n.25, 326–27 nn.9, 10
planned economy, 76–77, 82–83, 85–86, 302 nn.27, 30
Planning Commission, 78–79, 85, 154
Playboy, 298–99 n.3
Pocha, Adi, 65–67, 69, 97, 118, 311 n.14; on Bedi, 120; on Das Gupta, 123–24; on imagery, 121, 122; on Robinson, 312 n.19; on structure vs. impact, 134–35
Polar Latex, 131
political science, 317 n.8
politics. *See* government; planned economy
populism, 85, 192, 302 n.30, 319–20 n.3
positioning, 22–23
postcolonial writing, 258–61, 325–26 nn.5–6
Poster, Mark, 105
postmodernism, 16–17, 42–43, 45, 161, 317 n.8
poststructuralism, 44
potentialities, 47–48, 297–98 n.8
Prakash, A., 128, 129
Prasad, Mahesh, 128–29
Press Council, 128–29
price. *See* value politics

Procter and Gamble, 88, 295 n.30,
306 n.46
production vs. consumption, 84,
87–88, 305 n.41
protectionism, 10–11
Public Distribution System, 291
n.14
publicity, 99–100, 191–92, 308 n.1
Public Law, 80, 81, 304 n.36
public service advertising, 91–98

Rabinow, Paul, 17
Rajagopal, Arvind, 121
Rakshit, Goutam, 150
Ram, 281, 329 n.21
Ramayana, 281, 329 n.21
Rambagh Palace Hotel, 138
Ramusack, Barbara, 316 n.5
Rao, P. V. Narasimha, 5, 215
Rao, Sunita, 180
Ray, Satyajit, 181, 312 n.25
Raymond, 64, 151–52, 299 n.4
real world vs. ivory tower, 34, 296–
97 n.36
reciprocity. *See* gift exchange
Reddy, Narayan, 307 n.53
Reed, Vergil, 34–36, 284–85
reforms, 5, 262, 289–90 n.3
Rekhi, Ragvinder S., 291 n.12
Resor, Stanley, 35, 36
Richardson Hindustan, 88, 306 n.46
RightAway, 165–67, 169–71, 174–
76, 180–84, 186–87, 195–200,
318 n.17
Robertson, Roland, 17
Robinson, Marc, 312 n.19
Rosenblum, Barbara, 257
Rothenberg, Randall, 183
Roy, Ghosh, 321 n.4
Rushdie, Salman: *Midnight's Chil-
dren*, 260, 326 n.6

Saatchi and Saatchi Advertising,
255

Sahlins, Marshall, 23–25, 26
Said, Edward, 139
Samara skin/hair products, 139
SamTech, 162, 163–65, 170, 201,
317 n.11, 317–18 n.14
Sangh Parivar, 6, 291 n.7, 292
n.15
Saran, Sathya, 245–46, 324 n.19
Sarna, S. R., 292 n.16
Schudson, Michael, 27–28, 257,
294 n.27, 303 n.31
Schwartz, Peter, 217–18
Second Five-Year Plan, 71
self-orientalism/self-orientalization,
139
self-rule. *See* swaraj
self-strengthening (atmashakti),
290 nn.5–6. *See also* swadeshi
Sen, Anindya, 290 n.3
Sen, Antara Dev, 152
Sengupta, Ranjana, 96
sensual pleasure vs. historical prog-
ress, 140–41, 143–44
servicing, 195, 320 n.10
sex in advertising, 132–33. *See also*
KamaSutra condoms
Shah, Amrita, 76
Shakti, 281, 329 n.21
Shankar, Ravi, 181
Sheshadri, G. R., 88
"Shoveling Smoke," meaning of,
34–36, 284–85
signification of goods, 21–22, 25,
26, 294 n.26
SIM cards, 165, 317 n.13, 318 n.16
Simoes, Frank, 106–7, 108–9, 116,
310–11 n.14
Singh, Iqbal, 157
Singhania, Gautam, 64, 96, 97,
120–21, 299 n.6
Singhania, Juggilal Kamlapat, 299
n.4
Sinha, Indra, 190
Sinha, Tara, 93

Sinha, Yashwant, 11
Sita, 281, 329 n.21
SJM (Swadeshi Jagaran Manch), 6, 8, 10, 291–92 n.15
Skaria, George, 264, 278, 328 n.16
Smith, Adam, 78; *Wealth of Nations*, 13
socialism, 13–14, 293 n.19
soft drinks, 225–28. *See also* Coca-Cola Company; Pepsi; Sparka; Thums Up
Sontag, Susan, 50–51
Sparka, 217, 222–33, 243, 322 n.7
spending. *See* value politics
Spirit, 39–41, 115–16, 143
STAR-TV, 215, 319 n.23
sterilization camps, 68, 300 n.15
Stronach (L. A.) and Co., 12
structuralism, 21–26, 293–95 nn.25–26
sugar, 291 n.14
Sunnex jeans, 327 n.14
swadeshi, 5–14, 207; and asceticism vs. hedonism, 295 n.29; BJP on, 5, 6, 10–12, 291–92 n.15; and the Bombay Club, 9–10; and British industry, 5, 290 n.5; criticism of, 8–9, 10–11, 291 n.11; and economic reforms, 9–11, 291 n.14; and family, 6, 8; M. K. Gandhi on, 5–6, 290 n.6; and global consumerism, 12; and globalization vs. Hindu nationalism/tradition, 5–9, 291 nn.9, 11; vs. McDonald's, 8, 291 n.12; and self-sufficiency/self-reliance, 5–6, 290 nn.5–6; SJM on, 6, 8, 10, 291–92 n.15; and swaraj (self-rule), 6, 13
Swadeshi Jagaran Manch. *See* SJM
Swamy, R. K., 84–85, 88–89, 305–6 n.43

swaraj (self-rule), 6, 13, 101, 309 n.3

Tagg, John, 50
Tagore, Rabindranath, 290 n.5
Taj Mahal Inter-Continental hotel, 113
Tamilnad Mercantile Bank, 7
Tandon, Prakash, 87–88, 325–26 n.5
tariffs, 306–7 n.49
taste, 103–6
technology, as value-free, 153–54
teenagers: Asian vs. Western, 242, 323–24 n.15; and family values/Indian culture, 242–45, 246, 248; as a market, 217–22, 228–33, 240, 321 n.3, 322 n.9; materialism of, 243, 244–45. *See also* focus groups
telecommunications, 153–56, 184, 316–17 n.6. *See also* cellular phones; EMW; television
television, 72–76, 81–82, 98, 301 n.22, 302 n.26, 310 n.12, 313–14 n.28. *See also* Channel V; Doordarshan; MTV India; STAR-TV
Thapar, Raj, 300 n.15
Thompson (J. Walter), 12, 305–6 n.43, 307 n.52
thriftiness, 272–75
Thums Up cola, 221–22, 225–26, 321–22 n.4
Titan watches, 199–200
totalization narrative, 38–45, 46, 49, 55, 297 n.3. *See also* particulars vs. universals
tourist sites, 316 n.5
trademarks, 185
tradition. *See* Indianness; swadeshi
transnational corporations. *See* MNCS
Trikaya Grey, 13, 292 n.17

William Mazzarella is Assistant Professor of
Anthropology at the University of Chicago.

Library of Congress Cataloging-in-Publication Data
Mazzarella, William.
Shoveling smoke : advertising and globalization in
contemporary India / by William Mazzarella.
p. cm.   Includes bibliographical references and index.
ISBN 0-8223-3109-8 (cloth : alk. paper)
ISBN 0-8223-3145-4 (pbk. : alk. paper)
1. Advertising — India. 2. Advertising — Social aspects —
India. 3. Marketing — India. 3. Consumption (Economics) —
India. 5. Globalization — Economic aspects — India. I. Title.
HF5813.I4M39 2003   659.1'0954 — dc21   2003000435